directed at the cognition, not at the formation, of law. As a true science, it describes its object and refrains from prescriptions.

With the reception of Roman law, traditional jurisprudence took over the distinction between "subjective" law (the rights of a person) and "objective" law (the system of norms). Throughout history this dualism has been a handy tool for placing the concept of law in the service of politics, especially of rulers or parties in power. The pure theory of law destroys this dualism. It is a scientifically exact structural analysis of positive law, free of ethical and political value judgments.

The natural-law theory considers law as a transcendental phenomenon: as absolutely just because God-made; and it calls on man to observe and apply this God-made law. Man's law thus becomes in effect the human child of a divine parent. The pure theory of law does not recognize such a metaphysics of law. It sees the rationale of law not in God (or nature) but in a certain juristic hypothesis which Kelsen calls "basic norm," established by a logical analysis of actual juristic thinking.

Professor Kelsen (right) with his book and his translator.

Professor Hans Kelsen, born 1881 in Prague, and a citizen of the United States since 1945, is best known as the creator of the Pure Theory of Law and as the author of the Austrian Democratic Constitution, which was introduced in 1920, abolished during the Nazi regime, restored in 1945, and is in force today. He has written more than forty works on law and legal philosophy; if translations and scientific essays are included, the bibliography of his works contains more than five hundred titles.

The author was legal adviser to the last Austrian emperor and to the first republican government, the creator and permanent adviser of the Supreme Constitutional Court of Austria, and Dean of the Law Faculty of the University of Vienna. He has taught law at the University of Cologne, the Institute of International Studies in Geneva, the University of Prague; and in the United States at Harvard, Wellesley College, the University of California, and the Naval War College.

Professor Kelsen holds honorary doctorates from the universities of Utrecht, Harvard, Chicago, California, Mexico, Salamanca, Berlin, Vienna, Paris, Rio de Janeiro, and the New School of Social Research of New York. He is a member of distinguished scientific societies, including the Accademia Nazionale dei Lincei in Rome, and the recipient of high honors and decorations.

Max Knight studied under Professor Kelsen both at the University of Vienna (Constitutional Law) and at the University of California (International Law) ; he gained his law degree (J.D.) in 1933. A member of the University of California Press since 1950, he is the editor of works on legal philosophy by the author and by the Kelsen scholars Professor Alf Ross (Copenhagen) and Professor Julius Stone (Sydney), and has contributed articles on legal and economic subjects to journals in the United States and abroad.

UNIVERSITY OF CALIFORNIA PRESS
Berkeley 94720

PURE THEORY OF LAW

PURE THEORY OF LAW

by HANS KELSEN

Translation from the Second
(Revised and Enlarged) German Edition by
MAX KNIGHT

UNIVERSITY OF CALIFORNIA PRESS

BERKELEY AND LOS ANGELES : 1967

K
237
.K42313
1967

UNIVERSITY OF CALIFORNIA PRESS, BERKELEY AND LOS ANGELES, CALIFORNIA
CAMBRIDGE UNIVERSITY PRESS, LONDON, ENGLAND
© 1967 BY THE REGENTS OF THE UNIVERSITY OF CALIFORNIA
TRANSLATED FROM *Reine Rechtslehre* (VIENNA: VERLAG FRANZ DEUTICKE,
1960; SECOND, REVISED AND ENLARGED EDITION. FIRST
EDITION PUBLISHED 1934 BY DEUTICKE, VIENNA)
LIBRARY OF CONGRESS CATALOG CARD NUMBER: 67-10234
PRINTED IN THE UNITED STATES OF AMERICA

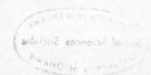

TRANSLATOR'S PREFACE

The present work is a translation of the second German edition of Hans Kelsen's *Reine Rechtslehre*, published in 1960, a completely revised version of the first edition, published in 1934. In the first edition Kelsen confined himself to formulate the characteristic results of his Pure Theory of Law. In the second edition he attempts to solve the fundamental problems of a general theory of law according to the principles of methodological purity of jurisprudential cognition and to determine to a greater extent than before the position of the science of law in the system of the sciences.

It stands to reason that a theory whose first draft was contained in Kelsen's *Hauptprobleme der Staatsrechtslehre*, published in 1911, does not remain entirely unchanged during such a long time. Some changes were incorporated earlier—in Kelsen's *General Theory of Law and State* (Cambridge, Mass., 1945) and in the French translation of the first edition by Professor Henri Thevenaz, *Théorie Pure du Droit* (Paris, 1953). In the present work, the most important changes are pointed out in the footnotes, usually changes pertaining to a more rigorous exposition of principles—to the results of a development originating from tendencies that are immanent in a theory which, in itself, has remained essentially unchanged. (Many polemical footnotes, however, were omitted in this translation.)

With the diversity of the contents of positive legal orders increasing, a general theory of law is in danger of missing some legal phenomena among its fundamental legal concepts; some of these concepts may turn out to be too narrow, others too wide. Kelsen is much aware of this danger and has stressed that he welcomes constructive criticism. He regards even the present edition not as the final word but as an enterprise that would benefit by continued additions, refinements, or improvements in general.

This translation, carefully checked by the author, represents a compromise between a contents-conscious author and a form-conscious translator. Kelsen's immense experience with misinterpretations of his works as a result of "elegant" translations had to be the deciding factor when seemingly repetitious or Germanic-sounding passages, expunged from or rephrased in an earlier draft of the translation as too literally mirroring the original, were restored. In view of the detailed Contents page an index was dispensed with.

A personal note may be permitted. It was my good fortune to study under Professor Kelsen both at the University of Vienna and at the University of California. My admiration for the scope, integrity, and consistency of his theory has been matched only by my respect for his humanity and modesty, and my affection for the man himself. The long working association with him provided me with my most rewarding intellectual experience.

I would like to express my appreciation to Professor Albert Ehrenzweig of the University of California Law School in Berkeley whose initiative made this work possible, and whose good offices secured the sponsorship of the Institute of Social Sciences and of the Law School's Committee for International Legal Studies.

Max Knight

CONTENTS

vii

IV. THE STATIC ASPECT OF LAW   108

VIII. INTERPRETATION   348

I

LAW AND NATURE

1. The "Pure" Theory

The Pure Theory of Law is a theory of positive law. It is a theory of positive law in general, not of a specific legal order. It is a general theory of law, not an interpretation of specific national or international legal norms; but it offers a theory of interpretation.

As a theory, its exclusive purpose is to know and to describe its object. The theory attempts to answer the question what and how the law *is*, not how it ought to be. It is a science of law (jurisprudence), not legal politics.

It is called a "pure" theory of law, because it only describes the law and attempts to eliminate from the object of this description everything that is not strictly law: Its aim is to free the science of law from alien elements. This is the methodological basis of the theory.

Such an approach seems a matter of course. Yet, a glance upon the traditional science of law as it developed during the nineteenth and twentieth centuries clearly shows how far removed it is from the postulate of purity; uncritically the science of law has been mixed with elements of psychology, sociology, ethics, and political theory. This adulteration is understandable, because the latter disciplines deal with subject matters that are closely connected with law. The Pure Theory of Law undertakes to delimit the cognition of law against these disciplines, not because it ignores or denies the connection, but because it wishes to avoid the uncritical mixture of methodologically different disciplines (methodological syncretism) which obscures the essence of the science of law and obliterates the limits imposed upon it by the nature of its subject matter.

1

2. THE ACT AND ITS LEGAL MEANING

If we differentiate between natural and social sciences—and thereby between nature and society as two distinct objects of scientific cognition the question arises whether the science of law is a natural or a social science: whether law is a natural or a social phenomenon. But the clean delimitation between nature and society is not easy, because society, understood as the actual living together of human beings, may be thought of as part of life in general and hence of nature. Besides, law—or what is customarily so called—seems at least partly to be rooted in nature and to have a "natural" existence. For if you analyze any body of facts interpreted as "legal" or somehow tied up with law, such as a parliamentary decision, an administrative act, a judgment, a contract, or a crime, two elements are distinguishable: one, an act or series of acts—a happening occurring at a certain time and in a certain place, perceived by our senses: an external manifestation of human conduct; two, the legal meaning of this act, that is, the meaning conferred upon the act by the law. For example: People assemble in a large room, make speeches, some raise their hands, others do not—this is the external happening. Its meaning is that a statute is being passed, that law is created. We are faced here with the distinction (familiar to jurists) between the process of legislation and its product, the statute. To give other illustrations: A man in a robe and speaking from a dais says some words to a man standing before him; legally this external happening means: a judicial decision was passed. A merchant writes a letter of a certain content to another merchant, who, in turn answers with a letter; this means they have concluded a legally binding contract. Somebody causes the death of somebody else; legally, this means murder.

3. THE SUBJECTIVE AND OBJECTIVE
MEANINGS OF THE ACT;
ITS SELF-INTERPRETATION

The legal meaning of an act, as an external fact, is not immediately perceptible by the senses—such as, for instance, the color, hardness, weight, or other physical properties of an object can be perceived. To be sure, the man acting rationally, connects his act with a definite meaning that expresses itself in some way and is understood by others. This subjective meaning may, but need not necessarily, coincide with its objective meaning, that is, the meaning the act has according to the law. For example, somebody makes some dispositions, stating in writing what is to happen to his belongings when he dies. The subjective meaning of this act is a testament. Objectively, however, it is not, because some legal formalities were not observed. Suppose a secret organization intending to rid the nation of subversive elements, condemns to death a man thought to be a traitor, and has a member execute what it subjectively believes to be and calls "a death penalty"; objectively and legally, however, not a death penalty but a Feme murder was carried out, although the external circumstances of a Feme murder are no different from the execution of a legal death penalty.

A written or spoken act can even say something about its own legal meaning. Therein lies a peculiarity of the objects of legal cognition. A plant is unable to tell the classifying botanist anything about itself. It makes no attempt to explain itself scientifically. But an act of human conduct can indeed carry a legal self-interpretation: it can include a statement indicating its legal meaning. The men assembled in parliament can expressly declare that they are enacting a statute; a man making a disposition about his property may call it "last will and testament"; two men can declare that they are making a contract. The scientist investigating the law, sometimes finds a legal self-interpretation which anticipates his own interpretation.

4. The Norm

a) *The Norm As a Scheme of Interpretation*

The external fact whose objective meaning is a legal or illegal act is always an event that can be perceived by the senses (because it occurs in time and space) and therefore a natural phenomenon determined by causality. However, this event as such, as an element of nature, is not an object of legal cognition. What turns this event into a legal or illegal act is not its physical existence, determined by the laws of causality prevailing in nature, but the objective meaning resulting from its interpretation. The specifically legal meaning of this act is derived from a "norm" whose content refers to the act; this norm confers legal meaning to the act, so that it may be interpreted according to this norm. The norm functions as a scheme of interpretation. To put it differently: The judgment that an act of human behavior, performed in time and space, is "legal" (or "illegal") is the result of a specific, namely normative, interpretation. And even the view that this act has the character of a natural phenomenon is only a specific interpretation, different from the normative, namely a causal interpretation. The norm which confers upon an act the meaning of legality or illegality is itself created by an act, which, in turn receives its legal character from yet another norm. The qualification of a certain act as the execution of the death penalty rather than as a murder—a qualification that cannot be perceived by the senses—results from a thinking process: from the confrontation of this act with the criminal code and the code of criminal procedure. That the mentioned exchange of letters between merchants constitutes legally a contract, results exclusively from the fact that such an exchange conforms with conditions defined in the civil code. That a document is objectively *as well* as subjectively a valid testament results from the fact that it conforms to conditions stipulated by this code. That an assembly of people is a parliament, and that the meaning of their act is a statute, results from the conformity of all these facts with the norms laid down in the constitution. That means, that the contents of actual happenings agree with a norm accepted as valid.

b) *Norm and Norm Creation*

Those norms, then, which have the character of legal norms and which make certain acts legal or illegal are the objects of the science of law. The legal order which is the object of this cognition is a normative order of human behavior—a system of norms regulating human behavior. By "norm" we mean that something *ought* to be or *ought* to happen, especially that a human being ought to behave in a specific way. This is the meaning of certain human acts directed toward the behavior of others. They are so directed, if they, according to their content, command such behavior, but also if they permit it, and—particularly—if they authorize it. "Authorize" means to confer upon someone else a certain power, specifically the power to enact norms himself. In this sense the acts whose meaning is a norm are acts of will. If an individual by his acts expresses a will directed at a certain behavior of another, that is to say, if he commands, permits, or authorizes such behavior— then the meaning of his acts cannot be described by the statement that the other individual *will* (future tense) behave in that way, but only that he *ought* to behave in that way. The individual who commands, permits, or authorizes *wills;* the man to whom the command, permission, or authorization is directed *ought to.* The word "ought" is used here in a broader than the usual sense. According to customary usage, "ought" corresponds only to a command, while "may" corresponds to a permission, and "can" to an authorization. But in the present work the word "ought" is used to express the normative meaning of an act directed toward the behavior of others; this "ought" includes "may" and "can". If a man who is commanded, permitted, or authorized to behave in a certain way asks for the reason of such command, permission, or authorization, he can only do so by saying: Why "ought" I behave in this way? Or, in customary usage: Why may I or why can I behave in this way?

"Norm" is the meaning of an act by which a certain behavior is commanded, permitted, or authorized. The norm, as the specific meaning of an act directed toward the behavior of someone else, is to be carefully differentiated from the act of will whose meaning the norm is: the norm is an *ought,* but the act of will is an *is.* Hence the situation constituted by such an act must be described by the statement: The one individual wills that the other individual ought to behave in a certain way. The first part of this sentence refers to an *is,* the existing fact of the first individual's act of volition; the second part to an *ought,* to a norm as the meaning of that act. Therefore it is incorrect to assert—as is often done—that the statement: "An individual ought" merely means that another individual wills something; that the *ought* can be reduced to an *is.*

The difference between *is* and *ought* cannot be explained further. We are immediately aware of the difference. Nobody can deny that the statement: "something is"—that is, the statement by

which an existent fact is described—is fundamentally different
from the statement: "something ought to be"—which is the statement by which a norm is described. Nobody can assert that from
the statement that something is, follows a statement that something ought to be, or vice versa.

This dualism of is and ought does not mean, however, that there
is no relationship between *is* and *ought*. One says: an *is* conforms
to an ought, which means that something is as it ought to be; and
one says: an *ought* is "directed" toward an is—in other words:
something ought to be. The expression: "an is conforms to an
ought" is not entirely correct, because it is not the is that conforms
to the ought, but the "something" that one time is and the other
time ought to be—it is the "something" which figuratively can be
designated as the content of the is or as the content of the ought.

Put in different words, one can also say: a certain something—
specifically a certain behavior—can have the quality of is or of
ought. For example: In the two statements, "the door is being
closed" and "the door ought to be closed," the closing of the door
in the former statement is pronounced as something that is, in the
latter as something that ought to be. The behavior that is and the
behavior that ought to be are not identical, but they differ only so
far as the one is and the other ought to be. Is and ought are two
different modi. One and the same behavior may be presented in
the one or the other of the two modi. Therefore it is necessary to
differentiate the behavior stipulated by a norm as a behavior that
ought to be from the actual behavior that corresponds to it. We
may compare the behavior stipulated by the norm (as content of
the norm) with the actual behavior; and we can, therefore, judge
whether the actual behavior conforms to the norm, that is, to the
content of the norm.

The behavior as it actually takes place may or may not be equal
to the behavior as it ought to be. But equality is not identity. The
behavior that is the content of the norm (that is, the behavior that
ought to be) and the actual behavior (that is, the behavior that
is) are not identical, though the one may be *equal* to the other.
Therefore, the usual way to describe the relation between an
actual behavior and a norm to which the behavior corresponds:
the actual behavior is the behavior that—according to the norm—

ought to be, is not correct. The behavior that is cannot be the behavior that ought to be. They differ with respect to the modus
which is in one case the is, in the other the ought.

Acts whose meaning is a norm can be performed in various
ways. For example, by a gesture: The traffic policeman, by a motion of his arms, orders the pedestrian to stop or to continue; or by
a symbol: a red light constitutes a command for the driver to halt,
a green light, to proceed; or by spoken or written words, either in
the imperative form—be quiet!—or in the form of an indicative
statement—I order you to be silent. In this way also permissions or
authorizations may be formulated. They are statements about the
act whose meaning is a command, a permission, an authorization.
But their meaning is not that something is, but that something
ought to be. They are not—as they linguistically seem to be—
statements about a fact, but a norm, that is to say, a command, a
permission, an authorization.

A criminal code might contain the sentence: Theft is punished
by imprisonment. The meaning of this sentence is not, as the
wording seems to indicate, a statement about an actual event; instead, the meaning is a norm: it is a command or an authorization,
to punish theft by imprisonment. The legislative process consists
of a series of acts which, in their totality, have the meaning of a
norm. To say that acts, especially legislative acts, "create" or
"posit" a norm, is merely a figure of speech for saying that the
meaning or the significance of the act or acts that constitute the
legislative process, is a norm. It is, however, necessary to distinguish the subjective and the objective meaning of the act.
"Ought" is the subjective meaning of every act of will directed at
the behavior of another. But not every such act has also objectively
this meaning; and only if the act of will has also the objective
meaning of an "ought," is this "ought" called a "norm." If the
"ought" is also the objective meaning of the act, the behavior at
which the act is directed is regarded as something that *ought* to be
not only from the point of view of the individual who has performed the act, but also from the point of view of the individual at
whose behavior the act is directed, and of a third individual not
involved in the relation between the two. That the "ought" is the
objective meaning of the act manifests itself in the fact that it is

supposed to exist (that the "ought" is valid) even if the will ceases
to exist whose subjective meaning it is—if we assume that an individual ought to behave in a certain way even if he does not know
of the act whose meaning is that he ought to behave in this way.
Then the "ought," as the objective meaning of an act, is a valid
norm binding upon the addressee, that is, the individual at whom
it is directed. The ought which is the subjective meaning of an act
of will is also the objective meaning of this act, if this act has been
invested with this meaning, if it has been authorized by a norm,
which therefore has the character of a "higher" norm.

The command of a gangster to turn over to him a certain
amount of money has the same subjective meaning as the command of an income-tax official, namely that the individual at
whom the command is directed ought to pay something. But only
the command of the official, not that of the gangster, has the meaning of a valid norm, binding upon the addressed individual. Only
the one order, not the other, is a norm-positing act, because the
official's act is authorized by a tax law, whereas the gangster's act is
not based on such an authorizing norm. The legislative act, which
subjectively has the meaning of *ought*, also has the objective
meaning—that is, the meaning of a valid norm—because the constitution has conferred this objective meaning upon the legislative
act. The act whose meaning is the constitution has not only the
subjective but also the objective meaning of "ought," that is to
say, the character of a binding norm, if—in case it is the historically first constitution—we presuppose in our juristic thinking that
we ought to behave as the constitution prescribes.

If a man in need asks another man for help, the *subjective*
meaning of this request is that the other ought to help him. But in
an objective sense he ought to help (that is to say, he is morally
obliged to help) only if a general norm—established, for instance,
by the founder of a religion—is valid that commands, "Love your
neighbor." And this latter norm is objectively valid only if it is
presupposed that one ought to behave as the religious founder has
commanded. Such a presupposition, establishing the objective
validity of the norms of a moral or legal order, will here be called
a *basic norm* (*Grundnorm*).[1] Therefore, the objective validity of

---
[1] Cf. § 34a.

a norm which is the subjective meaning of an act of will that men ought to behave in a certain way, does not follow from the factual act, that is to say, from an *is,* but again from a norm authorizing this act, that is to say, from an *ought.*

Norms according to which men ought to behave in a certain way can also be created by custom. If men who socially live together behave for some time and under the same circumstances in the same way, then a tendency—that is, psychologically, a will—comes into an existence within the men to behave as the members of the group habitually do. At first the subjective meaning of the acts that constitute the custom is not an *ought.* But later, when these acts have existed for some time, the idea arises in the individual member that he ought to behave in the manner in which the other members customarily behave, and at the same time the will arises that the other members ought to behave in that same way. If one member of the group does not behave in the manner in which the other members customarily behave, then his behavior will be disapproved by the others, as contrary to their will. In this way the custom becomes the expression of a collective will whose subjective meaning is an *ought.* However, the subjective meaning of the acts that constitute the custom can be interpreted as an objectively valid norm only if the custom has been instituted by a higher norm as a norm-creating fact. Since custom is constituted by human acts, even norms created by custom are created by acts of human behavior, and are therefore—like the norms which are the subjective meaning of legislative acts—"posited" or "positive" norms. Custom may create moral or legal norms. Legal norms are created by custom, if the constitution of the social group institutes custom—a specially defined custom—as norm-creating fact.

Finally it is to be noted that a norm need not be only the meaning of a real act of will; it can also be the content of an act of thinking. This is the case if the norm is only presupposed in our thinking. Just as we can imagine things which do not really exist but "exist" only in our thinking, we can imagine a norm which is not the meaning of a real act of will but which exists only in our thinking. Then, it is not a positive norm. But since there is a correlation between the ought of a norm and a will whose meaning it is, there must be in our thinking also an imaginary will whose meaning is the norm which is only presupposed in our thinking—as is the basic norm of a positive legal order.[2]

c) *Validity and Sphere of Validity of the Norm*

By the word "validity" we designate the specific existence of a norm. When we describe the meaning or significance of a norm-creating act, we say: By this act some human behavior is ordered, commanded, prescribed, forbidden, or permitted, allowed, authorized. If we use the word *ought* to comprise all these meanings, as has been suggested, we can describe the validity of a norm by saying: Something ought to, or ought not to, be done. If we describe the specific existence of a norm as "validity," we express by this the special manner in which the norm—in contradistinction to a natural fact—is existent. The "existence" of a positive norm—that is to say, its "validity"—is not the same as the existence of the act of will, whose objective meaning the norm is. A norm can be valid, even if the act of will whose meaning the norm is, no longer exists. Indeed, the norm does not become valid until the act of will whose meaning the norm is has been accomplished and hence has ceased to exist. The individual who has created a legal norm by an act directed at the behavior of others, need not continue to will this conduct in order that the norm be valid. When the men who act as legislators have passed a statute regulating certain affairs and have put this statute into "force" (i.e., into validity), they turn in their decisions to the regulation of other affairs; and the statutes put into validity may be valid long after these men have died and therefore are unable to will anything. It is incorrect, therefore, to characterize norms in general, and legal norms in particular, as the "will" or the "command" of the legislator or state, if by "will" or "command" a psychological act of will is meant. The norm is the *meaning* of an act of will, not the act of will.

Since the validity of a norm is an *ought* and not an *is*, it is necessary to distinguish the validity of a norm from its effectiveness. Effectiveness is an "is-fact"—the fact that the norm is actually applied and obeyed, the fact that people actually behave according to the norm. To say that a norm is "valid," however, means some-

---

[2] Cf. p. 23.

thing else than that it is actually applied and obeyed; it means that it *ought* to be obeyed and applied, although it is true that there may be some connection between validity and effectiveness. A general legal norm is regarded as valid only if the human behavior that is regulated by it actually conforms with it, at least to some degree. A norm that is not obeyed by anybody anywhere, in other words a norm that is not effective at least to some degree, is not regarded as a valid legal norm. A minimum of effectiveness is a condition of validity. "Validity" of a legal norm presupposes, however, that it is possible to behave in a way contrary to it: a norm that were to prescribe that something ought to be done of which everyone knows beforehand that it must happen necessarily according to the laws of nature always and everywhere would be as senseless as a norm which were to prescribe that something ought to be done of which one knows beforehand that it is impossible according to the laws of nature.

Nor do validity and effectiveness coincide in time. A legal norm becomes valid before it becomes effective, that is, before it is applied and obeyed; a law court that applies a statute immediately after promulgation—therefore before the statute had a chance to become "effective"—applies a valid legal norm. But a legal norm is no longer considered to be valid, if it remains permanently ineffective. Effectiveness is a condition of validity in the sense that effectiveness has to join the positing of a legal norm if the norm is not to lose its validity.

By effectiveness of a legal norm, which attaches a sanction to a certain behavior and thus qualifies the behavior conditioning the sanction as illegal, that is, as "delict," two facts may be understood: (1) that this norm is *applied* by the legal organs (particularly the law courts), which means, that the sanction in a concrete case is ordered and executed; and (2) that this norm is *obeyed* by the individuals subjected to the legal order, which means, that they behave in a way which avoids the sanction. If the stipulation of sanctions intends to prevent the commission of delicts, we are faced with the ideal case of the validity of a legal norm if this norm is never applied, because the awareness among those subjected to the legal order of the sanction to be executed in case of the commission of a delict has become the motive to refrain from committing the delict. In this situation, the effectiveness of the legal

norm is confined to obedience to it. But obedience to the legal
norm can be induced by other motives. If, for instance, the legal
delict is at the same time a religious delict, obedience to the law
may be caused not by the wish to avoid the legal sanction, but to
avoid the religious sanction. In this case the law is effective, that is,
actually obeyed, because religion is effective. The relation between validity and effectiveness will be discussed later.[3]

Let us take the statement: "The norm refers to a certain human
behavior." If by this behavior we mean the behavior that constitutes the content of the norm, then the norm can also refer to
other facts than human behavior—however, only to the extent that
these are *conditions* or (if existent in reality) *effects* of human
behavior. For example: A legal norm can prescribe that in the
event of a natural catastrophe those not immediately affected are
obliged to render aid to the victims as much as possible. If a legal
norm establishes the death penalty for murder, then the delict as
well as the sanction do not only consist in a certain human
behavior—directed toward the death of another human being
—but also in a specific effect of such behavior, namely the death of
a human being, which is a physiological event, not a human behavior. Since human behavior, as well as its conditions and effects,
occur in space and time, the legal norm must refer to space and
time. The validity of norms regulating human behavior in general, and the validity of legal norms in particular, therefore, must
be defined in terms of space and time, since these norms refer to
spatial and temporal events in their content. That a norm is
"valid" means always that it is valid for some specified space and
time; it means that it relates to a behavior that can take place only
somewhere and sometime (although it may perhaps not actually
take place).

The relation of the norm to space and time is the spatial and
temporal *sphere of validity* of the norm. This sphere of validity can
be limited or unlimited. The norm can be valid either for a definite space and time (that is, determined by the norm itself or by a
higher norm): it regulates, then, only those events that occur
within a certain space and during a certain time; or the norm can

---

[3] Cf. § 34g. To conclude from the fact that a norm is valid only if it is effective
to some extent, that effectiveness and validity are identical, would be as fallacious
as concluding from the assumption that "pleasure" and only "pleasure" is "good,"
that "good" and pleasure are identical.

be valid everywhere and always, that is, it can refer to events no matter where and when they occur. This latter alternative would be the meaning of a norm which does not contain any spatial or temporal limitations. Such a norm is not valid beyond space and time; the sphere of its validity in that case, does not lack space and time; it merely is not limited to a specific space or a specific time—its spatial and temporal sphere of validity is unlimited. The sphere of validity of a norm is an element of its content; and this content, as we shall see, can to some extent be predetermined by another, higher norm.[4]

As for the temporal sphere of validity of a positive norm, it is necessary to distinguish between the time before and after the enactment of the norm. In general, norms refer only to future behavior, but they may also refer to the past. For example, a legal norm which attaches a sanction to a certain behavior may prescribe that an individual ought to be punished even for behavior that had occurred before the legal norm was enacted whereby the behavior is qualified as a delict.[5] In this case we say that the norm is retroactive. But a legal norm may refer to the past not only with respect to the delict but also with respect to the sanction. A legal norm may stipulate not only that under certain conditions, fulfilled before its enactment, a coercive act as a sanction ought to be executed in the future, but also that under these conditions a coercive act that actually has been performed in the past without being prescribed by a norm then valid, ought to have been performed; so that the character of a sanction is conferred upon this coercive act with retroactive force. For example: In Nationalist-Socialist Germany certain coercive acts which at the time of their performance were legally murder, were subsequently retroactively legitimized as "sanctions"; and the behavior of the victim which elicited the murder was subsequently qualified as a "delict."

A legal norm can retroactively annul the validity of an earlier norm in such a way that the coercive acts carried out as sanctions under the earlier norm are divested of their character as punishments or civil executions; and that the human behavior that was the condition of the sanction is divested of its character as a delict. For example: A government that has come to power by revolution

[4] Cf. § 35.
[5] Cf. § 27b.

can, by a retroactive statute, repeal a statute enacted by the over-
thrown government, under which certain acts committed by members of the revolutionary party had been punished as political
crimes. Of course, that which had been done cannot be undone;
but the normative interpretation in general, and the legal qualifications in particular, of acts can be subsequently changed on the
basis of norms which are enacted after the acts have been performed.

In addition to a spatial and temporal sphere of validity of a
norm, a personal and material sphere of validity is to be distinguished. For the behavior that is regulated by norms is the behavior of human beings and every behavior regulated by a norm
contains a personal and a material element: the *individual* who
ought to behave in a certain way, and the *manner* in which he
ought to behave. Both elements are inseparably linked. In this respect it must be carefully observed that the norm does not refer to
the individual as such, but to a definite behavior of an individual.
The personal sphere of validity refers to the personal element of
the behavior determined by the norm. This sphere of validity,
again, can be unlimited or limited: a moral order may claim to be
valid for all individuals; that is, the norm of this order regulates
the behavior of all individuals and not only of individuals specifically qualified by the order; this is usually expressed by saying that
this order addresses itself to all individuals. On the other hand, the
behavior determined by the norms of a national legal order is only
the behavior of individuals who live within the state territory and
of the state's citizens who happen to be abroad. This is expressed
by saying that the national legal order regulates only the behavior
of human beings determined in this way—only these human beings
are subject to the national legal order; in other words: the personal sphere of validity is limited to these individuals.

We speak of the material sphere of validity when we have in
mind the various provinces of human behavior that are subject to
regulation such as economic, religious, political behavior. A norm
that regulates the economic behavior of men is said to be regulating the economy, one that regulates religious behavior to be
regulating religion, and so on. One speaks of different objects of
regulation and means by this the different directions of the behavior regulated by norms. What the norms of an order regulate is

always human behavior—only *it* can be regulated by norms. Facts
other than human behavior can be made the content of norms
only in connection with human conduct—only as a condition or as
the effect of it. The concept of a material sphere of validity is applied, for example, when a total legal order—such as that of a federal state comprising several member states—is articulated into
several partial legal orders, whose spheres of validity are delimited
with respect to the objects to be regulated by these partial orders:
For example, if the legal orders of the member states are competent to regulate only those objects which are specifically enu-
merated by the constitution; if—in other words—the regulating of
these objects falls within the competence of the member states,
whereas the regulation of all other objects is reserved for the legal
order of the federation, which, in itself is also a partial legal order.
The material sphere of validity of a total legal order is always unlimited, in the sense that such an order, by its very nature, can
regulate the behavior of the individuals subjected to it in all directions.

d) Positive and Negative Regulations: Commanding, Authorizing, Permitting

The behavior regulated by a normative order is either a definite
action or the omission (nonperformance) of such an action.
Human behavior, then, is either positively or negatively regulated
by a normative order. Positively, when a definite action of a definite individual or when the omission of such an action is commanded. (When the omission of an action is commanded, the
action is forbidden.) To say that the behavior of an individual is
commanded by an objectively valid norm amounts to the same as
saying the individual is obliged to behave in this way. If the individual behaves as the norm commands he fulfills his obligation—he
obeys the norm; if he behaves in the opposite way, he "violates"
the norm—he violates his obligation. Human behavior is positively
regulated also, when an individual is authorized by the normative
order to bring about, by a certain act, certain consequences determined by the order. Particularly an individual can be authorized
(if the order regulates its own creation) to create norms or to participate in that creation; or when, in case of a legal order provid-

ing for coercive acts as sanctions, an individual is authorized to
perform these acts under the conditions stipulated by the legal
order; or when a norm permits an individual to perform an act,
otherwise forbidden—a norm which limits the sphere of validity of
a general norm that forbids the act. An example for the last-
mentioned alternative is self-defense: although a general norm
forbids the use of force of one individual against another, a special
norm permits such use of force in self-defense. When an individual
acts as he is authorized by the norm or behaves as he is permitted
by a norm, he "applies" the norm. The judge, authorized by a
statute (that is, a general norm) to decide concrete cases, applies
the statute to a concrete case by a decision which constitutes an *individual* norm. Again, authorized by a judicial decision to execute
a certain punishment, the enforcement officer "applies" the individual norm of the judicial decision. In exercising self-defense,
one applies the norm that permits the use of force. Further, a
norm is also "applied" in rendering a judgment that an individual
does, or does not, behave as he is commanded, authorized, or permitted by a norm.

In the broadest sense, any human behavior determined by a
normative order as condition or consequence, can be considered as
being authorized by this order and in this sense as being positively
regulated. Human behavior is regulated negatively by a normative
order if this behavior is not forbidden by the order without being
positively permitted by a norm that limits the sphere of validity of
a forbidding norm, and therefore is permitted only in a negative
sense. This merely negative function of permitting has to be distinguished from the positive function of permitting—"positive,"
because it is the function of a positive norm, the meaning of an act
of will. The positive character of a permission becomes particularly apparent when the limitation of the sphere of validity of a
norm that forbids a certain conduct is brought about by a norm
that permits the otherwise forbidden conduct under the condition
that the permission has to be given by an organ of the community
authorized thereto. The negative as well as positive function of
permitting is therefore fundamentally connected with the function of commanding A definite human behavior can be *permitted* only within a normative order that *commands* different
kinds of behavior.

"To permit" is also used in the sense of "to entitle (*berechtigen*)." If *A* is commanded to endure that *B* behaves in a certain way, it is said that *B* is permitted (that is, entitled) to behave in this way. And if *A* is commanded to render a certain service to *B*, it is said that *B* is permitted (that is, entitled) to receive the service of *A*. In the first example, then, the sentence "*B* is permitted to behave in a certain way" says the same as the sentence: "*A* is commanded to endure that *B* behaves in a certain way." And in the second example, the sentence: "*B* is permitted to receive a certain service from *A*" says the same as the sentence: "*A* is commanded to render a service to *B*." The quality of *B's* behavior "to be permitted" is merely the reflex of the quality of *A's* behavior "to be commanded." This kind of "permitting" is not a function of the normative order different from its function of "commanding." [6]

e) Norm and Value

If a norm stipulates that a certain behavior "ought" to take place, in the sense of "commanding" the behavior, the actual behavior may or may not conform to the norm. The behavior conforms to the norm, if it is such as it ought to be according to an objectively valid norm; it does not conform, if it is not such as it ought to be according to an objectively valid norm because it is the opposite of the behavior that conforms to the norm. The judgment that an actual behavior is such as it ought to be according to an objectively valid norm is a value judgment—a positive value judgment. It means that the actual behavior is "good." The judgment that an actual behavior is the opposite of the behavior that conforms to the norm, is a negative value judgment. It means that the actual conduct is "bad" or "evil." An objectively valid norm according to which a certain behavior "ought to be," constitutes a positive or negative value. The behavior that conforms to the norm has a positive value, the behavior that does not conform a negative value. The norm that is regarded as objectively valid, functions as a standard of value applied to actual behavior. *Value* judgments affirming that an actual behavior conforms to an objectively

---

[6] Concerning this "permitting" (in the sense of "entitling") I formerly rejected the distinction between "imperative" and "permissive" law. This distinction, however, has to be maintained with respect to the other meanings of the word "permitting," especially when "permitting" means "authorizing." Cf. § 6a.

valid norm and is, in this sense, "good," or does not conform and is, in this sense, "bad," must be distinguished from judgments about reality that affirm—without reference to a norm regarded as objectively valid, which means, in the last analysis: without reference to a presupposed basic norm—that something is and how it is.

The actual behavior to which the value judgment refers—the behavior that constitutes the object of the valuation and that has a positive or negative value—is a fact existing in time and space, a part of reality. Only such a fact can, when compared with a norm, be judged to be good or bad. Only such a fact can have a positive or negative value. It is reality that is being valued. Inasmuch as the norms that are the basis of the value judgments are enacted by human, not superhuman, will, the values constituted by them are arbitrary. Other human acts of will can create other norms opposite to the former ones; and these other norms, then, constitute values that are opposite to those constituted by the former. That which is "good" according to the one norm may be "bad" according to another. Therefore the norms, enacted by men and not by divine authority, can only constitute relative values. This means: The validity of a norm according to which a certain behavior ought to be, as well as the value constituted by this norm, does not exclude the possibility of the validity of a norm according to which the opposite behavior ought to be constituting an opposite value. For example, a norm could be valid forbidding to commit suicide or to lie under all circumstances, and another norm could be valid permitting or even commanding suicide or lies under certain circumstances, yet it would be impossible to prove rationally that only one of these two norms, but not the other, is the truly valid one.

If however, the norm prescribing a certain behavior and thus constituting a certain value is supposed to emanate from a superhuman authority—from God or from a nature created by God— then this norm claims that the possibility of a norm prescribing the opposite behavior is excluded. The value constituted by such a norm is described as "absolute," in contrast to the value constituted by a norm enacted by human will. The object of a scientific theory of value can only be norms enacted by human will and values constituted by these norms.

If the value is constituted by an objectively valid norm, then the judgment that something real, an actual human behavior, is "good" or "bad," expresses the idea that this behavior conforms with an objectively valid norm: that the behavior ought to be the way it is; or that it does not conform with the objectively valid norm: that the behavior ought not to be the way it is. Then the value as an "ought" is placed in juxtaposition to the reality as the "is"—value and reality belonging to two different spheres, just as the "ought" and the "is."

If the statement that a behavior conforms or does not conform with an objectively valid norm is designated as "value judgment," then this value judgment must be distinguished from the norm that constitutes the value. The value judgment can be true or untrue, because it refers to a norm of a valid order. For example, the judgment that according to Christian morality it is "good" to love one's friends and to hate one's enemies is untrue because a norm of the valid Christian morality commands to love not only one's friends but also one's enemies. The judgment that it is legal to inflict upon a thief the penalty of death is untrue if the valid law in question commands to punish a thief by deprivation of freedom but not by deprivation of life. A norm, however, cannot be either true or untrue, but only valid or not valid.

The "judgment"—so-called—pronounced by a judge, is no more a judgment in the logical sense of the word, than the norm that he applies. That "judgment" is, instead, a norm—an *individual* norm, limited in its validity to a concrete case, as distinguished from a general norm, called a "law."

The value constituted by an objectively valid norm must be distinguished from the value that consists (not in the relation to a norm, but) in the relation of an object to the wish or will of an individual directed at this object. If the object is in accordance or not in accordance with the wish or will, it has a positive or negative value: it is "good" or "bad." If the judgment describing the relation of an object to the wish or will of an individual, is designated as a value judgment and the object which is in accordance with the wish or will as "good," the object which is not in accordance with the wish or will as "bad," then this value judgment is not different from a judgment about reality. For it describes only the relation between two facts, not the relation between a fact and an objectively valid norm; it is only a special judgment about reality.

If somebody says that something is good or bad, but if this statement is merely the immediate expression of his emotional attitude toward a certain object, if it expresses that he wishes something or does not wish it but its contrary, then the statement is no value "judgment," because it is not a function of cognition, but a function of the emotional component of consciousness; and if this emotional reaction refers to the behavior of another individual, then it is the expression of an emotional approval or disapproval, akin to the exclamation "bravo!" or "phooey!"

The value that consists in the relation of an object—particularly of behavior—to the wish or will of an individual can be designated as *subjective* value, in contradistinction to the value that consists in the relation of a behavior to an objectively valid norm that can be designated as *objective* value. If the judgment that a behavior is good merely means that it is wished by another individual, and if the judgment that a behavior is bad merely means that the opposite behavior is wished by an individual, then the values "good" and "bad" exist only for the individual who wishes the behavior, but not for the individual whose behavior is wished. If a judgment that a behavior is "good" means that the behavior conforms with an objectively valid norm (and if the judgment that a behavior is "bad" means that it does not conform with an objectively valid norm), then the values "good" and "bad" exist for the individuals whose behavior is being judged, that is, for all individuals whose behavior is regulated by the objectively valid norm regardless of whether these individuals themselves wish this behavior or not. Their behavior, then, has a positive or negative value, not because it is wished or not wished, but because it conforms, or does not conform, with a norm. The act of will, whose objective meaning the norm is, does not come into consideration as far as the value judgment is concerned.

Value in the subjective sense, that is, the value that consists in the relation of an object to the wish or will of an individual is distinguished from value in the objective sense (that is, the value that consists in the relation of a behavior to an objectively valid norm) also by the fact that the subjective value can have various degrees. For the wish or will of an individual is capable of different degrees of intensity. But a graduation of an objective value is not possible because a behavior can only conform or not conform with an objectively valid norm, but cannot do so more or less.[7]

Value judgments that state an objective value are designated as objective-value judgments; those that state a subjective value as subjective-value judgments. If thus defined, the adjectives "objective" and "subjective" refer to the stated values, not to the judgment function as a function of cognition. As a function of cognition any judgment has to be objective, that is, it must be performed without regard to the wishes of the judging individual. This is possible. It is possible to determine the relationship of a specific human behavior to a normative order—namely whether the behavior does or does not conform to the order—without taking an emotional position, either approving or disapproving, toward this order. Take for example, the question whether according to Christian morality, it is good to love one's enemies. The answer to this question, and therefore the value judgment that goes with it, can and must be given without regard to whether the one who has to give the answer approves or disapproves loving the enemy. Or another example: The answer to the question whether according to a valid law the death penalty ought to be imposed upon a murderer and consequently whether—legally—the death penalty in case of murder is valuable, can and must be given without regard to whether the one who has to give the answer approves or disapproves of the death penalty. Only then is the value judgment objective.

To sum up: If the judgment pronounces the relationship of an object (especially of human behavior) to the wish or will of an

[7] If a norm prescribes a behavior which is possible in differing degrees, it looks as if the norm could be obeyed in differing degrees, that is, more or less. This is a fallacy, however. If, for example, a norm prescribes that murder ought to be punished by twenty years in prison, and if, then, one court punishes murder by life-long imprisonment and another court punishes murder by ten years' imprisonment, then it is not true that one judgment is "more" in conformity with the norm to be applied and the other "less," but neither is in conformity. And if a norm prescribes only that murder ought to be punished by prison, without determining the length of imprisonment, then a judgment imposing life-long prison is not "more" in conformity with the norm to be applied and a judgment imposing twenty or ten years not "less," but all three judgments are equally in conformity with the norm. The "more" and "less" do not refer to the conforming but to the punishment.

individual (that is, a subjective value), then this value judgment is "objective" if the judging individual pronounces it without regard of whether he himself approves or disapproves of the behavior, but simply ascertains the fact that one individual or many individuals wish or will an object (or its opposite), particularly that they approve or disapprove a specific behavior.

We are making a distinction, then, between value judgments that state an *objective* value describing a relationship between a behavior and a norm regarded as objectively valid, and are therefore fundamentally different from a judgment about reality; and value judgments that state a *subjective* value by describing a relationship between an object (specifically a behavior) and the fact that an individual or many individuals wish this object or its opposite (specifically approve or disapprove a definite behavior) —these latter value judgments therefore being merely specific judgments about reality. Against this distinction it is objected that the former value judgments are also judgments about reality, because—so it is said—the norm that is the basis of the value judgment is created by a human command or by custom, therefore by facts of empirical reality. It is further argued that the relation of a fact (specifically of actual behavior) to a norm is therefore merely the relation between facts of empirical reality. This objection fails to distinguish between the fact of the act of command or the acts constituting the custom and the norm that is created by these acts: the former is a fact, the latter a meaning. Therefore the relation between an actual behavior and a norm; and the relation between this behavior to the fact whose meaning the norm is, are two different relations. It is entirely possible to describe the relation between a behavior and the norm stipulating that this behavior ought to be, without taking into consideration the act of command or custom by which the norm was created. This is obvious, for example, when we think of norms that were established a long time ago; of norms created by the acts of men long dead or forgotten; or of norms, especially, created by the custom of earlier generations, so that the men whose conduct is regulated by these norms are aware of them only as meanings. When a specific conduct is judged to be morally good or bad (because conforming or not conforming to a moral norm regarded as valid), one is usually not aware of the custom that created the moral norm on which the judgment is based. Above all, however, the acts by which legal norms are created come into consideration as objects of legal cognition only so far as they are determined by legal norms; and the basic norm, the ultimate reason for the validity of these norms, is not created by a real will at all, but is presupposed in legal thinking.[8]

By "value" we also mean the relation of something, specifically human behavior, as a means to a certain end or purpose. Suitableness, that is, to be suitable for a certain purpose, is the positive value; unsuitableness, the negative value. The purpose may be objective or subjective. An objective purpose is one that *ought* to be realized, that means, a purpose that has been stipulated by a norm regarded as objectively valid—a purpose, in other words, prescribed for nature in general or for man in particular by a supernatural or superhuman authority. A *subjective* purpose is one established by man himself, a purpose that he wishes to achieve. The value, therefore, that consists in the conformity with a purpose, is identical either with the value that consists in conformity with a norm or with the value that consists in conformity with a wish.

If we disregard that a realized purpose is something that conforms to a norm or to a wish, then the relation between means and end manifests itself as a relation between cause and effect. Something is suitable for a purpose if it is fit to realize the purpose—to bring about, as cause, the effect that constitutes the purpose. The judgment that something is purposeful can be a subjective or objective value judgment, depending on the subjective or objective character of the purpose. But such a value judgment is possible only on the basis of an insight into the causal relationship between the facts that are regarded as means and those regarded as end. If it is recognized that a relation of cause and effect exists between *a* and *b* (that *a* is the cause and *b* the effect), then, and only then, can we arrive at the (subjective or objective) value judgment: If *b* is wished as a purpose or "ought to be" according to a norm, then *a* is purposeful, that is, suitable for the purpose. The judgment concerning the relation between *a* and *b* is a—subjective or objective—value judgment only to the extent that *b* is presupposed as a subjective or objective purpose.

[8] Cf. § 6c and § 34.

5. The Social Order

a) Social Orders Prescribing Sanctions

The behavior of an individual can be—but need not be—in relation to other individuals: a man can behave in a certain way toward another man, but he can do so also toward animals, plants, and inanimate objects. The relation of one individual to other individuals can be direct or indirect. Murder is the behavior of a murderer toward the murdered—a direct relation between one individual and another. He who destroys a valuable object acts directly in relation to a thing, but indirectly in relation to men who are interested in the object, particularly its owners. A normative order that regulates human behavior in its direct or indirect relations to other human beings, is a social order. Morals and law are such social orders.

On the other hand, logic has as its subject matter a normative order that does not have a social character. For the acts of human thought, which are regulated by the norms of this order, do not refer to other human beings; one does not think "toward" another man in the way that one acts toward another man.

The behavior of one individual toward others may be useful or detrimental for them. From a psychological-sociological point of view, the function of every social order is to bring about a certain behavior of the individuals subject to this order; to motivate them to refrain from certain acts deemed detrimental "socially," that is, to other individuals; and to perform certain acts deemed socially useful. This motivating function is rendered by the idea men have of norms, which command or forbid certain human acts.

Depending on the manner in which human acts are commanded or forbidden, different types may be distinguished—they are ideal types, not average types. The social order may command a certain human behavior without attaching any consequence to the obeying or disobeying of the command. Or the social order may command a definite human behavior and at the same time connect with that behavior the granting of an advantage, a reward; or with the opposite behavior a disadvantage, punishment in the broadest sense of the word. The principle, to react upon a certain human behavior with reward or punishment, is the principle of retribution. Reward and punishment may be called "sanctions," but usually only punishment, not reward, is so called.

Finally, a social order may—and a legal order does—command a certain behavior by just attaching a disadvantage to the opposite behavior, for example, deprivation of life, health, freedom, honor, material goods, that is, by punishment in the broadest sense of the word. Therefore, one may say that a certain behavior is "commanded" by a social order and—in case of a legal order—is legally commanded, only insofar as the contrary behavior is a condition of a sanction (in the narrower sense of the word). If a social order—like the legal order—commands a behavior by prescribing a sanction in case of the opposite behavior, this set of circumstances can be described by a sentence stating that in the event of a certain behavior a certain sanction *ought* to be executed. By this is implied that the behavior conditioning the sanction is prohibited, the opposite behavior commanded: The behavior which is "commanded" is not the behavior which "ought" to be executed. That a behavior is "commanded" means that the contrary behavior is the condition of a sanction which "ought" to be executed. The execution of the sanction is *commanded* (i.e., it is the content of a legal obligation), if the nonexecution is the condition of a sanction. If this is not the case, the sanction is only authorized, not commanded. Since this regression cannot go on indefinitely, the last sanction in this chain can only be authorized, not commanded.

It follows that within such a normative order the same behavior may be—in this sense—commanded and forbidden at the same time, and that this situation may be described without logical contradiction. This is the case if a certain conduct is the condition of a sanction and at the same time the omission of this conduct is also the condition of a sanction. The two norms: "*a* ought to be" and "*a* ought not to be" exclude each other insofar as they cannot be obeyed or applied by the same individual at the same time; only one can be valid. But the two norms: "If *a* is, *x* ought to be" and "If non-*a* is, *x* ought to be" are not mutually exclusive. These two norms can be valid at the same time. Under a legal order a situation may exist in which a certain human behavior and at the same time the opposite behavior is the condition of a sanction which ought to be executed. The two norms can be valid side by side. They can be described without logical contradiction, but they express two conflicting political tendencies, a teleological conflict. The situation is possible, but politically unsatisfactory. Therefore legal orders usually contain rules according to which one of the two norms is invalid or may be invalidated.

Insofar as the evil that functions as a sanction—the punishment in the widest sense—has to be inflicted against the will of the affected individual; and insofar as, in case of resistance, the evil has to be inflicted by force, the sanction has the character of a coercive act. A normative order, which prescribes coercive acts as sanctions (that is, as reactions against a certain human behavior), is a coercive order. But coercive acts can be prescribed—and are so prescribed in a legal order, as we shall see—not only as sanctions, but as reactions against socially undesirable facts that do not have the character of human behavior and are therefore not to be regarded as prohibited.

From a sociological-psychological point of view, reward or punishment are ordered to make the desire for reward and the fear of punishment the motives for a socially desirable behavior. But actually this behavior may be brought about by other motives. According to its inherent meaning, the order may prescribe sanctions without regard to the motives that actually, in each single case, have brought about the behavior conditioning the sanctions. The meaning of the order is expressed in the statement that in the case of a certain behavior—brought about by whatever motives—a sanction (in the broader sense of the word, that is, reward or punishment) ought to be executed. Indeed, an order may attach a reward to a behavior only if it had not been motivated by the desire for reward. For example, a moral order may honor only the one who does good deeds for their own sake, not for honor's sake.

Since in the foregoing pages the validity of a social order has been distinguished from its effectiveness, it should be noted that a social order prescribing rewards or punishments is effective in the literal sense of the work insofar only as the behavior conditioning the reward is caused by the desire for the reward, and the behavior avoiding the punishment is caused by the fear of punishment. However, it is usual to speak of an effective order also if the behavior of the individuals subjected to the order by and large corresponds to the order, that is to say, if the individuals by and large by their behavior fulfill the conditions of the rewards and avoid the conditions of the punishments, without regard to the motive of their behavior. Used in this way the concept of effectiveness has a normative, not a causal, meaning.

b) *Are There Social Orders without Sanctions?*

Distinctly different from a social order prescribing sanctions (in the wider sense of the word) is one that commands a certain behavior without attaching reward for it or punishment for its opposite—that is, an order in which the principle of retribution is not applied. Usually the moral order is considered to be such a social order, and is thereby distinguished from the legal order. Jesus, in his Sermon on the Mount, does not seem, at first glance, to posit a moral order with sanctions, because he decidedly rejects the retribution principle of the Old Testament—evil for evil, good for good: "You have heard that it was said, 'An eye for an eye and a tooth for a tooth.' But I say to you, Do not resist one who is evil. . . . You have heard that it was said, 'You shall love your neighbor and hate your enemy.' But I say to you, Love your enemies . . . For if you love those who love you, what reward have you? Do not even the tax collectors do the same?" [9] Evidently, Jesus refers here to the heavenly reward, and therefore even in this moral order of highest standard the principle of retribution is not entirely excluded. Heavenly (although not secular) reward is promised to the one who renounces the application of the principle of retribution in this world—who does not requite evil with evil, and not only the good with good. Also punishment in the other world is included in this moral order which does not provide for punishment in this world. It is not a moral order without sanctions, but an order with transcendental sanctions, and in that sense a religious order.

In order to judge the possibility of a sanctionless moral order, it must be noted that: if a moral order commands a certain behavior, it commands simultaneouly that the commanded behavior of the one subject is to be approved by the others, the opposite behavior disapproved. If somebody disapproves the commanded behavior or approves the opposite behavior, then he behaves immorally and must himself be morally disapproved. Approval and disapproval

---

[9] Matt. V: 38 ff.

by the fellow members of the community are sensed as reward and punishment and may therefore be interpreted as sanctions. Sometimes they are more effective sanctions than other forms of reward and punishment, because they satisfy or hurt man's desire for reputation, which is one of the most important components of the instinct for self-preservation. It is to be noted that the two moral norms—the one commanding a certain behavior and the one prescribing disapproval for the opposite behavior—are essentially connected, and form a unity. It is therefore doubtful whether a distinction between social orders with and without sanctions is possible. The only relevant difference between social orders is not that some prescribe sanctions and the others do not, but that they prescribe different types of sanctions.

c) Transcendental and Socially Immanent Sanctions

The sanctions prescribed by a social order are either transcendental or socially immanent. Transcendental sanctions are those that according to the faith of the individuals subjected to the order originate from a superhuman authority. Such a faith is a specific element of a primitive mentality. Early man interprets natural events that affect his immediate interest according to the principle of retribution: favorable events as rewards for the observance, unfavorable events as punishment for disregard of the existing social order.[10] Originally it was probably the spirits of the dead which, according to the religious ideas of early man, reward socially good behavior with success in the hunt, a rich harvest, victory in battle, health, fertility, and long life; and which punish bad behavior with disease and death. Nature, socially interpreted, appears as a normative social order connecting a definite human behavior with definite sanctions. This order has a religious character. But even within religions of the highest standards, such as the Judeo-Christian, the normative interpretation of nature plays a part that is not to be underestimated. Even modern man, when hit by misfortune, will often instinctively ask: What have I done to deserve such punishment? He will be inclined to interpret his good fortune as reward for conscientious observance of God's commands. In this respect higher developed religions are distinguished

---

[10] Cf. § 19.

from the primitive ones only so far as they add to the sanctions to be executed in this world those that are imposed in the other world—by God rather than by the spirits of the dead. These sanctions are transcendental not only in the sense that they originate from a superhuman and therefore supersocial authority, but that they are executed outside society and even outside this world within a transcendental sphere.

Different from the transcendental sanctions are those that not only take place in this world and within society, but are executed by the members of the society and may therefore be described as "socially immanent" sanctions. These may consist merely in the approval or disapproval expressed by the fellow members or in specific acts directed against others, that is, in acts to be performed by certain individuals designated by the social order in a procedure regulated by this order. Then one can speak of socially organized sanctions. The oldest sanction of this kind is blood revenge as practiced in primitive society. This is a sanction by which the primitive social order reacts against the fact that a member of a group constituted by blood relationship (the narrower or wider family) kills the member of another group of this kind in a natural way or by magic. It is to be executed by the members of the latter against the members of the former group. Murder within a group originally was probably sanctioned only by the revenge taken by the spirit of the murdered on the murderer. But insofar as the spirit of the dead has power only within his own group, a murder committed by a member of another group can be revenged only by acts of the victim's relatives. Only the nonfulfillment of the obligation for revenge is subject to the transcendental sanction of revenge from the soul of the murdered. It should be noted that blood revenge, this oldest socially organized sanction, originally worked only in the relation between groups. It developed to a sanction functioning within one and the same group only when the social community comprised several groups constituted by blood relationship and hence was larger than a mere family group.

Sociologically, the religious development was characterized by centralization of the superhuman authority, increase of its power, and increase of the distance between the authority and man. The many spirits of the dead were reduced to a few gods and finally to

one all-powerful God transferred to another world. How much the
social idea of retribution dominated this development shows the
fact that when man in his faith imagined in addition to this world
another world, then this other world, in accordance with the principle of reward and punishment, split into a heaven for the good
and a hell for the evil.

It is remarkable that of the two sanctions, reward and punishment, the latter plays a much more important role in social reality
than the former. This is shown not only by the fact that the most
important social order, the legal order, essentially makes use only
of punishment, but especially clearly under a social order which
still has a purely religious character, that is, a social order guaranteed only by transcendental sanctions. The morally or legally correct behavior of primitive men, especially in the observance of the
numerous prohibitions—the so-called tabus—is determined primarily by the fear of misfortunes imposed by a superhuman authority—the spirits of the dead—as a reaction against the violation
of the traditional order. The hope of reward, if compared with the
fear that dominates the life of the primitives, plays only a subordinate role. In the religious beliefs of civilized man, too, according to
which divine retribution is not (or not only) imposed in this
world but in the world beyond, fear of punishment after death
takes first place. The image of hell as the place of punishment is
much more vivid than the usually vague idea of a life in heaven
which is the reward for piety. Even when no limits are imposed on
man's wish-fulfilling phantasy, it produces a transcendental order
which is not fundamentally different from that of the empirical
society.

6. THE LEGAL ORDER

a) The Law: An Order of Human Behavior

A theory of law must begin by defining its object matter. To
arrive at a definition of law, it is convenient to start from the usage
of language, that is, to determine the meaning of the word "law"
as equivalent to the German word *Recht,* French *droit,* Italian
*diritto.** Our task will be to examine whether the social phenomena

* *Translator's Note:* This is the translation of the German text ". . . die Bedeutung
festzustellen, die das Wort 'Recht' in der deutschen Sprache und seine Aequivalenten
in anderen Sprachen (*law, droit, diritto* usw.) haben." The English word "law" is
not confined to the legal sense but is also used for law of nature.

described by these words have common characteristics by which they may be distinguished from similar phenomena, and whether these characteristics are significant enough to serve as elements for a concept of social-scientific cognition. The result of such an investigation could conceivably be that the word "law" and its equivalents in other languages designates so many different objects that they cannot be comprehended in one concept. However, this is not so. Because, when we compare the objects that have been designated by the word "law" by different peoples at different times, we see that all these objects turn out to be *orders of human behavior*. An "order" is a system of norms whose unity is constituted by the fact that they all have the same reason for their validity; and the reason for the validity of a normative order is a basic norm—as we shall see—from which the validity of all norms of the order are derived. A single norm is a valid legal norm, if it corresponds to the concept of "law" and is part of a legal order; and it *is* part of a legal order, if its validity is based on the basic norm of that order.

The norms of a legal order regulate human behavior. At first sight it seems as if this sentence applied only to the social orders of civilized peoples, because in primitive societies the behavior of animals, plants, and even inanimate objects is also regulated by a legal order. For example, we read in the Bible that an ox that has killed a man ought to be killed—evidently as a punishment. In ancient Athens, there was a special court, in which a stone or spear or any other object could be tried by which a man—presumably inadvertently—had been killed. In the Middle Ages it was possible to sue an animal, for example a bull that had caused the death of a man or grasshoppers that had destroyed a harvest. The accused animal was condemned and executed in formal legal procedure, exactly like a human criminal. If the sanctions, provided by the legal order, are directed not only against men but also against animals, this means that not only human behavior, but also the behavior of animals is legally commanded. This means further: if that which is legally commanded is to be regarded as the content of a legal duty,[11] then not only men, but also animals are regarded as being obliged to behave in a certain way. This, in our modern point of view, absurd legal content is the result of animistic ideas, according to which not only men, but also animals, and

---

[11] Cf. § 28.

inanimate objects have a "soul" and are therefore basically not different from human beings. Consequently sanctions, and therefore norms that establish legal duties, are applicable to men as well as animals and things. Although modern legal orders regulate only the behavior of men, not of animals, plants, and things, it is not excluded that these orders prescribe the behavior of man toward animals, plants, and things. For example, the killing of certain animals (in general or at specific times), the damaging of rare plants or historically valuable buildings may be prohibited. But these legal norms do not regulate the behavior of the protected animals, plants, and things, but of the men against whom the threat of punishment is directed.

This behavior may be a positive action or nonaction—a lack of action, an omission, a forbearance, a refrainment from action. The legal order, as a social order, regulates positively [12] the behavior of individuals only so far as it refers, directly or indirectly, to other individuals. The object of regulation by a legal order is the behavior of one individual in relation to one, several, or all other individuals—the mutual behavior of individuals. The relation of the behavior of one man to others may be an individual one: for example, the norm that obliges every man to refrain from killing other men; or the norm that obliges the debtor to pay the creditor; or the norm that obliges everybody to respect the property of others. But the relation may also have a collective character. For example, the behavior prescribed by the norm obliging a man to do military service, is not the behavior of an individual versus another individual, but versus the entire social community—versus all individuals subject to the legal order. The same is true where suicide attempt is punishable. And in the same way the mentioned norms protecting animals, plants, and inanimate objects may be interpreted as social norms. The legal authority commands a certain human behavior, because the authority, rightly or wrongly, regards such behavior as necessary for the human legal community. In the last analysis, it is this relation to the legal community which is decisive for the legal regulation of the behavior of one individual to another. For the legal norm obliges the debtor not only and, perhaps, not so much in order to protect the creditor, but in order to maintain a certain economic system.

---

[12] Cf. § 4d.

b) The Law: A Coercive Order

The first characteristic, then, common to all social orders designated by the word "law" is that they are orders of human behavior. A second characteristic is that they are *coercive orders*.
This means that they react against certain events, regarded as undesirable because detrimental to society, especially against human
behavior of this kind, with a coercive act; that is to say, by inflicting on the responsible individual an evil—such as deprivation of
life, health, liberty, or economic values—which, if necessary, is imposed upon the affected individual even against his will by the
employment of physical force. By the coercive act an evil is inflicted in the sense that the affected individual ordinarily regards it
as such, although it may occasionally happen that this is not so.
For example, somebody who has committed a crime may regret his
action so much that he actually wishes to suffer the punishment of
the law and therefore does not regard it as an evil; or somebody
commits a crime in order to go to jail where he can be sure of food
and shelter. But these are, of course, exceptions. Since, ordinarily,
the affected individual regards the coercive act as an evil, the social
orders, designated as "law" are coercive orders of human behavior.
They command a certain human behavior by attaching a coercive
act to the opposite behavior. This coercive act is directed against
the individual who behaves in this way (or against individuals
who are in some social relation to him). That means: the coercive
order authorizes a certain individual to direct a coercive act as a
sanction against another individual. The sanctions prescribed by
the legal order are socially immanent (as distinguished from transcendental) sanctions; besides, they are socially organized (as distinguished from mere approval or disapproval).

By prescribing coercive acts, a legal order may not only react
against a certain human behavior, but also against other socially
detrimental facts, as will be described later. In other words:
Whereas the coercive act prescribed by the legal order is always
the behavior of a certain individual, the condition to which the
coercive act is attached need not necessarily be the behavior of an
individual but may be another fact, regarded as socially detrimental. As we shall see, the coercive act prescribed by the legal order

may be interpreted as an action of the community constituted by the legal order and especially as a reaction of the legal community against a socially detrimental fact. That means that the coercive act may be *attributed* to this community; which is a figurative expression of the mental operation by which we refer the coercive act prescribed by the legal order to this legal order, the unity of which we personify as an acting entity. If the socially detrimental fact against which the community reacts with a coercive act is a definite human behavior, the reaction is interpreted as a sanction. That the law is a coercive order means that the legal norms prescribe coercive acts which may be attributed to the legal community. This does not mean that the execution of the sanctions each time requires the application of physical force; this is necessary only if execution meets resistance, which ordinarily does not happen.

Modern legal orders sometimes contain norms that provide for rewards, such as titles or decorations, for certain meritorious acts. But rewards are not an element common to all social orders designated as law; they are not an essential function of these orders. Within these coercive orders they play a subordinate role. Besides, these norms authorizing certain organs to confer titles or decorations on individuals who have distinguished themselves in some way or another have a fundamental connection with the sanction-prescribing norms: For the use of a title or the display of a decoration is either legally not prohibited, that is, negatively permitted; or—and this is the usual situation—it is positively permitted, which means it is forbidden, unless expressly permitted. The legal situation, then, can only be described as a norm-stipulated restriction of the validity of a prohibitive norm; in other words, by referring to a coercive norm.

As a coercive order, the law is distinguished from other social orders. The decisive criterion is the element of force—that means that the act prescribed by the order as a consequence of socially detrimental facts ought to be executed even against the will of the individual and, if he resists, by physical force.

The coercive acts prescribed by the legal order as sanctions

Insofar as the coercive act prescribed by the legal order has the function of a reaction against a human behavior determined by the legal order, then this coercive act has the character of a sanction. The human behavior against which the coercive act is directed is to be considered as prohibited, illegal—as a delict. It is the opposite of *that* behavior that is regarded as commanded or legal, namely the behavior that avoids the application of the sanction. That the law is characterized as a "coercive order" does not mean —as is sometimes asserted—that it "enforces" the legal, that is, the commanded, behavior. This behavior is not enforced by the coercive act, because the coercive act is to be executed precisely when an individual behaves in the prohibited, not the commanded, manner. It is exactly for this case that the coercive act as a sanction is prescribed. Perhaps, however, the mentioned assertion should be taken to mean that the law, by prescribing sanctions, tries to induce men to behave in conformity with its command, in that the wish to avoid the sanctions becomes the motive that brings about this behavior. However, the motivation in question is only a possible, not a necessary, function of the law; the legal—that is, the commanded—behavior may be brought about by other motives also, especially by religious and moral ones. And this happens frequently enough. The coercion that is implied in the motivation is a psychic coercion, which is a possible effect of the idea an individual has of the law, and which takes place within this individual. And this psychic coercion must not be confused with the prescription of the coercive act, which takes place within the legal order. Every effective social order exerts some kind of psychic coercion, and some orders—such as the religious order—in much higher degree than the legal order. This psychic coercion, then, is not a characteristic that distinguishes the law from other social orders. The law is not a coercive order in the sense that it exerts a psychic coercion; but in the sense that it prescribes coercive acts, namely the forcible deprivation of life, freedom, economic and other values as a consequence of certain conditions. These conditions are in the first place—but not exclusively—a definite human behavior, which precisely by being a condition of a sanction assumes the character of legally prohibited (illegal) behavior—a delict.

The monopoly of force of the legal community
Although the various legal orders largely agree about the coercive acts which may be attributed to the legal community—they always

consist in the deprivation of the mentioned goods—these orders differ concerning the conditions to which the coercive acts are attached. They differ particularly concerning the human behavior whose opposite should be brought about by stipulating the sanctions, that is, concerning the socially desired status, which consists in the legal behavior prescribed by the legal order; in other words, concerning the *legal value* constituted by the legal norms. The development of the law from primitive beginnings to its present stage in the modern state displays, concerning the legal value to be realized, a tendency that is common to all legal orders. It is the tendency gradually and increasingly to prohibit the use of physical force from man to man. Use of force is prohibited by making it the condition for a sanction. But the sanction itself is a use of force. Therefore the prohibition of the use of force can only be a limited one; and one must distinguish between a permitted and a prohibited use of force. It is permitted as a reaction against a socially undesirable fact, especially against a socially detrimental human behavior, as a sanction, that is, as an authorized use of force attributable to the legal community. This distinction does not yet mean, however, that the use of force other than legally authorized as reaction against an undesirable fact, is prohibited and therefore illegal. Primitive legal orders do not prohibit all other kinds of use of force. Even the killing of men is prohibited to only a limited degree. Only the killing of free fellow countrymen is considered to be a crime in primitive societies, not the killing of aliens or slaves. The killing of the latter, insofar as it is not prohibited, is—in the negative sense—permitted. But it is not authorized as a sanction! Gradually, however, the principle is recognized that every use of physical force is prohibited unless—and this is a limitation of the principle—it is especially authorized as a reaction against a socially detrimental fact attributable to the legal community. In this case, the legal order determines exhaustively the conditions under which (and the men by whom) physical force may be used. Since the individual authorized to use force may be regarded as an organ of the legal order (or of the community constituted by the legal order), the execution of coercive acts by these individuals may be attributed to the community.[13] Then we are confronted with a monopoly of force of the legal community. The monopoly is de-

---

[13] Cf. § 30c.

centralized if the individuals authorized to use force do not have
the character of special organs acting according to the principle of
division of labor but if the legal order authorizes all individuals to
use force who consider their interests violated by the illegal conduct of others; in other words if the principle of self-help still prevails.

Legal order and collective security

When the legal order determines the conditions under which, and
the individuals by whom, physical force is to be used, it protects
the individuals who live under this order against the use of force
by other individuals. When this protection has reached a certain
minimum we speak of collective security, because the security is
guaranteed by the legal order as a social order. This minimum of
protection against the use of physical force can be regarded as existing even when monopoly of force is decentralized, that is, even
when self-help still prevails. It is possible to consider such a state as
the lowest degree of collective security. However, we may speak of
collective security only in a narrower sense if the monopoly of
force of the legal community has reached a minimum of centralization, so that self-help is excluded, at least in principle. Collective
security, in this narrower sense, exists when at least the question of
whether in a concrete situation the law was violated and of who is
responsible for it, is not answered by the parties involved, but by a
special organ, an independent court; when, therefore, the question
of whether in a concrete case, the use of force is a delict or legal
and an act that may be attributed to the community, particularly
a sanction, can be objectively decided.

Collective security, then, can have different degrees depending
on the degree of centralization of the procedure by which in concrete cases the existence of the conditions is determined to which
the coercive action of a sanction is attached; and by which this coercive action is carried out. Collective security reaches its highest
degree when the legal order installs law courts with compulsory
jurisdiction and central executive organs whose coercive means are
so effective that resistance ordinarily is hopeless. This is the situation in the modern state, which represents a highly centralized
legal order.

The aim of collective security is peace, because peace is the ab-

sence of the use of physical force. By determining the conditions
and the executive organs for the use of force, by establishing a
monopoly of force of the legal community, the legal order pacifies
this community. But the peace of law is only a relative peace. The
law does not exclude the use of physical force of man versus man.
The law is not a forceless order, as postulated for by utopian anarchism. The law is an order of coercion and, as a coercive order—
according to its evolution—an order of security, that is, of peace.
But precisely as the concept of collective security may be defined
in a narrower sense and applied only where the monopoly of force
of society is centralized, so we may assume that a pacification of the
legal community takes place only on that level of legal development in which self-help is prohibited, at least in principle, and collective security in the narrower sense of the word prevails. Actually, we can hardly assume even a relative pacification of the legal
community as long as the law is still in a primitive condition. As
long as no courts exist that objectively ascertain whether a prohibited use of force has taken place; as long as every individual
who considers his rights violated by another is authorized to use
force as a sanction; as long as the individual against whom force
was used is authorized to react against this use of force by the use
of force, which he can justify as a sanction (that is, as a reaction
against a wrong suffered); as long as blood revenge is a legal institution and the duel legally permitted and even regulated by law;
as long as only the killing of free fellow countrymen, but not the
killing of aliens and slaves is regarded as a crime; as long, finally,
as war is not prohibited by international law in the relations between states: one cannot very well assert that the state of law is
necessarily a state of peace and that the securing of peace is an essential function of the law.[14] All one can say is that the development of the law runs in this direction. Therefore, even if peace is
regarded as an absolute moral value or as a value common to all
positive moral orders—which, as we shall see later, is not the case—
the securing of peace, the pacification of the legal community,
cannot be considered as an essential moral value common to all
legal orders; it is not the "moral minimum" common to all law.

The prohibition of all use of force reveals the tendency to en-

---

[14] This constitutes a significant modification of my view on the relation between
law and peace as presented in my *General Theory of Law and State*, pp. 22 ff.

large the sphere of facts that are established by the legal order as
condition of coercive acts; this tendency has developed far beyond
this prohibition, by the attachment of coercive acts as consequences not only to the use of force, but also to other acts, and
even to omissions of acts. If the coercive act established by the law
is a reaction against socially detrimental behavior and if the function of such an establishment is to prevent such a behavior (individual or general prevention), then this act has the character of a
sanction in the specific and narrower sense of the word; and the
fact that a certain behavior is made the condition for a sanction in
this sense means that this behavior is legally prohibited, a delict.
There is a correlation between this concept of sanction and the
concept of delict. The sanction is the consequence of the delict;
the delict is the condition of the sanction. In primitive legal orders
the reaction of the sanction against the delict is entirely decentralized. The reaction is left to the discretion of the individuals whose
interests have been violated by the delict. They are authorized to
identify *in concreto* as a delict what has been so identified by the
legal order only *in abstracto;* and they are authorized to execute
the sanction established by the legal order. The principle of self-
help prevails. In the course of evolution this reaction against the
delict is increasingly centralized, in that the identification of the
delict and the execution of the sanction is reserved for special organs: the courts and executive authorities. Thereby the principle
of self-help is limited, but it cannot be entirely eliminated. Even
in the modern state, in which centralization has reached the highest degree, a minimum of self-help remains: self-defense. Besides,
there are other cases in modern, centralized legal orders—cases that
have been largely ignored in legal theory—in which, to a limited
extent, the use of physical force is not reserved for special organs,
but left to the discretion of individuals interested in it. We speak
of the right of corporal punishment that even modern legal orders
concede to parents as a means of educating their children. It is
limited to the extent that it must not harm the child's health; but
the decision, which behavior of the child is a condition of corporal punishment, that is, which behavior is pedagogically and
hence socially undesirable, is in principle left to the parents who
may pass this right to professional educators.

Coercive acts other than sanctions

As the state develops from a judicial to an administrative community,[15] the sphere of facts that are made conditions for coercive acts grows. Now not only socially undesirable actions and omissions but also other facts, not having the character of delicts, are included. Among those facts is the suspicion that a definite individual has committed a delict. Special organs, having the character of police agents, may be legally authorized to deprive the suspected individual of his liberty in order to safeguard legal proceedings against him, in which it will be decided whether he has, in fact, committed the delict of which he is suspected. The condition for the deprivation of liberty is not a definite behavior of the individual, but the suspicion of such a behavior. Similarly, the police may be authorized by the legal order to take persons in so-called protective custody, that is, to deprive them of their liberty, in order to protect them against illegal aggression that threatens them. Further, modern legal orders prescribe the forced internment in institutions of insane individuals constituting a public danger, and in hospitals of persons with contagious diseases. Further, property may be expropriated if necessary in the public interest, domestic animals may be destroyed if infected with an epidemic illness, buildings may be torn down by force to prevent their collapsing or the spread of a conflagration. The legal order of totalitarian states authorizes their governments to confine in concentration camps persons whose opinions, religion, or race they do not like; to force them to perform any kind of labor; even to kill them. Such measures may morally be violently condemned; but they cannot be considered as taking place outside the legal order of these states. All these acts constitute the same forced deprivation of life, liberty, and property as the sanctions of the death penalty, imprisonment, and civil execution. But, as we have said, they differ from sanctions insofar as they are not the consequence of a legally ascertained, socially undesirable action or omission of an individual; the condition is not a legally ascertained delict committed by an individual. Delict is a definite human behavior (an action or omission) which, because socially undesirable, is prohibited by the legal order; and it is prohibited insofar as the legal order attaches

---

[15] Cf. p. 297.

to it (or, more correctly formulated: to the fact that it is ascertained in a legal procedure) a coercive act, as this fact is made by the legal order the condition of a coercive act. And this coercive act is a sanction (in the sense of a reaction against a delict) and as such distinguishable from other legally established coercive acts only in that the conditioning fact of the former is a legally ascertained human behavior, whereas the coercive acts which have not the character of sanctions are conditioned by other facts.[16] Some of the coercive acts belonging to the second category may be interpreted as sanctions, if the concept of "sanction" is not limited to reactions against a definite human behavior whose actual existence is legally ascertained, but is extended to situations in which the coercive act is provided for as reaction against a delict—but against a delict whose commission by a definite individual has not yet been legally ascertained, though the individual may be suspected of having committed it and may therefore be arrested by the police; and to situations in which the coercive act is a reaction against a delict that has not even been committed yet, but is expected in the future as a possibility—as in the cases of internment of dangerous psychopaths or persons of undesired opinions, religions, and races, insofar as they are interned in concentration camps to prevent them from a socially undesired behavior of which, rightly or wrongly, in the opinion of the legal authority, they are considered capable. Apparently, this motive is the basis for the limitations of liberty to which, in a war, the citizens of the one belligerent party living on the territory of the other are subjected by the latter. If we extend the concept of "sanction" in this sense, it is no longer congruent with "consequence of a delict." Sanction in this wider sense of the word does not necessarily *follow* the delict.

Finally, the concept of sanction may be extended to include all coercive acts established by the legal order, if the word is to express merely that the legal order reacts with this action against socially undesirable circumstances and qualifies in this way the circumstances as undesirable. This, indeed, is the common characteristic of all coercive actions commanded or authorized by legal orders. The concept of "sanction," understood in this broadest sense, then, the force monopoly of the legal community, may be formu-

---

[16] Cf. § 29 f.

lated by the alternative: "The use of force of man against man is either a delict or a sanction."

The minimum of liberty

As a sanction-prescribing social order, the law regulates human behavior in two ways: in a positive sense, commanding such behavior and thereby prohibiting the opposite behavior; and, negatively, by not attaching a coercive act to a certain behavior, therefore not prohibiting this behavior and not commanding the opposite behavior. Behavior that legally is not prohibited is legally permitted in this negative sense. Since human behavior is either prohibited or not prohibited, and since, if not prohibited, is to be regarded as permitted by the legal order, any behavior of an individual subjected to a legal order may be regarded as regulated by it—positively or negatively. Insofar as the behavior of an individual is permitted by the legal order in the negative sense—and that means: not prohibited—the individual is legally free.

The freedom left to the individual by the legal order simply by not prohibiting a certain behavior must be distnguished from the freedom which is positively guaranteed to the individual by that order. The freedom of an individual which consists in permitting him a certain behavior by not prohibiting it, is guaranteed by the legal order only to the extent that the order commands the other individuals to respect this freedom; the order forbids them to interfere in this sphere of freedom, that is, the order forbids a behavior by which an individual is prevented from doing what is not prohibited and what therefore in this sense is permitted to him. Only then can the nonprohibited (in a negative sense permitted) behavior be looked upon as rightful: that is to say, as the content of a right, which is the reflex of a corresponding obligation.[17]

However, not every behavior so permitted—in the negative sense of not being forbidden—is safeguarded by the prohibition of the opposite behavior of others; not every permitted behavior of one individual corresponds to an obligation of another individual. It is possible that a behavior is not prohibited by the legal order (and therefore, in this sense, permitted), without an opposite behavior of others being prohibited by the legal order, so that this opposite behavior is also permitted. A behavior may not be prohib-

---

[17] Cf. p. 125.

ited, for example, because it is not related to other individuals or at least does not hurt anybody. But not even every behavior that *does* hurt others is prohibited. For example, it may not be prohibited that the owner of a house install a ventilator into a wall situated directly at the borderline of his property. But, at the same time, it may not be prohibited that the owner of the neighboring property builds a house whose one wall directly adjoins the ventilator-equipped wall of the first house and thereby nullifies the effect of the ventilator. In this example, one party is permitted to prevent what the other party is permitted to do—namely to pipe air into one of his rooms by a ventilator.

If a behavior opposite to the not prohibited behavior of another individual is not prohibited, then a conflict is possible against which the legal order makes no provision. The legal order does not seek to prevent this conflict, like other conflicts, by prohibiting the opposite behavior. Indeed, the legal order cannot try to prevent all possible conflicts. Only one thing is prohibited practically universally by modern legal orders: to prevent another individual by force from doing what is not prohibited. For the exercise of physical force—coercive action—is prohibited in principle, except where it is positively permitted for certain authorized individuals.

A legal order—like any normative social order—can command only specific acts or omissions of acts; therefore, no legal order can limit the freedom of an individual with respect to the totality of his external and internal behavior, that is, his acting, wishing, thinking, or feeling. The legal order can limit an individual's freedom more or less by commanding or prohibiting more or less. But a minimum of freedom, that is, a sphere of human existence not interfered by command or prohibition, always remains reserved. Even under the most totalitarian legal order there exists something like inalienable freedom; not as a right innate and natural, but as a consequence of the technically limited possibility of positively regulating human behavior. This sphere of freedom, however, can be regarded as legally guaranteed only to the extent that the legal order prohibits interference. In this respect the constitutionally guaranteed so-called civil liberties are politically particularly important. They are established by provisions of the constitution that limit the competence of the legislators to the extent that the latter are not authorized (or so authorized only under exceptional

conditions) to issue norms that command or forbid a certain behavior, such as the practice of a certain religion or the expression
of certain opinions.[18]

c) *The Law As a Normative Coercive Order;* *Legal Community and Gang of Robbers*

The law as a coercive order is sometimes characterized by the
statement that the law commands a certain behavior "under
threat" of coercive acts, that is, of certain evils. But this formulation ignores the normative meaning with which coercive acts in
general and sanctions in particular are stipulated by the legal
order. The meaning of a threat is that an evil *will be* inflicted
under certain conditions; the meaning of a legal order is that certain evils *ought to be* inflicted under certain conditions or—
expressed more generally—that certain coercive acts ought to be
executed under certain conditions. This is not only the subjective
meaning of the acts by which the law is established but also their
objective meaning. Only because this normative meaning is the
objective meaning of these acts, do they have the character of law-
stipulating, norm-creating, or norm-executing acts. The action of
a highwayman who under threat commands somebody to surrender his money also has the subjective meaning of an "ought." If
the situation created by such a command is described by saying
that one individual expresses a will directed toward the behavior
of another individual, then one merely describes the action of the
first as an actually happening event. The behavior of the other individual, however, which is intended by the will of the first, cannot be described as something that actually takes place, because he
does not yet behave and may not behave at all in the way that the
first one had intended. It can only be described as something that
according to the subjective meaning of the command ought to
take place.

In this way every situation must be described in which one individual expresses a will directed toward the behavior of another
individual. In this respect (namely, so far as only the subjective
meaning of the acts are considered), there is no difference between describing the command of a robber and the command of a

---

[18] Cf. § 29 f.

legal organ. The difference appears only when the objective meaning of the command is described, the command directed from one individual toward another. Then we attribute only to the command of the legal organ, not to that of the robber, the objective meaning of a norm binding the addressed individual. In other words, we interpret the one command, but not the other, as an objectively valid norm; and then we interpret in the one case the connection of the nonfulfillment of the command with a coercive act merely as a "threat" (i.e., a statement that an evil *will be* inflicted), whereas in the other case, we interpret this connection to mean that an evil *ought to be* inflicted. Therefore we interpret the actual infliction of the evil in the second situation as the application or execution of an objectively valid norm, stipulating a coercive act as a sanction, but in the first situation—if we offer a normative interpretation—as a crime.

But why do we interpret the subjective meaning of the one act also as its objective meaning, but not so of the other act? Why do we suppose that of the two acts, which both have the subjective meaning of an "ought," only one established a valid, that is, binding, norm? In other words: What is the reason for the validity of the norm that we consider to be the objective meaning of this act? This is the decisive question.

By analyzing the judgments that interpret the acts as legal (that is, as acts whose objective meaning is norms) we get the answer to the question. Such an analysis reveals the *presupposition* that makes such an interpretation possible.

Let us start from the earlier-mentioned interpretation of the killing of one individual by another as the execution of a death sentence and not as murder. Our interpretation is based on the recognition that the act of killing constitutes the execution of a court decision that has commanded the killing as a punishment. This means: We attribute to the act of the court the objective meaning of an individual norm and in this way interpret the individuals who perform the act, as a court. We do this, because we recognize the act of the court as the execution of a statute (that is, of general norms stipulating coercive acts) in which we see not only the subjective but also the objective meaning of an act that had been established by certain individuals whom we consider, for this reason, as legislators. For we regard the act of legislation as the execution of the constitution, that is, of general norms that, according to their subjective meaning, authorize these individuals to establish general norms prescribing coercive acts. In this way we interpret these individuals as legislative organs. By regarding the norms authorizing the legislative organ not only as the subjective but also as the objective meaning of an act performed by definite individuals, we interpret these norms as "constitution." For the historically first constitution such an interpretation is possible only, if we *presuppose* that one ought to behave according to the subjective meaning of the act, that one ought to perform coercive acts only under the conditions and in the manner the constitution stipulates; if, in other words, we presuppose a norm according to which (a) the act whose meaning is to be interpreted as "constitution" is to be regarded as establishing objectively valid norms, and (b) the individuals who establish this act as the constitutional authorities. As will be developed later,[19] this norm is the basic norm, of the national legal order. It is not established by a positive legal act, but is presupposed, *if* the act mentioned under (a) is interpreted as establishing a constitution and the acts based on the constitutions are interpreted as legal acts. To make manifest this presupposition is an essential function of legal science. This presupposition is the ultimate (but in its character conditional and therefore hypothetical) reason for the validity of the legal order.

By making these statements we are considering, at this point, only a national legal order, that is, a legal order whose territorial sphere of validity is limited to the territory of a state. The reason for the validity of international law, whose territorial sphere of validity is not so limited, and the relationship of the international legal order to the national legal orders, are, for the present, outside our discussion.[20]

It was observed earlier that the validity of a norm (which means that one ought to behave as the norm stipulates) should not be confounded with the effectiveness of the norm (which means that one, in fact, does so behave); but that an essential relation may exist between the two concepts, namely, that a coercive order, presenting itself as the law, is regarded as valid only if it is by and large effective. That means: The basic norm which is the reason

---

[19] Cf. § 34.
[20] Cf. § 34h–j and 43d.

for the validity of a legal order, refers only to a constitution which is the basis of an effective coercive order. Only if the actual behavior of the individuals conforms, by and large, with the subjective meaning of the acts directed toward this behavior—if, in other words, the subjective meaning is recognized as the objective meaning—only then are the acts interpreted as legal acts.

Now we are ready to answer the question why we do not attribute to the command of a robber, issued under threat of death, the objective meaning of a valid norm binding on the addressed victim; why we do not interpret this act as a legal act; why we regard the realization of the threat as a crime, and not as the execution of a sanction.

An isolated act of one individual cannot be regarded as a legal act, its meaning cannot be regarded as a legal norm, because law, as mentioned, is not a single norm, but a system of norms; and a particular norm may be regarded as a legal norm only as a part of such a system. How about a situation, however, in which an organized gang systematically jeopardizes a certain territory by forcing the people living there, under threat, to surrender their money? In this situation we will have to distinguish between the order that regulates the mutual behavior of the members of this robber gang and the external order, that is, the commands that the members of the gang direct at outsiders under the threat of inflicting evils. For it is only in relation to outsiders that the group behaves as a *robber* gang. If robbery and murder were not forbidden in the relations between the robbers, no community, no robber *gang* would exist. Nevertheless, even the internal order of the gang may be in conflict with the coercive order, considered to be a legal order, valid for the territory in which the gang is active. Why is the coercive order that constitutes the community of the robber gang and comprises the internal and external order not interpreted as a legal order? Why is the subjective meaning of this coercive order (that one ought to behave in conformity with it) not interpreted as its objective meaning? Because no basic norm is presupposed according to which one ought to behave in conformity with this order. But why is no such basic norm presupposed? Because this order does not have the lasting effectiveness without which no basic norm is presupposed. The robbers' coercive order does not have this effectiveness, if the norms of the legal order in whose territorial sphere of validity the gang operates are actually applied to the robbers' activity as being illegal behavior; if the members of the gang are deprived of their liberty or their lives by coercive acts that are interpreted as imprisonment and death sentences; and if thus the activity of the gang is terminated—in short, if the coercive order regarded as the legal order is more effective than the coercive order constituting the gang.

If the validity of this coercive order is restricted to a certain territory and if it is effective within this territory in such a way that the validity of any other coercive order of this kind is excluded, then the coercive order may indeed be regarded as a legal order and the community constituted by it may be regarded as a "state" —even if its external activity is illegal according to positive international law. Thus, from the sixteenth to the beginning of the nineteenth century so-called pirate states existed along the northwest coast of Africa (Algiers, Tunis, Tripolis) whose ships preyed upon navigation in the Mediterranean. These communities were "pirates" only with respect to their exercise of force on ships of other states, in defiance of international law. Yet, their internal order presumably prohibited mutual employment of force, and this prohibition was by and large obeyed, so that the minimum of collective security existed which is the condition for the existence of a relatively lasting community constituted by a normative order.

Collective security or peace—as we have said—is a function that the coercive orders designated as "law" have in various degrees when they have reached a certain level of development. This function is an objectively determinable fact. The scientific statement that a legal order is pacifying the legal community, is not a value judgment. Specifically, this statement does not mean that the realization of justice is essential to the law; this value, therefore, cannot be made an element of the concept of law and can therefore not serve as a criterion for the distinction between a legal community and a robber gang. This, however, is the distinction made by St. Augustine who says in his Civitas Dei: "Set justice aside then, and what are kingdoms but thievish purchases? because what are thieves' purchases but little kingdoms?" [21] A state,

---

[21] Saint Augustine, *The City of God*, trans. by John Healy (Edinburgh: 1909), Vol. I, Book iv, chap. 4.

which is according to Augustine a legal community, cannot exist without justice. "Where true justice is wanting, there can be no law. For what law does, justice does, and what is done unjustly, is done unlawfully." But what is justice? "Justice is a virtue distributing onto everyone his due. What justice is that then, that takes man from the true God and gives him unto the condemned fiends? Is this distribution according to due? Is not he that takes away thy possessions and gives them to one that has no claim to them, guilty of injustice, and is not he so likewise, that takes himself away from his Lord God, and gives himself to the service of the devil?" [22]

According to this reasoning, the law is a just coercive order and is distinguished from the coercive order of the robbers by the justice of its content.

That justice cannot be the criterion distinguishing law from other coercive orders follows from the relative character of the value judgment according to which a social order is just. Saint Augustine recognizes as "just" only that order which gives each his due, and applies this empty formula by saying that an order is just only when it gives the true God—who, to him, is the Judeo-Christian God, not the gods of the Romans—what is his due, namely the worship that is expressed in a certain cult; therefore, according to Augustine, an order that does not conform with this postulate, cannot be law, and the community based on this order cannot be a state, but only a robber gang. With this, Roman Law is denied the character of law. If justice is assumed to be the criterion for a normative order to be designated as "law," then the capitalistic coercive order of the West is not law from the point of view of the Communist ideal of justice, nor the Communist coercive order of the Soviet Union from the point of view of the capitalist ideal of justice. A concept of law with such consequences is unacceptable by a positivist legal science. A legal order may be judged to be unjust from the point of view of a certain norm of justice. But the fact that the content of an effective coercive order may be judged unjust, is no reason to refuse to acknowledge this coercive order as a legal order. After the victory of the French Revolution in the eighteenth century and after the victory of the Russian Revolution in the twentieth, the other states showed the distinct inclination not to interpret the coercive orders established by the revolu-

---

[22] *Ibid.*, Vol. II, Book xix, chap. 21.

tion as legal orders and the acts of the revolutionary governments
as legal acts, because the one government had violated the monar-
chic principle of legitimacy and the other had abolished private
property of the means of production. For the last-named reason,
even American courts refused to acknowledge acts of the revolutionary Russian government as legal acts; the courts declared that
these were not acts of a state, but of a robber gang. However, as
soon as the revolution-born coercive orders turned out to be effective, they were recognized as legal orders, the governments as state
governments, and their acts as state acts, that is, legal acts.

d) *Legal Obligations without Sanctions?*

If the law is conceived of as a coercive order, then the formula by
which the basic norm of a national legal order is expressed runs as
follows: "Coercion of man against man ought to be exercised in
the manner and under the conditions determined by the historically first constitution." The basic norm delegates the first constitution to prescribe the procedure by which the norms stipulating
coercive acts are to be created. To be interpreted objectively as a
legal norm, a norm must be the subjective meaning of an act performed in this procedure, hence in accordance with the basic
norm; besides, the norm must stipulate a coercive act or must be
in essential relation to such a norm. Together with the basic norm
the definition of law as a coercive order is presupposed.[23] From the
definition of law as a coercive order follows that a behavior may be
regarded as legally commanded (i.e., as the content of a legal obligation) only if the contrary behavior is made the condition of a
coercive act directed against the individual thus behaving. It is to
be noted, however, that the coercive act itself need not be commanded in this sense: its ordering and executing may be merely
authorized.

Against the definition of law as a coercive order, that is, against
the inclusion of the element of coercion into the concept of law,
the objections have been raised (1) that legal orders actually contain norms that do not stipulate coercive acts: norms that permit
or authorize a behavior, and also norms that command a behavior

---

[23] But the basic norm is not identical with this definition. As a norm the basic
norm is not a concept.

without attaching to the opposite behavior a coercive act; and (2) that the nonapplication of the norms that stipulate coercive acts are frequently not made the condition for coercive acts functioning as sanctions.

The second objection is not valid, because the definition of law as a coercive order can be maintained even if the norm that stipulates a coercive act is not itself essentially connected with a norm that attaches, in a concrete case, a sanction to the nonordering or nonexecuting of the coercive act—if, therefore, the coercive act stipulated in the general norm is to be interpreted objectively not as commanded but only as authorized or positively permitted (although the subjective meaning of the act by which the general norm stipulates the coercive act is a commanding). As for the first objection, the definition of law as a coercive order can be maintained even with respect to norms that authorize a behavior not having the character of a coercive act; or norms that positively permit such a behavior insofar as they are *dependent* norms, because they are essentially connected with norms that stipulate the coercive acts. A typical example for norms cited as arguments against the inclusion of coercion into the definition of law are the norms of constitutional law. It is argued that the norms of the constitution that regulate the procedure of legislation do not stipulate sanctions as a reaction against nonobservance. Closer analysis shows, however, that these are dependent norms establishing only one of the conditions under which coercive acts stipulated by other norms are to be ordered and executed.[24] Constitutional norms authorize the legislator to create norms—they do not command the creation of norms; and therefore the stipulation of sanctions do not come into question at all. If the provisions of the constitution are not observed, valid legal norms do not come into existence, the norms created in this way are void or voidable. This means: the subjective meaning of the acts established unconstitutionally and therefore not according to the basic norm, is not interpreted as their objective meaning or such a temporary interpretation is annulled.[25]

The most important case of norms which according to traditional science of law constitute legal obligations without stipulat-

[24] Cf. § 6c.
[25] Cf. § 35j.

ing sanctions, is the so-called natural obligation. Natural obligations are obligations whose fulfillment cannot be asserted in a
court, and whose nonfulfillment is not the condition of a civil execution. Still, one speaks of a legal obligation, because that which,
in fulfillment of a so-called natural obligation, has been given by
one individual to another cannot be recovered as an unjustified
enrichment. If this is so, however, it merely means: A general
norm is valid stipulating that: (1) if the beneficiary of a performance to which the performer was legally not obligated refuses resti-
tution, civil execution ought to be directed into the property of
the beneficiary; and (2) the validity of this coercion-stipulating
norm is restricted with respect to cases determined by the legal
order. This situation, therefore, can be described as a restriction of
the validity of a sanction-stipulating norm; it is not necessary to
assume the existence of a sanctionless norm.

It is possible, of course, for a legislator to establish, in a procedure conforming with the basic norm, an act whose subjective
meaning is a behavior-commanding norm, without (1) establishing an act whose subjective meaning is a norm prescribing a sanction as a reaction against the opposite behavior; and without (2)
the possibility of describing the situation as "restriction of the validity of a sanction-stipulating norm." In this case the subjective
meaning of the act in question cannot be interpreted as its objective meaning; the norm, which is the act's subjective meaning cannot be interpreted as a legal norm, but must be regarded as legally
irrelevant.

And there are other reasons why the subjective meaning of an
act established in conformity with the basic norm may be regarded
as legally irrelevant: namely, if the subjective meaning of such an
act is not a norm that commands, permits, or authorizes human behavior. A law, established strictly according to the constitution,
may have a content that is not a norm, but the expression of a
religious or political theory—for example, the statement that the
law is given by God or that the law is just or that the law realizes
the interest of the entire population. Or, to give another example,
in the form of a constitutionally established statute the nation's congratulations may be conveyed to the head of the state on the occasion of an anniversary of his accession to power; this may be done
in this form merely to invest the congratulations with special

solemnity. After all, since constitutionally established acts are expressed by words, the acts may have any meaning whatever, not only the meaning of norms. If law is defined as norm at all, legal science cannot dispense with the concept of legally irrelevant contents.

Since the law regulates the procedure by which it is itself created, one might distinguish this legally regulated procedure as *legal form* from the *legal content* established by the procedure, and speak of a legally irrelevant legal content. In traditional science of law this thought is expressed to some extent by the distinction between law in the formal sense and law in the material sense. This distinction acknowledges the fact that not only general behavior-regulating norms are issued in the form of laws, but also administrative decisions, such as the naturalization of a person, the approval of the state budget, or judicial decisions (when, in certain cases, the legislator acts as a judge). But it would be more correct to speak of form of law and content of law rather than of law in the formal and in the material sense. However, the words "legal form" and "legal content" are unprecise and even misleading in this respect; in order to be interpreted as a legal act it is not only required that the act be established by a certain procedure, but also that the act have a certain subjective meaning. The meaning depends on the definition of law, presupposed together with the basic norm. If the law is not defined as a coercive order, but only as an order established according to the basic norm (and if, therefore, the basic norm is formulated as: one ought to behave as the historically first constitution prescribes), then sanctionless legal norms could exist, that is, legal norms that under certain conditions command a human behavior without another norm stipulating a sanction as a reaction against nonobservance. In this case the subjective meaning of an act, established in accordance with the basic norm—if this meaning is not a norm and in no relation to a norm—would be legally irrelevant. Then, a norm established by the constitutional legislator and commanding a certain behavior without attaching a coercive act to its nonobservance, could be distinguished from a moral norm only by its origin; and a legal norm established by custom could not be distinguished from a customarily established moral norm at all.

If the constitution has established custom as a law-creating fact, then all moral norms created by custom constitute a part of the legal order.

Therefore, then, a definition of law, which does not determine law as a coercive order, must be rejected (1) because only by including the element of coercion into the definition of law is the law clearly distinguished from any other social order; (2) because coercion is a factor of great importance for the cognition of social relationships and highly characteristic of the social orders called "law"; and, (3) particularly, because by defining law as a coercive order, a connection is accounted for that exists in the case most important for the cognition of the law, the law of the modern state: the connection between law and state. The modern state is essentially a coercive order—a centralized coercive order, limited in its territorial validity.[26]

Norms that are the subjective meaning of legislative acts and that command a certain behavior without the opposite behavior being made the condition of a sanction are very rare in modern legal orders. If the social orders designated as law *did* contain significant numbers of sanctionless norms, then the definition of law as a coercive order could be questioned; and if from the existing social orders designated as law the element of coercion were to disappear—as predicted by Marx's socialism—then these social orders would indeed fundamentally change their character. They would —from the point of view of the offered definition of law—lose their legal character, and the social orders constituted by them would lose their character as states. In Marxian terms the state—and along with the state, the law—would wither away.

e) Dependent Legal Norms

It was pointed out earlier that: if one norm commands a certain behavior and a second norm stipulates a sanction as reaction against nonobservance, the two norms are tied to each other. This is particularly true if a social order—as the legal order—commands a certain behavior specifically by attaching a coercive act as sanction to the opposite behavior. Therefore a behavior according to such an order may be regarded as commanded—and in case of a legal order as legally commanded—only so far as the opposite be-

---

[26] Cf. § 41a.

havior is the condition of a sanction. If a legal order, such as a statute passed by parliament, contains one norm that prescribes a certain behavior and a second norm that attaches a sanction to the nonobservance of the first, then the first norm is not and independent norm, but fundamentally tied to the second; the first norm merely designates—negatively—the condition under which the second stipulates the sanction; and if the second one positively designates the condition under which it stipulates the sanction, then the first one is superfluous from the point of view of legislative technique. For example: If a civil code contains the norm that a debtor ought to pay back the received loan to the creditor; and the second norm that a civil execution ought to be directed into the property of the debtor if the debtor does not repay the loan; then everything prescribed by the first norm is contained conditionally in the second. Modern criminal codes usually do not contain norms that prohibit, like the Ten Commandments, murder, adultery, and other crimes; they limit themselves to attach penal sanctions to certain behavior. This shows clearly that a norm: "You shall not murder" is superfluous, if a norm is valid: "He who murders ought to be punished"; it shows, further, that the legal order indeed prohibits a certain behavior by attaching to it a sanction or that it commands a behavior by attaching a sanction to the opposite behavior.

Dependent are also those legal norms that positively permit a certain behavior. For—as shown before—they merely limit the sphere of validity of a legal norm that prohibits this behavior by attaching a sanction to the opposite. The example of self-defense has been cited earlier. Another example is found in the United Nations Charter. Article 2, paragraph 4, forbids all members to use force: the Charter attaches to the use of force the sanctions stipulated in Article 39. But the Charter permits in Article 51 the use of force as individual or collective self-defense by limiting the general prohibition of Article 2, paragraph 4. The named articles form a unit. The Charter could have combined them all in a single article forbidding all members to use force which does not have the character of individual or collective self-defense by making the thus restricted use of force the condition of a sanction. Yet another example: A norm prohibits the sale of alcoholic beverages, that is, makes it punishable; but this prohibition is restricted by another norm according to which the sale of these beverages, if a license is obtained, is not forbidden; that means that the sale is not punishable.

The second norm, restricting the sphere of validity of the first, is a dependent norm; it is meaningful only in connection with the first; both form a unit. Their contents may be expressed in the single norm: "If somebody sells alcoholic beverages without a state license, he ought to be punished." The function of the merely negative permission, consisting in the nonprohibition by the legal order of a certain behavior, need not be considered here because negative permission is not granted by a positive norm.

A legal norm may not only restrict the sphere of validity of another norm, but may entirely annul the validity. These derogating norms too are dependent norms, meaningful only in connection with other, sanction-stipulating norms. Further, legal norms authorizing a certain behavior are dependent norms likewise, if "authorizing" is understood to mean: confer upon an individual a legal power, that is, the power to create legal norms. These authorizing norms designate only one of the conditions under which —in an independent norm—the coercive act is prescribed. These are the norms that authorize the creation of general norms: (1) the norms of the constitution which regulate legislation or institute custom as a law-creating fact; and (2) the norms that regulate judicial and administrative procedures in which the general norms created by statute or custom are applied by authorized courts and administrative officials through individual norms created by these organs.

To give an example: Suppose the legal order of a state prohibits theft by attaching to it in a statute the penalty of imprisonment. The condition of the punishment is not merely the fact that a man has stolen. The theft has to be ascertained by a court authorized by the legal order in a procedure determined by the norms of the legal order; the court has to pronounce a punishment, determined by statute or custom; and this punishment has to be executed by a different organ.The court is authorized to impose, in a certain procedure, a punishment upon the thief, only if in a constitutional procedure a general norm is created that attaches to theft a certain punishment. The norm of the constitution, which authorizes the creation of this general norm, determines a condition to which the sanction is attached. The rule of law that describes this situation says: "If the individuals authorized to legislate have issued a general norm according to which a thief is to be punished in a certain way; and if the court authorized by the Code of Criminal Proceedings in a procedure prescribed by this code has ascertained that an individual has committed theft; and if that court has ordered the legally determined punishment; then a certain organ ought to execute the punishment." By thus phrasing the rule of law that describes the law, it is revealed that the norms of the constitution which authorize the creation of general norms by regulating the organization and procedure of legislation; and the norms of a Code of Criminal Procedure which authorize the creation of the individual norms of the judicial court decisions by regulating the organization and procedure of the criminal courts, are dependent norms; for they determine only conditions under which the punitive sanctions are to be executed. The execution of all coercive acts stipulated by a legal order—including those that are ordered by an administrative procedure and those that do not have the character of sanctions—is conditioned in that manner. The constitutional creation of the general norms to be applied by courts and administrative agencies, and the creation of the individual norms by which these organs have to apply the general norms, are as much conditions of the execution of the coercive act as the ascertainment of the fact of the delict or as other circumstances which the legal norms have made the condition of coercive acts that are not sanctions. But the general norm that stipulates the coercive act under all these conditions is an independent legal norm—even if the coercive act is not commanded because its nonexecution is not made the condition of a further coercive act. If we say that in this case the coercive act is authorized, then the word "authorized" is used in a wider sense. It then does not merely mean conferring a legal power in the sense of a power to create legal norms, but also conferring the power to perform the coercive acts stipulated by the legal norms. In a wider sense, then, this power may also be designated as a legal power.

Dependent norms are, finally, also those that further determine the meaning of other norms, by defining a concept used in a second norm or by authentically interpreting a second norm otherwise. For example, a Criminal Code might contain an article saying: "By murder is to be understood the behavior of an individual which intentionally causes the death of another individual." This article defines murder; however, the article has normative character only in connection with another article that says: "If a man commits murder, the authorized court ought to impose the death penalty." And this article, again, is inseparably connected with a third article that says: "The death penalty is to be carried out by hanging."

It follows, that a legal order may be characterized as a coercive order, even though not all its norms stipulate coercive acts; because norms that do not themselves stipulate coercive acts (and hence do not command, but authorize the creation of norms or positively permit a definite behavior) are dependent norms, valid only in connection with norms, that *do* stipulate coercive acts. Again, not all norms that stipulate a coercive act but only those that stipulate the coercive act as a reaction against a certain behavior (that is, as a sanction), command a specific, namely the opposite, behavior. This, therefore, is another reason [27] why the law does not have exclusively a commanding or imperative character. Since a legal order, in the sense just described, is a coercive order, it may be described in sentences pronouncing that under specific conditions (that is, under conditions determined by the legal order) specific coercive acts ought to be performed. All legally relevant material contained in a legal order fits in this scheme of the rule of law formulated by legal science—the *rule of law* which is to be distinguished from the *legal norm* established by the legal authority.[28]

---

[27] Cf. p. 16.
[28] Cf. p. 71.

II

LAW AND MORALS

7. Moral Norms As Social Norms

By determining law—so far as it is the subject of a specific science of law—as norm, it is delimited against nature; and science of law against natural science. But in addition to legal norms, there are other norms regulating the behavior of men to each other, that is, social norms; and the science of law is therefore not the only discipline directed toward the cognition and description of social norms. These other social norms may be called "morals," and the discipline directed toward their cognition and description, "ethics." So far as justice is a postulate of morals, the relationship between justice and law is included in the relationship between morals and law. It should be noted that in the common usage of language, morals is often mixed up with ethics, just as law is mixed up with the science of law; and that to ethics is attributed what is a function of morals: that it regulates human behavior, that it stipulates duties and rights, in other words, that it authoritatively posits norms, whereas actually its function is the cognition and description of the norms that have been created by a moral authority or by custom. The methodological purity of the science of law is jeopardized not only because the bar that separates it from natural science is ignored, but even more so because the science of law is not (or not clearly enough) separated from ethics—that no clear distinction is made between law and morals.

The social character of morals is sometimes called in question by pointing to those moral norms that prescribe a behavior not toward other individuals but toward oneself—such as the norms that prohibit suicide or prescribe courage or chastity. But even these norms occur only in the awareness of socially living people.

59

The behavior of the individual, which these norms prescribe, refers directly—it is true—only to this individual; but indirectly to other members of the community. For this behavior becomes the object of a moral norm in the consciousness of the community, only because of its consequences on the community. Even the so-called obligations toward oneself are social obligations. They would be meaningless for an individual living in isolation.

8. MORALS AS REGULATION OF INTERNAL BEHAVIOR

A distinction between morals and law cannot relate to the behavior to which the norms of these two social orders obligate man. Suicide may be forbidden not only by morals, but also by law; courage and chastity may be moral as well as legal obligations. Nor is the frequently asserted opinion correct that law prescribes external and morals internal behavior. The norms of both orders determine both kinds of behavior. The moral virtue of courage consists not merely in the internal quality of fearlessness, but also in an external behavior conditioned by this quality. And if, on the other hand, a legal order prohibits murder, it prohibits not only the bringing about a man's death by the external behavior of another, but also an internal behavior, namely the intention to bring about such a result. The "internal" behavior—postulated morally according to some moral philosophers—is supposed to consist in a behavior which, in order to be qualified as "moral," must be directed against one's inclinations or against one's egoistical interest. So far as this merely means an obligation created by a moral norm to behave in a certain way exists—that is to say that this norm is valid, even if inclination or egoistical interest are opposed to the commanded behavior—then this also applies to obligations created by legal norms. It is unavoidable that a social order will prescribe a behavior that is possibly directed against some inclinations or egoistical interests of the individuals whose behavior the order regulates. It would be superfluous to prescribe only a behavior that conforms to all inclinations and interests of those subjected to the norm. People follow their inclinations or try to realize their interests even without being obliged to do so. A social order is meaningful only if a situation is aimed at other than the one that results when everybody follows his inclinations or tries to realize his interests, which would be present without the validity and effectiveness of a social order.

It is to be noted that, if individuals subjected to a social order actually behave in conformity with the norms of that order, they do so only because this behavior conforms with their inclination or an egoistical interest, which was elicited by the social order and is possibly—but not necessarily—opposed to the inclination or interest that would be present without the interference of the social order. A man may have contradictory inclinations or interests. His actual behavior then depends on which inclination is more intensive, which interest stronger. No social order is able to eliminate man's inclinations and egoistical interests as motives of his actions and omissions. The social order can only create, if it is to be effective, the inclination or the interest to behave according to the social order and oppose them to inclinations and egoistical interests that would be present without that order.

The mentioned ethical doctrine is sometimes understood to mean that only a behavior directed against inclination or egoistical interest has any moral value. Since "to have a moral value" means to conform with a moral norm, the doctrine implies that morals prescribe to suppress one's inclinations and not to realize one's egoistical interests, but to act from other motives. This means that the moral norm refers only to the motive of one's behavior. Apart from the fact that the fulfillment of the postulate to act from motives other than inclinations and egoistical interest is psychologically impossible, a moral order whose norm relates only to the motive of the behavior presupposes a different social order, which prescribes an external behavior. A norm of morals which relates only to the motive of the external behavior, is incomplete; it can be valid only together with the norms that prescribe the external behavior, and these norms, too, must be moral norms. Not every behavior is moral when it is performed against inclination and egoistical interest. If one obeys somebody else's command to commit murder, then this act cannot have any moral value, even if performed against his inclination or egoistical interest, as long as murder is morally forbidden. A behavior can have moral value only if not merely the motive but the behavior itself conforms to a moral norm. In pronouncing a moral judgment, the motive and the motivated behavior cannot be separated. For this reason, too, the concept of morals cannot be limited to the norm: "Suppress your inclinations, forego the realization of your egoistical interest." But only by so limiting the concept is it possible to distinguish morals and law as the former relating to internal behavior and the latter prescribing also an external behavior.

9. MORALS, A POSITIVE NONCOERCIVE ORDER

Nor is it possible to distinguish law and morals by reference to the creation and application of their norms. Moral norms, precisely like legal norms, are created by custom and by acts of will (for example, of a prophet or the founder of a religion, such as Jesus). In this sense morals, like the law, because actually posited, are positive, and only positive morals are the object of scientific ethics, even as only positive law is the object of the science of law. It is true that a moral order does not provide for organs working according to the principles of division of labor, that is, central organs for the application of norms. This application consists in the moral evaluation of other individuals' behavior as regulated by this order. But, a primitive legal order too is decentralized and, in this respect, is indistinguishable from a moral order. It is significant that the entirely decentralized general international *law* sometimes is considered merely as international *morals*.

A difference between law and morals cannot be found in *what* the two social orders command or prohibit, but only in *how* they command or prohibit a certain behavior. The fundamental difference between law and morals is: law is a coercive order, that is, a normative order that attempts to bring about a certain behavior by attaching to the opposite behavior a socially organized coercive act; whereas morals is a social order without such sanctions. The sanctions of the moral order are merely the approval of the norm-conforming and the disapproval of the norm-opposing behavior, and no coercive acts are prescribed as sanctions.

10. LAW AS A PART OF MORALS

Once law and morals are recognized as different kinds of normative systems, the question of the relationship of law and morals arises. This question has two meanings: One, What *is* the relationship between the two? The other, What *ought* it be? If both questions are intermingled, misunderstandings result. The first question is sometimes answered by saying that law by its very nature is moral, which means that the behavior commanded or prohibited by legal norms is also commanded or prohibited by the moral norms. Furthermore, that if a social order commands a behavior prohibited by morals or prohibits a behavior commanded by morals, this order is not law, because it is not just. The question is also answered, however, by stating that the law may, but need not, be moral—in the mentioned sense, that is, "just"; that a social order that is not moral (which means: just) may nevertheless be law, although the postulate is admitted that the law ought to be moral, which means: just.

If the question of the relationship between law and morals is understood as a question concerning the content of law and not as a question concerning its form; if it is said that law according to its nature has a moral content or constitutes a moral value; then one asserts by these statements that law is valid within the sphere of morals, that the legal order is a part of the moral order, that law is moral and therefore by its nature just. So far as such an assertion aims at a justification of law—and this is its true meaning—it must presuppose that only one moral order is valid constituting an absolute moral value; and that only norms that conform with this moral order and therefore constitute an absolute moral value, can be regarded as "law." This means: one proceeds from a definition of law, which determines law as a part of morals, which identifies law and justice.

11. RELATIVITY OF MORAL VALUE

But if an absolute value in general and an absolute moral value in particular is rejected from the point of view of scientific cognition, because an absolute value can be assumed only on the basis of religious faith in the absolute and transcendent authority of a deity; if one must admit that, from this viewpoint, an absolute moral order excluding the possibility of the validity of another moral order does not exist; if one denies that what is good or just according to that moral order is good under all circumstances, and what is evil according to that order is evil under all circumstances; if, further, one admits that at different times and with different nations and even within the same nation, depending on various classes and professions, very different and contradictory moral systems are valid; if one grants that under different circumstances different behavior may be considered good or evil, just or unjust, and nothing has to be considered good or evil, just or unjust, under all possible circumstances; if, in short, one acknowledges that moral values are only relative: then, the assertion that social norms must have a moral content, must be just in order to qualify as law, can only mean that these norms must contain something common to all possible moral systems, as systems of justice. In view of the extraordinary heterogeneity, however, of what men in fact have considered as good or evil, just or unjust, at different times and in different places, no element common to the contents of the various moral orders is detectable. It has been said that all moral systems postulate to preserve the peace, to inflict force on no one. But already Heraclitus taught that war is not only the "father," that is, the cause, of everything, but also the "king," that is, the highest norm-creating authority, the highest value, hence "good"; that right is fight, and fight therefore just. And even Jesus says: "Do you think that I have come to give peace on earth? No, I tell you, but rather division."

Jesus proclaims thereby that peace is not the highest value, at least not for the moral order of this world. Is it possible to deny that even today many are convinced that war has moral values because it makes possible the practice of virtues and the realization of ideals that are higher than the value of peace? Or is the morality of pacifism uncontested? Does the philosophy of liberalism— that competition, contest, guarantee the best status of society— conform with the ideal of peace? This ideal does not represent the highest value in all moral systems, and no value at all in some. But even if one could detect an element common to all moral systems valid so far, there would not be sufficient reason to regard as not "moral" or not "just" and therefore not as "law" a coercive order that does not contain this element, that commands a behavior that so far in no community has been considered to be good or just and that prohibits a behavior that so far in no community has been considered to be evil or unjust. For if one does not presuppose an a-priori, that is, absolute, moral value, one is unable to determine what must be considered good and evil, just and unjust, under all circumstances. And then, undeniably, also that which the mentioned coercive order commands may be considered as good and just, and that which it prohibits as evil and unjust; so that this order too is—relatively—moral or just. All moral orders have only one thing in common: namely, that they are social norms, that is, norms that order a certain behavior of men—directly or indirectly—toward other men. All possible moral systems have in common their form, the "ought": they prescribe something, they have normative character. Morally good is that which conforms with the social norm that prescribes a certain human behavior; morally evil that which is opposed to such a norm. The relative moral value is established by a social norm that men ought to be behave in a certain way. Norm and value are correlative concepts.

Under these presuppositions the statement "law is moral by nature" does not mean that law has a certain content, but that it is norm—namely a social norm that men ought to behave in a certain way. Then, in this relative sense, every law is moral; every law constitutes a—relative—moral value. And this means: The question about the relationship between law and morals is not a question about the content of the law, but one about its form. Then one cannot say, as is sometimes said, that the law is not only norm (or command) but also constitutes or realizes a value—such an assertion is meaningful only if an absolute, divine value is presupposed. For the law constitutes a value precisely by the fact that it is a norm: it constitutes the *legal value* which, at the same time, is a (relative) moral value; which merely means that the law is norm.

The theory, however, that the law in its essence represents a moral minimum—that a coercive order, to be regarded as law, must fulfill a minimum moral postulate—is not thereby accepted. For to assume the existence of this postulate presupposes an absolute morality, determined by its content, or at least a content common to all positive moral systems—usually the ideal of peace. From what has been said it follows that the legal value, as used here, does not represent a moral minimum in this sense—that, specifically, the peace value is not an element essential for the concept of law.

12. Separation of Legal
and Moral Orders

If it is assumed that law *is* moral by nature, then, presupposing an absolute moral value, it is meaningless to demand that the law *ought* to be moral. Such a postulate is meaningful only (and the presupposed morality represents a yardstick for the law only), if the possibility of the existence of an immoral law is admitted—if, in other words, the definition of law does not include the element of moral content. If a theory of positive law demands a distinction between law and morals in general, and between law and justice in particular, then this theory is directed against the traditional view, regarded as obvious by most jurists, which presupposes that only *one* absolutely valid moral order and therefore only one absolute justice exists. The demand for a separation between law and morals, law and justice, means that the validity of a positive legal order is independent of the validity of this one, solely valid, absolute moral order, "the" moral order, the moral order *par excellence.* If only relative moral values are presupposed, then the postulate that the law *ought* to be moral, that is, just, can only mean that the formation of positive law ought to conform to one specific moral system among the many possible systems. This, however, does not exclude the possibility of the postulate that the formation of positive law ought to conform with another moral system—and actually perhaps conforms with it—while it does not conform with a moral system that is different from it. If, presupposing only relative values, the demand is made to separate law and morals in general, and law and justice in particular, then this demand does not mean that law and morals, law and justice, are unrelated; it does not mean that the concept of law is outside the concept of the Good. For the concept of the "good" cannot be defined otherwise than as that which ought to be: that which conforms to a social norm; and if law is defined as norm, then this implies that what is lawful is "good." The postulate, made under the supposition of a relativistic theory of value, to separate law and morals and therefore law and justice, merely means this: (1) If a legal order is judged to be moral or immoral, just or unjust, these evaluations express the relation of the legal order to one of many possible

moral systems but not to "the" moral system and therefore constitute only a relative, not an absolute, value judgment; and (2) the
validity of a positive legal order does not depend on its conformity
with some moral system.

A relativistic theory of value is often misunderstood to mean
that there are no values and, particularly, that there is no justice.
It means rather that values are relative, not absolute, that justice is
relative not absolute; that the values as established by our norm-
creating acts cannot claim to exclude the possibility of opposite
values.

It is obvious that merely relative morals cannot render the function—consciously or unconsciously demanded—to provide an absolute standard for the evaluation of a positive legal order. Such a
standard of evaluation simply cannot be found by scientific cognition. But this does not mean that there is no such standard—every
moral system can serve as such. But one must be aware, in judging
a positive legal order from a moral point of view (as good or bad,
as just or unjust) that the standard of evaluation is relative and
that an evaluation based on a different moral system is not excluded; further, that a legal order evaluated on the basis of one
moral system as unjust may well be evaluated as just on the basis
of another moral system.

13. JUSTIFICATION OF LAW THROUGH MORALS

A justification of positive law through morals is possible only if a
contrast can exist between the moral and the legal norms—if there
can be a morally good and a morally bad law. If a moral order, like
the one proclaimed by Paul in his Letter to the Romans prescribes
to observe under all circumstances the norms enacted by the legal
authority and thereby excludes any discrepancy between it and
positive law, then it is not possible to legitimize the positive law by
the moral order. For if all positive law, as willed by God, is just
(like everything else that exists is good insofar as it is willed by
God); and if no positive law is unjust, because nothing that exists
can be evil; if law is identified with justice; and if that which *is* is
identified with that which *ought* to be, then the concept of justice
as well as the concept of the Good have lost their meanings. If
nothing bad (unjust) exists, then nothing good (just) can exist.

The postulate to differentiate law and morals, jurisprudence and ethics, means this: from the standpoint of scientific cognition of positive law, its justification by a moral order different from the legal order, is irrelevant, because the task of the science of law is not to approve or disapprove its subject, but to know and describe it. True, legal norms, as prescriptions of what ought to be, constitute values; yet the function of the science of law is not the evaluation of its subject but its value-free description. The legal scientist does not identify himself with any value, not even with the legal value he describes.

If the moral order does not prescribe to obey the positive legal order under all circumstances, if, in other words, a discrepancy between a moral and a legal order is possible, then the postulate to separate law and morals, science of law and ethics means that the validity of positive legal norms does not depend on their conformity with the moral order; it means, that from the standpoint of a cognition directed toward positive law a legal norm may be considered valid, even if it is at variance with the moral order.

It is paramount and cannot be emphasized enough to understand that not only one moral order exists, but many different and even conflicting ones; that a positive legal order may on the whole conform with the moral views of a certain group of the population (especially the ruling one), yet may conflict with the moral views of another group; and that, above all, the judgment of what is morally good or evil, morally justifiable or unjustifiable, is subject to continuous change, as is the law, and that a legal order (or some of its norms) that at the time of its validity may have conformed with the postulates of the moral order then prevalent, may still be judged to be immoral today. The thesis, widely accepted by traditional science of law but rejected by the Pure Theory of Law, that the law by its nature must be moral and that an immoral social order is not a legal order, presupposes an absolute moral order, that is, one valid at all times and places. Otherwise it would not be possible to evaluate a positive social order by a fixed standard of right and wrong, independent of time and place.

The thesis that law is moral by nature—in the sense that only a moral social order is law—is rejected by the Pure Theory of Law not only because this thesis presupposes an absolute moral order, but also because in its actual application by the science of law pre-

vailing in a certain legal community, this thesis amounts to an uncritical justification of the national coercive order that constitutes
this community. For it is taken for granted that one's own national
coercive order is a legal order. The dubious standard of an absolute morality is applied only to the coercive order of other nations.
Only they are disqualified as immoral and therefore as nonlaw,
when they do not conform with certain postulates with which
one's own coercive order conforms—for example, when they recognize or do not recognize private property, or when they are democratic or not democratic. But since one's own coercive order is
law, then, according to the above-mentioned thesis, it must also be
moral. Such justification of the positive law may politically be
convenient, even though logically inadmissible. From the point of
view of a science of law it must be rejected, because it is not the
task of this science to justify the law by absolute or relative morals;
but to know and to describe it.

III

LAW AND SCIENCE

14. Legal Norms As the Object of the Science of Law

The obvious statement that the object of the science of law is the law includes the less obvious statement that the object of the science of law is *legal norms,* but human behavior only to the extent that it is determined by legal norms as condition or consequence, in other words, to the extent that human behavior is the content of legal norms. Interhuman relations are objects of the science of law as legal relations only, that is, as relations constituted by legal norms.[29] The science of law endeavors to comprehend its object "legally," namely from the viewpoint of the law. To comprehend something legally means to comprehend something as law, that is, as legal norm or as the content of a legal norm —as determined by a legal norm.

15. Static and Dynamic Legal Theory

We distinguish a static and a dynamic theory of law, depending on whether the one or the other alternative is emphasized—the human behavior regulated by norms or the norms regulating human behavior (that is, whether the cognition is directed toward the legal norms created, applied, or obeyed by acts of human behavior or toward the acts of creation, application, or obedience determined by legal norms).[30] According to the first alternative, the object of the theory of law is the law as a system of valid norms— the law in its state of rest. According to the second, the object of

---

[29] Cf. § 32.
[30] Cf. § 27 and § 34a–d.

70

the legal theory is the process in which law is created and applied —the law in motion. Whereby it is to be noted that this process itself is regulated by law. For it is a most significant peculiarity of law that it regulates its own creation and application. The creation of the general legal norms—the process of legislation—is regulated by the constitution; the formal or procedural statutes regulate the application of the material statutes by the courts and administrative organs. Therefore, the acts of law creation and law application [31] that constitute the legal process are considered by legal cognition only to the extent that they form the content of legal norms—that they are determined by legal norms; hence the dynamic theory of law is also directed toward legal norms, namely toward those that regulate the creation and application of the law.

16. LEGAL NORM AND RULE OF LAW

The science of law, by comprehending human behavior only to the extent that it is the content of—which means, determined by —legal norms, represents a normative interpretation of its object. The science of law describes the legal norms created by acts of human behavior and to be applied and obeyed by such acts; and thereby describes the norm-constituted relations between the facts determined by the norms. The sentences by which the science of law describes these norms and relationships must be distinguished as "rules of law" from the legal *norms* that are created by the legal authorities, applied by them, and obeyed by the legal subjects. Rules of law (in a descriptive sense), on the other hand, are hypothetical judgments stating that according to a national or international legal order, under the conditions determined by this order, certain consequences determined by the order ought to take place. Legal *norms* are not judgments, that is, they are not statements about an object of cognition. According to their meaning they are commands; they may be also permissions and authorizations; but they are not instructions as is often maintained when law and jurisprudence are erroneously equated. The law commands, permits, or authorizes, but it does not "teach." However, when legal norms are linguistically expressed in words and sentences, they may ap-

[31] Cf. § 35 f.

pear in the form of assertions stating facts. For example, the norm
that theft ought to be punished is frequently formulated by the
legislator in the sentence: "Theft is punished by imprisonment";
the norm that the head of state is authorized to conclude treaties is
expressed by saying: "The head of state concludes treaties." Important, however, is not the linguistic form, but the meaning of
the law-creating, norm-positing act. The meaning of the act is
different from the meaning of the law-describing rule of law. The
differentiation between "rule of law" (in German: Rechts-*Satz*)
and "legal norm" (in German Rechts-*Norm*) expresses the difference between the function of legal cognition and the entirely
different function of legal authority represented by the organs of
the legal community. The science of law has to know the law—as it
were from the outside—and to describe it. The legal organs, as
legal authorities, have to create the law so that afterward it may be
known and described by the science of law. It is true that the law-
applying organs also have to know—as it were from the inside—the
law they are applying. The legislator who applies the constitution
ought to know the constitution, and the judge who applies the law
ought to know the law. But this knowledge is not the essential element of their functions; it is only the preparation for their functions.[32]

It is further true that, according to Kant's epistemology, the
science of law as cognition of the law, like any cognition, has constitutive character—it "creates" its object insofar as it comprehends
the object as a meaningful whole. Just as the chaos of sensual per-
ceptions becomes a cosmos, that is, "nature" as a unified system,
through the cognition of natural science, so the multitude of general and individual legal norms, created by the legal organs, becomes a unitary system, a legal "order," through the science of law.
But this "creation" has a purely epistemological character. It is
fundamentally different from the creation of objects by human
labor or the creation of law by the legal authority.

The difference between the function of the science of law and
the function of the legal authority, and thereby the difference between the product of the one and that of the other, is frequently
ignored. Linguistically law and science of law are often used
synonymously. For example by speaking of "classical international

---

[32] Cf. § 35g, subsection "The constitutive character of the judicial decision."

law" one actually means a certain theory of international law; or by speaking of science of law as a source of law, one means that the science of law can make a binding decision of a law case. But the science of law can only *describe* the law, it cannot *pre*scribe a certain behavior like the law created by the legal authority (in the form of general or individual norms). No jurist can deny the essential difference between a law published in the official legal gazette and a scientific commentary to this law—between the penal code and a textbook on criminal law. The statements formulated by the science of law that, according to a certain legal order, something ought to be done or not to be done, do not impose obligations nor confer rights upon anybody; they may be true or false. But the norms enacted by the legal authority, imposing obligations and conferring rights upon the legal subjects are neither true nor false, but only valid or invalid; just as facts are neither true nor false, but only existent or nonexistent, and only *statements about* facts can be true or false. For example, the statement contained in a text on civil law that a person who does not fulfill a promise of marriage has to compensate for the damage caused or else a civil execution ought to be directed into his property, is false if the law of the state, which is described in this legal text, does not establish such an obligation because it does not prescribe such a civil execution. The answer to the question of whether such a legal norm is valid within a legal order can be—indirectly— verified, because the norm, to be valid, must have been created by an empirically identifiable act. But the norm enacted by the legal authority (prescribing compensation for the damage and civil execution in case of nonfulfillment) cannot be true or false, because it is not an assertion about a fact—not a *de*scription of an object but a *pre*scription—and is as such the object to be described by the science of law. The norm constituted by the legislator (prescribing execution against a person who does not fulfill a marriage promise and does not compensate for the damage) and the statement formulated by the science of law and describing this norm (that execution ought to be carried out against a person who does not fulfill his marriage promise and does not compensate for the damage caused)—these expressions are logically different. It is therefore convenient to differentiate them terminologically as "legal norm" and "rule of law." It follows from what has been said that the rules of law formulated by the science of law are not simply repetitions of the legal norms created by the legal authority. The objection that rules of law are superfluous is not so obviously unfounded, however, as the view that a natural science is superfluous beside nature, for nature does not manifest itself in spoken and written words, as the law does. The view that a rule of law formulated by the science of law is superfluous beside the legal norm created by the legislator can be met only by pointing out that such a view would amount to the opinion that a scientific presentation of a criminal law is superfluous beside this criminal law, that the science of law is superfluous beside the law.

Since legal norms, being prescriptions (that is, commands, permissions, authorizations), can neither be true nor false, the question arises: How can logical principles, especially the Principle of the Exclusion of Contradiction and the Rules of Inference be applied to the relation between legal norms, if, according to traditional views these principles are applicable only to assertions that can be true or false. The answer is: Logical principles are applicable, indirectly, to legal norms to the extent that they are applicable to the rules of law which describe the legal norms and which can be true or false. Two legal norms are contradictory and can therefore not both be valid at the same time, if the two rules of law that describe them are contradictory; and one legal norm may be deduced from another if the rules of law that describe them can form a logical syllogism.*

This is not incompatible with the fact that these rules of law are ought-statements and must be ought-statements, because they describe norms prescribing that something ought to be. The statement describing the validity of a norm of criminal law that prescribes imprisonment for theft would be false if it were to say that according to that norm theft is punished by imprisonment—it would be false, because there are circumstances in which despite the validity of that norm theft is, in fact, not punished: for example, when the thief is not caught. The rule of law describing this

---

* *Translator's Note:* As for the applicability of the logical principle of the exclusion of contradiction to positive legal norms, see the article by Hans Kelsen, "Derogation" in *Essays in Jurisprudence in Honor of Roscoe Pound,* ed. by Ralph Newman under the aegis of the American Society for Legal History (Indianapolis and New York: Bobbs-Merrill, 1962), pp. 339–355. With respect to the application of the rule of inference to norms, see "Recht und Logik," *Forum,* XII: 142 (Vienna, October, 1965), pp. 421–425, and XII: 143 (November, 1965), pp. 495–500.

norm can be formulated only in this way: If somebody steals, he ought to be punished. But the "ought" of the legal rule does not have a prescriptive character, like the "ought" of the legal norm— its meaning is descriptive. This ambiguity of the word "ought" is overlooked when ought-statements are identified with imperative statements.

17. CAUSAL SCIENCE AND NORM SCIENCE

By defining law as a norm (or, to be precise, as a system of norms or as a normative order) and by limiting the science of law to the cognition and description of legal norms and to the norm-constituted relations between the norm-determined facts, the law is delimited against nature, and the science of law as a science of norms is delimited against all other sciences that are directed toward causal cognition of actual happenings. Thereby a criterion has been ascertained according to which society can be clearly differentiated from nature, and social science from natural science.

One of the many definitions of nature identifies it as an order of things, or a system of elements, that are linked as cause and effect, which means they are connected according to the principle of causality. The so-called laws of nature by which science describes nature are applications of this principle—for example the statement that a metallic body expands when heated. The relation between heat and expansion is that of cause and effect.

If a social science, different from natural science, exists, it must describe its object according to a principle different from causality. Society as the object of such a science, different from natural science, is a normative order of human behavior. There is no cogent reason, however, why human behavior should not be understood also as an element of nature, as determined by the principle of causality—why it should not be explained like the facts of nature as cause and effect. It cannot be doubted that such an explanation is possible at least to a certain extent, and has actually been given. So far as a science describes and explains human behavior in this manner, and is defined as social science because it has the mutual behavior of men as its object, such a social science cannot be considered to be essentially different from the natural sciences.

If we analyze our statements about human behavior, however, we discover that we connect acts of human behavior toward each other and toward other facts not only according to the principle of causality (i.e., as cause and effect), but also according to a principle entirely different from that of causality—a principle for which science does not as yet have a generally accepted word. If we succeed in proving that such a principle exists in our thinking and is applied by the sciences that have as their object mutual human behavior as determined by norms (that is, by sciences that have as their object the norms which determine the behavior) then we are entitled to consider society as an order or system different from that of nature and the sciences concerned with society as different from natural sciences. Only if society is understood as a normative order of human behavior can society be conceived of as an object different from the causal order of nature; only then can social science be opposed to natural science. Only if the law is a normative order of mutual behavior can it be differentiated from nature, as a social phenomenon; only then can the science of law as a social science be differentiated from natural science.

18. Causality and Imputation; Law of Nature and Legal Law

The principle, different from causality, that we apply when describing a normative order of human behavior, may be called *imputation*. By analyzing legal thinking it can be demonsrated that in the rules of law (the sentences by which the science of law *describes* its object, the law; in contradistinction to legal norms which are prescriptions) a principle is applied which, although analogous to causality, is nevertheless characteristically different from it. It is analogous in that this principle has a function in the rules of law similar to the function of the principle of causality in the laws of nature. For example, the following statement is a rule of law: If an individual commits a crime, he ought to be punished; or: If an individual does not pay his debt a civil execution ought to be directed into his possessions; or: If an individual contracts an infectious disease he ought to be interned in an institution. Generally formulated: Under conditions determined by the legal order a coercive act, determined by the legal order, ought to take place.

This is the earlier-mentioned basic form of the rule of law. Precisely like a law of nature, the rule of law connects two elements. But the connection expressed in the rule of law has a meaning entirely different from causality, the connection expressed in a law of nature. Quite patently crime and punishment, civil delict and civil execution, disease and internment of the sick individual are not connected as cause and effect. The rule of law does not say, as the law of nature does: when A is, "is" B; but when A is, B "ought" to be, even though B perhaps actually is not. The reason for the different meaning of the connection of elements in the rule of law and in the law of nature is that the connection described in the rule of law is brought about by a legal authority (that is, by a legal norm created by an act of will), whereas the connection of cause and effect is independent from such human interference.

The difference does not appear within the framework of a religious-metaphysical view of the world, where cause and effect are connected by the will of a divine creator. According to this view the laws of nature describe *norms* that express the divine will— norms, that is, which command nature to behave in a certain way. Consequently a metaphysical theory of law pretends to discover a natural law immanent in nature. From the point of view of a scientific view of the world, however, within which only a positivistic theory of law can be established, the difference between the (causal) law of nature and the rule of law must be maintained with all emphasis. If the rule of law is formulated: "Under certain conditions certain consequences *ought* to take place"; if, in other words, the norm-created connection of the facts determined in a legal norm as condition and consequence is expressed by the word "ought," then this word is not used in its usual sense, as has been said before.[33] "Ought" usually expresses a command, not an authorization or permission. The legal "ought," however, the conjunction which in the rule of law connects condition and consequence, embraces all three meanings: the command, the authorization, and the positive permission of a consequence. The "ought" of the rule of law designates all three normative functions. This "ought" merely expresses the specific meaning in which the two sets of facts are connected by a legal norm, which means *in* a legal

---

[33] Cf. p. 5.

norm. The science of law cannot express this norm-created connection—particularly the connection between delict and sanction—otherwise than by the copula "ought." To render the specific meaning in which the legal norm addresses the legal organs and legal subjects, the science of law cannot formulate the rule of law otherwise than by saying: "According to a certain positive legal order and under certain conditions a certain consequence ought to take place." It is not correct to say, as has been said: the science of law merely asserts that a legal norm of a legal order is "in force" at a certain time, therefore it does not—in contradistinction to a legal norm—assert an "ought" but an "is." Since an assertion that a norm commanding, authorizing, or positively permitting a certain behavior "exists" or is "valid" cannot mean that this behavior actually takes place, it can only mean that this behavior "ought to take place."

Specifically, the science of law is not in a position to assert that, according to a certain legal order, under the condition that a delict has been committed, a sanction is actually executed. If the science of law were to make such an assertion it would conflict with reality: delicts are committed very frequently without the sanction taking place as stipulated by the legal order; and reality is not the object to be described by the science of law. This is still true even if the legal norms to be described by the science of law are valid, that is to say that the behavior determined by them *ought* (in an objective sense) to take place only if the behavior actually conforms with the legal order in some measure. The effectiveness of the legal order—it must be stressed—is only the condition of the validity, not the validity itself. If the science of law has to represent the validity of the legal order—that is, the specific meaning with which the legal order addresses itself to the individuals subject to it; it can only state that according to a certain legal order under the condition that a certain delict determined by that legal order has been committed, a certain sanction determined by that legal order ought to take place; thereby the word "ought" covers both: the situation that the execution of the sanction is merely authorized or positively permitted and the situation that the execution is commanded. The rules of law to be formulated by the science of law can only be ought-statements. But in this respect we have to grapple with a logical difficulty: By using the word "ought," the rule of law formulated by the science of law does not assume the authoritative meaning of the legal norm described by the rule; the "ought" in the rule of law has only a descriptive character. On the other hand, from the fact that the rule of law describes something does not follow that what is described is an actual fact, because not only actual facts, but also norms, that is, the specific meanings of facts, may be described. Specifically, the rule of law is not an imperative; it is, rather, a judgment, a statement about an object of cognition. Nor does the rule of law imply any approval of the described legal norm. The jurist who describes the law scientifically does not identify himself with the legal authority enacting the norm. The rule of law remains objective *de*scription; it does not become *pre*scription. The rule does no more than state, like the law of nature, the link between two elements, a functional connection.

Although the object of the science of law is legal norms and therefore the legal values constituted by these norms, the rules of law are nevertheless, like the laws of nature of the natural sciences, a value-free description of their object. This means, that the description has no relation to a meta-legal value and does not imply any emotional approval or disapproval. If a jurist, describing, from the point of view of legal science, a positive legal order, asserts that under a condition determined by the legal order a sanction ought to be executed determined by this order, he asserts this even if he regards the imputation of the sanction to the condition as unjust, and therefore disapproves of it. The norms that constitute the legal value must be differentiated from the norms according to which the formation of the law is evaluated. If the science of law is called upon at all to answer the question of whether a concrete behavior does or does not conform to the law, the answer can only be an assertion to the effect that this behavior, in the legal order described by the science of law, is commanded or prohibited, authorized or not authorized, permitted or not permitted—regardless of whether this behavior is judged by the one who makes the assertion to be morally good or bad, and whether he approves or disapproves of it.

Since the rule of law in a descriptive sense, like the law of nature (of the natural science) expresses a functional connection, it can also be designated as legal law (meaning law in a legal sense, German: *Rechtsgesetz*), in analogy to law of nature. As was emphasized earlier, the rule of law by using the word "ought" expresses merely the specific meaning in which condition and consequence, particularly delict and sanction, are connected by the legal norm; whereby the connection described by the legal law is analogous, yet different, from the connection of cause and effect expressed in a law of nature.

Precisely as the law of nature (the assertion describing nature) is not the described object, so the legal law (the assertion describing the law or, in other words, the rule of law formulated by the science of law) is not the described object, namely the law, the legal norm. The latter—although designated as "law" when it has general character—is not a law in a sense analogous to a law of nature. For the legal norm is not an assertion *de*scribing a functional connection. The legal norm is not an assertion at all, but the meaning of an act by which something is *pre*scribed and by which the functional connection between facts is first established—a connection described by the rule of law, the legal law.

The rule of law that presents itself as a legal law has a general character, like the law of nature, which means that the legal law describes the general norms of the legal order and the relationships constituted by these norms. The individual legal norms, created by judicial decision or administrative acts, are described by the science of law as a concrete experiment is described by natural science by referring to a law of nature that manifests itself in the experiment. A textbook on physics might, for example, contain the words: "Since, according to a law of nature, a metallic body expands when heated, the metallic sphere that physicist X dropped before heating through a wooden ring, did not pass through it after heating." Or a text on German criminal law might say: "According to a legal law to be formulated with reference to German law, an individual who committed theft ought to be punished by a court by imprisonment; therefore the Court X in Y, having determined that A has committed theft, has decided that A ought to be forcibly confined in prison Z for one year." By saying that "A having committed a certain theft ought to be forcibly confined in prison Z for one year" the individual norm is described which Court X in Y has enacted.

If the connection between condition and consequence, expressed by the word "ought" in the rule of law, is called "imputation," then perhaps a new word but not a new concept is introduced into a discipline which always used the concept designated here by the word "imputation." This is implied in the concept "responsibility." That an individual is responsible for his behavior means that he may be punished for this behavior; and that he is irresponsible, or not responsible, means that he, for the same behavior—because he is a minor or insane—may not be punished. That means, that in the first case a definite behavior *is*, in the second case this behavior is *not*, connected with punishment; that the behavior is or is not a condition for punishment; that punishment is or is not *imputed* to the behavior. It is true that by saying: an individual is responsible or not responsible for his behavior, one means that the behavior is or is not imputed to the individual. But the behavior in question is imputed or not imputed to the individual (which means: the individual is responsible or not responsible for his behavior) only by the fact that in the former case the behavior is connected with a sanction and thereby qualified as a delict, whereas this is not done in the latter case; so that, therefore an irresponsible individual cannot commit a delict. This means, however, that imputation merely consists in this connection between delict and sanction. Imputation, which expresses itself in the concept of responsibility, is therefore not the connection between a certain behavior and an individual who thus behaves—as assumed by traditional theory; for this, no connection by a legal norm is necessary, because the behavior and the behaving individual cannot be separated; even the behavior of a not responsible man is still his behavior (his action or his refraining from action), even if it is not an imputable delict. Imputation, implied in the concept of responsibility, is the connection between a certain behavior, namely a delict, with a sanction. Therefore it is possible to say: the sanction is imputed to the delict, but the sanction is not "effected by" (is not "caused by") the delict. It is obvious that the science of law does not aim at a causal explanation of the legal phenomena delict and sanction. In the rules of law by which the science of law describes these phenomena, it is not the principle of causality which is employed, but another principle that we designated as imputation.

19. THE PRINCIPLE OF IMPUTATION IN
THE THINKING OF PRIMITIVE MAN

An investigation of primitive societies and of primitive mentality
shows that the same principle is at the basis of the interpretation
of nature by primitive men.[34] Primitive man probably did not ex-
plain natural phenomena according to the principle of causality.
This principle, the fundamental principle of natural science—like
natural science itself—is the achievement of a relatively advanced
civilization. Early man interpreted facts perceived by his senses
according to the same principles which regulated the relationships
to his fellow men, namely according to social norms.

When men live together in a group the idea arises that a certain
behavior is good and another is bad; in other words: that the
members of the group ought to behave under certain conditions in
a certain manner so that the individual who in a concrete situation
desires the opposite behavior and actually behaves according to
this desire, is aware not to have behaved as he ought to. This
means that in the consciousness of socially living men the idea exists that norms binding the individuals regulate their mutual behavior. Furthermore, men living together in a group judge their
mutual behavior according to such norms that actually come into
being by custom, even though they are interpreted as the commands of a superhuman authority. The oldest norms of mankind
are probably those aiming at a restriction of the sexual impulse
and the desire of aggression. Incest and murder are probably the
oldest crimes, outlawry and blood revenge the oldest socially
organized sanctions. These sanctions were based on a rule that
dominated the social life of primitive man: the rule of retribution.
It included both punishment and reward. It may be formulated
roughly as follows: If you behave rightly, you ought to be rewarded, that is, a benefit ought to be bestowed on you; if you behave wrongly, you ought to be punished, that is, an evil ought to
be inflicted on you. In this basic rule, condition and consequence
are not connected with each other according to the principle of
causality, but according to the principle of imputation. So far as

---

[34] Cf. Hans Kelsen, *Vergeltung und Kausalität* (Den Haag: 1941), pp. 1 ff. and
Society and Nature (Chicago: 1943), pp. 1 ff.

any need for an explanation of phenomena existed in the mind of
primitive men at all, it was met by the principle of retribution. If
an event was regarded as harmful, it was interpreted as a punishment for bad behavior; if an event was regarded as beneficial, it
was interpreted as a reward for good behavior. In other words:
Misfortune—that is, detrimental events like poor harvest, unsuc-
cessful hunt, defeat in war, illness, or death—were imputed, as
punishment, to the wrong behavior of the members of the group;
whereas beneficial events—a good harvest, successful hunt, victory,
health, long life—were imputed, as reward, to the right behavior of
the members. If an event occurred which, in the consciousness of
primitive men, required an explanation—and this was only an
event that directly affected their interests—they did not ask:
"What is the cause of it?" but "Who is responsible for it?" Theirs
was not a causal, it was a normative interpretation of nature; and
since the norm of retribution, according to which this interpretation takes place, is a specifically social principle regulating the
mutual behavior of men, this kind of interpretation of nature may
be characterized as socionormative interpretation of nature.

So-called animism of primitive man is his view that not only
human beings have a soul, but all things, including objects that according to our view are inanimate; that in the things, or behind
them invisible but powerful spirits exist, which means that all
things are persons. This view implies that things behave toward
men in the same way that men behave toward each other, namely
according to the principle of retribution. Primitive men believe
that these souls or spirits create misfortune for men as punishment, and fortune as reward. The link that exists according to the
belief of primitive men between wrong behavior and misfortune
as punishment, and between right behavior and fortune as reward,
is based on the idea that mighty superhuman but personal beings
operate nature in this way, that is, according to the principle of
retribution. The essence of animism is personalistic, that is, socionormative, interpretation of nature—an interpretation according
to the principle of imputation, not according to the law of causality.

Consequently, the concept of nature as an order of elements connected together according to the principle of causality, cannot be
formed in the thinking of primitive man. To him nature is part of

his society as a normative order whose elements are connected with one another according to the principle of imputation. The dualism of nature as a causal, and society as a normative, order is unknown to him. That such a dualism exists in the thinking of civilized man is the result of an intellectual development during which human and other beings, persons and things, are distinguished, and the causal explanation of the relationships between things is separated from the normative interpretation of the relationships between men. Modern science of nature is the result of its emancipation of the normative from the social interpretation of nature, and that means from animism. Paradoxically formulating this process we might say: At the beginning of evolution, during the animistic period of mankind, there existed only society (as a normative order); nature as a causal order was created by science only after the latter liberated itself from animism. The instrument of this liberation is the principle of causality.

20. The Origin of the Principle of Causality in the Principle of Retribution

The Law of Causality probably has its origin in the Norm of Retribution.[35] This development is the result of a transformation of the principle of imputation according to which in the norm of retribution the wrong behavior is connected with punishment and the right behavior with reward. This process of transformation began in the philosophy of nature of the ancient Greeks. It is significant that the Greek word for cause, *aitia*, originally meant guilt: the cause is "guilty" of the effect, is responsible for the effect; the effect is imputed to the cause in the same way that the punishment is imputed to the delict. One of the earliest formulations of the law of causality is the famous fragment of Heraclitus: "If the Sun will overstep his prescribed path, then the Erinyes, the handmaids of justice, will find him out." Here the law of nature still appears as a rule of law: If the Sun does not follow his prescribed path he will be punished. For the Erinyes are the demons of revenge of the Greek religion and Dike is the goddess of retribution. The decisive step in the transition from a normative to a causal interpreta-

---

[35] Kelsen, *Vergeltung und Kausalität*, pp. 259 ff. and *Society and Nature*, pp. 249 ff.

tion of nature, from the principle of imputation to the principle of causality, consists in man becoming aware that the relations between things (as distinguished from relations between men) are independent of a human or superhuman will, or, which amounts to the same, are not determined by norms—it consists in man becoming aware that the behavior of things is neither prescribed nor permitted by any authority. Only gradually could the principle of causality divest itself of all slags of animistic, that is, personalistic, thinking. For example, the idea that causality means an absolutely necessary relation between cause and effect—an idea that still prevailed at the beginning of the twentieth century—is certainly a consequence of the view that it is the will of an absolute all-powerful transcendental authority beyond the realm of human experience which connects the cause with the effect. If this view is abandoned, then nothing stands in the way of eliminating the element of necessity from the concept of causality and of replacing it by the element of mere probability. If, however, the element of necessity is retained, it must undergo a change of meaning—it must change from the absolute necessity of a divine will, expressed in the cause-and-effect relation, to a necessity of human thinking, that is, to the exceptionless validity of a postulate of human cognition.

21. CAUSAL AND NORMATIVE SOCIAL SCIENCE

Once the principle of causality is recognized, it is also applicable to human behavior. Psychology, ethnology, history, sociology are disciplines that have human behavior as their object so far as it is determined by causal laws, which means, so far as it occurs in the realm of nature or natural reality. When a discipline is characterized as "social science" because it is directed toward the mutual behavior of men, this science, so far as it attempts to explain human behavior causally, is not essentially different from the natural sciences like physics, biology, or physiology. How far such causal explanations of human behavior are possible is another question. The difference existing in this respect between the mentioned social sciences and natural sciences is only one of degree, not of principle. An essential difference exists only between nat-

ural sciences and those social sciences that do not interpret the
mutual behavior of men according to the principle of causality,
but according to that of imputation; these are the sciences that do
not describe how human behavior, determined by causal laws,
takes place in the realm of natural reality, but how it ought to take
place, determined by "positive," that is, man-made norms. If we
oppose the sphere of values with which we are here concerned to
that of natural reality, then these values are constituted by positive
norms; therefore, the object of these social sciences is by no means
unreal—it also has a reality, but its reality is different from the natural reality: it is a social reality. Such social sciences are ethics (the
science of morals) and jurisprudence (the science of law). If we
designate them as normative sciences, this does not mean that they
prescribe norms for human behavior and thereby command, authorize, or positively permit a certain conduct, but that they describe certain man-made norms and the relationships between
men thereby created. The social scientist is not a social authority.
His task is not to regulate human society, but to know and understand it. Society as the object of a normative social science is a
normative order of the mutual behavior of men. These belong to a
society, so far as their behavior is regulated by such an order, that
is, commanded, authorized, or positively permitted by the order.
If it is said that a certain society is constituted by a normative
order regulating the mutual behavior of a multitude of men, one
must remain aware that order and society are not two different
things; that they are one and the same thing, that society consists
in nothing but this order, and that, if society is designated as a
community, then essentially that which these men have "in common" is nothing else but the order regulating their mutual behavior.

This becomes particularly clear in the case of a legal order (or
the legal community constituted by it) which includes men of
different tongues, races, religions, views of the world, and—
particularly—men belonging to different antagonistic groups of
interests. They all form one legal community so far as they are
subject to the same legal order, that means, so far as their mutual
behavior is regulated by the same normative order. It is true that a
normative order is considered valid only if it is by and large effective; and that, if a normative order, especially a legal order, is

effective one can say: If the conditions, determined by the norms of the social order, actually exist, the consequences connected with these conditions will probably occur; or, in case of an effective legal order: if a delict determined by the legal order has been committed, then the sanction prescribed by the legal order will probably take place. Assuming that the relation between cause and effect is not one of absolute necessity, but of mere probability, and the essence of causality consists in the possibility to predict future events, then it appears as if legal laws are no different from laws of nature and should therefore be formulated as "is-sentences" and not as "ought-sentences." Precisely as the former predict how nature will behave in the future, so the latter predict how society (or the state) will behave in the future. A law of nature says: "If a metallic body is heated, it will expand"; a legal law says: "If a man steals, he will be punished by a law court." Starting from this assumption some distinguished American representatives of the so-called realistic school of jurisprudence assert that the law is nothing but a prediction about what the courts will decide—that the law is a science of prediction.[36] In opposition to this view it must be said: the statement that legal law like laws of nature are assertions about future events cannot refer to norms enacted by the legal authority—neither to the general norms established by the legislator nor to the individual norms created by court decisions; that means, it cannot refer to the law, but only to rules of law formulated by the science of law, describing the law. Legal norms, as stressed earlier, are not assertions—neither assertions about future nor about past events. True, they usually refer to future human behavior, but they do not assert that this behavior will take place; instead, they command, authorize, permit it. On the other hand, the legal rules formulated by the science of law are indeed assertions—not assertions, however, to the effect that something actually will happen (like laws of nature) but assertions to the effect that something *ought* to happen according to the law described by the science of law. It is not correct to object that legal norms are recognized by the science of law as valid only if they are effective and that, if the legal rules describe only effective legal norms, the legal rules are assertions about actual happenings. For validity and effectiveness are not identical. A legal norm is valid

[36] Cf. Kelsen, *General Theory of Law and State*, pp. 165 ff.

even if it is not wholly effective—it suffices if it is effective "by and large," that is, if it is applied and obeyed to some degree. The possibility of the norm being ineffective—that in individual cases it may not be applied or obeyed—must always be present. Precisely in this respect does the difference between legal law and law of nature become apparent. If a fact is found that is in conflict with the law of nature, then science must abandon that law as inaccurate and replace it by another that conforms with the fact. But if some behavior is not in conformity with the legal norm—provided such behavior is relatively infrequent—the science of law has no reason to regard as invalid the violated legal norm, no reason to replace the rule of law describing the law by another rule of law. The laws of nature formulated by natural science *must* conform to the facts, but the facts of human action and refrainment *ought* to conform to the legal norms described by the science of law. It is for this reason that the law-describing legal rules must be ought-statements.

The mingling of law and science of law, which is characteristic for the so-called realistic jurisprudence, demonstrates the need for the distinction between the concept of legal norm and the concept of rule of law, the latter being a legal law analogous to, but not identical with, the law of nature. Besides, there is doubt whether laws of nature actually are predictions about future events. A causal law of nature is verified if it is possible to base on it the prediction of a future event. However, it functions primarily as an explanation of an event that already took place—as the effect of an event designated as its cause by this law of nature. In this respect it refers to the past. Laws of nature are based on experience, and our experience lies in the past, not in the future. As a prediction of the future, a law of nature is applicable only under the doubtful premise that the past will repeat itself in the future. However, we need not pursue this problem here. At any rate, the science of law does not have the task of predicting court decisions. It is directed not only at the cognition of the individual norms actually issued by the courts, but also, and primarily so, at the general legal norms created by legislators and custom; the creation of these general norms can hardly be predicted because the constitution ordinarily does not predetermine [37] the content of laws, but only the proce-

[37] Cf. § 35a.

dure of legislation. A prediction of a judicial decision, however, essentially rests on the fact that the courts by and large apply the general norms created by legislator or custom; the prediction therefore consists merely in the statement that the courts will decide as they ought to decide according to the valid general norms. The predictions of realistic jurisprudence differ from the rules of law of normative jurisprudence (normative science of law) only in that these predictions are *is*-statements not *ought*-statements, but—being is-statements—do not render the specific meaning of the law. To the extent that courts create new law by their decisions, predictions are just as impossible as predictions of general norms to be created by legislators. General norms, however, constitute the bulk of the law with which the science of law is concerned. But even to the extent that predictions are possible, these are not the task of the science of law, which is able to describe individual and general norms only after they have been created and become valid. The prediction of a future court decision might be considered part of the business of a practical lawyer counseling his client. But cognition of the law must not be confounded with legal advice. Even if a by and large effective legal order could be described by statements which, like laws of nature, assert that under certain conditions certain consequences actually take place (in other words: that, if something is done which according to this legal order is defined by the law-applying organ as a delict, the sanction prescribed by the legal order will be executed) still, it is not the science of law that aims at such a description. For the science of law, by formulating rules of law, does not describe a causal connection but a normative connection between the elements of its object: namely, imputation.

22. DIFFERENCES BETWEEN THE PRINCIPLES OF CAUSALITY AND IMPUTATION

The linguistic form in which both the principle of causality and the principle of imputation is presented, is a hypothetical judgment, in which a certain condition is connected with a certain consequence. But, as we have seen, the meaning of the connection is different in the two cases. The principle of causality says: "If *a* is, then *b* is (or will be)." The principle of imputation says: "If *a* is, then *b* ought to be." As an example of the application of the principle of causality in a definite law of nature may serve the earlier-mentioned physical law that describes the effect of heat on metals.

Following are examples, in the realm of normative social sciences, for the application of the principle of imputation: If someone has rendered to you a good service, you ought to show gratitude; if someone has sacrificed his life for his country, his memory ought to be honored; if someone has sinned he ought to do penance. These are ethical sentences or moral laws that express positive norms, that is, norms enacted by a religious leader or created by custom.

Following are examples of legal rules or legal laws in which postive legal norms are expressed, that is, norms enacted by a legislator or created by custom: If someone has committed a crime he ought to be punished; if someone does not pay his debt, civil execution ought to be directed into his property.

The difference between causality and imputation consists, as mentioned before, in the fact that the relationship between the condition as cause and the consequence as effect, expressed in a law of nature, is not brought about by a man-made norm (as is the relation between condition and consequence in a moral or legal law), but is independent of man's interference. Since the specific meaning of the act by which the relation between condition and consequence in a moral or legal law is brought about is a "norm," we can speak of a "normative" relation, as distinguished from a "causal" relation. "Imputation" means a normative relation. This, and nothing else, is expressed by the word "ought" when it is used in a moral or legal law.

Another difference between causality and imputation is this: Each concrete cause must be regarded as the effect of another cause, and each concrete effect as the cause of another effect, so that the chain of cause and effect is endless in both directions in conformity with the essence of causality. To this must be added that every concrete event lies at the intersection of a theoretically unlimited number of causal chains.

The situation is different with respect to imputation. The condition to which the consequence in a moral or legal law is imputed—such as patriotic death to which honor, benefits to which gratitude, sin to which penance, crime to which punishment are imputed—all these conditions are not necessarily also consequences which must be imputed to other conditions. And the consequences —honor, gratitude, penance, punishment—need not necessarily be conditions to which further consequences are to be imputed. The number of links of an imputation chain is not unlimited as the links of a causal chain, but limited. There is an end point in the imputation chain, but nothing of the kind in the causal chain. The supposition of a first cause, a *prima causa*—analogous to the end point in the imputation chain—is incompatible with the idea of causality, or, at any rate, with that idea of causality as expressed in the laws of classical physics. The idea of a first cause which, as the creative will of God or as the free will of man, plays a decisive role in religious metaphysics, is likewise a residue of primitive thinking, in which the principle of causality is not yet emancipated from that of imputation.

23. THE PROBLEM OF THE FREEDOM OF WILL

On the fundamental difference between imputation and causality, namely that imputation has an end point whereas causality has not, rests the contrast between the necessity prevailing in nature and the freedom existing in society and so essential for the normative relations between men. That man, as part of nature, is not free means that his behavior, looked upon as a natural fact, is caused by other facts according to the law of nature—that his behavior must be regarded as the effect of these facts and therefore determined by them. But that man, as a moral or legal person, is "free" and therefore responsible has a different meaning. If a man is held responsible, morally or legally, for his moral or immoral, his legal or illegal behavior, that is, if human behavior is interpreted according to a moral or legal law as merit, sin, or delict; and if to the merit is imputed a reward, to sin a penance, and to the delict a sanction, then this imputation ends in the behavior interpreted as merit, sin, or delict. To be true, it is customary to say that the merit, sin, and delict are imputed to the man responsible for this behavior. But the real meaning of this statement is that the man ought to be rewarded for his merit (more precisely: that the merit of this man ought to be rewarded); that the man ought to do penance for his sin (more precisely: that the sin of this man ought to have its penance); that the criminal ought to be punished (more precisely: that his crime ought to get the punishment it deserves). It is not behavior defined as merit, sin, or crime that is imputed to the man—such an imputaton would be superfluous, since human behavior cannot be separated from the behaving human being. If the question of imputation is raised after a man has behaved meritoriously, has sinned, or has committed a crime, then this question is not: *who* has performed the meritorious deed, who has committed the sin or the crime?—this would be a question of fact; the moral or legal question of imputation is rather: who is responsible for the behavior? And this question means: who ought to be rewarded or who ought to do penance or be punished? It is the reward, the penance, the punishment that are imputed as specific consequences to specific conditions. And the condition is the behavior that represents the merit, sin, or crime. The imputation of the reward to the merit, of the penance to the sin, and of the punishment to the crime includes the imputation to the man, although only this imputation is clearly expressed in the common usage of language.

The problem of moral or legal responsibility is fundamentally connected with that of retribution; retribution is imputation of reward to merit, of penance to sin, of punishment to crime. The principle of retribution connects a behavior which is in conformity to a norm with a reward, a behavior which is in conflict with a norm with penance or punishment. Thus it *presupposes* a norm that commands or prohibits this behavior or *is* a norm that prohibits the behavior just by attaching a punishment to it. But the behavior that constitutes the immediate condition for the reward, the penance, or the punishment may itself be commanded or prohibited as consequence of a definite condition. If by imputation we understand every connection of a human behavior with the condition under which it is commanded or prohibited in a norm,[38] then also the behavior to which, as to its immediate condition, the reward, the penance, or the punishment is imputed, may be imputed to the condition under which it is commanded or prohibited.

---

[38] Cf. § 24 and § 30c.

For example: Morals command that if someone is in need he ought to be helped; if someone obeys this command, his behavior ought to be approved, if he disobeys, his behavior ought to be disapproved. The sanctions of approval and disapproval are imputed to their immediate condition—the commanded aid and the prohibited nonaid; the commanded aid is imputed to the fact whose immediate conditon it is: namely that somebody is in need. This fact is the mediate condition of the approval (functioning as sanction) of rendering aid and of the disapproval of not rendering it. Another example: The law commands that if someone receives a loan and does not repay it, civil execution—as a sanction—ought to be directed into his property. The sanction of civil execution is imputed to the nonrepayment of the loan, defined as a delict—the nonrepayment being the immediate condition for this sanction; the commanded repayment of the loan is imputed to its immediate condition, the receipt of the loan. This fact is the mediate condition of the sanction of the execution. Beyond this mediate condition of the sanction no imputation takes place. But the reward, penance, punishment (including civil execution) are not imputed to their mediate condition, but only to their immediate condition—merit, sin, delict. Reward, penance, punishment are not imputed to the condition under which a certain behavior is commanded as meritorious or prohibited as sinful or unlawful; they are imputed to the man who behaves in conformity or in conflict with the command, or, more precisely: his behavior in conformity with the command is rewarded, his opposite behavior penanced or punished. In this behavior ends the imputation that constitutes his moral or legal responsibility.

If, however, a certain event is the effect of a cause, and if this cause, as always, itself has a cause, then this cause, too, as *causa remota,* is a cause of the event in question. This event is not only referred to its immediate cause, but also to all its mediate causes, and thus is interpreted as the effect of all those causes that form an infinite chain. The decisive point is: the behavior that, under a normative (i.e., a moral or legal) order, is the end point of an imputation, is, under the causal order, no end point (neither as cause nor as effect) but only a link in an infinite chain.

This, then, is the true meaning of the idea that man, as the subject of a moral or legal order, that is, as a member of a society and as a moral or legal person, is "free." That man, subjected to a moral or legal order, is "free" means: he is the end point of an imputation that is possible only on the basis of this normative order. According to the usual view, however, freedom is understood as the opposite of causal determination. To be "free" means: not to be subjected to the law of causality. It is usually said: Because man is free or has a free will—and this means according to the usual view that his behavior is not subjected to the law of causality that determines it, insofar as his will is the cause of effects, but not the effect of causes—he is responsible, which means, capable of moral or legal imputation. Only because man is free can he be made responsible for his behavior: punishable for crimes, expected to do penance for sins, eligible to be rewarded for merits. The assumption, however, that only man's freedom (that is, the fact that he is not subjected to the law of causality) makes responsibility (and that means: imputation) possible is in open conflict with the facts of social life. The establishment of a normative, behavior-regulating order which is the only basis of imputation, actually presupposes that man's will is causally determinable, therefore not free. For it is the undoubtable function of such an order to induce human beings to observe the behavior commanded by the order—to turn norms that command a certain behavior into possible motives determining man's will to behave according to the norms. But this means that the idea of a norm commanding a certain behavior becomes the cause of a norm-conforming behavior. Only because the normative order (as the content of the ideas of men whose conduct the order regulates) inserts itself in the causal process, in the chain of cause and effects, does the order fulfill its social function. And only on the basis of a normative order, that presupposes such causality with respect to the will of the human beings subject to it, is imputation possible.

Earlier [39] it has been said it would be senseless to issue a norm commanding that something ought to be done of which it is known beforehand that, under a law of nature, it must necessarily, always and everywhere, take place. This seems to admit that normativity and causality are mutually exclusive. However, this is not so. The norm that we ought to speak the truth is not senseless, for we have no reason to assume a law of nature according to which

---

[39] Cf. p. 11.

men must speak the truth always and everywhere; we know that
men sometimes speak the truth and at other times lie. But when a
man speaks the truth or when he lies, then in both cases his behavior is causally determined, that means, determined by a law of
nature. Not by a law of nature according to which one must always
speak the truth or always lie, but by another law of nature, for example by one according to which man chooses that behavior from
which he expects the greatest advantage. The idea of the norm
that one ought to speak the truth can be—in conformity with this
law of nature—an effective motive for behavior according to the
norm. A norm that would prescribe that man ought not to die
would be senseless because we know beforehand that all men
must die according to a law of nature. The idea of such a norm
cannot be an effective motive for a behavior according to the norm
but in contradiction to the law of nature. The idea of such a norm
is senseless, precisely because of the lack of the possibility of causal
effectiveness.

Sometimes it is admitted that man's will, like all happenings, is
actually causally determined, but it is asserted that, in order to
make moral-legal imputation possible, man must be regarded *as if*
his will were free; that means, one believes it necessary to maintain freedom of will (that is, causal nondetermination) as a necessary fiction.

However, when imputation is recognized as a connection of facts
different from causality but by no means in conflict with it, this
fiction becomes superfluous.

Since the objective determination of the will according to the
laws of causality cannot be denied, some writers believe to be able
to base the possibility of imputation upon the subjective fact that
man, although not free, erroneously believes himself to be free;
they base the assumption that he believes himself to be free on the
fact that he feels remorse when he has committed a legal or moral
wrong. But this is not correct. By no means do all men feel remorse as a result of a committed wrong. Above all, many do not
regard as a wrong that which, according to the legal or moral order
under which they are living, is a wrong; besides, what is wrong is
different according to different legal or moral orders. Men feel remorse even if they are aware that they have committed a deed they
themselves regard as a wrong, forced by a motive that was stronger

than the one that pressed them to refrain from committing the deed. Even a convinced determinist can feel remorse when he has done something that he considers to be wrong; just as even a con-vinced determinist does by no means draw from his view the con-clusion that a behavior forbidden by morals or law must not be disapproved or not be punished—that no imputation must take place. Imputation presupposes neither the fact or fiction of causal nondetermination, nor the subjective error of man to be free.

Some writers believe they can use the following way to solve the problem of the conflict between freedom of will as an indispensa-ble supposition of imputation and the principle of causality that determines all events: A man is morally or legally responsible for a happening if it was caused either by his act of will or by his failure to perform an act of will that could have prevented the happen-ing. He is not responsible for a happening when it was not caused by his act of will or his failure to perform an act of will that could have prevented the happening. That man is free merely means, according to these writers, his awareness to be able to act as he wishes. These facts, they maintain, are entirely compatible with strict determinism because the act of will or the failure to act are considered as causally determined.

The attempt to maintain the idea of freedom of will by inter-preting it as the awareness of the possibility to act as one wishes must fail. For the awareness to be able to act as one wishes, is the knowledge that our acts are caused by our will. But the question is not whether our action is caused by our will—indeterminism does not deny this; but, rather, whether our will is causally determined or not. If the mentioned attempt is not merely a denial of freedom of will, but is to represent a solution of the problem while main-taining the supposition that responsibility is possible only under the condition of freedom of will, then we are merely confronted with a shift of the problem. By presenting the problem in this way, it is merely proved that a moral-legal imputation is possible and actually occurs though the will is causally determined.

The supposition that man has a free will (that is, a causally not determined will), is necessary—so it is frequently argued—to ex-plain why only men, not things, animals, and natural events are made morally-legally responsible; why imputation takes place only with respect to man. However, imputation takes place only with respect to man because and insofar as moral and legal orders command only human behavior; and they do so because it is assumed that the idea of their norms create acts of will only in man—acts that, in turn, cause the commanded behavior. The explanation, therefore, is not the freedom of will, but, to the contrary, the causal determinability of the human will.

Another argument in favor of the dogma of the freedom of will is the reference to the fact that modern legal orders exempt certain cases from responsibility (and that means, from imputation), because, it is said, in these cases it cannot be assumed that a free act of will takes place. Thus, children and the mentally ill are not held responsible for their conduct and its effects, and even mentally sane adults if they are placed under "irresistible compulsion." The explanation for the first two cases is the assumption that children and the mentally ill (because of the condition of their consciousness) cannot, or not sufficiently, be caused, by the idea of legal norms, to behave in conformity with these norms; other motives are usually stronger than these ideas especially since these individuals do not even know of legal norms. For mentally sane adults, however, it may be assumed that usually the idea of legal norms and of the evil consequences of their violation is a stronger motive than the motives that lead to an illegal behavior. To be sure, these latter motives may also be stronger in an adult and a mentally sane individual, but this would be the exception. Modern legal orders presuppose an average human being and an average set of external circumstances under which people act causally determined. If such a human being under such circumstances exhibits a conduct that the legal order prohibits, then this human being is responsible for his conduct and its effects according to this legal order. If he, causally determined by circumstances other than those presupposed by the legal order, exhibits a conduct prohibited by the legal order, then he is said to act under irresistible compulsion. Actually man always acts under irresistible compulsion, because his actions are always causally determined; and causality, by its very nature, is irresistible compulsion. That which is called "irresistible compulsion" in legal terminology actually is only a special case of irresistible compulsion—namely that for which the legal order does not stipulate responsibility. When imputation takes place, irresistible compulsion is always present. But imputation does not take place in every case of irresistible compulsion.

Finally we must mention the view that determinism and moral-legal responsibility can be considered to be compatible only by referring to the fact that our knowledge of the causal determination of human behavior is inadequate—that we do not know, or not know sufficiently, the causes that determine human behavior. If we fully knew these causes we would not be in a position to hold a person responsible for his behavior and their consequences; therefore the proverb: "To understand everything means to forgive everything." To understand the behavior of a human being means: to know its causes; to forgive him means: to renounce to hold him responsible for his behavior, to renounce to blame or punish him, to renounce to link his behavior with a sanction—that is, to renounce imputation. But in many cases in which the causes of his behavior are known and hence his behavior is understood, imputation is not renounced, the behavior is not forgiven. The proverb rests on the error that causality excludes imputation.

It follows that it is not freedom, i.e., nondetermination of will, but its very opposite, causal determinability of will, that makes imputation possible. One does not impute a sanction to an individual's behavior because he is free, but the individual is free because one imputed a sanction to his behavior. Imputation and freedom (in this sense) are indeed essentially linked. But this freedom cannot exclude causality, and does in fact not exclude it. If the assertion that man as a moral or legal personality is free, is to have any meaning, then this moral or legal freedom must be compatible with the causal determination of his behavior. Man is free insofar and because reward, penance, or punishment are imputed as consequence to a certain human behavior; not because this conduct is causally indetermined, but although it is causally determined, nay, *because* it is causally determined. Man is free because his behavior is an end point of imputation. And this behavior can be an end point of imputation even if it is causally determined. Therefore the causality of the natural order and freedom under a moral and legal order are not incompatible with each other; even as the natural order and the legal-moral orders are not contradictory—and cannot be contradictory, because the one is an order of something that *is* and the others are orders of something that *ought* to be. Incompatibility as consequence of logical contradiction can exist only between an assertion that something *is* and an assertion that it *is not,* or between an assertion that something *ought* to be and an assertion that it *ought not to be;* but not between an assertion that something *is* and that it *ought not to be.*

24. FACTS OTHER THAN HUMAN BEHAVIOR AS CONTENT OF SOCIAL NORMS

The principle of imputation, in its original meaning, connects two acts of human behavior: the behavior of one individual with that of another, such as the moral law which connects reward with merit or the rule of law (see section 16) which connects punishment with crime; or it connects the behavior of an individual with another behavior of the same individual, such as the rule of a religious order which connects penance with sin. In all these cases the human behavior prescribed by a norm is conditioned by another human behavior; condition and consequence are acts of human behavior. But the norms of a social order need not only refer to human behavior—they can also refer to other facts. As we mentioned in a different connection, a norm may forbid a certain behavior that has a certain effect (such as murder), and a norm may command a certain behavior that is not only conditioned by the behavior of another individual, but also by other facts, such as the moral norm of loving your neighbor: if somebody is suffering you ought to deliver him from his suffering; or the legal norm: if somebody is a public danger because he is mentally ill, he ought to be forcibly interned. The imputation which takes place on the basis of the principle of retribution (and which represents moral and legal responsibility) is only a special, albeit the most important, case of imputation in the wider sense (namely, the link between a human behavior with the condition under which this behavior is commanded by a norm). All retribution is imputation, but not all imputation is retribution. Besides, it is to be noted that norms may refer to individuals without referring to their behavior as for example in the case of liability for the delict of someone else and, especially, in the case of collective liability.

If in the statement that under certain conditions a certain hu-

man behavior ought to take place, the conditions do not, or not exclusively, represent a human behavior; and if, further, in this case too the connection between the conditioning fact and the conditioned human behavior is designated as "imputation," then this concept is used in a wider sense than the usual one. For the consequence is not only imputed to a human behavior (or, to use the usual terminology: the consequence is not only imputed to a person), but to facts or external circumstances. But it is always human behavior that is imputed.

25. Categorical Norms

Apparently some social norms command a certain behavior unconditionally—under all circumstances—and in this sense are categorical norms, in contradistinction to hypothetical norms. These are certain norms commanding a certain omission (refrainment), such as: Thou shalt not kill, not steal, not lie. If these norms actually did have the character of categorical norms, it would not be possible to interpret normatively the social situation, created by such norms, in a statement that connects two elements as condition and consequence; then the principle of imputation would not be applicable. But even norms prescribing refrainment cannot be categorical. A positive action, obviously, cannot be prescribed unconditionally, because an action is possible only under certain conditions. But even refrainment cannot be unconditionally prescribed; otherwise the norms concerned could be unconditionally obeyed or violated. Refrainment, too, is possible only under certain conditions. A man cannot kill, steal, lie under all circumstances, but only under certain conditions—and therefore he can refrain from killing, stealing, or lying only under these conditions. The condition, under which refraining from a certain action is prescribed, is the totality of all circumstances under which such action is possible. Besides, in an empirical society no prescriptions (and this includes prescriptions for refrainment) are possible that do not permit of exceptions. Even such fundamental prohibitions as not to kill, not to take someone else's property without his permission, not to lie, are valid only with certain reservations. Positive legal orders always must stipulate the conditions under which it is not prohibited to kill, to take property, or to lie. This, too,

demonstrates that all general norms of an empirical social order (including general norms of refrainment) can prescribe a certain behavior only under certain conditions. Therefore every general norm establishes a relationship between two sets of facts, which may be described in the statement: Under certain conditions certain consequences ought to take place. This is, as was shown, the formulation of the principle of imputation, as distinguished from the principle of causality. Only individual norms can be categorical in the sense that they command, authorize, or positively permit a certain behavior of a certain individual without condition; for example, when a court decides that a certain organ has to direct a certain civil execution into a certain property; or that a certain organ has to imprison a certain criminal for a certain time. However, even individual norms may be hypothetical, that is, they may prescribe a certain behavior of a certain individual only conditionally: for example, when the judge orders civil execution into the property of the tardy debtor only under the condition that the debtor does not pay the owing amount within a certain time; or when the judge orders the carrying out of the punishment of a certain individual under the condition that the individual commits a punishable delict within a set time.

26. The Denial of the Ought; the Law as Ideology

The possibility of a normative science of law (of a science of law that describes the law as a system of norms) is sometimes questioned by advancing the argument that the concept of the "ought" (whose expression the norms is) is senseless or merely ideological fallacy. From this it is concluded that a normative science of law (a science of law directed at the cognition of norms) cannot exist —that science of law is possible only as legal sociology. Legal sociology relates facts not to valid norms but to other facts as causes and effects. Sociology investigates, for example, what causes induce a legislator to issue these and not other norms and what effects legislative acts have. Legal sociology investigates in what way economic facts or religious ideas influence the activities of the legislators and judges, and which are the motives that cause men to conform or not conform with the legal order. Therefore, not law itself is the object of cognition for legal sociology, but certain parallel phenomena in nature. Likewise a physiologist, who investigates chemical or physical processes which condition or accompany certain feelings, does not grasp these feelings themselves which, in fact, cannot be chemically or physically grasped, because they are psychological phenomena. The Pure Theory of Law, as specific science of law, is directed toward the legal norms; it is not directed toward facts; it is not directed toward the acts of will whose meaning the legal norms are, but toward the legal norms as the meanings of acts of will. And the Pure Theory is concerned with facts only so far as they are determined by legal norms which are the meanings of acts of will; and these meanings and their mutual relations are the subject of the Pure Theory of Law.

If the concept of the "ought" is rejected as senseless, then the law-creating acts can merely be perceived as the means of bringing about a certain behavior of men to whom these acts are addressed; therefore as causes of certain effects. One believes, then, to be able to understand the legal order merely as the regularity of a certain course of human behavior. One purposely ignores the normative meaning of the law-creating acts believing that the meaning of an "ought" different from one of "is" cannot be assumed. In that case, however, the meaning of an act in which the legal authority commands, authorizes, or positively permits can scientifically be described only as an attempt to create in men certain ideas whose motivating power causes them to behave in a certain way. The norm that one "ought" not to steal or that a thief "ought" to be punished is reduced to the statement that some individuals seek to induce others not to steal or to punish the thief; and that men usually refrain from stealing, and that a thief is punished if, as an exception, theft is committed. The law—in its relation between law-creating and law-obeying men—is viewed as an enterprise comparable to, say, that of a hunter who places a bait to catch game. The comparison is apt not only because in both processes the fact of motivation is essential; it is apt also because, in the view of law here characterized, a deception takes place in the presentation (by the legislator or by the science of law) of the law as a norm. From this viewpoint "norms" do not "exist" and the statement that this or that "ought" to be has no meaning, not even a specific positive-legal meaning, different from a moral meaning. From this viewpoint, merely the natural, causally connected, events and the legal acts merely in their actuality, but not their specific meaning, are taken into consideration. This specific meaning, the "ought," is—according to the sociological interpretation—an ideological fallacy and therefore has no place in a scientific description of the law.

Such fallacy indeed is present if the legal "ought" is interpreted to constitute an absolute value. But one cannot speak of an ideological fallacy if the "ought" in the law-describing rule of law merely has the meaning of a specific functional connection. It has been shown above that such a specific functional connection, different from a causal connection, is the imputation. The causal connection which legal sociology describes, consists (if it exists at all) between certain economic or political facts and the law-creating acts on the one hand and between these acts and the human behavior that they intend to bring about on the other. In the latter case, the causal connection exists only if the behavior is actually motivated by men's ideas about the intention of the law-creating acts, a motivation which by no means is always the case because obedience to the law is frequently caused by other motives. Above all, however, two other facts are connected by legal imputation: not the law-creating act with the law-obeying behavior, but the fact determined by the legal order as a condition with the consequence determined by that order. Imputation, like causality, is a principle of order in human thinking, and therefore just as much or just as little an illusion or ideology as causality, which—to use Hume's or Kant's words—is only a thinking habit or category of thinking.

That the subjective meaning of law-creating acts is an "ought" cannot be seriously denied if these acts are looked upon according to their meaning as commands, as imperatives.[40] Questionable is only whether this can be also interpreted as their objective meaning; whether the "ought" may be looked upon as an objectively valid norm that imposes obligations and confers rights upon individuals. The question is in what way law-creating acts differ from other commands, for example from the command of a highway-

---

[40] Cf. pp. 7 f.

man. In the preceding pages the condition was shown under which this differentiation is possible: the condition is: presupposition of the basic norm.

If all meaning is denied to the norm (looked upon as objectively valid) which constitutes the connection called "imputation" —if all meaning is denied to the "ought"—then it would be senseless to say: "this is legally permitted, that is forbidden"; "this belongs to me, that to you"; "X is entitled and Y is obligated." The thousands of statements in which the law is expressed daily would be senseless. In contrast to this, the fact is undeniable that everybody understands readily that it is one thing to say: "A is legally obligated to pay $1,000 to B," and quite another: "There is a certain chance that A will pay $1,000 to B." Everybody understands that it is one thing to say: "This behavior is a delict according to the law and ought to be punished according to the law"; and quite a different thing to say: "He who has done this will probably be punished." The immanent meanings of the acts directed by the legislator to the law-applying organ, by this organ—in the judicial decision or the administrative act—to the subject, by the subject— in the legal transaction—to the other subject is not comprehended in the statement about a probable course of future behavior. Such a statement is issued from a point of view that transcends the law. It does not answer the specifically legal question of what ought to happen according to the law, but the meta-legal question of what actually happens and what probably will happen. The legal statements that one ought to behave in a certain way cannot be reduced to statements about present or future facts, because the former do not refer to such facts, not even to the fact that certain individuals wish that one ought to behave in a certain way. The legal judgments refer to the specific meaning which the fact of such an act of will has; and the "ought," the norm, is precisely this meaning that is different from this act of will. Only if "ideology" is understood as a contrast to the reality of facts—that is, if ideology is understood as everything that is not causally determined reality or a description of this reality—then the law as a norm (that is, as the meaning of these acts, different from the causally determined acts) is an ideology. And then the subject of the science of law that describes only the norms and not the acts in their causally determined connection with other facts—and describes them in rules of law that do not assert causal connections like the laws of nature, but links of imputation—is an ideology. Then the Pure Theory of Law has opened the way to that viewpoint from which the law may be understood as an "ideology" in this specific sense:—as a system of connections different from that of nature.

The possibility and necessity of such a discipline directed toward the law as a normative meaning is proved by the fact that the science of law has been in existence for millennia—a science which, as dogmatic jurisprudence, serves the intellectual needs of those who deal with the law. There is no reason to leave these entirely legitimate needs unsatisfied and to give up such a science of law. To replace this science by legal sociology is impossible, because the latter is concerned with an entirely different problem. As long as a religion exists, there must be a dogmatic theology that cannot be replaced by religious psychology or religious sociology; in precisely the same manner there will be a normative science of law as long as there is a law. The rank of this science in the total system of the sciences is a subordinate question. What is important is not: to give up this science of law together with the categories of the "ought" or the norm; but: to confine this science of law to its subject and to clarify critically its methods.

If we do not understand by "ideology" everything that is not natural reality or its description, but nonobjective presentation of the subject influenced by subjective value judgments and glorifying or disfiguring the subject of cognition; and if we designate as "reality" not only the natural reality as the subject of natural science, but every subject of cognition including the subject of the science of law, namely positive law, as legal reality; then a presentation of positive law must keep itself free from ideology (in the second meaning of the word). If positive law is looked upon as normative order in relation to the reality of actual happenings, which, according to the claim of positive law ought to conform to it (although, actually, it does not always conform to it) then positive law may be characterized as "ideology" (in the first meaning of the word). If positive law is looked upon in its relation to a "higher" order, which claims to be the "ideal law," the "right" law, and demands that the positive law ought to be in conformity with this order—for example, in relation to natural law or to some type of other justice—then the positive law (that is, the law created by human acts, the valid law, the law that is by and large applied and obeyed) presents itself as the "real" law; and then a theory of positive law which mixes the latter with natural law or any other type of justice in order to justify or disqualify the positive law must be rejected as "ideological" (in the second meaning of the word). In this sense the Pure Theory has an outspoken anti-ideological tendency. The Pure Theory exhibits this tendency by presenting positive law free from any admixture with any "ideal" or "right" law. The Pure Theory desires to present the law as it is, not as it ought to be; it seeks to know the real and possible, not the "ideal," the "right" law. In this sense, the Pure Theory is a radical realistic theory of law, that is, a theory of legal positivism. The Pure Theory refuses to evaluate the positive law. As a science, the Pure Theory regards itself as obligated to do no more than to grasp the essence of positive law and, by an analysis of its structure, to understand it. Specifically, the Pure Theory refuses to serve any political interests by supplying them with an "ideology" by which the existing social order is justified or disqualified. In this way the Pure Theory prevents that, in the name of the science of law, a higher value is attributed to positive law than it actually has, by identifying it with an ideal law; or by denying positive law any value, and thus any validity, by claiming that it contradicts an ideal law. Thereby the Pure Theory places itself in sharpest contrast to traditional jurisprudence which, consciously or unconsciously, sometimes more, sometimes less, has an "ideological" character in the second meaning of the word. Precisely this anti-ideological tendency shows that the Pure Theory of Law is a true science of law. For science as cognition has the immanent tendency of revealing its subject. Ideology, however, veils reality either by glorifying it with the intent to conserve and to defend, it or by misrepresenting it with the intent to attack, to destroy, and to replace it by another. Such ideology is rooted in Wishing, not in Knowing; it springs from certain interests or, more correctly, from interests other than the interest in truth—which, of course, is not intended to say anything about the value or dignity of those other interests. The authority that creates the law and which therefore attempts to preserve it may not appreciate an ideology-free cognition of its product; likewise, the forces that try to destroy the existing order and wish to replace it by another, thought to be better, may not have much use for such a cognition of the law. A true science of law, however, does not care about the one or the others. To be such a science of law is the aim of the Pure Theory of Law.

IV

THE STATIC ASPECT OF LAW

27. The Sanction

a) *The Sanctions of National and International Law*

If the law is conceived as a coercive order, that is, as an order stipulating coercive acts as sanctions, then the law-describing rule of law appears as the statement that under certain conditions, determined by the legal order, a certain coercive act, likewise determined by that order, ought to be performed. "Coercive acts" are acts executed even against the will of the affected individual and, in case of resistance, by the use of physical force. From the preceding pages it follows that two kinds of coercive acts must be distinguished:

First, coercive acts that are sanctions—they are stipulated as reactions against an action or refrainment determined by the legal order, such as imprisonment for theft; and, second, coercive acts that do not have this character, such as the forced internment of individuals afflicted with an illness constituting a public danger or individuals considered dangerous because of their race, political views, or religious convictions; and forcible destruction or deprivation of property in the public interest. In the latter cases, the conditions of the coercive act include no action or refrainment of a definite individual determined by the legal order.

"Sanctions" in the specific sense of the word appear—within national legal orders—in two different forms: as punishments (in the narrower sense of the word) and as civil executions. Both types consist in the forcible infliction of an evil or, expressed negatively, in the forcible deprivation of a value: in case of capital punishment the taking away of an individual's life; in case of corporal punishment, as customary in earlier times, blinding, amputation of a part of the body; in case of imprisonment the deprivation of liberty; in case of a fine, the taking away of assets, especially property. The deprivation of other rights can also be stipulated as a punishment, such as the loss of an office or of political rights.

Civil execution too is the forcible infliction of an evil. It is distinguished from punishment in that civil execution is carried out in order to, as is usually said, "righting a wrong." The so-called righting of a wrong consists in the ending of the state of affairs that was caused by the unlawful behavior and in bringing about a state of affairs that conforms with the law. This state of affairs may be the same as the one that should have been brought about by a lawful behavior of the delinquent; but if it is impossible to bring about such a state of affairs, another one can function as a substitute. Examples for the former case are: A fails to fulfill his duty to render to B an object in A's possession; the sanction of civil execution consists in the forcible taking away of the object from A and rendering it to B; or: A fails to meet his duty of appearing before the court as a witness; the sanction consists in forcibly bringing A before the court, which means that A will be deprived of his freedom for this purpose. An example for the latter of the above-mentioned cases: A fails to meet his obligation of rendering B an objects not in A's possession or to perform a certain work for B. The sanction of civil execution consists in forcibly taking away from A a piece of property equivalent in value to the object or work that A owes to B, and in rendering to B proceeds from auctioning off that piece of property. If the unlawful behavior consists in causing damage to another individual (as in the first and last example), then the sanction of the execution consists in repairing the illegally caused damage. In that case, there is a certain similarity between the fine and the civil execution. Both are enforcement procedures directed against property. They differ from each other in that: in case of the fine, which usually has the character of a pecuniary penalty, this money goes into a public fund, whereas in case of a civil execution it is given to the illegally damaged individual in order to repair the material or moral damage. In this case a definite purpose determined by the legal order is manifest, which is not so in case of the punishment. It is hardly possible to define the concept of punishment according to its purpose, because the purpose of the punishment is not—or not directly—

evident from the content of the legal order. That this purpose consists in preventing (by deterring) the commission or omission of an action is an interpretation which is possible also in case of a criminal legal order, whose establishment was not consciously determined by the idea of prevention but simply by the principle of retribution: to retaliate evil with evil. Capital punishment and imprisonment remain the same whether they were stipulated with the purpose of prevention or without it.

In this respect there is no essential difference between punishment and civil execution, because the latter, felt as an evil by the affected individual, may have a preventive effect too, so that in this case the compensatory and preventative effects may be combined. Both kinds of sanctions—punishment and civil execution—have to be ordered by the judicial or administrative authorities in a procedure set up for this purpose. Therefore it is necessary to distinguish judicial punishments to be ordered by criminal courts, and administrative punishment to be ordered by administrative authorities, judicial civil execution to be ordered by civil courts and civil executions to be ordered by administrative authorities. It is also necessary to distinguish the act by which the sanction of the punishment or civil execution is ordered, from the act by which the norm, created by this act, is applied—the punishment or civil execution is carried out. The latter act is always performed by an administrative authority.

The sanctions of general international law, reprisals and war (as discussed later), are neither defined as punishment nor as civil execution, but they also represent a forcible deprivation of values or, in other words, a violation, stipulated by the legal order, of otherwise protected interests of one state by another. If it is assumed that according to positive international law one state may resort to reprisals or to war against another state only if the latter refuses to repair the illegally caused damage; and that these coercive acts (reprisals and war) may be executed only for the purpose of obtaining reparation; then a certain similarity between the sanctions of general international law and civil execution may be acknowledged. It is, however, disputed whether reprisals and war may be interpreted as sanctions of international law, and whether, therefore, international law may be regarded as a legal order.[41]

---

[41] Cf. § 42a.

b) *The Delict (the Wrong) is Not Negation but Condition of the Law*

According to the preceding discussion, the action or refrainment constituting the condition of the coercive act ordered by the legal order represents the delict (usually called "the wrong"), and the coercive act represents the sanction. An action or refrainment assumes the character of a delict only if the legal order makes it the condition of a coercive act as a sanction. A coercive act assumed the character of a sanction only if the legal order makes it the consequence of a definite action or refrainment. As mentioned before, coercive acts stipulated by the legal order as the consequence of other facts, are not "sanctions" in the specific meaning of the word; and the conditioning facts—since they are not legally determined actions or refrainments of certain individuals—do not have the character of delicts.

Therefore, a definite action or refrainment is not—as traditional jurisprudence assumes—connected with a coercive act because this action or refrainment is a delict, but a definite action or refrainment is a delict because it is connected with a coercive act, that is, with a sanction as its consequence. No immanent quality, no relation to a meta-legal natural or divine norm is the reason for qualifying a specific human behavior to be regarded as a delict; but only and exclusively the fact that the positive legal order has made this behavior the condition of a coercive act—of a sanction.

The doctrine prevailing in traditional jurisprudence that a moral value element is immanent in the concepts of delict and sanction—the idea that a delict necessarily must mean something immoral and that punishment must necessarily be something dishonorable—is untenable, if for no other reason than because of the very relative character of the respective value judgments. It may well be that the behavior which, according to a positive legal order, is the condition of a sanction is considered immoral by certain groups, but moral by other groups. For example, a man who kills his adulterous wife or her lover is a criminal according to most positive legal orders, but his action may by no means be disapproved by all, and may even be approved by many as the exercise of his natural right to defend his honor. The duel, punishable under the law, is regarded within a certain stratum of society by no means immoral but, to the contrary, a moral obligation, and the jail sentence pronounced as the consequence, is not regarded as dishonorable. Insofar as the civil delict and its sanctions (civil execution) are concerned, traditional jurisprudence does not even attempt to maintain the doctrine of the essential moral qualification of the delict. From the point of view of a theory of positive law, there is no fact that by itself—that is, regardless of a consequence stipulated by the legal order—is a delict. There are no *mala in se,* but only *mala prohibita.* This is only the consequence of the principle, generally recognized in criminal law: *nullum crimen sine lege, nulla poena sine lege;* and this principle which is valid not only for criminal law, not only for criminal but for all delicts, not only for punishment but for all sanctions, is merely a consequence of legal positivism. The very same fact may be a delict according to one legal order because this order attaches a sanction to it, but not according to another that provides for no such consequence. It is self-evident that the legal order makes a certain human behavior the condition of a sanction, because the legal authority regards this behavior as harmful to society, hence undesirable. But from the point of view of an analysis of the immanent meaning of the legal order, this circumstance is irrelevant for the concept of the delict. If a certain behavior has been made the condition of a sanction, the action is to be regarded as a delict, even by a jurist who may not regard it as detrimental at all and perhaps even as useful, and vice versa. The distinction between a fact that is a delict because it is punishable according to positive law and a fact that is punishable because it is, by its very nature, a delict—this distinction is based on a natural-law doctrine. It presupposes that the character of delict, the negative value, is immanent in certain facts and postulates prescription of punishment by positive law. When the natural-law doctrine of values being immanent in reality is rejected, then the distinction collapses.

Such words as "illegality," "breaking" or "violating" the law, express the thought of a negation of the law; they give the idea of something that is outside the law and directed against it, threatening, interrupting, or even abolishing the existence of law. This idea is misleading; it is caused by the fact that the relationship between a norm that prescribes a certain behavior and an actual

behavior which is the contrary of the prescribed one are interpreted as logical contradiction. But a logical contradiction can
exist only between two statements of which one says that *a* is, and
the other that *a* is not. Both statements cannot be true. Between
the norm-describing statement that a man *ought* to behave in a
certain way and the statement that he *actually* does not so behave,
no logical contradiction exists. Both statements can stand side by
side, both can be true at the same time. The existence or validity
of a norm commanding a certain behavior is not "broken" by the
opposite behavior—in the way that a chain might be broken that
fetters a man. The chain of law fetters even the man who "breaks"
the law; the norm is not "violated," as a human being can be violated (that means, injured in his existence) by an enforcement action directed against him. If a normative order commands a certain behavior merely by attaching a sanction to its opposite, then
the essential facts are exhaustively described by a conditional
statement that says: "If a certain behavior is present, then a certain sanction ought to be executed." In this statement, the delict
appears as a condition, not as a negation of the law; and this shows
that the delict is not a fact standing outside, much less in opposition to, the law, but a fact inside the law and determined by it—it
shows that the law, according to its nature, refers specifically to
this fact. Like everything else, so the delict (in German: *Unrecht*,
literally "unlaw," like "unaction") can *legally* be understood
only as law. If we speak of "unlawful" behavior, we mean by this
the behavior that is the condition for a coercive act as a sanction; if
we speak of "lawful" behavior, we mean the opposite, a behavior
by which the coercive act is avoided.

The Pure Theory of Law, by reinterpreting the delict—which in
the naïve, prescientific thinking is conceived of as a negation of the
law, as "un-law"—as a condition determined by the law, fulfills
a similar function as theology toward the problem of theodicy, the
problem of evil in the world created by all-good and all-powerful
God. Since everything that exists must be conceived as willed by
God, the question arises: How can evil be conceived as willed by
the good God? The answer given by a consistent monotheistic theology is that evil must be interpreted as a condition necessary for
the realization of the good. The assumption that evil is not the
work of God, but directed against God, the work of the devil, is

not compatible with the monotheistic hypothesis, because such an assumption would imply the concept of an anti-God.

Since the delict is not the only condition to which a sanction is attached, since the conditioning fact—as we shall see—may be composed of many parts, including human behavior that cannot be defined as delict (such as, for example, the legislative act creating the general norm which determines the delict; and the judicial act determining the existence of a concrete delict), the question arises how the behavior to be defined as delict is to be distinguished from other behavior that occurs as a part of the conditioning facts. Ordinarily, the delict is the behavior of the individual against whom the coercive act, functioning as sanction, is directed. However, this definition of delict applies only if the sanction is directed against the delinquent, that is, the individual who, by his behavior, has committed the delict. This is the case—discussed later —of liability for one's own behavior. But the sanction need not always be directed against the delinquent, or not only against him alone, but may also be directed against another individual or several others. This is the case of liability for someone else's behavior. In this case the legal order must determine the relationship between the delinquent and the individual liable for the delict of the former. The legal order may make liable the father, the spouse, or other members of the narrower or wider family of the delinquent. If we designate, for purposes of linguistic simplification, as "relatives" all those individuals who are in a legally determined relation to the delinquent (members of the family, clan, state), then delict may be defined as the behavior of that individual against whom, or against whose relatives, the sanction is directed as a consequence.

28. Legal Obligation (Duty) and Liability

a) Legal Obligation and Sanction

The behavior commanded by a social order is that which an individual is obligated to adopt: An individual has the obligation (or duty) to behave in a certain way, if this behavior is commanded by the social order. To say "a behavior is commanded" is synonymous with saying "an individual has the obligation to behave in a certain way." Since the legal order is a social order, the behavior which an individual is obligated to adopt is a behavior which, directly or indirectly, has to take place toward another individual. If the law is conceived as a coercive order, then a behavior can be looked upon as objectively legally commanded (and therefore as the content of a legal obligation) only if a legal norm attaches a coercive act as a sanction to the opposite behavior. To be true, legal norm and legal obligation are usually differentiated, and it is said that a legal norm stipulates a legal obligation. But the legal obligation to behave in a certain way and the legal norm that prescribes this behavior are not two different facts; the legal obligation *is* this legal norm. The statement: "An individual is legally obligated to behave in a certain way" is identical with the statement: "A legal norm commands a certain behavior of an individual." And a legal order commands a certain behavior by attaching a sanction to the opposite behavior.

The legal obligation, like the legal norm which is identical with it, has a general or an individual character. The legal norm which commands compensation for damage, stipulates (or, more correctly: *is*) a general legal obligation. The judicial decision—that is, the individual legal norm—which prescribes in a concrete case that an individual *A* has to compensate an individual *B* with a sum of money for a damage which *A* had caused *B*—this judicial decision stipulates (or, more correctly: *is*) the individual legal obligation of *A;* whereby it is merely stated, however, that the rendering of a sum of money by *A* to *B* is the content of an individual legal norm. Usually, a legal obligation is mentioned only in case of an individual legal norm, and since traditional theory considers only general legal norms and ignores the existence of individual norms, the identity of legal norm and legal obligation is overlooked, and the legal obligation is regarded as an object of legal cognition different from the legal norm albeit somehow connected with the latter.

The attempt to characterize the legal obligation in this way leads into error. It leads, for example, to the assumption that the legal obligation is an impulse immanent in man; that it is the urge to behave in a way that he feels as commanded; that it is the obligation (or binding; from *ligare,* to bind) caused by an innate, natural, or divine norm whose observance is merely "secured"

through the legal order by stipulating a sanction. However, a legal
obligation is nothing else but the positive legal norm which commands the behavior of an individual by attaching a sanction to the
opposite behavior. And the individual is legally obligated to adopt
the commanded behavior, even if the idea of this legal norm does
not create any impulse toward the commanded behavior, even if
he has no idea of the obligating legal norm at all, as long as the
positive-legal principle prevails that ignorance of the law is no
excuse.

Thereby the concept of legal obligation is determined. It is fundamentally connected with that of the sanction. Legally obligated
is the individual who, by his behavior, is able to commit the delict
and thereby bring about the sanction—the potential delinquent;
or the individual who by the opposite behavior is able to avoid the
sanction. In the first case we speak of violation of an obligation, in
the second case of fulfillment of an obligation. The individual
who fulfills the obligation imposed on him by a legal norm, obeys
the norm; the individual who, in case of a violation executes the
sanction stipulated by the legal norm, applies the norm. Both the
obeying of the legal norm and the applying of it represent a behavior in conformity with the norm. If by "effectiveness" of a legal
order we understand the fact that individuals behave according to
this order, then the effectiveness manifests itself (a) in the actual
obeying of the legal norms (that is, in the fulfillment of the legal
obligations stipulated by the norms) and (b) in the application of
the norms (that is, in the execution of the sanctions stipulated by
them).

Normally, the content of a legal obligation is the behavior of
only one individual; but it can also be the behavior of two or
more. This is the case, if an obligation may be fulfilled by one *or*
the other individual, and if the obligation is violated if it is fulfilled by neither; or if the obligation can only be fulfilled by the
cooperation of all, and is violated if this cooperation does not take
place.

Traditional theory employs, beside the concept of legal obligation, also the concept of a "subject" or "holder" of the obligation
in the same way as it employs, beside the concept of subjective
right, the concept of a subject or holder of the right. Both are included in the concept of a person having rights and obligations

stipulated by the legal order. Normally, it is the individual whose behavior constitutes the content of the obligation, who is designated as the subject or holder of the obligation. But this individual is not somebody who has or holds the obligation as something different from himself. It is not the individual as such at all with whom we are concerned when describing the facts of the legal obligation, but only a certain behavior of an individual—only the personal element of a behavior which, inseparably connected with the material element, constitutes the content of the legal obligation. Only in this sense is the concept of a "subject of the obligation" admissible. The subject of a legal obligation is the individual whose behavior is the condition to which, as a consequence, is attached a sanction directed against this individual or his relatives. It is the individual who, by his behavior, can violate the obligations, that is, can bring about the sanctions, and who therefore can also by his behavior fulfill the obligation, that is, avoid the sanctions.

b) *Legal Obligation and "Ought"*

With the German word "Pflicht"—English: obligation or duty—is associated, especially since Kant's ethics, the concept of an absolute moral value. The principle that man should always fulfill his obligation or obligations, evidently presupposes that absolute obligations exist, obvious to anyone. If it were admitted that a single absolute morality does not exist, but different, and contradictory, moral orders, which prescribe different, contradictory, behavior, the mentioned principle, which is the central thesis of Kant's moral philosophy, would amount to the tautology that man ought to do what is ordered by the respective moral order, which means, he ought to do what he ought to do. The concept of a legal obligation refers exclusively to a positive legal order and has no moral implication whatever. A legal obligation may, but need not, have as its content the same behavior as an obligation established by a moral order, but it may also have the opposite behavior as its content, so that a "conflict of legal obligation and moral obligation" arises, as one is wont to assume. To avoid this possibility of such a conflict it has even been asserted that "obligation" (or "duty") is not a legal concept at all, and that only morals but not the law im-

pose obligations; and that the specific function of the law—in contradistinction to morals—is to confer rights. But as soon as it is recognized that the obligation to behave in a certain way means
merely that this behavior is commanded by a norm; and that the
legal order—like every normative order—commands a certain
human behavior, then "to impose an obligation" must be regarded as an essential function of the law and must even be
acknowledged as the primary function, as will be shown in the
analysis of the function of "conferring a right," that follows below.

Since norms not only command or prohibit, but may also authorize behavior, it may not be superfluous to point out that, if an
individual is authorized to behave in a certain way, he thereby
need not necessarily be obliged to this behavior. Since "to authorize" means, in the context of a legal order, to confer the power
to create law, only positive action, not the refraining from action,
can be the subject of an authorization; a command, on the other
hand, can refer both to action and refrainment. Therefore one
may be legally obligated to do something or to refrain from doing
something; but one can be *authorized* only to do something. However, one may be legally obligated to make use of one's authorization; an action to which an individual is authorized by the legal
order may, at the same time, be commanded, that is, it may be
made the content of his obligation. The judge is authorized—that
is, the legal order has conferred upon him, and upon him only, the
authority—to impose punishment under certain conditions. He
may, but need not, be obligated to impose this punishment; and
he is legally obligated to do so, if his not doing so is placed under
sanction by the legal order. The same is true, if a certain behavior
is positively permitted (by a norm that makes an exception to a
general prohibition). The legal order may, but need not, stipulate
an obligation to make use of this permission.

In this connection it might be permitted to repeat: if the rule of
law is formulated in the sentence that under certain conditions a
certain coercive act "ought" to be performed, the word "ought"
does not say whether the performing of the coercive act is the content of a legal obligation, a positive permission, or an authorization; all three cases are covered by it. If the word "ought" is used
to designate the meaning of all three cases, that is: if the sentence
"somebody ought to behave in a certain way" only means that this

behavior is stipulated in a norm, then the statement that somebody is legally obligated (has a legal duty) to behave in a certain
way, refers to a behavior which is the opposite of the behavior that
is the condition of a coercive act as a sanction. And there is a legal
obligation to execute this act if the nonexecution is the condition
of another coercive act as a sanction; otherwise the execution of
the coercive act is only authorized or positively permitted. Legal
obligation is not, or not immediately, the behavior that ought to
be.[42] Only the coercive act, functioning as a sanction, ought to be.
If we say: "He who is legally obligated to a certain behavior,
'ought' to behave in this way according to the law," we only express the idea that a coercive act as a sanction ought to be executed
if he does not behave in this way.

c) Liability

The concept of legal responsibility, or liability, is essentially connected, but not identical with, the concept of legal obligation. An
individual is legally obligated to behave in a certain way, if his
opposite behavior is made the condition of a coercive act. But this
coercive act need not be directed against the obligated individual
—the "delinquent"—but may be directed against another individual related to the former in a way determined by the legal
order. The individual against whom the sanction is directed is said
to be "liable" or legally responsible for the delict. In the former
case he is liable for his own delict—in which case the obligated and
the liable individual are identical: the potential delinquent is
liable. In the second case an individual is liable for a delict committed by someone else—the obligated and the liable individual
are not identical. An individual is obligated to a lawful behavior,
and he is liable for an unlawful behavior. The obligated individual can bring about or avoid the sanction by his behavior. The
individual, however, who is only liable for nonfulfillment of another individual's obligation (that is, for the delict committed by
somebody else) can neither bring about nor avoid the sanction by
his own behavior. This is obvious in case of criminal liability for
someone else's delict, that is, when the sanction has the character of
a punishment. But it also applies to civil liability for the delict of

---

[42] Cf. p. 25.

someone else, when the sanction has the character of a civil execution. A is obliagated to render 1,000 to B, if the legal order stipulates that a civil execution is to be directed into the property of A or C in the event that A does not render the 1,000 to B. C cannot bring about the sanction by his behavior, because the condition of the sanction is the behavior of A, not that of C. Nor can C avoid the sanction by his behavior, if he is only liable for A's civil delict. This would be the case if the legal order were to stipulate that the sanction is to take place against C if A fails to render 1,000 to B, even if C renders 1,000 to B; this means: if the legal order does not accept the fulfillment of A's obligation by C as substitute. Not only may C be liable if A does not fulfill his duty to render 1,000 to B, but he may also be obligated to render 1,000 to B, if A does not fulfill his duty. This will occur if the legal order stipulates (as it usually does) that civil execution is to be directed into C's property, if either A or C fails to render 1,000 to B. In this case, C—as the subject of the obligation to render 1,000 to B—is able to bring about or to avoid the sanction by his behavior. In case of liability for the nonfulfillment of a legal duty constituted by civil execution into a property, two possibilities must be distinguished: (a) that the property into which the civil execution has to be directed is the property of the individual against whom the coercive act is directed; and (b) that the property is that of someone else over which this individual is able to dispose. In the former case the individual is liable with his person and his property; in the latter case two individuals have to be considered for liability—the one who has the authority to dispose over the property, and the other who is the subject of the rights which constitute the property. One is liable with his person, the other with his property.

In the case of liability for someone else's delict, the behavior that is the condition for the sanction is not a behavior of the individual against whom the sanction is directed, but the behavior of another individual. The individual who is liable for someone else's delict is not the subject of a behavior determined by the legal order as the condition for a sanction; he is only the object of a behavior determined by the legal order as the consequence of a delict, namely the object of the coercive action of the sanction. In this respect a certain similarity exists between this set of facts and that which is present if the legal order stipulates the earlier-mentioned coercive acts which do not have the character of sanctions: In these cases, too, the individual against whom the coercive act is directed is not the subject of a behavior determined by the legal order as the condition for the coercive act; but only the object of a behavior determined by the legal order as consequence, namely the object of the coercive acts directed against this individual. The difference is that in case of liability for someone else's delict, the conditions of the coercive act include a certain behavior of a certain individual, whereas in the case of coercive acts that do not have the character of sanctions, the conditions do not include such behavior.

d) Individual and Collective Liability

The difference between obligation (duty) and liability expresses itself linguistically too. One is obligated *oneself* to behave in a certain way; one cannot be obligated that someone else behaves in a certain way. But one can be liable not only for one's own behavior, but also for the behavior of someone else. Liability for a delict committed by someone else can have a preventive effect only if a relationship exists between the two that allows the assumption that the obligated individual (the potential delinquent) regards the execution of the sanction as an evil even if directed against another individual. For example, if the sanction is directed against a member of the family, clan, or nation, that is, against the member of a group whose members more or less identify themselves with each other—if the obligated and the liable individual belong to the same collective group. Such a relation is usually presupposed when the legal order stipulates liability for someone else's delict. In this sense, liability for a delict committed by another may be characterized as collective liability. But one can restrict the concept of collective liability to cases in which the sanction is not directed against a single individual, but against many or all members of a group, to which the delinquent belongs; for example in case of blood revenge, which may be executed against all members of the murderer's family; or in the case of the sanctions of international law (reprisals and war), which are directed against the members of a state whose organ has committed a violation of international law.

Collective liability is a characteristic element of primitive legal orders and is closely connected with primitive man's collectivistic thinking and feeling. Because of the lack of a sufficiently strong ego consciousness the primitive man identifies himself so much with the members of his group that he interprets any significant deed of a group member as a deed of "the group"—as something that "we" have done; and he therefore claims the reward for the group in the same manner as he accepts the punishment of the whole group. But individual liability prevails if the sanction is directed exclusively against the delinquent—the one who by his behavior has committed the delict.

e) Liability Based on Fault and Absolute Liability

It is customary to distinguish liability based on fault and absolute liability. Where the legal order makes an action or refrainment by which an undesirable event is caused or not prevented (e.g., death of a man) the condition for a sanction, it is possible to distinguish between the case in which the event was intended or foreseen by the individual whose behavior is being considered and the case in which the event happened without his intention or foresight, "accidentally" as we usually say. The first case is liability based on fault, the second is absolute liability. If the undesirable event is intended, it is possible to distinguish whether the intention of the perpetrator was subjectively "malicious"—that is, whether the event was caused or not prevented with the intention to do harm; or, to the contrary, with the intention of doing good, for example, if a doctor causes the death of an incurably sick patient in order to terminate his suffering. "Fault" is a specific element of the delict: it consists in a certain positive relationship between the psychic behavior of the delinquent and the event brought about or not prevented by his exterior behavior—it consists in his intention or foresight. But we speak of absolute liability if no such relationship exists, if the event is neither foreseen nor intended.

Liability based on fault usually includes the case of so-called negligence. Negligence is present when the bringing about or nonprevention of an event that is undesirable from the viewpoint of the legal order is forbidden, although the event was neither foreseen nor intended by the individual, but could normally have been foreseen and could not have been brought about or could be prevented. This means, that the legal order commands to foresee certain undesirable events which, as the result of a certain behavior can be foreseen, and consequently demands that such an event is not brought about or is prevented. Negligence consists in the omission of a foresight commanded by the legal order. Negligence is not—like foresight or intention—a positive relation between the mind of the delinquent and the undesirable event brought about or not prevented by his actual behavior. Negligence consists in the lack of this kind of relation. In this sense negligence is a delict of omission for which the legal order stipulates absolute liability.

f) The Obligation of Reparation

Frequently the legal obligation of an individual to repair a material or moral damage caused by him or someone else has been interpreted as a sanction, and therefore this obligation has also been designated as "liability." Such a construction, however, confuses the concepts of obligation, sanction, and liability. A sanction per se is not an obligation—it can but need not be stipulated as such—but it is a coercive act which a norm attaches to a certain behavior, whose opposite is therefore legally commanded, that is, the content of a legal obligation. This can also be expressed by saying: the sanction is the coercive act that constitutes the legal obligation. Liability is no obligation either, as has been mentioned, but the relation between an individual against whom a coercive act is directed and the delict committed by him or someone else. Obligation of an individual is: to omit the behavior which constitutes the delict. The legal order may oblige individuals not to inflict damage on others, without stipulating an obligation to repair the unlawfully caused damage. An obligation to make reparation exists only, if not only the causing of damage, but also the nonreparation of the unlawfully caused damage was made the condition of a sanction. The fact that the legal order establishes an obligation to make reparation is correctly described in the rule of law: "If an individual causes damage to another and does not repair it, then a coercive act ought to be directed against the property of an individual"; that is, an individual ought to be forcibly deprived of property and this ought to be rendered to the damaged individual as reparation for the caused damage. It was mentioned that an individual could be obliged not to damage another, without being obliged to repair the illegally caused damage. This would be the case if the individual could not avoid the sanction by making reparation for the damage. Normally, however, an individual can, according to positive law, avoid the sanction by making reparation for the damage. This means, the individual is not only obligated to refrain from causing damage to another but, if he has caused damage, he is also obligated to make reparation. The sanction of civil execution constitutes two obligations: The obligation not to cause damage (this is the main obligation) and to make reparation for the damage illegally caused (this is the substitute obligation, which takes the place of the violated main obligation). The obligation to make reparation for the damage is not a sanction, but a substitute obligation. The sanction of civil execution takes place only when this obligation is not fulfilled. If the sanction of civil execution is directed into the property of the individual who has caused damage by his behavior but has not made reparation, then he is liable for his own delict that consists in not making reparation for the damage caused by his behavior. But for this delict another individual can be liable too; this is the case if the sanction of civil execution is to be directed into the property of another individual when the first one does not fulfill his duty to make reparation. The second individual is liable only if he cannot avoid the sanction by himself making reparation for the damage caused by the first individual. According to positive law, however, he usually can avoid the sanction by doing so. For he normally is not only liable for nonreparation of the damage caused by the individual primarily obligated, but is also secondarily obligated to make reparation for the damage caused by the first if the latter has not done so. Only as subject of this obligation, not as object of the liability, can he avoid the sanction by his behavior. But he then is not only liable for the illegal nonreparation by the first individual, but also for the violation of his own obligation of reparation. Neither this, his obligation to make reparation for the damage, nor his liability for the fulfillment of this duty, is a sanction. The sanction occurs only if neither the first nor the second individual makes reparation for the illegally caused damage.

g) Collective Liability As Absolute Liability

If the sanction is not directed against the delinquent but—as in collective liability—against another individual, then the liability is absolute. For no inner connection exists between the liable individual and the undesirable event brought about or not prevented by the illegal behavior of someone else. The liable subject must have neither foreseen nor intended the event. But it is possible that the legal order stipulates liability for a delict committed by someone else only if the delict was culpably committed by the delinquent. In this case the liability has the character of liability based on fault with respect to the delinquent, and of absolute liability with respect to the object of liability.

29. LAW IN A SUBJECTIVE SENSE; RIGHT AND AUTHORIZATION

a) Right and Obligation

It is usual to oppose to the concept "obligation" the concept "right," and to cede priority of rank to the latter. Within the sphere of law we speak of "right and duty," and not of "duty and right," as within the sphere of morals, where greater stress is laid on duty; and we speak of a right as somthing different from law. But the right *is* law—law in a subjective sense of the word in contradistinction to "law" in an objective sense, that is, a legal order or system of norms. In describing the law, the right is so much in the foreground that the obligation almost disappears; in German and French legal language, the same word, namely *Recht* and *droit,* is used to designate "right" as well as "law," as a system of norms forming a legal order. Hence, in order to distinguish right and law, it is necessary to speak in German of *subjektives Recht* and *objektives Recht* (subjective law and objective law) or of *Recht im subjektiven Sinne and Recht im objektiven Sinne* (law in a subjective sense and law in an objective sense); and in French of *droit subjectif* and *droit objectif.*

To understand the essence of the German term *subjektives Recht* is difficult because so many different sets of facts are covered by this term. To one set of facts refers the statement that an individual has *das Recht,* that is, the "right" to behave in a certain way. Nothing more may be meant by this than the negative fact that the individual is legally not forbidden (he is, in this sense, negatively permitted) to act or refrain from acting in this way— that he is free to perform or to refrain from a certain action. But the statement may mean also that a certain individual is legally obligated—or, indeed, that all individuals are legally obligated—to behave in a certain way toward another individual (that is, toward the entitled individual, or the subject of the right). The behavior which is the immediate obligation of an individual toward an-other, may be a positive or negative behavior, that is, it may be a specific action or refrainment. The action consists in rendering a performance by the obligated individual toward another individ-ual. The performance may consist in transferring a certain thing (in German: *Sachleistung*) or in rendering a service (*Dienstleis-tung*). The refrainment which is the obligation of an individual vis-à-vis another individual may either be the refraining from a certain action (for example, killing another individual); or the refraining from preventing or impairing the behavior of another individual (especially preventing or impairing another individual in his behavior toward a certain thing). In the latter case we speak of tolerating the behavior of one individual by another, and we juxtapose the obligation to perform (*Leistungspflicht*) to the ob-ligation to tolerate something (*Duldungspflicht*).

The obligated behavior of one individual toward another corre-sponds with a certain behavior of the other individual. The latter may demand the behavior of the former. In the case of an obliga-tion to perform something, the other individual may receive the transferred thing or rendered service. In the case of an obligation to tolerate something, the behavior that corresponds to the obli-gated behavior consists in the behavior to be tolerated; in the case of tolerating a certain behavior in relation to a certain thing: in the use of the thing; if it is food, in consuming it; finally even in destroying it.

The behavior of one individual that corresponds to the ob-ligated behavior of the other is usually designated as the content of a "right"—as the object of a "claim" that corresponds to the obligation. The behavior of the one individual that corresponds to the obligated behavior of the other particularly the claiming of the obligated behavior, is designated as exercising a right. However, in case of an obligation to refrain from an action, such as to refrain from murder or burglary, one does not usually speak of a right or claim "not to be murdered" or "not to be burglarized." In case of an obligation to tolerate something, the behavior of the one corresponding to the obligation of the other is spoken of as "enjoyment" (German: *Genuss*) of the right. Particularly we speak of enjoyment of a right, when we deal with the use, consummation, or even destruction of a thing, which another individual is obligated to tolerate.

This "right" or "claim" of an individual, however, is merely the obligation of the other individual or individuals. If the right or claim of an individual is spoken of as if it were different from the obligation of the other, the impression of two legally relevant facts is created where only one is present. The fact in question is exhaustively described as the legal obligation of one individual to behave in a certain way toward another. That an individual is obligated to behave in a certain way means that in case of the opposite behavior a sanction ought to take place; his obligation is the norm that commands this behavior, by attaching a sanction to the opposite behavior. If an individual is obligated to render a performance to another, then the performance to be received by the other constitutes the content of the obligation; one can render unto another only that which the other accepts. And if an individual is obligated toward another to tolerate a certain behavior of the other, then the tolerance of this behavior is the content of the obligation. This means: the behavior corresponding to the obligated behavior, of the individual toward whom the obligation exists, is codetermined in the behavior that constitutes the content of the obligation. If one designates as "right" the relationship of one individual toward whom another individual is obligated to a certain behavior, then this right is merely a reflection of this obligation.

It is to be noted that the "subject" in this relationship is only the obligated individual—the one who can violate or fulfill the obligation by his behavior; the "entitled" individual—the one toward whom the behavior is to take place—is only the object of the behavior which, because corresponding to the obligated behavior, is codetermined by the latter. The concept of a right which is only the reflection of a legal obligation—the concept of a "reflex right" —may facilitate, as an auxiliary concept, the description of the legal situation; but from the point of view of a scientifically precise description of the legal situation, it is superfluous. This is evident from the fact that one does not in all cases of a legal obligation assume a "reflex right." If the obligated behavior of the one individual does not refer to a specifically designated other individual (that is, if it does not have to take place with respect to a specifically determined individual) but refers only to the legal community as such, then—although one sometimes speaks of a "right of the community" (especially of the state) to the behavior of the obligated individual, such as the obligation to do military service—one is satisfied in other cases to assume a legal obligation without a corresponding reflex right: for example in case of the legal norms that prescribe a certain human behavior toward some animals, plants, or inanimate objects by pain of punishment. It is forbidden to kill certain animals at certain times (or altogether), to pick certain flowers, to cut certain trees, or to destroy certain historical monuments. These are obligations which—indirectly— exist toward the legal community interested in these objects. But no reflex rights are assumed on the part of the animals, plants, or monuments. The argument that the protected animals, plants, and inanimate objects are not subjects of the reflex rights because these objects are not "persons," is not correct. For "person," as we shall see, means legal subject; and if the subject of a reflex right is the individual toward whom the behavior of an obligated individual has to take place, then animals etc. toward whom men are obligated in a certain way are indeed "subjects" of a right to this behavior in the same sense in which the creditor is the subject of the right that consists in the obligation of the debtor. But, as has been said, if a man is obligated to behave in a certain way toward another man, only the former, not the latter is a "subject," namely the subject of an obligation. Since the reflex right is identical with the obligation, the individual toward whom the obligation exists cannot be regarded as a "subject," because he is not the subject of this obligation. The individual toward whom the obligated behavior has to take place, is only the object of the behavior, in the same way as the animal toward which the individual is obligated to behave in a certain way. Also untenable is the argument that animals cannot "make a claim" that would correspond to the obligation. For it is not essential for the existence of a reflex right that the obligated behavior is being claimed. The fact that a claim is not being made or cannot be made for some reason does not change the legal situation.

A claim to be made in a legal relevant act exists only if the non-fulfillment of the obligation can be asserted in a lawsuit. Then, however, a situation prevails which is entirely different from a mere reflex right; it will be discussed later. A reflex right, at any rate, cannot exist without the corresponding legal obligation. Only if an individual is legally obligated to behave in a certain way toward another, has the other one a "right" to this behavior. Indeed, the reflex right of the one consists solely in the obligation of the other.

The traditional view that the right and the obligation are two different objects of legal cognition, that, in fact, the former has a priority in relation to the latter, is probably rooted in the natural-law doctrine. This doctrine assumes the existence of natural rights, inborn in man, that are valid before any positive legal order is established. Among these natural rights, the right of individual property plays a major role. The function of a positive legal order (i.e., of the state), which terminates the state of nature, is—according to this doctrine—to guarantee the natural rights by stipulating corresponding obligations. This view has influenced the representatives of the School of Historical Jurisprudence, who inaugurated the legal positivism of the nineteenth century and decisively influenced the concept of a general theory of law. Thus, Dernburg says: "Historically, subjective rights existed long before a self-conscious national legal order (a state) had developed. They were based on the personality of the individual and in the recognition which they were able to achieve and to enforce for the person and his property. Only by abstraction was the concept of a legal order gradually derived from the existing subjective rights. The view, therefore, that subjective rights are merely derived from an objective law is unhistorical and erroneous." [43] If the assumption of the existence of natural rights is rejected, and if subjective rights are recognized only when established by a positive legal

---

[43] Heinrich Dernburg, *System des Römischen Rechts (der Pandekten achte, umgearbeitete Auflage)*, Part I (1911), p. 65.

order, then it becomes evident that a subjective right (as a reflex right) presupposes a corresponding legal obligation—that indeed, it *is* this legal obligation.

b) *Jus ad rem* and *Jus in personam*

Influenced by Roman jurisprudence we usually distinguish between a right to a thing (*jus ad rem*) and a right against a person (*jus in personam*). This distinction is misleading, because every right to a thing is also a right against a person. If in order to maintain this distinction (German: *Sachenrecht* and *Personenrecht*), the former is defined as the right of an individual to dispose over a certain thing, one overlooks that this right consists merely in the legal obligation of other individuals to tolerate these dispositions, so that the right to a thing is also a right against a person. It is the relation between individuals which is of primary importance, and this relation is implied in the right to a thing. It is constituted by the obligation of other individuals to tolerate the disposition over a certain thing by a definite individual. The relation to the thing is of secondary importance, because it merely serves to clarify the definition of the first relation.

The typical right to a thing (or real right), which is the basis for the distinction, is the property right. Traditional science of law defines it as the exclusive dominion of a person over a thing and thereby distinguishes this right from the right to claim which is the basis only of personal legal relations. This distinction, so important for civil law, has an outspoken ideological character.

Since the law as a social order regulates the behavior of individuals in their direct or indirect relations to other individuals,[44] property, too, can legally consist only in a certain relation between one individual and other individuals. This relation is: the obligation of these other individuals not to disturb the first one in his disposition over a certain thing. What is described as the exclusive "dominion" of an individual over a thing is the legally stipulated exclusion of all others from the disposition over this thing. The dominion of the one is legally merely the reflex of the exclusion of the others. The dominion is a relation between these others and the one, in the usual terminology: a relation between persons; and

[44] Cf. § 5 and § 6.

only secondarily a relation to a thing, namely a relation of the others to the thing, by which their relation to the one (the "owner") is established. Nevertheless, the traditional definition of property as exclusive dominion of a person over a thing is maintained and the legally essential relation is ignored. The reason for this is, apparently, that the definition of property as a relation between an individual and a thing veils the economically decisive function of this relation—a function which (if it refers to ownership of the means of production)—is, rightly or wrongly, labeled as "exploitation" by socialist theory; which function certainly is present in the relation of the owner toward all other subjects who are excluded from the disposition of the thing and are obligated by the law to respect the owner's exclusive power of disposition. Traditional science of law is stubbornly opposed to acknowledge the right of the one merely as a reflex of the obligation of the other, because traditional science of law believes that it ought to stress, if only for ideological reasons, the primary character of the right.

It is preferable, because devoid of any ideological tendency, to speak of relative and absolute reflex rights, when describing the two sets of facts characterized by traditional science of law as *jus in personam* and *jus ad rem*. To behave in a certain way toward an individual may be the obligation of an individual; this is so, for example, in the relation of debtor to creditor, for here only the debtor is obligated to render performance to the creditor and therefore only the creditor has a reflex right to the performance. The obligation of the debtor and the reflex right of the creditor exist only in relation to a specific individual and is therefore only relative. If, however, the behavior refers to a specific thing, then it may be the obligation of all other individuals to behave in a certain way toward a specific individual. This is the case of the right of property; for here, all others are obligated not to prevent a definite individual from, or disturb him in, his disposition over a thing. The reflex right that consists in the obligation of these others is directed against all these others and is, in this sense, an absolute right. Terminologically the distinction between relative and absolute reflex rights is not a very felicitous one, because so-called "absolute" rights are also only relative; they consist only in the relation of the many to the one. The reflex right of ownership actually is not an absolute right; it is the reflex of a multitude of obligations of an indeterminate number of individuals toward one individual with respect to one thing, in contradistinction to a claim, which is the reflex of only one obligation of a specific individual toward another specific individual.

The secondary relation to a thing, however, is not limited to cases of the so-called *jus ad rem* but may also be present in the case of claims or *jus in personam:* for example, if a debtor is obligated to render a specific thing to the creditor, let us say, if somebody is obligated by a contract of sale to transfer the ownership of a specific piece of movable property or real estate to somebody else. In this case the right of the creditor is differentiated from the *jus ad rem* in that his right corresponds merely to the obligation of a specific individual.

In this analysis only the reflex right is considered. It plays a decisive role in the traditional doctrine, although this "right" of the one is nothing but the obligation of another or of all others to behave in a certain way toward the first. If, however, the right of property is defined as the legal power of the owner to exclude all others from the disposition over a thing, then we are no longer dealing with a mere reflex right. An individual has this legal power only if the law authorizes him to assert in court that the obligation not to prevent him from his disposition of a certain thing had been violated.

c) The "Right" As a Legally Protected Interest

The definition of the law in a subjective sense as a legally protected interest, frequently presented by traditional science of law, refers to the right as the reflex of a legal obligation. This definition clearly displays the dualism characteristic for traditional science of law: the right, that is, the law in a subjective sense, is juxtaposed with the law in an objective sense. This dualism contains an insoluble contradiction. If the law in an objective sense is a norm or system of norms (a normative order); and if the right as the law in a subjective sense is something entirely different, namely interest, then law in an objective sense and right as law in a subjective sense cannot be subsumed under a common concept. This contradiction cannot be avoided by admitting a relation between law in an objective sense and right as law in a subjective sense, namely that the latter is an interest protected by the former. If the law is conceived as a norm, the law—even in a "subjective sense"—cannot be a law-protected interest, but only the protection of this interest—that is, the law in an objective sense. The protection consists in the legal order attaching a sanction to the violation of this interest—which means, in stipulating a legal obligation not to violate the interest; such as, for example, the legal obligation of the debtor to pay back to the creditor the loan received. According to the interest theory, the right of the creditor is his interest, protected by the legal obligation of the debtor, in the repayment of the loan. But his right as a reflex right is nothing but this legal obligation of the debtor.

From the point of view of the interest theory, the assumption of a reflex right does not seem to be possible if the act to which one is obligated toward the other consists in inflicting an evil on him. This is the case if the act has the character of a sanction prescribed by the legal order, and if the commanding and executing of the sanction in concrete situations has been made the content of the official obligation of the law-applying organs. Normally, nobody is interested in the suffering of an evil. If an interest is protected by the obligation in question, it cannot be an interest of the individual against whom the sanction is directed; in the mentioned example it cannot be the interest, and therefore not the right, of the debtor who does not fulfill his obligation; the interest, and therefore the right, of the creditor is protected by the legal obligation of the debtor to repay the loan. In the case of a criminal sanction it cannot be the interest, and therefore not the right, of the wrongdoer, that is protected by the obligation of the law-applying organ to punish the wrongdoer. If nevertheless one assumes such a right —as is sometimes done—if one says that the wrongdoer has a right to be punished, has a claim to the legally stipulated punishment (that is, to the fulfillment of the obligation to punish him), then this view rests on interpreting the community's interest of reacting against a delict by a sanction, as the interest (the "well-understood" interest) of the delinquent. But usually the interest of the community, or, more correctly, the protection of this interest by the official duty of the law-applying organs, is not designated as subjective reflex right; in common language one does not in all cases of a legal obligation speak of a corresponding reflex right.

d) The "Right" As Legal Power

In traditional jurisprudence, the interest theory is opposed by the so-called will-power theory, according to which the "right," i.e., the law in a subjective sense, is a will power conferred by the legal order. Thereby, however, an object is defined that is different from the one to which the interest theory refers, namely an authorization, a legal power conferred upon the individual by the legal order. A "right" in this sense is present if the conditions of the sanction that constitutes a legal obligation includes a motion, normally of the individual in relation to whom the obligation exists; the motion is aimed at the execution of the sanction and has the form of a law suit brought before the law-applying organ. Then this organ may apply the general norm (that is, enact the individual norm that attaches a concrete sanction to a concrete delict established by the organ) if an authorized individual—the plaintiff —makes such motion which starts the procedure of the law-applying organ, specifically the judicial procedure. In this case the law, that is, the general legal norm, to be applied by the legal organ, is at the disposal of a specific individual; and in this sense, the law is indeed "his" law, which means: his right. If in presenting this situation we make use of the auxiliary concept of "reflex right," then we can say that the right—the reflex of the legal obligation—is equipped with the legal power of the entitled individual to bring about by a law suit the execution of a sanction as a reaction against the nonfulfillment of the obligation whose reflex is his right; or—as it is usually, but not quite correctly, formulated: to bring about, by a law suit, the enforcement of the fulfillment of this obligation.

This situation is not exhaustively described by presenting the obligation of one individual to behave in a certain way toward another individual. For the essential element is the legal power bestowed upon the latter by the legal order to bring about, by a law suit, the execution of a sanction as a reaction against the nonfulfillment of the obligation. Only this legal power is something different from the legal obligation against whose nonfulfillment the former is exercised; only in the exercise of this legal power is the individual the "subject" of a right different from a mere reflex of the legal obligation. Only if the legal order confers such a legal power are we faced by a "right" in a specific, technical sense of the word, which is the legal power conferred for the purpose of bringing about by a law suit the execution of a sanction as a reaction against the nonfulfillment of an obligation. To make use of this legal power is "exercise of rights" in the specific sense of the word. This exercise is not codetermined by the behavior that constitutes the content of the obligation against whose nonfulfillment the exercise of the legal power is directed. In traditional linguistic usage, to be sure, another behavior of the individual in relation to whom the obligation exists is designated as "exercise of rights," namely the behavior that corresponds to the obligated behavior and is codetermined by it. It is the exercise of the reflex right.

According to traditional theory, each right of an individual contains a "claim" to the behavior of another individual—namely to that behavior to which the second individual is obligated toward the first: the behavior that constitutes the content of the legal obligation identical with the reflex right. But a "claim" in a legally relevant sense is asserted only in exercising the legal power with which a reflex right must be equipped to be a so-called law in the subjective sense of the word. If an individual, toward which another individual is obligated to a certain behavior, does not have the legal power to bring about by a law suit the execution of a sanction as a reaction against the nonfulfillment of the obligation, then the act by which he demands fulfillment of the obligation has no specific legal effect; the act is legally irrelevant, except for not being legally prohibited. Therefore, a "claim" as legally effective act exists only when a so-called law in a subjective sense exists, which means that an individual has the just characterized legal power.

Neither this so-called law in a subjective sense nor the legal obligation is different from, and independent of, the law in an objective sense. The former, like the legal obligation, is a legal norm: the legal norm which confers a specific legal power upon a certain individual. That this individual "has" a right, i.e., a specific legal power, merely means that a legal norm has made a certain act of this individual the condition for certain consequences. If traditional theory characterizes the right as a legal power conferred by the legal order, then the theory has in mind the legal power exercised in the law suit. But not only this legal power alone is understood by right (i.e., the law in a subjective sense), but this power in connection with the reflex right, that is, the obligation against whose nonfulfillment the exercise of the legal power is directed; in other words: a reflex right equipped with this legal power. The emphasis here is on the reflex right. As has been demonstrated above, however, the essence of the right that is more then a mere reflex of a legal obligation consists in the fact that a legal norm confers upon an individual the legal power to bring about by a law suit the execution of a sanction as a reaction against the nonfulfillment of the obligation. We mean this legal norm conferring a legal power upon an individual, when in the following we speak of a right in the technical sense.

The establishment of such rights, unlike the establishment of legal obligations, is not an essential function of law. To establish such rights represents only a possible, not a necessary function of law—a special legal technique. It is the specific technique of the capitalist legal order, insofar as this order guarantees the institution of private property and therefore considers especially individual interests. This technique does not prevail in all parts of the capitalist legal order, and appears fully developed only in the realm of so-called private law and in some parts of administrative law. Modern criminal law does not, or only exceptionally, make use of this technique. In the case of murder or manslaughter, the individual against whom the prohibited behavior has taken place, has ceased to exist and therefore cannot bring an action against the murderer or manslayer; but also in other cases of criminal behavior the individual who is the victim of the crime is replaced by an organ of the state who, as prosecutor *ex officio* starts the procedure that leads to the execution of the sanction. Hence the essence of the right characteristic for private law consists in this: the legal order confers a specific legal power upon an individual (not an "organ" of the community, but an individual traditionally designated as a "private person"), and usually upon the individual toward whom another individual is obligated to behave in a certain way—namely the legal power to start the procedure that leads to a court decision in which a concrete sanction is ordered as reaction against the violation of the obligation.

Like the subject of an *obligation,* the subject of a *right* also may be not only one individual, but two or several individuals. Subject of a right are two or more individuals if the obligation (identical with the reflex right) constitutes a behavior toward two or more individuals; and if the legal power to bring about by a law suit the execution of a sanction as a reaction against the nonfullfillment of the obligation may be exercised by one individual *or* the others, alternatively or in joint cooperation of all of them.

This legal power conferred upon an individual regularly includes the authorization to appeal against an unfavorable court judgment (in a so-called appeal proceedings) on the grounds that the judgment is not in conformity with the law; by this act a procedure is started that may set aside the attacked judgment and replace it by another. Such legal power is not only granted to the individual in relation to whom the obligation exists, but also to the subject of the alleged legal obligation. According to modern procedural law, not only the plaintiff, but also the defendant may appeal against a judgment unfavorable to him. The legal power of the defendant is exercised to oppose the action of the plaintiff, to prevent the enforcement of an obligation which, in the view of the defendant, does not exist. In this case, we do not characterize the legal power of the defendant as a "right" in the specific technical sense.

According to modern administrative law, an analogous power is conferred upon the individual toward whom an administrative order is directed, which, in his opinion, has no legal basis—that is, toward whom an individual norm is directed by the administrative authority prescribing a certain behavior of this individual. The affected individual is authorized to appeal against the administrative order and thereby to start a procedure that may lead to the enactment of another individual norm by which the former is rescinded or modified. In this case, too, we do not usually speak of a "right" in the technical sense of the word.

e) The "Right" As a Positive Permission

By the statement that an individual has the right to behave in a certain way (specifically: to carry on a certain activity) may be meant, as we have said, that such activity is legally not prohibited to this individual or that others are obligated not to prevent this activity, or that the entitled individual has a legal power to start legal proceedings in case of a violation of the corresponding obligation. The "right" may also consist in that an activity, for instance the exercise of a business, in order to be lawful, is conditioned by a permission called "concession" or "license" given by an organ of the community, a governmental authority, either within its free discretion or only if some requirements are fulfilled. To carry on the activity without this official permission is prohibited, that is, subject to a sanction. This permission does not consist in the mere negative fact of not being prohibited, but in the positive act of a community organ. It plays an important role in modern administrative law. This right, based on an official permission, is not a reflex right; it is not the function of a corresponding obligation. It involves a legal power to the extent that it constitutes an authorization to perform certain legal transactions, such as the sale of liquor or of certain drugs, dependent on a license or concession obtained from the authorities.

f) The Political Rights

The so-called "political rights" represent a special category. They are usually defined as the power to influence the formation of the will of the state; this means: to participate directly or indirectly in the formation of the legal order in which the "will of the state" expresses itself. In applying this definition, however, one considers only the general norms of this order: the statutes. Participation in legislation that is, the creation of the general legal norms, by those subjected to the norms is the essential element of the democratic form of government, in contrast to autocratic government in which the subjects are excluded from sharing in the formation of the will of the state, and therefore have no political rights. Democratic legislation may be effected directly by "the people," that is, those subjected to the norms. In this case we speak of a direct democracy in which the individual has the right to take part in the legislative popular assembly, join in the discussion, and in voting. Or, the people participate in legislation only indirectly, which means that this function is exercised by a parliament elected by the people. In this case the process of the formation of the will of the state—the creation of general legal norms—has two stages: election of parliament and legislation by members of parliament. Therefore in this case two rights exist of the individuals forming the constituency: the right to vote and the right of the elected to be members of parliament and to join in the discussion and decisions there. These are the political rights.

If the essence of these rights consists in granting individuals the capacity of participating in the formation of the will of the state (in the creation of legal norms), then the rights established by private law, the private rights, too, are political rights; for they too allow the entitled individual to take part in the formation of the will of the state.

The latter is expressed in the individual norm of a court decision no less than in the general norm of the statute.

There are other political rights besides the right to vote for and in parliament. Not only legislative but also governmental, administrative, and judicial organs may—according to a democratic constitution—be called to their positions by election. Insofar as the functions of these organs is the creation of law, the respective rights to vote represent, like the parliamentary right to vote, the legal power to participate (indirectly) in the creation of those legal norms which the organs are authorized to create.

To subsume the private right (that is, the legal power to bring about by a law suit the execution of a sanction as a reaction against the nonfulfillment of an obligation) and the political right (which, too, is a legal power) under one and the same concept, namely, the right as the law in a subjective sense, is possible only insofar as both express the same legal function: participation of those subjected to the law in the creation of the law. In doing so one must keep in mind that the private right differs from the political right also insofar as the function of the legal power is different in the two cases. The creditor is authorized by the legal order to participate, by bringing a law suit before the court, in the creation of the individual norm of the judicial decision, in order to bring about—as it is normally formulated—the enforcement of the fulfillment of the obligation of his debtor. The subject of the political right, such as the voter, has the legal power to participate in the creation of general legal norms; but the purpose of this is not the enforcement of the fulfillment of another individual's obligation toward the voter. The execution of this legal power may, but need not be, guaranteed by a legal obligation imposed upon another individual, just as the exercise of an authorization may be, but need not be, the content of a legal obligation of the authorized individual. The judge may be obligated to accept the creditor's law suit; and he is legally obligated to do so if his refusal is subject to a disciplinary punishment as a reaction against a violaton of his official duty. But the legal power conferred upon the creditor, which is his right, does not serve the enforcement of the fulfillment of this official duty but the enforcement of the fulfillment of the debtor's obligation. A polling clerk can be obligated to receive and count the votes of the voters; and he *is* so obligated if the non-performance of this function has a sanction as a consequence. But the legal power implied in the political right to vote does not serve to enforce the fulfillment of this official duty. Its purpose—in contradistinction to the legal power constituting the private right—is not to react against the nonfulfillment of an individual legal obligation, but—indirectly—to participate in the creation of general norms by which legal obligations are established.

The political rights include the so-called fundamental rights or liberties stipulated by most modern constitutions. They guarantee equality before the law, freedom (i.e., inviolability) of property, of the person, of speech (especially of the press), of conscience (especially of religion), of assembly, and others. All these constitutional guarantees do not in themselves confer rights—neither mere reflex rights nor private rights in the technical sense. They are prohibitions insofar as they forbid the violation by statutes or statutory orders of the guaranteed rights, that is, to limit or rescind them; but these "prohibitions" do not in the main consist in imposing the legal obligation upon the legislative organ to refrain from enacting such statutes; they consist in the possibility that such statutes or statutory orders, if enacted, may be repealed as "unconstitutional" in a special procedure established for this purpose.[45] The constitutional guarantees of fundamental rights are provisions of the constitution by which the content of statutes enacted by the legislator and statutory orders issued by administrative organs is determined negatively, and a procedure established by which statutes and statutory orders not conforming with these provisions may be repealed. Fundamental rights and liberties may be violated not only by statutes or statutory orders but also by executive orders, administrative acts, or judicial decisions; that is, norms which are not enacted in the form of statutes or statutory orders may have an unconstitutional content and may be annulled for this reason. Even if not enacted on the basis of an unconstitutional statute but having no statute at all as their basis, they may be annulled for this formal reason alone and not only in case their content is in conflict with a material "prohibition" of the constitution.

The constitutionally guaranteed equality of the individuals subject to the legal order does not mean that these ought to be treated equally in the norms especially in the statutes issued on the basis of the constitution. Such equality is not intended because it would be absurd indiscriminately to impose the same obligations and the same rights upon all individuals—children and adults, the sane and the insane, men and women. As for equality *in* the statutes, the constitution can guarantee it only by prescribing that certain differences, such as differences of race, religion, status, or property must not be made in the statutes—that statutes which do make such differences may be annulled as unconstitutional. If the constitution does not determine specific differences that must not be made in the statutes and if the constitution contains a formula proclaiming the equality of all individuals, then this constitutionally guaranteed equality can hardly mean anything else but equality *before* the statutes, so-called "equal justice under the law." The guarantee of this equality means only that the law-applying organs are permitted to consider only those differences which the statutes to be applied by them expressly recognize. Thereby nothing else is stipulated but the general principle of the lawfulness of the application of the law, immanent in all law; and the principle of the legality of the application of statutes, immanent in all statutes; more generally formulated: the tautological principle

---

[45] Cf. § 35j, subsection "The 'unconstitutional' statute."

that a norm ought to be applied in conformity with this norm, a principle which expresses only the meaning immanent in each norm. A judicial decision which does not inflict upon an individual a punishment provided for in the statute to be applied only because the delinquent is a white, not a Negro, a Christian, not a Jew, although the statute in determining the delict does not consider the race or the religion of the delinquent—such a judicial decision is illegal and subject to appeal for the same reason as a judicial decision inflicting a punishment upon an individual who has not committed a delict determined *in abstracto* in the statute and ascertained *in concreto* by the courts; or as a judicial decision inflicting upon an individual who *has* committed such a delict a punishment not provided for in the statute to be applied. The unconstitutionality of the decision in this case does not represent grounds for appeal or annulment different from those of its illegality.

A constitutional provision stipulating inviolability of property may merely mean that statutes authorizing the government to deprive an individual of his property against his will without compensation (except in case of deprivation of property as a sanction) may be annulled as "unconstitutional." Such a constitutional provision is not actually a prohibition of expropriation. It refers only to uncompensated expropriation and does not stipulate a legal obligation of the legislator to refrain from enacting such statutes. The "unconstitutional" statute is a valid law until it is individually or generally annulled. It is not void, but voidable.[46] The situation is analogous when the constitution guarantees freedom of religion. Such a guarantee means that a statute prohibiting the exercise of a certain religion may be annulled as unconstitutional.

An effective guarantee of these so-called fundamental rights and liberties exists only if the guaranteeing constitution may not be changed by ordinary legislation but only by a special procedure, which differs from the ordinary by requiring special conditions rendering the enactment of a statute more difficult, such as a qualified majority of the members of the legislative body or more than a single resolution.[47] For if the constitution may be changed by ordinary statutes, then no statute, and hence no judicial decision

---

[46] Cf. pp. 271 ff.
[47] Cf. pp. 221 ff.

and no administrative act based on a statute, can be annulled as "unconstitutional," because the constitution is set aside by the statute for its sphere of validity. Therefore there is no true guarantee for fundamental rights and liberties even if the constitution, changeable only under more difficult conditions, guarantees the "liberty" merely to the extent that it is not limited by a statute—if, in other words, the constitution authorizes to stipulate, in the way of ordinary legislation, uncompensated expropriation, to recognize differences, prohibited by the constitution, in ordinary statutes imposing obligations and conferring rights and to limit in such statutes, certain liberties. Such a pseudoguarantee is present if, for example, the constitution says: "The inviolability of property is guaranteed. Uncompensated expropriation in the public interest is permitted only if authorized by a statute"; or: "Everybody has the right, within the limitations established by statute freely to express his opinions"; or: "All citizens have the right to assemble and to form associations. The exercise of this right is regulated by statute."

As long as the constitutional guarantee of the fundamental rights and liberties means nothing more than the fact that the statutory restriction of these rights and liberties is rendered more difficult, no rights are present; not even reflex rights, because the "prohibition" of restricting legislation pronounced by the constitution, does not constitute a legal obligation; and therefore no rights in the technical sense either if by such rights is understood the legal power of bringing about by law suits the enforcement of the fulfillment of obligations. A fundamental right (or liberty) represents a right in the sense of a legal power if the legal order confers upon the individual affected by an unconstitutional statute the legal power to initiate the procedure that leads to the annulment of the unconstitutional statute. Since the meaning of the act by which a norm is repealed is a norm itself, we can say: the so-called fundamental right or liberty is the legal power to participate in the creation of this norm. Thus, for example, the constitutionally guaranteed right of religious liberty is a right in the specific technical sense, if the procedure for the repeal of a statute that restricts religious freedom may be initiated by any individual affected by it through a kind of *actio popularis*. But this right, as a political right, as the political right to vote, is distinguished from the subjective right in the technical sense, which is a private right, in that the former does not serve, as the latter, to bring about by law suit the enforcement of the fulfillment of an obligation toward the subject of the right. For technical reasons alone it is hardly possible to obligate a legislative body to refrain from enacting unconstitutional statues, and this, in fact, is never done. But it is possible, and actually happens, that the head of the state (whose task it is to approve or promulgate statutes passed by parliament) and members of the cabinet (who have to countersign the acts of the head of the state) are made responsible for the constitutionality of the statutes they have approved, promulgated, or countersigned. This means, that, in case the statute is unconstitutional, a special court may inflict upon them specific punishments such as loss of office or of political rights. Then these organs are legally prohibited from performing such acts, that is, from participating in the passage of unconstitutional statutes. But as a rule it is not the individuals affected by an unconstitutional statute who has the legal power to start the procedure that leads to the execution of these sanctions. If the constitutionally guaranteed equality of freedom is violated by an administrative act or a judicial decision—in other words, if an individual norm is created on the basis of an unconstitutional statute; and if only the individual affected by this individual norm has the legal power to initiate a procedure leading to the repeal of the individual norm; then the so-called fundamental right is a right of the individual inasmuch as the repeal of the individual norm implies the repeal of the unconstitutional statute for that concrete case, or is somehow connected with a general repeal of that statute. If the individual norm of the administrative or judicial decision by which the fundamental right or liberty guaranteed by the constitution is violated, is not based on an unconstitutional statute but is enacted without any legal basis, then the right of the individual (his legal power) to bring about a repeal of the individual norm is in no way different from any right consisting in the legal power to bring about the annulment of an administrative act or a judicial decision for being illegal. The procedure initiated by the individual's complaint or appeal does not lead to an individual or general repeal of an unconstitutional statute but only to the repeal of an illegal individual norm. Only if the individual has the legal power to bring about the individual or general repeal of a statute that violates the constitutionally guaranteed equality or freedom, only then is the so-called fundamental right a right (in the specific technical sense) of the individual.

Summarizing one may say: The right of an individual is either a mere reflex right—the reflex of a legal obligation existing toward this individual; or a private right in the technical sense—the legal power bestowed upon an individual to bring about by lawsuit the enforcement of the fulfillment of an obligation existing toward him (i.e., the legal power to participate in the creation of the individual norm by which the sanction is ordered that is attached to the nonfulfillment of the obligation); or a political right—the legal power granted an individual (1) to participate directly, as a member of the legislative popular assembly in the creation of general legal norms known as statutes, or (2) as subject of a parliamentary or administrative voting right to participate indirectly in the creation of legal norms for whose creation the elected organ is authorized, or (3) to participate in the creation of the norm by which the validity of an unconstitutional statute that violates the guaranteed equality or freedom is repealed generally (i.e., for all possible cases) or individually (i.e., only for a concrete case). Finally, a positive permission given by a governmental authority may also constitute a right in a technical sense of the term.

30. Capacity to Act; Competence; the Concept of "Organ"

a) Capacity to Act (Handlungsfähigkeit)

The legal power, discussed in the preceding pages as "right" (that is, as private or political right), is only a special case of that function of the legal order described here as "authorization." From the point of view of a legal science that describes the legal order by rules of law, the function of the legal order consists in connecting certain conditions, determined by the legal order, with a coercive act, also determined by the legal order, as a consequence. This coercive act is the consequence par excellence. To be sure, among those conditions are some, which in turn are conditioned by facts determined by the legal order and which, in this sense, are relative consequences. For example, if the legal order prescribes a man ought to be punished if he appropriates a found object and does not report to the police that he has found it, then the fact of the appropriating of the found object is the condition for the fact of nonreporting—a fact which in itself, together with its condition, is the condition for a coercive act. The coercive act alone is consequence without itself being condition; it is the last consequence, the legal consequence; and if the coercive act is a sanction, then the legal consequence is the consequence of an illegal act. In stipulating that the coercive act—which is an act of human behavior—ought to be performed, the law has the character of a normative order regulating human behavior.

The function of the legal order described as authorization relates only to human behavior. Only human behavior is authorized by the legal order. In the broadest sense, a certain behavior by a certain individual is "authorized" by the legal order not only if a legal power is conferred upon him (that is, the capacity of creating legal norms), but also generally, if the individual's behavior is made the direct or indirect condition of the coercive act as the legal consequence, or if this behavior is in itself the coervice act. Other facts determined by the legal order as conditions are not to be regarded as "authorized." When the legal order stipulates: "If a man is suffering from an infectious disease he ought to be confined to a hospital," then the legal order authorizes an individual to execute the act of internment; but it does not authorize anybody to get sick. In this broadest sense, any human behavior, determined by the legal order as a condition or consequence may be regarded as being "authorized" by the legal order. The man who can exhibit such a behavior is enabled by the legal order to behave in this way. He has a capacity conferred upon him by the legal order. If this capacity is designated as "authorization," this word does not imply approval. Even the capacity of committing a delict is a capacity conferred by the legal order only upon certain qualified individuals to commit delicts by their behavior, which means: to realize a condition of the coercive act that functions as a sanction —of the act which is directed against them (or their relatives) as a consequence of their behavior. Only the individuals qualified by the legal order can commit delicts—only they are enabled by the legal order to do so. But the behavior that constitutes the delict is prohibited by the legal order in that the behavior is made the condition of a sanction—and, being prohibited, it is not approved.

However, the word "authorization" is also used in a narrower sense when it *does* imply approval; in this sense "authorization" does not include the capacity of committing a delict; in this sense traditional theory speaks of capacity to act (*Handlungsfähigkeit*) in contradistinction to "capacity to commit a delict" (*Deliktsfähigkeit*), defining the former as the capacity of a man to bring about legal effects by his behavior. Since these "effects" are not effects in the causal sense, the capacity to act consists in a man's capacity conferred by the legal order to bring about legal consequences by his behavior, that is, consequences which the legal order attaches to this behavior. These legal consequences are, however, not the sanctions which as a consequence of a behavior are directed against the individual behaving in this way (i.e., against the delinquent or his relatives). The capacity to bring about a sanction by one's behavior is the capacity to commit a delict and is distinguished from the capacity to act. The legal consequences to which the concept of the capacity to act refers are, according to traditional science of law, essentially obligations and rights created by legal transactions. The capacity to act is primarily the capacity to conduct legal transactions (*Geschäftsfähigkeit*); but capacity to act also means the capacity to influence judicial procedure by a law suit or an appeal (*Prozessfähigkeit*).

This last-mentioned capacity is a power conferred by the legal order to participate in the creation of an individual legal norm established by a judicial decision. It is, then, a legal power, and conferring this power means "authorization" in the narrowest, most specific, sense of the word.

But also the legal capacity to conduct legal transactions, that is to say, the capacity of creating obligations and rights, is such a legal power. For legal obligations and rights are established by legal norms, and such norms are created by legal transactions. An analysis of the typical legal transaction, the contract, demonstrates this. The contract stipulates that the contracting parties ought to behave in their mutual relations in a certain way; the contract of sale, for example, stipulates that the seller ought to render an object to the buyer, and the buyer a sum of money to the seller. The contract is an act whose subjective meaning is an "ought." The

legal order, in authorizing individuals by general norms to conclude contracts, elevates the subjective meaning of the transaction
to an objective one. The contract creates obligations of the contracting parties, because the legal order attaches sanctions to a behavior contrary to the terms of the contract. In this sense, the
norm created by the transaction is a dependent norm. The contract creates rights of the contracting partners, because the legal
order—by authorizing the individuals to conclude contracts—
confers upon the contracting parties the legal power to bring
about by a law suit the enforcement of the fulfillment of the obligation created by the contract, which means: to bring about by a
law suit the execution of a sanction as a reaction against the violation of the obligation created by the contract, and thus to participate in the creation of the individual norm of the judicial
decision. The capacity to conduct legal transactions is the capacity, conferred upon individuals by the legal order, to create,
on the basis of general legal norms, legal norms of a lower level
and to participate in the creation of individual norms to be created by the law courts. This capacity is a true legal power.

If capacity to act is understood to mean the capacity of bringing
about legal consequences by one's behavior, and if one regards as a
consequence of a legal transaction the legal obligation—and that
means an individual norm—created by this act, then the capacity
of fulfilling legal obligations, that is, the capacity of avoiding the
sanction by one's own behavior, may also be understood as capacity to act. Therein lies the—negative—legal consequence of fulfillment of an obligation.

b) Competence

It is readily to be seen that the exercise of this legal power has
essentially the same character as the function of a legislative organ,
authorized by the legal order, to create general legal norms; and as
the functions of the judicial and administrative organs, authorized
by the legal order, to create individual legal norms by applying
those general ones. In all these cases, just as in the case of the so-
called capacity to act, an authorization is present to create, or to
participate in the creation of, legal norms—in all these cases the
legal order confers a legal power upon certain individuals. But not

in all cases of conferring a legal power does traditional theory speak of "capacity to act." In some cases, especially with respect to the functions of organs of the community such as law courts or administrative authorities, traditional theory speaks of "jurisdiction" or "competence." The legal power conferred upon a "private person" to create legal norms by a legal transaction or to participate in the creation of legal norms by law suit, appeal, or exercise of the right of voting, his rights in the technical sense of the term are not called "jurisdiction" or "competence."

This limitation of the concept of competence is not justified as far as the function is concerned which consists in the exercise of the legal power conferred by the legal order. The capacity to conduct legal transactions, and rights in the technical sense of the term (private or political rights) of an individual, are "competence" in the same sense as the capacity of certain individuals to enact statutes, to make judicial decisions, or to issue administrative orders. Traditional terminology blurs the essential similarity between all these functions exercising legal power. If the individuals who conduct some legal transactions, or if the parties who in a judicial or administrative procedure bring a law suit against somebody (or who give notice of appeal, or who make a complaint) are considered to be "private persons" and not "organs" of the legal community, and if, for this reason, the legal power conferred upon them is not designated as "jurisdiction" or "competence," the reason of this cannot be a difference in the content of the functions. The content is the same: namely the creation of legal norms. And it is to be noted that not only individual but also general norms may be created by legal transactions conducted by "private persons" authorized thereto by the legal order; and that the creation of general norms by treaties, concluded by states authorized by international law, play an important role within the international community. And yet neither the states, in exercising this function, nor the individuals authorized by national law to conduct legal transactions are called "organs" of the legal community; nor is the legal power conferred upon them called "jurisdiction" or "competence." Since, in these cases the individuals exercising the function are not called organs of the legal community, then something that is different from the *content* of the function must be decisive for the concept of "organ" used here.

c) The Concept of "Organ"

"Organ" of a community is an individual who performs a function that can be attributed [48] to the community; it is a function which, therefore, is said to be exercised by the community (thought of as a person) through the individual that functions as the community's organ. This is a fiction, because it is not the community, but a human being that exercises the function. The "community" is nothing but the normative order regulating the behavior of a multitude of individuals. True, it is usually said that the order constitutes the community, but order and community are not two different things. A community of individuals, that is: that which those individuals have in common, consists exculsively in the order which regulates their mutual behavior. The behavior of an individual can be attributed to the community (and this means—expressed without using a fiction—can be referred to the normative order) only if this behavior is stipulated as a condition or consequence in a norm of the order that—as it is usual to say—constitutes the community. By attributing the behavior of an individual to the community, by interpreting it as an act of the community, the community is presented as an acting subject, as a person. This means: the attribution of a function determined by a normative order and rendered by an individual to the community constituted by this order, implies the personification of that community; nothing else is expressed by this personifying attribution [49] than that the behavior attributed to the community is determined in the order that constitutes the community and is therefore authorized by it. To attribute an act of human behavior to the community merely means to refer this act to the order that constitutes the community—to understand it as an act authorized by the normative order. Therefore, every behavior of an individual, determined by the normative order and thus authorized (in

---

[48] In earlier publications I called the mental operation in question "imputation" (*Zurechnung*). But since this word primarily describes the normative connection between two facts, in analogy to the causal connection, I was forced to differentiate between the imputation of a function to a community as "central imputation" from the normative connection of two facts as "peripheral imputation." This terminology is not very satisfactory and leads to misunderstandings. I therefore now confine the word "imputation" to the normative connection between two facts.

[49] Cf. § 33c.

the broadest sense) by it, can be attributed to the community constituted by the normative order, can be interpreted as function of
the community; and every individual whose behavior is determined in the normative order—and this means every member of
the community—can be regarded as an organ of the community.
An individual is an organ of the community, if and to the extent
that, he renders a behavior that can be attributed to the community; and a behavior can be attributed to the community if it is
determined as a condition or a consequence in the normative
order that constitutes the community. This is the primary, the
basic, concept of the function of an organ—it is "organ function"
in the broadest sense. And it is the concept of "organ *function*,"
not of the "organ," which refers to the essential facts, especially in
the realm of legal science. The concept of organ expresses the idea
of a subject or "holder" (German: *Träger*) of the function; i.e.,
the personal element of the behavior that represents the function;
this function, like any human behavior, consists [50] of a personal
and a material element. The concept of the organ as the subject or
holder of a function different from this holder is a concept of substance and as such to be used with the awareness that, from the
point of view of scientific cognition, substance is to be reduced to
function. In the concept of the organ as the holder of the function,
the personal element is detached from the material element, although the two are inseparably connected. Only with this reserva-
tion can the concept of the organ be used as an auxiliary concept
which facilitates the presentation of the facts to which the concept
of "organ" refers.

The concept of "organ function" which appears in traditional
legal terminology (and which is not uniform in its usage) is narrower, however, than that presented here as primary or basic concept. Since the latter relates to every behavior determined by the
normative order—so far as it is a behavior determined by the legal
order and therefore a function of the legal community—it includes
also the behavior which, as a condition for a sanction, i.e., as a delict, is legally prohibited. Usually, however, one does not attribute
a delict to a legal community. The view according to which the
prohibited behavior is illegal (unlawful; in German: *Unrecht*—a
kind of negation of the law) is repugnant to the view that the

---
[50] Cf. pp. 14 and 116 f.

legal community commits an illegal act. There is a tendency to attribute to the community only a human behavior which is determined in the normative order, but is not determined as a delict, that is, prohibited.[51] If the word "authorizing" is used in the broader sense that includes also the capacity "to order, to permit positively," then one can say that a tendency exists to attribute to a legal community only *that* behavior of an individual to which he is "authorized" by the legal order—that is, a behavior by which legal norms are created or applied, an ordered behavior, not a prohibited behavior, and a positively permitted behavior; so that an individual is considered to be the organ of a legal community only insofar as he manifests a behavior "authorized" in this sense. However, as we shall see, linguistic usage is not consistent in this respect. Occasionally a delict is attributed to the legal community, especially when the community is regarded as the subject of obligations, because the capacity to assume obligations presupposes the capacity to commit a delict.[52] But the thesis that the *legal* community cannot commit a delict, i.e., cannot behave *il-legally*, implies that the attribution to a legal community is limited to human behavior "authorized" in the just described sense; it implies that the delict, although determined by the legal order, is not attributed to the community, because not "authorized" in the narrower sense. If the attribution to the legal community is thus limited, then the individual committing a delict is not interpreted to be a community organ, and his behavior not as the function of an organ (an "organ function"). To the legal community, then, only *that* behavior is attributed which refers to the concept of "capacity to act"—which does not include the capacity to commit a delict.[53]

If we thus exclude the committing of a delict from the organ functions attributable to a legal community, then any behavior determined by the legal order constituting the legal community may be regarded as a function of the community if it does not consist in committing a delict: This behavior may consist not only in the creation and application of legal norms, including the partici-

[51] For how to distinguish the condition of the sanction qualified as "delict" from other conditions of the sanction, see p. 114.

[52] As for the capacity of a corporation as a juristic person to commit a delict, see § 33e, subsection "Obligations of the juristic person."

[53] Cf. pp. 302 f.

pation in the creation and application of legal norms by law suit, appeal, complaint and the execution of coercive acts—all this is the law-creating and law-applying function; but it may also consist in the fulfillment of legal obligations, in the exercise of reflex rights, and in the exercise of those rights that consist in a positive permission—functions that may be designated as law-observing functions. Every individual, therefore, who performs a legal function in the narrower or broader sense, is a legal organ. Therefore the individual who exercises a legal power by bringing a law suit against somebody or by conducting a legal transaction may be designated as "legal organ" and the legal power bestowed upon him as his "competence"—in the same sense in which the legislator, judge, or administrative functionary are designated as "organs," and the legal power bestowed upon them, as their "competence" (or "jurisdiction"). Even the individual who fulfills his legal obligation, or exercises a reflex right, or makes use of a positive permission, may be regarded as a legal organ. This concept of "organ function" expresses only the relationship of the function to the normative order determining the function.

However, in legal terminology the concept of organ is used in a still narrower sense than here described. Not every behavior determined by the legal order, and not being qualified as delict, is interpreted as a function of the legal community; not every individual who performs such a function is designated as an "organ" in this narrower sense. His behavior is attributed to the legal community as its function only (and the individual is designated as an "organ" only), if this individual is qualified in a certain way.

If a function determined by a normative order is to be performed not by any individual subject to this order but only by a qualified one, then a functional division of labor is established. Only functions exercised by individuals qualified in a certain way are attributed to the legal community; only these individuals are designated as "organs" in this narrower sense. Communities which have "organs" are designated as "organized" communities. But every community must have organs—even though not the kind that functions according to the principle of division of labor— because a community can only function through organs, that is, through individuals determined by the normative order. If a normative order determines that certain functions under certain conditions may be performed by every individual subject to the order, then every individual in the exercise of this function may be regarded as an organ, the function may be attributed to the community, although no division of labor is established. But according to prevailing terminology individuals who do not function by division of labor are not called "organs," their functions are not attributed to the community.

The qualifications of the individuals who—according to actual legal terminology—are designated as "organs of the community," are of various kinds. They are determined by nature, if the legal order prescribes that certain functions must be performed only by a man or woman or only by an individual of a certain age, of physical or mental health, or by an individual of certain descent (if the position or organ is inherited). But the legal order can also make certain moral qualifications or specific skills of an individual the condition of conferring the function upon him. Of particular importance is the qualification which is constituted by the provision that the individual to be designated as "organ" is to be called to the function in a definite way determined by the legal order. The calling of the individual to the function may have a direct or an indirect character. It has a direct character if the constitution, a statute, or a norm of customary law refers to an individually determined man and stipulates that a certain function ought to be exercised only by this man—for example, if the historically first constitution prescribes: "*A* shall be the head of state"; or: "The Constituent National Assembly shall be the assembly of people who actually convened at a certain day at a certain place and actually adopted a definite constitution." The calling of an individual to a certain function has an indirect character if the constitution, a statute, or a norm of customary law requires a certain act (e.g., nomination, election, drawing lots) by which an individual is called to the function and thus made an organ of the legal community. In this way an organ is created. But even in the case of direct calling we are dealing with the creation of an organ. *A,* by taking over the office of the head of state, establishes himself, according to the constitution, as the organ provided for by the constitution. The assembly referred to in the historically first constitution, by adopting this constitution establishes itself—according to this constitution—as the Constituent National Assembly provided for by the constitution. Direct calling of an individual (or of individuals) to a function implies self-creation of the organ concerned.

A minimum of division of labor is present if the legal order—e.g., a primitive legal order—stipulates that certain functions, such as the ascertainment of the existence of a delict in a concrete case and the execution of the sanction provided for in the law, ought to be performed not by each of the individuals subject to the order, but only by men of a certain age; or if, according to existing law, a law-creating custom shall be established not by the behavior of all individuals subject to the order, but by the majority of those who have the legal capacity to act; or, again, if according to existing law only individuals who have reached a certain age and are mentally sound are capable to regulate their mutual economic relationships by legal transactions. But this minimum of labor division which not even the most primitive legal order can forego, is not sufficient, according to legal terminology, to designate as "organs" the individuals authorized to perform the function; nor to attribute their functions to the community. According to this terminology a function is attributed to a community only (the individual is an "organ" only), if the individual is called—directly or indirectly—to the function.

If the general norms of a primitive legal order are not created by a legislative organ but by custom, and are applied not by law courts but the individuals themselves whose rights had been infringed, then the individuals who constitute by their behavior the law-creating custom and the individuals who apply the custom-created norms are not regarded as "organs," and their functions are not attributed to the legal community. In this case it is usual to say that the law is created and applied by the individuals themselves who are subjected to legal order. One speaks of "organs" creating general legal norms and of "organs" applying the law only if an individual or an assembly of individuals has been called to the function of legislation and if certain individuals have been called to the function of applying the law as judges. The functions of law creation and law application are the same in both instances. But only in the second case are the individuals performing the functions called to their functions by special acts.

The legal terminology is particularly apparent if a technically highly developed legal order institutes a democratically elected parliament or head of state. The constitution may stipulate that every male, mentally sound citizen of a certain age and previously not convicted has the right to vote. The election of a parliament or a president, establishing a law-creating organ, is an essential part of the law-creating procedure, and is therefore a paramount legal function in the narrower sense of the word. Nevertheless, not the voter but the parliament or president is described as organ of the state; not the function of the voter, but the function of the parliament or president is described as function of the state. True, it is said that the state (through parliament) makes laws and that the state (through the president) issues decrees; but one does not say that the state elects the parliament, although, considering the content of the voter's function (as stipulated in the legal order), he could be regarded as an organ of the state no less than the parliament or president elected by him, although the voter's function as well as the function of parliament or president could be attributed to the state. The difference between the function of the voter and that of the elected organ is this: the member of parliament or the president does not merely have to meet certain natural conditions (sex, age, mental health), but has to be called to his function by a special act.

This, evidently, is also the reason why (1) the legal transactions executed by the individuals authorized by the legal order (that is, the individual and general legal norms created by legal transactions) are not regarded as being enacted by the legal community, but are regarded as being created by "private persons" although there is a tendency to regard all law (except international law) as state law and although there should, consequently, also be a tendency to regard as state organs all individuals who execute legal transactions; why (2) when the legal procedure has to be initiated by a specific act directed toward it we speak in one case of a private plaintiff, in another case of a public prosecutor (the act of an organ of the state), although the functions of both are essentially the same; why (3) international law created by custom (established by acts of state) and by treaties (concluded by states) is not described as law created by the international community but by the subjects of the international order, namely the individual states; and why these individual states are not regarded as organs of the international community in their law-creating and law-applying functions.

Beside the concept of "organ" whose criterion—in addition to certain conditions, such as sex, age, etc.—is the fact that the individual concerned is (directly or indirectly) called to a function determined in the legal order, traditional terminology also employs a concept of organ whose criterion, in addition to these qualifications, is a specific personal status of the individual who exercises the functions concerned. The individual so qualified is called "an official"; later we will investigate this special qualification of an official.[54] We therefore distinguish organs of the state who have and those who have not the status of officials. The elected members of a legislative body are organs of the state but not state officials. Not only legal functions in the narrower sense of law-creating and law-applying functions, but also law-*observing* functions are attributed to the state and designated as "state functions," if they are rendered by an individual qualified as state official. Functions of very different types constitute the content of the official duties for which these individuals are responsible. They play an important role within the state function called "administration." [55]

So far as division of labor means that certain functions cannot be rendered by just anybody—not by every individual subjected to the normative order—but only by certain individuals qualified in a certain way by the order; and that the function under these circumstances is regarded as relatively centralized, so far, then, division of labor and relative centralization coincide.[56] In common parlance only relatively centralized functions are attributed to the community; only relatively centralized organs are designated as community organs, and only relatively centralized communities as "organized" communities.

It is needful to reëmphasize that with respect to the problem of community organs in general, and of state organs in particular, we largely have to deal with the common use of language—and that this usage is not always consistent. This is so because the attribution of a legally determined function to the legally constituted community is only a possible, not a necessary, mental operation.

[54] Cf. pp. 296 ff.
[55] § 35i.
[56] For the problem of centralization and decentralization, see § 41d.

The function-performing individual may, but need not, be designated as an organ of the legal community; its function may, but need not, be attributed to the legal community. The legal situation can be described without the aid of this mental operation. Relevant for a scientific cognition of the law is only an understanding of the essence of this operation which consists in attributing a function to the legal community, and thereby an understanding of the essence of the concept of "organ."

31. LEGAL CAPACITY (*Rechtsfähigkeit*); REPRESENTATION

Traditional theory designates as legal capacity the capacity of an individual to have rights and legal duties or to be the subject of rights and duties. Under modern law, says the theory, every human individual can be the subject of rights and duties; individuals who lack legal capacity—such as slaves—no longer are said to exist under modern law. But not every individual is said to have "the capacity to act" (*Handlungsfähigkeit*)—for example, children and the mentally ill. Therefore, according to modern law, these individuals must have representatives who in their behalf exercise rights, fulfill duties, and create rights and duties for them by legal transactions (so-called statutory representation). According to the traditional theory the capacity to act and legal capacity are not identical.

This theory cannot stand up under critical analysis. If an individual is legally obliged to behave in a certain way—if his opposite behavior is the condition of a sanction directed against him (or his relations), which means: if he is able to bring about by his behavior a sanction as a legal consequence—then he must have the capacity to act, and he must have the capacity to commit a delict in order to have the capacity to assume an obligation. But children and the mentally ill are not capable of committing a delict and therefore not capable of assuming an obligation. Their behavior is not the condition for a sanction. If the behavior of a child or a mentally ill person causes the death of an individual, then neither of them nor any other individual is being punished "because" of such behavior. Neither the child, nor the mentally ill, nor anybody else is liable for the deed. If, for example, the child's father is punished, then the punishable delict is not the killing of the individual, but the violation of the father's duty to supervise the child and to prevent an antisocial behavior of the child. The behavior of the child or mentally ill, which, if exhibited by an individual capable of acting, constitutes the crime of murder, is not murder. The child and the mentally ill do not have the legal duties constituted by punitive sanctions because their behavior is not the condition of a punitive sanction—because they cannot behave in a way that can bring about a punitive sanction; they are not capable of committing a delict (are not responsible for tort), and in this sense not capable of acting.

This, however, does not seem to apply to delicts which are constituted by a fine or civil execution. For these sanctions consist in a forced deprivation of assets, particularly of property; and, according to the traditional theory, an individual incapable of acting still can have property rights. He has no acting capacity, but he has legal capacity. Hence, a child or insane individual is said to be the owner of a house and its furnishings; if the property tax is not paid, civil execution may be directed into the property of the individual. From this one might deduce that the individual incapable of acting, if he can be the subject of property rights, can also be the subject of the obligation to pay the property tax. By the same reasoning an individual incapable of acting, could, if he is regarded as the subject of property rights at all, also be regarded as the subject of all legal obligations constituted by civil execution.

However, if only *that* individual is considered to be the subject of a legal obligation who, by his own behavior can fulfill or violate the obligation—and if the obligation can only be fulfilled or violated by the representative—then the subject of the obligation is the representative, not the individual incapable of acting. From the fact that the latter individual can be the subject of property rights could only be deduced that he is liable for the violation of financial obligations and that he can be liable—insofar as his representative is authorized to dispose of his property—only with his property, not with his person. If we assume that an incapable individual cannot be the subject of a legal obligation, and that an individual is the subject of a financial obligation only if he has to fulfill the obligation from his own property (if we, therefore, refuse to regard the representative as the subject of the obligation), then we are confronted with an obligation without a subject, for whose nonfulfillment the legal representative is liable only with his person, not with his property. Traditional theory refuses to regard the representative as the subject of the obligation which he has to fulfill from the property of the individual whom he represents and which he can violate by nonfulfillment. On the other hand, the theory attempts to avoid the assumption of an obligation without a subject.[57] The theory regards the individual incapable of acting as the subject of the obligation, which means that the obligation is attributed to this individual. The obligation whose content is the behavior of the representative is attributed to the represented individual, because it is to be fulfilled from the property which, according to traditional theory, is the property of the individual and not of the representative; and because the sanction, in case of nonfulfillment, is directed into this property. That is to say: The representative—assuming that the property concerned is interpreted as belonging to the individual—has to fulfill the obligation *for* the individual, that is, in his interest; for the representative, by fulfilling the obligation, avoids the forcible deprivation of property considered to belong to the individual. The possibility of regarding the obligation as being the obligation of the individual is based, therefore, on the possibility of regarding that individual as the subject of rights.

If by "right" is understood the legal power, that is, the capacity, conferred upon an individual by the legal order to assert by an action the fulfillment of a legal obligation that another individual has toward him, then the individual incapable of acting cannot have a right, for he does not have this capacity. Only his statutory representative has this capacity. Upon the latter, not upon the child or the insane does the legal order confer this legal power. But he is obligated to exert this power in the interest of the represented individual. In the case of property rights, the obligations whose violation can be asserted in court by the statutory representative, are obligations toward the representative who is entitled to dispose of the property. All others are obligated to tolerate this disposition, that is, not to prevent or otherwise to impair it. But the representative is obligated to dispose of the property only in

[57] Cf. pp. 161 f.

the interest of the represented individual, especially to yield the use or consumption of the property to the represented individual to the extent of the latter's ability. In case of a claim as the reflex of an obligation to perform something, the performance has to be rendered to the representative, but he is obligated to give the represented individual the benefit of the performance. It is because of these limitations, imposed upon the representative, that the traditional theory does not recognize him as the subject of the rights concerned, but attributes them to the individual. If, however, the concept of "right" is not defined as legal power, but as a legally protected interest, then it is indeed possible to regard the individual, in whose interest the representative exercises the legal power conferred upon him, as the subject of the right, without any fictitious attribution and therefore as having legal capacity. However, the definition of "right" as legally protected interest is not acceptable, for the reasons here stated.

If one holds to the view that only that individual is legally obligated to behave in a certain way who by his own opposite behavior can violate the obligation and by his own conforming behavior can fulfill the obligation and therefore must have the capacity to act; and that, further, a right, as a specific legal power, can be conferred only upon an individual who has the capacity to act, then the obligations and rights concerned can be interpreted—without fictitious attribution—only as obligations and rights of the legal representative, who, however, must fulfill or exercise them only in the interest of the represented individual. Of the same type are the obligations and rights created by legal transactions, which the representative performs on behalf of the represented individual. If the obligations and rights, because of the limitations imposed upon the representatives, are not interpreted as his obligations and rights, then they can only be regarded as obligations and rights without a subject. Precisely in order to avoid this consequence does traditional theory attribute them to the represented individual. This attribution represents a mental operation analogous to that with which a function determined by the legal order performed by an individual is attributed to the legal community. The difference between them is that the latter function is attributed to a (thereby personified) community, the former to an individual. Statutory representation and organ function are related concepts. An individual is regarded as organ of the community because the situation is presented *as if* the community would perform the function which actually is performed by the individual; and an individual is regarded as a representative of the individual incapable of acting, because the situation is presented *as if* this individual, while not by himself, but through the representative, could fulfill obligations and exercise rights; *as if* he, while not personally, but through his statutory representative, could conduct legal transactions creating obligations and rights which are *his* obligations and rights. The attribution of the function of the organ to the community, just as the attribution of the function of the representative to the represented individual incapable of acting, is a fiction. For just as it is not the community, but the individual designated as organ, so it is not the individual, but his representative, who displays the legally relevant behavior. Only with the aid of this fiction can the community be regarded as an acting person, and can the individual incapable of acting be regarded as having the capacity to act and thereby as having legal capacity.

In addition to statutory representation of the individuals incapable of acting, a representation of individuals *capable* of acting exists, established by a legal transaction (contractual representation). It is different from the former in that, in a concrete case, it is not mandatory, does not take place directly by law (as the statutory representation in which the child's father or a guardian performs functions designated as "representation" for the individual) but it is optional, created by a legal transaction. By this transaction an individual capable of acting authorizes another individual to fulfill certain obligations, to exercise certain rights, and—especially—to create obligations and rights by certain legal transactions for the former. With respect to legal transactions, direct and indirect representation are sometimes distinguished. Representation is characterized as indirect when the obligations and rights created by the legal transaction of the representative at first become his obligations and rights and are then, by a further legal transaction, transferred by him to the authorizing individual. However, this is not representation in the specific sense, because there is not attribution—neither of the act of legal transaction nor of the obligations and rights created by the act to the authorizing individual. The legal transaction is regarded as being performed by the authorized, not by the authorizing, individual, and the obligations and rights created by the transaction are not fictitiously attributed to the authorizing individual, but are actually transferred to him. Direct representation is present when the legal transaction, performed on the basis of an authorization, has, according to the law, direct legal effect for the authorizing individual, so that the obligations created by the legal transaction of the representative can be fulfilled or violated, and the rights created by the legal transaction of the representative be exercised only by the authorizer (the principal). Representation in the specific sense of the word is present only, if the facts are described in such a way as if the authorizer acted through the authorized. If this attribution is rejected as fictitious, then one should not speak of "representation," but of a legal transaction, particularly of a contract obligating or benefiting another party. A legal transaction obligating or benefiting another is one by which obligations and rights are created of somebody other than the one who executes the transaction; whereby this other individual must have the capacity to act in order to be able to become the subject of these obligations and rights. There is, therefore, no reason for attribution, in contradistinction to the case of statutory representation where fictitious attribution to the individual does take place, in order to make him appear as having legal capacity, despite his incapacity to act.

32. THE LEGAL RELATION

According to traditional theory, the concept of "legal relation" is closely tied to the concepts of obligation and right. It is defined as the relation between legal subjects, that is, between the subject of an obligation and the subject of the corresponding right or—and this is not the same—the relation between an obligation and a corresponding right (whereby the words "obligation" and "right" are understood in the traditional sense). The "corresponding" of obligation and right means that the right is a reflex of the obligation, that a relation exists between the individuals in which the one is obligated to a certain behavior toward the other. In both cases it is a relation constituted by the legal order. If it is conceived as a relation between individuals, then the traditional definition is too narrow. For the legal order establishes not only relations between legal subjects (in the traditional sense of the word), that is, between one individual obligated to a certain behavior and another individual toward whom this behavior is obligatory, but also between one individual who is authorized to create a norm and another individual who is authorized to apply this norm; and also between one individual who is authorized to create or apply a norm and an individual who is obligated or entitled by this norm. Such legal relations exist, for example, between the individuals authorized to create general norms and the individuals authorized to apply them as between legislative organs and judges or administrative organs; but also between the judges and administrative organs on the one hand, and the subjects obligated and entitled by the norms created by the legislative organs; and also between the individuals authorized to execute the coercive acts and the individuals against whom the coercive acts are directed.

Traditional jurisprudence distinguishes between private and public legal relations and sees the difference in that the one is a relation between equals and the other a relation between a superior and an inferior (between state and subject). Traditional theory evidently has the difference in mind that in one case the relation exists between the subject of an obligation and the subject of a corresponding right, and in the other case between an individual authorized to create or apply a legal norm and an individual obligated or entitled by this norm. If the individuals authorized to create or apply legal norms are legally obligated to exercise their function and thus are also legal subjects (in the traditional sense)—which, however need not be the case and never is the case for legislators—then, the relations between these individuals and the individuals obligated or entitled by the norm created or applied by the former, are indeed also relations between legal subjects; however, these relations are, primarily, relations between subjects of obligations—between, that is, subjects of the obligation to create or apply legal norms and subjects of the obligations established by these norms; and, secondarily, are they relations between the subjects of the obligation to create or apply legal norms and the subjects of the rights established by these norms; and these rights are not reflexes of those obligations (that is, the obligations of the organs to create or apply the legal norms), but reflexes of the obligations established by these norms. Besides, in this case we cannot speak of a relation between superiors and inferiors, because the norm-creating or -applying individuals (as subjects of the obligation to create or apply legal norms) are on the same level as the subjects of the obligations or rights established by these norms. This is particularly true for relations in which—according to the traditional formulation—the state as the subject of a legal transaction, for example as buyer or seller, is confronted by a private individual—if the act of one of the two partners is attributed to the state as a "juristic person." Only in the exercise of a legal power, that is, in the creation or application of norms, could individuals be considered as superior to those who are obligated or entitled by the norms created or applied by the others. However, "superior" to those obligated or entitled by the norms are merely the obligation-establishing and right-establishing *norms,* not the norm-creating or -applying individuals, because these themselves are subject to the legal order, namely to the norms authorizing their functions. It is to be noted that by presenting individuals as "inferior" to the norms of the legal order, and the norms as "superior" to the individuals, we employ a figure of speech which merely expresses that the norms of the legal order command, authorize, or positively permit the behavior of individuals—that the norms of the legal order have the behavior of individuals as their contents. If the figure of speech is taken literally, a relation between the legal order and individual seems to exist, whose behavior is determined by the norms of the legal order. However, no relation can exist between a norm and the human behavior that is its content, because the norm and its contents form an indivisible unit.

From the point of view of cognition directed toward the law—that is, toward legal norms—relations between individuals are not at issue, but only relations between legal norms (created or applied by individuals) or between facts determined by the legal norms, among which human behavior represents only one special case, albeit a very important one. For the content of legal norms is not individuals, but their behavior; it is not human beings, but a certain human behavior and not only this behavior but also other facts in connection with human behavior. This is recognized in some degree in the definition of "legal relation" as a relation between a legal obligation and its corresponding reflex right. However, precisely in this case no legal *relation* exists, as a relation between two different, legally relevant phenomena. This is so because the legally relevant facts are sufficiently described by presenting the obligated behavior as the opposite of the behavior which is a condition for the sanction; and because the statement: somebody has a (reflex) right that somebody else should behave toward him in the obligated manner, says nothing else but that this other individual is obligated to behave toward the first in a certain manner. In other words, the reflex right of the one is identical with the obligation of the other—the concept of reflex right becomes superfluous. The reflex right is only the legal obligation, seen from the viewpoint of the individual toward whom the obligation has to be fulfilled. Therefore no relation between a legal duty and the corresponding reflex right exists.

A legal relation between two individuals—or, more correctly, between the law-determined behavior of two individuals—does exist in the case of a right in the specific technical sense of the word; this means, in case the legal order conveys to an individual toward whom another individual is obligated to behave in a certain manner the legal power to initiate, by taking a legal action, a procedure leading to issuing by a court an individual norm ordering the execution of a sanction, provided for by a general norm, to be directed against the individual who has violated his obligation. In that case a legal relation does exist between the individual invested with the legal power and the obligated individual. This relation, however, is nothing but the relation between the behavior that consists in the exercise of that legal power (the legal action) and the behavior against which the sanction is directed (the delict). This is the relation between two facts, designated by the legal order as conditions for the sanction. It is the typical legal relation designated as "private" by traditional theory. But so far as the difference between public and private legal relations rests on the difference between superordination and subordination on the one hand and coordination at the same level on the other, the relation between the individual invested with the legal power to sue and the obligated individual against whom the action is directed is a "public" legal relation in the same sense as the relation between the court functioning as an organ of the state and the obligated individual. For the legal power of the individual entitled to bring an action against another individual consists of his capacity to participate in the creation of the individual norm, which orders a sanction against the obligation-violating individual. If the function of the court is attributed to the state and if, therefore, the situation is interpreted as relation between the state in its capacity as legal authority and the defendant subjected to this authority, which means as a relation of super- and subordination, then—as pointed out—the function of the plaintiff can be interpreted in the same way. Attribution of the legal function to the legal community merely expresses the view that this function is determined by the legal order. The relation of superordination and subordination that, according to traditional theory, exists here between the state (represented by the court) and the defendant, also exists between the plaintiff and the defendant. This relation of super- and subordination is merely the super- and subordination existing between the legal order and the individuals whose behavior it regulates—hence nothing but a figurative expression for the fact that the behavior of the individuals forms the content of the legal norms. The authority manifested in this figure of speech is the authority of the legal order which, created and applied according to its own precepts by certain individuals, obligates and entitles other individuals. If the state is presented as superordinated to the individual, this merely means that individuals as organs of the state create and apply norms which regulate the behavior of other individuals—and which, specifically, obligate other individuals to behave in a certain way. If expressed without the use of the spatial figure of speech: this merely means that the legal order determines facts by which legal norms are created that connect a certain human behavior as condition with certain coercive acts as consequence.

A legal relation of a special kind exists where the obligation of one individual toward another is connected, by the law, with the obligation of the latter toward the former. This is so, for example, in a contract of sale where the obligation to deliver certain goods is tied to the obligation to pay the purchase price. Then a legal relation exists between the norm that obligates the buyer and the norm that obligates the seller, or, more correctly, between the law-determined behavior of the one and the law-determined behavior of the other.

Paralleling the theory that the right is a legally protected interest, is the theory that the legal relation is an actual relationship of a sexual, economic, or political nature, existing independently of the legal order in social reality, and merely regulated but not constituted by the legal order. However, just as the subjective right is not an interest protected by legal norms, but the protection that consists in these legal norms, in the same way is the legal relation not an actual relation existing in social reality, only regulated by legal norms, but a relation primarily constituted by legal norms. The legal relation of matrimony, for example, is not a complex of sexual and economic relations between two individuals of different sex merely shaped into a specific form by law. Without law there simply is no such thing as "matrimony." Matrimony as a legal relation is a legal institution, that is to say, a complex of legal obligations and rights in the specifically technical sense—this means, a complex of legal norms. The relations that concern us here are relations between legal norms or relations between facts determined by legal norms. For a cognition directed toward law as a system of norms, no other legal relations exist. But also from the point of view of a cognition directed toward actual reality it must be admitted that by law—and this means by the idea that men have of a legal order presupposed to be valid—actual relations between individuals can be created, which, without such an idea as a motive of behavior, did not and could not exist.

33. The Legal Subject; the Person

a) The Legal Subject

According to traditional theory a legal subject is he who is the subject of a legal obligation or of a right. If by "right" (Berechtigung) is understood not the mere reflex right, but the legal power to assert (by taking a legal action) the fulfillment of a legal obligation, that is, the legal power to participate in the creation of a judicial decision constituting an individual norm by which the execution of a sanction as a reaction against the nonfulfillment of an obligation is ordered; and if one takes into consideration that the subject of a legal power to create or apply legal norms is by no means always designated as a legal subject, then it is convenient to confine the concept of "legal subject" to the subject of a legal obligation and to differentiate between the concept of "subject of a legal obligation" from that of "subject of a legal power." To the extent that in traditional legal language the function of creating and applying legal norms is attributed to the legal community, the concept "subject of legal power" and the concept "legal organ" coincide.[58] It is to be noted that by the statement that "an individual is the subject of a legal obligation or has a legal obligation" is only meant that a certain behavior of this individual is the content of a legally established obligation and that by the statement that "an individual is the subject of a legal power" or "an individual has a legal power," is only meant that, according to the legal order, legal norms are created or applied by certain acts of this individual, or that certain acts of this individual participate in the creation or application of legal norms. As mentioned before, a cognition directed toward legal norms is concerned not with individuals per se, but with their legally determined actions which form the contents of the legal norms. When we say: "An individual, as a legal organ, creates or applies law; an individual, as legal subject, obeys or violates law," then this personifying language merely expresses the functional difference between the two different types of legally determined human behavior. The personal concepts of "legal subject" and "legal organ" [59] are not necessary concepts for the description of a legal order. They are merely auxiliary concepts that—like the concept of reflex right—facilitate the description. Their use is permissible only if one is aware of this, their nature. To awaken this awareness is the task of the Pure Theory of Law. If the Pure Theory employs these concepts, it is done only in the sense here described.

Just as traditional theory places "right" ahead of "obligation," so it regards the legal subject primarily as a subject of rights and only secondarily as a subject of legal obligations. In German legal theory, which distinguishes between law and right as between objective law and subjective law, the concept of "legal subject"— in German *Rechtssubjekt* (literally: subject of law)—is closely

---

[58] Note, however, that the legal terminology is not consistent, particularly that the plaintiff who exercises a true legal power is not called "organ."

[59] Cf. pp. 150 ff.

connected with the concept of *subjectives Recht* (subjective law). The concept of *Rechtssubjekt* as the possessor or "holder" (*Träger*) of a *subjektives Recht* (subjective law, i.e., a right) is only another version of the concept of "subjective" law which is essentially formed with regard to the concept of property right. Just as in the concept of *subjectives Recht* so in the concept of *Rechtssubjekt* the idea predominates of an entity different from, and independent of, the positive legal order—the idea of the existence of a legal subject which is to be found, so to speak, in the individual and in certain corporate bodies whom the positive law must recognize as subjects of certain rights in order to preserve its character as true law. This view implies an antagonism between the law as an objectively valid order, a system of binding norms (the objective law) and the subjective law (the right) as possessed by a subject; and this antagonism implies a logical contradiction. This contradiction manifests itself most clearly when the essence of being a legal subject is considered to be freedom, whereas the essence of the objective law is considered to be its binding force, even its coercive character, which is evidently the opposite of freedom. Thus, e.g. G. F. Puchta says: "The basic concept of law is freedom. . . . The abstract concept of freedom is: possibility of self-determination. . . . Man is subject of law [*Rechtssubjekt,* legal subject] because he has that possibility of self-determination, that means that he has a [free] will" (*Cursus der Institutionen,* 10th ed., 1873, 1, 4, 5, 6).

The fictitiousness of this definition of the concept of the subject of law is apparent. Because if one can talk at all about self-determination of the individual in his capacity as a legal subject, namely in the realm of so-called private law (with respect to the law-creating function of a legal contract), then legal self-determination, that is, autonomy, is present only in a very limited sense. For nobody can create rights for himself, because the right of the one presupposes the obligation of the other, and such legal relation can regularly only be established in the field of private law, according to the legal order by an agreement of two individuals. And even then only if the legal order conferred upon the agreement a law-creating function. Therefore the legal determination ultimately originates in the objective law and not in the legal subjects subordinated to it. Consequently there is no full self-determination even in private law.

The ideological function of this self-contradictory conception of the legal subject as the holder of rights is easily seen: The function is to maintain the idea that the existence of the legal subject as the holder of a right—and this means holder of a property right—is in a category that transcends the objective law, namely the positive law made by man and hence changeable by man; in other words, to maintain the idea that property is an institution protected by a barrier insurmountable by the legal order. The concept of a legal subject who, as the holder of a subjective right, is independent of the positive law, becomes all the more important if the legal order that guarantees the institution of private property is recognized as changeable and forever changing, created by human will and not by the eternal will of God or by nature—especially when the creation of the legal order is accomplished by a democratic procedure. The idea of a legal subject independent of the law, that is, the idea of a holder of a "subjective" law which is not less, perhaps even more, "law" than the "objective," that is, the positive law, is designed to protect the institution of private property from being rescinded by the legal order. It is easy to understand why the ideology of legal subjectivity seeks to establish a link with the ethical value of individual freedom and of an autonomous personality, if property is always included in this freedom. An order that refuses to recognize man as a free personality in this sense, that is, an order that does not guarantee the subjective right of property, is rejected by this ideology as not being a legal order at all.

b) The Physical Person

Traditional theory is identifying the concept of "legal subject" with that of "person." The definition of "person," according to traditional theory, is: the human being as a subject of rights and obligations. Since, however, not only a human being but also other entities, such as corporations, municipalities, and states, are presented as persons, a person is defined as the holder of rights and obligations, whereby as a holder not only a human being can function, but also these other entities. The concept of a "holder" of rights and obligations plays a decisive role in the traditional theory dealing with the concept of "legal person." If the holder of rights and obligations is a human being, traditional theory speaks of a "physical person"; if it is one of the other entities it speaks of a "juristic person." Whereby the physical person is juxtaposed as a "natural" person to the juristic as an "artificial" person—a person not "real" but only constructed by jurisprudence. Efforts have been made, to be sure, to prove that even juristic persons are "real." But these efforts are futile because analysis shows that even the so-called physical person is an artificial construction of jurisprudence—that even the so-called physical person is actually only a "juristic" person.

If in the case of the juristic person rights and obligations can be "held" by something that is not a human being, then also in the case of the so-called physical person that which holds the rights and obligations (and which the juristic person must have in common with the physical person, since both are "persons" as "holders" of rights and obligations) cannot be the human being, who is the "holder" in question, but something which the human being and the "juristic person" have in common.

It is said, too, that the human being has "personality," that the legal order invests man with personality—and not necessarily all men. Slaves are not "persons," they have no legal personality. Traditional theory does not deny that "person" and "human being" are two different concepts, though it asserts that according to modern law, as distinguished to ancient law, all men are persons or have legal personality. What, now, does the statement of traditional theory mean that the legal order invests the human being, or a group of human beings, with the quality of legal personality —with the quality of being a "person"? It means that the legal order imposes obligations upon, or confers rights to, human beings, that is, that the legal order makes human behavior the content of obligations and rights. "To be a person" or "to have a legal personality" is identical with having legal obligations and subjective rights. The person as a holder of obligations and rights is not something that is different from the obligations and rights, as whose holder the person is presented—just as a tree which is said to have a trunk, branches, and blossoms, is not a substance different

from trunk, branches, and blossoms, but merely the totality of
these elements. The physical or juristic person who "has" obligations and rights as their holder, *is* these obligations and rights—a
complex of legal obligations and rights whose totality is expressed
figuratively in the concept of "person." "Person" is merely the
personification of this totality.

If especially the facts are analyzed which are presented in traditional theory as "rights and obligations of a juristic person," and if
the word "right" is used in its specific technical sense of the word
(meaning a legal power or competence to be exercised by bringing an action against somebody), then we find that these rights
and obligations, exactly like those of a physical person, have
human behavior as their content, and are in this sense—and only
in this sense—rights and obligations of human beings. Only by
human behavior can a right be exercised or an obligation be fulfilled or violated. Therefore it cannot be the relation to a human
being which is the element that differentiates the physical or
natural person from the juristic or artificial person. Therefore,
too, the so-called physical person cannot—in contradistinction to
the juristic person—be defined as something like a qualified
human being, qualified, that is, by holding rights and obligations.
Such a definition is to be rejected just as the definition of the concept of right as "a legally protected interest." Just as the right is
not a (legally protected) interest but the legal protection of an interest, so is the physical person not the human being who has
rights and obligations, but a totality of rights and obligations
which have the behavior of a human being as its content and thus
form a unity. This unity is also expressed in the concept of the
legal subject which traditional theory identifies with that of the
juristic person. That the human being is a legal subject (subject
of rights and obligations) means nothing else, as has been emphasized, but that human behavior is the content of legal obligations
and legal rights—nothing else than that a human being is a person
or has personality. What we have in both cases—in that of the
physical and in that of the juristic person—is legal obligations and
legal rights that have human behavior as their content and constitute a unity. A legal person is the unity of a complex of legal obligations and legal rights. Since these obligations and rights are constituted by legal norms (more correctly: *are* these legal norms),

the problem of "person" is in the last analysis the problem of the unity of a complex of norms. The question is: what constitutes this unity in the one case and in the other?

The unity of obligations and rights (that is, the unity of the legal norms that concern us here) which is presented as a physical person, consists in the fact that it is the behavior of one and the same human being which constitutes the content of these obligations and rights—that it is the behavior of the same human being which is determined by these legal norms. The so-called physical person, then, is not a human being, but the personified unity of the legal norms that obligate or authorize one and the same human being. It is not a natural reality but a legal construction, created by the science of law—an auxiliary concept in the presentation of legally relevant facts. In this sense a physical person is a juristic person.

c) The Juristic Person (Corporation)

The essence of the so-called juristic person, juxtaposed by traditional jurisprudence to the physical person, is most clearly illustrated by an analysis of the typical case of such a juristic person, namely of the corporation. It is usually defined as a community of individuals upon which the legal order imposes obligations and bestows rights not to be regarded as the obligations and rights of the individuals who form the corporation as its members. Precisely because these obligations and rights concern in some way the interests of the individuals who form the corporation, and still are not—as traditional theory assumes—their obligations and rights, are these interpreted as obligations and rights of the corporation, and hence the latter is conceived as a person.

The legal relations of a juristic person are described as follows: It is said, for example, that a corporation rents a house or buys a piece of land. The right to use the house (i.e., to exclude non-members of the corporation from its use), the ownership of the land (i.e., the right to dispose about it and to exclude nonmembers from disposing about it), is a right of the corporation, not of its members. If this right is violated, then it is the corporation, not the individual member, which has to enter an action for trial; the compensation for the damage caused by the violation of law—the sum of money collected through civil execution—flows into the assets of the corporation, not into those of individual members. The obligation to pay the amount of rent to the owner of the house, the purchasing price to the seller of the piece of land, are the obligations of the corporation, not those of the members; for if the obligation is not fulfilled, that is, if the corporation commits a delict, then the law suit of the house owner or the seller is not directed against the members, but against the corporation; and the civil execution is directed not into the property of the members, but of the corporation. There are cases in which, if the assets of the corporation do not suffice, civil execution may also be directed into the property of the members, that is, cases in which the liability for the delict is not limited to the assets of the corporation, but in which the members too are liable for the delict with their own assets. However, it is precisely the case of the limited-liability of the corporation which seems to recommend the conception of a legal personality of the corporation.

In the description of the legal relations of a corporation as a juristic person, two different types of assertions are made: the assertion that the corporation, as an acting person, performs certain acts, especially legal acts; that the corporation performs a legal transaction, such as the conclusion of a contract, that it brings an action against somebody, that it fulfills a legal obligation, or that it by its behavior violates a legal obligation, i.e., commits a delict. And, secondly, the assertion that the corporation is the subject of legal obligations and legal rights, because the legal order imposes obligations and bestows rights on it. The first assertion describes always the behavior of a definite individual through whom the legal person acts.

It is the action or refrainment from action by an individual that is interpreted as the action or refrainment of the corporation—"attributed" to the corporation. The human being through whom the corporation acts as a juristic person, and whose behavior is attributed to the corporation, is called the "organ" of the corporation. The problem of the corporation as an acting person is the problem (already discussed) of the community organ; it is the problem of attributing to the community the function performed by an individual. Applied to the juristic person of the corporation, the problem is this: Under which conditions can the behavior of a human being be interpreted as the behavior of a corporation—can it be attributed [60] to the corporation? Which are the conditions under which a human being performs or refrains from performing a certain action in his capacity as an organ of the corporation? Closely connected with this problem is the problem of the corporation as the subject of obligations and rights. Since obligations and rights can only have human behavior as their content, the legal order can impose obligations and confer rights only upon human beings. The statement that a corporation is the subject of obligations and rights, describes the obligations and rights of definite human beings, which, however, are interpreted as obligations and rights of the juristic person—attributed to the juristic person. Therefore the assumption of traditional theory that the obligations and rights of the juristic person are not (or not at the same time) the obligations and rights of human beings—of "physical persons," in the terminology of traditional theory—is untenable.

d) The Juristic Person As an Acting Subject

If two or more individuals wish to pursue jointly some economic, political, religious, humanitarian, or other purposes within the sphere of validity of a national legal order, they form a community by submitting their cooperative behavior, according to the legal order, to a special normative order that regulates this behavior and thus establishes the community. The cooperation of the individuals of the community directed toward the realization of the community purpose can be organized according to the principle of division of labor. In this event the community is a corporation. For: a corporation is defined as an "organized" community, that is, a community constituted by a normative order, a "statute," prescribing that certain functions are to be exercised by individuals called in a way determined by the statute for this purpose—in other words, a normative order instituting organs who work according to the principle of division of labor.[61] The statute constituting the corporation is created by a legal transaction determined by the national legal order. Leaving aside international law, the

---

[60] Cf. § 30c.
[61] Cf. pp. 153 ff.

statute of a corporation represents a partial legal order, to be distinguished from the national legal order, which is a total legal order.

The statute regulates the behavior of individuals who are the "members of the corporation," "belong" to the corporation, "form" the corporation. These are figures of speech meaning merely that a certain behavior of these individuals is regulated by a partial legal order. As has been said, these individuals do not belong to the corporation with the totality of their existence, but only with the actions and omissions determined by the statute. Only an action or a refraining determined by the statute can be attributed to the corporation. For the attribution of an act of human behavior to the corporation merely expresses the relation of this act to the normative order that constitutes the community—the order which is personified by this attribution. Therefore any behavior determined by a normative order may be attributed to the community established by that order; any normative order regulating the behavior of a number of individuals (including one that does not establish organs functioning according to the principle of division of labor) may be personified, described as an acting person; and therefore any "member" of such a community may be looked upon as its "organ." But since in common usage of language only those functions are attributed to the community which are performed according to the principle of division of labor by the authorized individuals, and since only those individuals who perform these functions are designated as organs, therefore one can distinguish between the "organs" and the "members" of a corporation. It is to be noted that the organs of a corporation, according to the statute, may perform not only legal functions such as changing the statute, bringing an action, lodging an appeal, conducting legal transactions, but also other functions depending on the purpose of the corporation. If these functions are attributed to the corporation, if the corporation is described as an acting person, if it is said that the corporation "acts," although only a human being determined by the statute performs an act determined by the statute, then one uses in this anthropomorphic metaphor a fiction of the same kind as that in the attribution of legal acts of a statutory representative to the represented individual who lacks the capacity to act. The misinterpretation of the anthropomorphic metaphor "juristic person" as a real entity, as a kind of superman or organism, is the unpermissible hypostatization of a thinking aid or auxiliary concept constructed by jurisprudence merely for the purpose of simplifying and illustrating the description of a complex legal situation. Such hypostatization not merely results in obscuring the facts that are to be described, but also in the creation of sham problems whose solution jurisprudence vainly attempts. Such sham problems play a particularly fateful role when it is the state that is hypostatized as a juristic person, and when, then, the question is raised of the relationship of this reality to the law, as to "its" law. This will be discussed later.[62]

e) The Juristic Person As a Subject of Obligations and Rights

This metaphor is used not only to describe the corporation as an acting person, but also as a subject of obligations and rights; by "rights" traditional theory not only means rights in the technical sense of the word, that is, legal power, but also positive permission. These obligations and rights of the corporation are partly those established by the national legal order, partly those established on the basis of an authorization (by the national legal order) by the statute of the corporation. The former are external, the latter internal obligations and rights of the corporation. The statute, however, can also stipulate obligations and rights of the members which are not interpreted as those of the corporation, not attributed to the corporation. A corporation's obligation to pay taxes or a corporation's right to conduct legal transactions or the right to assert by an action the fulfillment of an obligation toward the corporation or a corporation's right to participate in a political election or a corporation's right to exercise a certain trade—all these are external obligations and rights. A corporation's obligation to distribute profits among its members or a corporation's right to collect membership fees—these are internal obligations and rights. The corresponding right, to receive a share of the profits and the corresponding obligation to pay a membership fee, however, are described as rights and obligations of the members, not of the corporation. For the question of the nature of the cor-

---

[62] Cf. § 41a.

poration as a juristic person, only those obligations and rights are relevant which are interpreted to be those of the corporation.

We have said that all obligations and rights have the behavior of human beings as their content. If the national legal order imposes obligations or bestows rights that are interpreted to be those of the corporation; and if we speak of the obligations and rights of the corporation—these can only be obligations that are fulfilled, and rights that are exercised, by the behavior of human beings who belong to the corporation. And if these obligations and rights are attributed to the corporation, then these individuals, in their role as organs of the corporation, must fulfill (or violate) the obligations or exercise the rights. Therefore the national legal order, in imposing obligations or bestowing rights upon a corporation, determines only the material element of the behavior that constitutes the content of the obligation or right, and leaves the determination of the personal element, that is, of the individual who is to fulfill the obligation or exercise the right, to the statute; so therefore the relationship between the national legal order and the obligated or authorized juristic person is the relationship between two legal orders, a total and a partial one. Thereby the manner in which the national legal order—to speak in terms of traditional terminology—obligates or authorizes a corporation as a juristic person, differs from the manner in which the national legal order obligates or authorizes a human being as a physical person. In the latter case the national legal order determines directly not only the material, but also the personal element of the behavior that constitutes the content of the obligation or right.

In case of internal obligations and rights of the corporation, the statute determines both the material and personal elements of the behavior that constitutes the content of the obligation or right. Internal obligations are stipulated when the statute prescribes a behavior to whose opposite the national legal order attaches a sanction. Internal rights are stipulated when the statute establishes obligations of the members whose fulfillment can be asserted, according to the national legal order, by an action entered by an individual, determined by the statute, in his capacity as organ of the corporation.

Obligations of the juristic person

In the preceding discussion it has been assumed that the legal order establishes an obligation to behave in a certain way if it makes the opposite behavior, as the behavior of a human being, the condition of a sanction. The behavior which is the condition of the sanction is delict; the sanction is the consequence of the delict. Subject of an obligation, therefore, is the individual who, by his own behavior, can bring about or avoid the sanction—can commit the delict or refrain from committing it: the potential delinquent. If this concept of legal obligation is accepted, then an individual may be regarded as capable of being obligated (*verpflichtungsfähig*) only if he is capable of committing a delict (*deliktsfähig*).[63]

The situation with which we are confronted when the legal order establishes an obligation interpreted to be an obligation of a corporation as a juristic person is this: the legal order determines a behavior and attaches a sanction to its opposite, but leaves the determination of the individual through whose behavior the sanction is brought about or avoided to the statute of a corporation; and prescribes the sanction in such a way that it can be interpreted as being directed not against this individual, but against the corporation, which means that the liability for the nonfulfillment of the obligation (the suffering of the evil that the sanction represents) is attributable to the corporation. We will discuss later the basis of this attribution; for the moment we may merely state that the obligation—without the aid of the fiction of attribution—is the obligation of the individual who, by his behavior, can fulfill or violate the obligation, but that for the nonfulfillment of the obligation *an other* individual or individuals are liable with their person or property. The statute, in determining the individual whose behavior can fulfill or violate the obligation (by enabling, which in the broader sense means authorizing, this individual, and only this one, to behave in this way), also determines, indirectly, his behavior. Therefore the behavior by which the individual fulfills or violates the obligation, and therefore the fulfilled or violated obligation, can be referred to the statute, that is, the normative partial order constituting the corporation.

---

[63] Cf. § 31.

This is the situation when the obligation is attributed to the corporation as a juristic person (is interpreted to be the subject of the obligation) and the individual who actually fulfills or violates the obligation is considered to be an organ of the corporation. With the aid of this fictitious attribution the juristic person is represented as having the capacity of being obligated and of committing a delict.

The problem of the corporation's capacity of being obligated and the much discussed and closely linked problem of its capacity of committing a delict are problems of attribution; and attribution is a mental operation which may, but need not be, performed; for the facts can be described without the aid of this mental operation, which in any case involves a fiction, particularly when a delict is attributed to a corporation. A delict is an act of human behavior and therefore can only be committed by a definite human being. In fact, as linguistic usage shows, the attribution of a human behavior, determined by the legal order, to a community constituted by this same order, is not carried out with consistency because it is not always carried out according to the same criterion. The attribution of human behavior can be far-reaching or restricted. If only a *specifically* functioning individual is regarded as an "organ" of the community; [64] if it is asumed, further, that his behavior is not attributable to the community when the behavior is not authorized by the normative order; and if, finally, it is assumed that the statute of corporation authorizes its organs only to fulfill, not to violate the obligations established by the national legal order—and, according to the national legal order, only *can* authorize the fulfillment, not the violation, of obligations—then the corporation is not capable of committing a delict. But since nothing stands in the way of attributing to the corporation the fulfillment of the obligation which the organ is authorized by the statute to fulfill, the corporation may be regarded as the subject of an obligation which it can fulfill but not violate; in this limited sense, then, can the corporation be described as having the capacity of being obligated without having the capacity of committing a delict. It may be objected that this is incompatible with the concept of legal obligation as developed in these pages, according to which only he is capable of being obli-

---

[64] Cf. pp. 151 f.

gated who is capable of committing a delict; but this objection is irrelevant because actually (without the fictitious attribution) not the corporation, but only *that* individual is legally obligated and capable of being obligated, whose behavior can fulfill or violate the obligation. From the fact that in the former case the individual is regarded as an organ of the corporation (i.e., that his behavior is attributed to the corporation) does not necessarily follow to regard him thus in the latter case. Such attribution is always only possible, never necessary. In fact, however, the corporation *is* regarded as capable of committing a delict; in common usage of language we attribute to the corporation the nonfulfillment of certain obligations stipulated by the national legal order. It is said, for example, the corporation as a juristic person failed to pay a tax and thereby committed a punishable delict; or that the corporation failed to pay rent for a rented house or the purchase price for a bought piece of land thus committing a civil delict. All this means that these delicts are attributed to the corporation; the corporation is regarded as the delinquent and may therefore also be regarded as the subject of the obligations violated. But if not only the fulfillment of an obligation, but also its violation is attributed to a corporation, then one has to recognize, as an organ of the corporation, the individual authorized by the statute to fulfill those obligations, even if he acts outside this authorization in the narrower sense—if he does not fulfill the obligation imposed upon the corporation, but violates it by his behavior. This is entirely feasible if one recognizes that the attribution of human behavior to a corporation merely expresses that this behavior is somehow determined in the statute constituting the corporation; if one recognizes that "to attribute the behavior of a certain individual to the corporation" only means referring this behavior to the statute. As has been shown in preceding explanations, the behavior by which an obligation of the corporation is violated, and which, according to the national legal order, is the condition of a sanction, is, indirectly, determined by the statute of the corporation insofar as the individual is determined by the statute who by his behavior can fulfill or violate the obligation. If, for example, the statute prescribes that the corporation's taxes ought to be paid by a certain organ from the corporation's treasury, then this organ alone can violate the corporation's obligation to pay the taxes; and thus, this behavior that violated the obligation of the corporation directly determined by the national legal order, is also determined, indirectly, by the statute.

If a delict is not attributed to a corporation, this is so because the statute which authorizes the behavior (like a contract which obligates a party to a legally prohibited behavior) is void or voidable according to the national legal order. But this need not necessarily be so. It is possible that, according to a national legal order, a statute is valid although it authorizes an organ to a behavior prohibited by the national legal order. If the organ is authorized or even obligated by the statute to a behavior prohibited by the national legal order, then we are confronted with the already discussed stiuation [65] that a certain behavior and also its opposite are made the condition for a sanction—namely: the behavior by which the organ fulfills the obligation imposed upon him by the statute as the condition of a sanction directed against the corporation, and the behavior by which the organ violates the obligation imposed upon him by the statute as a condition of a sanction directed against the organ.[66] The situation may be described in two rules of law which do not logically contradict each other. But from the point of view of legal politics such a situation is most undesirable. In order to avoid it the national legal order can stipulate that the statutory authorization and, particularly, the statutory obligation to a behavior contrary to the national legal order, is to be regarded as invalid, that is, void or voidable. If the legal order does not do this, then the delict committed by the organ in agreement with the statute can be attributed to the corporation even if the attribution is limited to a behavior authorized by the statute. Actually norms of the statute of a corporation are not always to be regarded as void or voidable if they authorize illegal behavior. For example, the shareholder's meeting of a stock company could decide on the basis of the opinion of its legal adviser not to pay a certain tax and to give the organ of the corporation orders accordingly. If thereupon the tax is not paid, and if, further, the fiscal authority in an administrative tax procedure directed against the company decides that nonpayment is a delict and, consequently, the company is ordered to pay the tax and a

---

[65] Cf. § 5a.

[66] Such a situation is also present in international law; cf. § 43b.

fine, and if, finally, execution is carried directly into the property
of the company because of lack of payment, then the illegal behavior of the organ is attributed to the corporation; and it is not
assumed that the illegal behavior took place outside of the statutory authorization; it is not assumed that the individual who behaved in that way did *not* act as an organ of the corporation, and it
is not assumed that the statute which had authorized the behavior
(especially the individual norm which had authorized or obligated
the organ to refuse payment), was invalid.

If the attribution to the community of a delict committed by an
organ or member of the community is made dependent on the delict having been authorized by the statute constituting the community, then the answer to the question whether attribution to
the community is possible depends on the interpretation of the
statute. This question may come up in judging political crimes
committed by members or organs of a political organization. Even
if the statute of this organization lacks a specific clause that authorizes the commitment of the crime to be judged, it still may be
assumed that the crime was committed in accordance with the
statute if the organ or member of the organization in committing
the crime acted according to the—while not specifically marked,
but—tacitly understood aims of the organization.

Besides, the attribution to the corporation of a statutorily authorized illegal behavior can also take place on the basis of an invalid statute. Since this optional mental operation is legally
irrelevant, even a statute that is illegal from the viewpoint of the
legal order may serve as a scheme of interpretation. This is the case
if crimes, committed by organs of members of political organizations which are active on the basis of secret statutes authorizing
their organs or members to commit such crimes, are attributed to
these organizations and if, consequently, the organizations are declared to be subversive and criminal.[67]

If the question of who is the "subject" of an obligation that is
described as an obligation of the corporation is to be answered

---

[67] The Charter of the International Tribunal, which is a part of the so-called
London Agreement for the Prosecution and Punishment of the Major War Criminals
of the European Axis, says in Article 9: "At the trial of any individual member
of any group or organization the Tribunal may declare (in connection with any
act of which the individual may be convicted) that the group or organization of
which the individual was a member was a criminal organization."

without the aid of attribution, then we can only consider as subject of the obligation—as we have done—the individual who, by his behavior, can fulfill or violate the obligation, in other words, the competent organ of the corporation. If we consider that the financial obligations (which are the ones usually concerned) are to be fulfilled from the property which is interpreted as that of the corporation, not from that of the organ, and if—as we shall see later—the property of the corporation may be considered as the collective property of the members of the corporation, then the obligation of the corporation may be considered as being the collective obligation of the members of the corporation. This means: The obligation in question can be attributed to the members of the corporation just as well as to the juristic person of the corporation. But for the description of the present set of facts neither the one nor the other attribution is needed.

Just as the obligation attributed to the corporation is not to be fulfilled from the property of the corporation organ, but from the property interpreted as the property of the corporation, so in case of nonfulfillment of the obligation the sanctions prescribed by the national legal order, the civil execution, is not directed into the property of the organ but into the property attributed to the corporation. According to this attribution we may speak of a sanction directed against the corporation and therefore of a liability of the corporation for the nonfulfillment of the obligation which an individual designated by the statute ought to fulfill in his capacity as an organ of the corporation.

Liability of the juristic person

If the corporation's capacity to commit a delict is excluded, this does not mean the exclusion of the possibility of the corporation's liability; only the liability, in this case, is not one for the corporation's own delict, that is, for a delict attributed to the corporation, but for someone else's delict, namely that committed by the individual designated by the statute to fulfill the obligation. Liable for the delict is the individual against whom the coercive act, conditioned by the delict, is directed. If the sanction consists in the coercive deprivation of property, then the individual who has the right to dispose of the property and against whom the coercive act is directed, is liable with his *person;* and the individual who is the subject of the rights which constitute the property is liable with the property into which the execution is to be directed. In case of a corporation, an organ of the corporation is competent to dispose of the property. If a civil execution into this property takes place as a reaction to the nonfulfillment of an obligation imposed by the national legal order upon the corporation, then the coercive act is directed against the organ who, therefore, is liable only with his person for the nonfulfillment of the obligation; whereas, if the corporation is regarded as the subject of this property, one can say that it is the corporation which is liable with its property. Actually, it is the corporation which is regarded as the subject of this property, that is, in common language, the rights that constitute this property are attributed to the corporation. However, as we shall see, these rights can also be interpreted as joint or collective rights of the corporation's members, that is, they can be attributed to the members as collective rights. This, at any rate, is a more realistic interpretation than one which constructs a fictitious person as the holder of these rights. It is, then, possible to say that the members of the corporation are liable with their collective property for the nonfulfillment of an obligation imposed upon the corporation by the national legal order. When we speak of the corporation's liability for the nonfulfillment of its obligation constituted by civil execution, we mean by this the following situation: an organ competent to dispose over the property into which the civil execution is to be directed is liable with his person, and the corporation or the members of the corporation are liable with the property which may be interpreted to be the property of the corporation or the collective property of the corporation members. When we speak of the liability of the corporation, then we attribute to the corporation the suffering of the evil that consists in the forcible deprivation of property interpreted to be the property of the corporation or the collective property of the members. If the fulfillment of the obligation stipulated by the national legal order has been made, by the statute, the content of the obligation of a definite organ, then this individual liability of the organ is added to the liability of the corporation.

If the corporation is looked upon as the subject of property rights, then the concept of the corporation's liability for delicts which are the condition for civil execution into the property presents no difficulties. A difficulty arises, however, when the question is raised whether a corporation can be liable for delicts which are the condition of *other* sanctions, such as imprisonment or even the death penalty, and if the delicts have been committed by individuals who have been authorized by a public or secret statute. To impose imprisonment or the death penalty upon a corporation indeed seems an absurd notion. But this is no longer paradoxical if we consider that it is not absurd to say that a fine is inflicted upon a corporation, whereby we say nothing else than that civil execution is directed into the corporation's property, which, realistically interpreted, is merely the collective property of the members. Hence the expression "the corporation is being punished for a delict" merely means that the members are collectively liable for the delict. A national legal order may deviate from the principle of individual liability, a principle usually adhered to in criminal law. It may stipulate: "If an individual in his capacity as a member or organ of an organization commits a crime, then not only this individual but all members or particularly prominent organs of this organization ought to be punished by imprisonment or death." That means: the legal order may establish collective liability. Then it is by no means more absurd to regard this collective liability of the members as a punishment to be executed against the organization, than to interpret the civil execution directed into the property of a corporation as being directed against the corporation, and to say, in case of a fine, that the juristic person has been punished. But, if a criminal code were to stipulate such collective liability as outlined here, then the suffering of imprisonment or the death penalty by the affected individuals would probably not be attributed to the organization—language would refuse in this case to give expression to a mental operation of attribution.[68]

Rights of the juristic person

If a right in the technical sense, that is, a legal power, is attributed to a corporation to assert, by taking an action, the nonfulfillment of an obligation, then this power is to be exercised by an organ designated by the statute. The subject of this right is the organ. To

---

[68] But note that in international relations it is said, as a matter of course, that one state conducts a war against another state, although the coercive acts which constitute war—killing, mutilation, capture—are directed only against individuals as members of the state, so that the suffering of these evils is attributed to the corporation as the juristic person of the state. Cf. § 42b and d.

attribute this right to the corporation expresses that the exercise of the legal power is determined by the statute. If it is an obligation to perform something, then the performance has to be rendered to the individual determined by the statute as entitled to receive the performance; if it is an obligation to tolerate something, particularly, in the case of property, if it is the obligation to tolerate the disposition of a certain object by another, then it is the organ of the corporation who is entitled, according to the statute, to make the disposition, toward whom the obligation to tolerate exists. But the statute can stipulate that the members are entitled to use the object—in which case this use by the members must be regulated. In this case the regulation is to be tolerated as a disposition of the object. When we speak of an obligation toward the corporation or of a reflex right of the corporation, we express in this attribution the fact that the statute determines the individuals toward whom an obligation to perform or to tolerate exists. Such attribution means, just as the attribution of legal power to the corporation, a reference to the thus personified partial legal order that constitutes the corporation.

Considering that the legal power is to be exercised in the interest of the members of the corporation and that the fulfillment of the obligations constituting the reflex rights eventually has to benefit the members, we may speak of "collective rights" of these members. And then we may characterize the property which consists of these rights as the property of the corporation or—which amounts to the same—as the collective property of the members; and a civil execution directed into this property constituting the liability of the corporation, as the collective liability of the members.

Therefore, then, the obligations and rights attributed by traditional jurisprudence to the corporation as a juristic person, are, like all obligations and rights, the obligations and rights of human beings, in the sense that their content is the behavior of particular human beings. It is not correct to assume that these obligations and rights must be attributed to the corporation as their holder, because they cannot be considered to be obligations and rights of men, that is, of the members of the corporation; for, as we have shown, they can be attributed to the members as collective obligations or rights. Still, there is a difference between these obligations and rights and those which, according to traditional theory, are not attributed to the corporation. The latter, unlike the former, are not collective obligations and rights of the members, but are *individual* obligations and rights, in contrast to collective ones; and the liability for the nonfulfillment of the obligations attributed by traditional theory to the corporation is *collective* liability of the members. They are liable with their collective property. It is possible—but not necessary—that *only* such a collective liability of the members for the nonfulfillment of the obligations attributed to the corporation is established. As has been mentioned, to this collective liability may be added the individual liability of the organ who is obligated by the statute to fulfill the obligation imposed upon the corporation by the national legal order; and the liability of the corporation need not be limited to the collective property of the members. If the property of the corporation (the collective property of the members) is not sufficient to repair the damage caused by the nonfulfillment of the obligations attributed to the corporation, individual liability of the members (i.e., liability with their individual property) may be stipulated. This is the difference between corporations with limited and with unlimited liability.

The attribution, to the corporation, of obligations to be fulfilled by an organ of the corporation and of rights to be asserted by an action taken by an organ of the corporation, is of the same type as the attribution to an individual lacking capacity to act, of obligations to be fulfilled by the statutory representative and of rights to be asserted by action taken by the representative. A difference exists only so far as in the former case the obligations and rights are attributed to a corporation, conceived of as a juristic person, in the latter case to a human being. The organ of the corporation "represents" the juristic person of the corporation. If it is recognized that the obligations and rights in question can be attributed to the members as collective obligations and rights, then the organ of the corporation can be looked upon as the representative of the corporation members, authorized by the statute. The creation of the statute is the legal transaction by which this relationship between the corporate organ and the members is established. The much-discussed question of the difference between being an organ and being a representative is a question of attribution. Being a rep-

resentative as well as being an organ is the result of attribution; an
individual is a representative if his acts are attributed to another
individual, and he is an organ if his acts are attributed to a corporation, that is, related to the unity of a normative order, personified by this attribution.

f) The Juristic Person As an Auxiliary Concept of Legal Science

According to the preceding analysis, the juristic person, as well as
the so-called physical person, are constructions of legal science.
The juristic person is neither a social reality nor, as is sometimes
assumed, a creation of the law. If it is said that the legal order "bestows legal personality on an individual" it merely means that the
legal order makes the individual's behavior the content of obligations and rights. Legal science expresses this unity of obligations
and rights by the concept of "physical person," different from the
concept of a human being. This concept of physical person may be
used as an auxiliary concept in the description of law, but it need
not be because the situation created by the legal order may also be
described without the aid of this conception. If it is said that the
legal order bestows juristic personality upon a corporation, this
means (1) that the legal order stipulates obligations and rights
which have as their content the behavior of human beings who are
organs or members of a corporation constituted by a statute and
(2) that this complicated set of facts may conveniently, because relatively simply, be described with the aid of a personification of
the statute that constitutes the corporation. But this personification and its result, the auxiliary concept of the juristic person, are
a product of legal science describing the law, not of law itself. This
remains true even though the legislator may use this concept, as
any other created by legal science. We have already said that any
normative order regulating the behavior of individuals can be personified; any thus regulated behavior and any obligations to be
fulfilled by this behavior or rights to be asserted may be referred
to the unity of this order—they may be attributed to the thus constructed juristic person. If we distinguish, as is sometimes done,
between associations that do and those that do not have juristic
personality, we do so because a narrower concept of juristic person

is used, one in which we speak of a juristic person only if the legal order contains special provisions, for instance, that the members are liable only (or primarily) with their collective property. But this narrower concept of juristic person is also a construction of legal science, an auxiliary concept which may but need not be used in describing the law. The law creates obligations and rights which have human behavior as their content—the law does not create persons. Just as functions of the law must not be attributed to the science of law, functions of the science of law must not be attributed to the law.

g) *The Abolition of the Dualism of Right and Obligation*

According to traditional jurisprudence the legal subject—the physical or juristic person—with "his" rights and obligations refers to the law in its subjective sense. It should be noted that the concept of "right," presented by traditional (especially German) jurisprudence, as "law in a subjective sense," is only a special case of this concept which comprehends also the concept of "obligation." The law in this subjective sense and the law in the objective sense (i.e., the legal order as a system of norms), are distinguished as two different spheres. The Pure Theory of Law eliminates this dualism by dissolving the concept of "person" as the personification of a complex of legal norms, by reducing obligation and subjective law (in the technical sense) to the legal norm which attaches a sanction to a certain behavior and makes the execution of the sanction dependent on an action directed at this execution; that means: by reducing the so-called law in the subjective sense to the law in the objective sense. By doing so, the Pure Theory eliminates that subjectivistic approach to law in whose service is the concept of law in the subjective sense—the looking upon the law only from the point of view of party interest, that is, from the point of view of what it means to the individual, whether it serves his interests or threatens him with an evil. This is the specific approach of Roman jurisprudence which, essentially the result of practicing jurists, was taken over together with the reception of Roman Law. The approach of the Pure Theory, in contrast, is objectivistic and universalistic. It aims at the totality of law in its objective validity and seeks to conceive each individual phenomenon in its systematic context with all others—to conceive in each part of the law the function of the total law. In this sense the Pure Theory is a truly organic legal theory. But if the Pure Theory conceives the law as an "organism," it does not mean by this some supra-empirical metaphysical entity (a conception behind which usually hide some ethical-political postulates), but exclusively this: the law is an order, and therefore all legal problems must be set and solved as order problems. In this way legal theory becomes an exact structural analysis of positive law, free of all ethical-political value judgments.

V

THE DYNAMIC ASPECT OF LAW

34. The Reason for the Validity of a Normative Order: the Basic Norm

a) *The Meaning of the Search for the Reason for Validity*

If the law as a normative order is conceived as a system of norms that regulates the behavior of men, the question arises: What constitutes the unity of a multitude of norms—why does a certain norm belong to a certain order? And this question is closely tied to the question: Why is a norm valid, what is the reason for its validity?

A norm referring to the behavior of a human being is "valid" means that it is binding—that an individual ought to behave in the manner determined by the norm. It has been pointed out in an earlier context that the question why a norm is valid, why an individual ought to behave in a certain way, cannot be answered by ascertaining a fact, that is, by a statement that something *is;* that the reason for the validity of a norm cannot be a fact. From the circumstance that something *is* cannot follow that something *ought* to be; and that something *ought* to be, cannot be the reason that something *is.* The reason for the validity of a norm can only be the validity of another norm. A norm which represents the reason for the validity of another norm is figuratively spoken of as a higher norm in relation to a lower norm. It looks as if one could give as a reason for the validity of a norm the circumstance that it was established by an authority, human or divine; for example, the statement: "The reason for the validity of the Ten Commandments is that God Jehovah issued them on Mount Sinai"; or: "Men ought to love their enemies, because Jesus, Son of God, issued this command in his Sermon on the Mount." But in both cases the reason for the validity is not that God or his son issued a certain norm at a certain time in a certain place, but the tacitly presupposed norm that one ought to obey the commands of God or his son. To be true: In the syllogism whose major premise is the *ought*-statement asserting the validity of the higher norm: "One ought to obey God's commands," and whose conclusion is the ought-statement asserting the validity of the lower norm: "One ought to obey God's Ten Commandments," the assertion that God had issued the Ten Commandments, an "is-statement," as the minor premise, is an essential link. The Major premise and the minor premise are both conditions of the conclusion. But only the major premise, which is an *ought*-statement, is the *conditio per quam* in relation to the conclusion, which is also an *ought*-statement; that is, the norm whose validity is stated in the major premise is the reason for the validity of the norm whose validity is stated in the conclusion. The *is*-statement functioning as minor premise is only the *conditio sine qua non* in relation to the conclusion; this means: the fact whose existence is asserted in the minor premise is not the reason for the validity of the norm whose validity is asserted in the conclusion.

The norm whose validity is stated in the major premise ("One ought to obey God's commands") is included in the supposition that the norms, whose reason for validity is in question, originate from an authority, that is, from somebody competent to create valid norms; this norm bestows upon the norm-creating personality the "authority" to create norms. The mere fact that somebody commands something is no reason to regard the command as a "valid" norm, a norm binding the individual at whom it is directed. Only a competent authority can create valid norms; and such competence can only be based on a norm that authorizes the issuing of norms. The authority authorized to issue norms is subject to that norm in the same manner as the individuals are subject to the norms issued by the authority.

The norm which represents the reason for the validity of another norm is called, as we have said, the "higher" norm. But the search for the reason of a norm's validity cannot go on indefinitely like the search for the cause of an effect. It must end with a norm which, as the last and highest, is presupposed. It must be *presup-*

posed, because it cannot be "posited," that is to say: created, by an authority whose competence would have to rest on a still higher norm. This final norm's validity cannot be derived from a higher norm, the reason for its validity cannot be questioned. Such a presupposed highest norm is referred to in this book as basic norm.[69] All norms whose validity can be traced back to one and the same basic norm constitute a system of norms, a normative order. The basic norm is the common source for the validity of all norms that belong to the same order—it is their common reason of validity. The fact that a certain norm belongs to a certain order is based on the circumstance that its last reason of validity is the basic norm of this order. It is the basic norm that constitutes the unity in the multitude of norms by representing the reason for the validity of all norms that belong to this order.

b) *The Static and the Dynamic Principle*

According to the nature of the reason for the validity two types of norm systems may be distinguished: a static and a dynamic type. The norms of the order of the first type are valid on the strength of their content: because their validity can be traced back to a norm under whose content the content of the norms in question can be subsumed as the particular under the general. Thus, for example, the validity of the norms "do not lie," "do not give false testimony," "do fulfill a promise," can be derived from a norm that prescribes to be truthful. From the norm to love one's neighbor one can derive the norm not to harm one's fellow man, not to damage him physically or morally, to help him in need, and—particularly—not to kill him. Perhaps one might reduce the norms of truthfulness and love for one's fellow man to a still higher norm, such as to be in harmony with the universe. On this norm a whole moral order may be founded. Since all norms of an order of this type are already contained in the content of the presupposed norm, they can be deduced from it by way of a logical operation, namely a conclusion from the general to the particular. This norm, presupposed as the basic norm, supplies both the reason for the validity and the content of the norms deduced from it in a logical operation. A system of norms, whose reason for validity

---

[69] Cf. p. 8.

and content is deduced from a norm presupposed as a basic norm, is a *static norm system*. The principle according to which the validity of the norms of this system is founded is a static principle.

However, the norm from whose content other norms are deduced in the described fashion can be regarded as basic norm only if its content is assumed to be directly evident. In fact, the reason for the validity and the content of norms of a moral system are frequently traced back to a norm considered to be directly evident. A norm is "directly evident" means that it is immanent in, or emanates from, reason. The concept of a directly evident norm presupposes the concept of a practical reason, that is, a norm-creating reason; but this concept is untenable, as will be shown, because the function of reason is knowing and not willing, whereas the creation of norms is an act of will. Therefore there can be no such things as norms which are valid only in virtue of their directly evident content. If a norm prescribing a definite human behavior is asserted to be directly evident, it is done because it is believed that it is created by the will of God or another superhuman authority or because it was created by custom and therefore—like everything customary—regarded as self-evident. It is, then, a norm created by an act of will. Its validity can, in the last analysis, be based only on a presupposed norm which prescribes that one ought to behave according to the commands of the norm-creating authority or according to the norms created by custom. This norm can supply only the reason for the validity, not the content of the norms based on it. These norms constitute a dynamic system of norms. The principle according to which the validity of the norms of this system is founded, is a dynamic principle.

The dynamic type is characterized by this: the presupposed basic norm contains nothing but the determination of a norm-creating fact, the authorization of a norm-creating authority or (which amounts to the same) a rule that stipulates how the general and individual norms of the order based on the basic norm ought to be created. For example: A father orders his child to go to school. The child answers: Why? The reply may be: Because the father so ordered and the child ought to obey the father. If the child continues to ask: Why ought I to obey the father, the answer may be: Because God has commanded "Obey Your Parents," and one ought to obey the commands of God. If the child now asks why one ought to obey the commands of God, that is, if the child questions the validity of this norm, then the answer is that this question cannot be asked, that the norm cannot be questioned— the reason for the validity of the norm must not be sought: the norm has to be presupposed. The content of the norm that started it—the child ought to go to school—cannot be derived from the basic norm. For the basic norm is limited to authorize a norm-creating authority, it is a rule according to which the norms of this system ought to be created. The validity of the norm that constituted the starting point of the question is not derived from its content; it cannot be deduced from the basic norm by a logical operation. It has to be created by an act of the father, and it is valid (if we formulate this according to tradition) because it was so created; or, formulated more correctly: because a basic norm is presupposed to be valid which authorizes this way of creating norms. A norm belongs to an order founded on such a basic norm, because it was created in a fashion determined by the basic norm— and not because it has a certain content. The basic norm supplies only the reason for the validity, but not at the same time the content of the norms constituting the system. Their content can only be determined by the acts by which the authority authorized by the basic norm, and the authorities in turn authorized by this authority, create the positive norms of this system. Another example: In a social community, a tribe, it is customary that a man who marries a girl pays a certain amount to her father or uncle. If the groom asks why he ought to do this, the answer is: because in this community such a payment has always been made, that is, because there is a custom to make this payment and because it is assumed to be self-evident that the individual member of the tribe ought to behave as all other members customarily do. This is the basic norm of the normative order that constitutes the community. It establishes custom as a norm-creating fact. The two examples illustrate the dynamic type of a norm system.

The static and dynamic principles may be combined in the same system if the presupposed basic norm, according to the dynamic principle, merely authorizes a norm-creating authority, and if this authority (or one authorized by it in turn) not only establishes norms by which other norm-creating authorities are delegated, but also norms in which the subjects are commanded to observe a certain behavior and from which further norms can be deduced, as from the general to the particular. The Ten Commandments not only establish parents as norm-creating authorities but also stipulate general norms from whose content special norms may be logically deduced without requiring a norm-creating act, such as, for example, Thou shalt not make unto thee any graven image, etc. A wealth of special moral norms may logically be deduced from the command to love one's enemy. In giving a reason for the validity of the norms deduced from such commands of God or Christ, the static principle is applied; in giving a reason for the validity of God's commands through the basic norm: "One ought to obey God's commands" and for the validity of Christ's commands through the basic norm: "One ought to obey Christ's commands," the dynamic principle is applied.

c) The Reason for the Validity of a Legal Order

The norm system that presents itself as a legal order has essentially a dynamic character. A legal norm is not valid because it has a certain content, that is, because its content is logically deducible from a presupposed basic norm, but because it is created in a certain way—ultimately in a way determined by a presupposed basic norm. For this reason alone does the legal norm belong to the legal order whose norms are created according to this basic norm. Therefore any kind of content might be law. There is no human behavior which, as such, is excluded from being the content of a legal norm. The validity of a legal norm may not be denied for being (in its content) in conflict with that of another norm which does not belong to the legal order whose basic norm is the reason for the validity of the norm in question. The basic norm of a legal order is not a material norm which, because its content is regarded as immediately self-evident, is presupposed as the highest norm and from which norms for human behavior are logically deduced. The norms of a legal order must be created by a specific process. They are posited, that is, positive, norms, elements of a positive order. If by the constitution of a legal community is understood the norm or norms that determine how (that is, by what organs and by what procedure—through legislation or custom) the general norms of the legal order that constitute the community are to be created, then the basic norm is that norm which is presupposed when the custom through which the constitution has come into existence, or the constitution-creating act consciously performed by certain human beings, is objectively interpreted as a norm-creating fact; if, in the latter case, the individual or the assembly of individuals who created the constitution on which the legal order rests, are looked upon as norm-creating authorities. In this sense, the basic norm determines the basic fact of law creation and may in this respect be described as the constitution in a logical sense of the word (which will be explained later) in contradistinction to the constitution in the meaning of positive law. The basic norm is the presupposed starting point of a procedure: the procedure of positive law creation. It is itself not a norm created by custom or by the act of a legal organ; it is not a positive but a presupposed norm so far as the constitution-establishing authority is looked upon as the highest authority and can therefore not be regarded as authorized by the norm of a higher authority.

If the question as to the reason for the validity of a certain legal norm is raised, then the answer can only consist in the reduction to the basic norm of this legal order, that is, in the assertion that the norm was created—in the last instance—according to the basic norm. In the following pages we would like to consider only a national legal order, that is, a legal order limited in its validity to a specific space, the so-called territory of the state, and which is regarded as "sovereign," that is, as not subordinated to any higher legal order. We shall discuss the problem of the validity of the norms of a national legal order, at first without considering an international legal order superordinated to or included in it.

The question of the reason for the validity of a legal norm belonging to a specific national legal order may arise on the occasion of a coercive act; for example, when one individual deprives another of his life by hanging, and now the question is asked why this act is legal, namely the execution of a punishment, and not murder. This act can be interpreted as being legal only if it was prescribed by an individual legal norm, namely as an act that "ought" to be performed, by a norm that presents itself as a judicial decision. This raises the questions: Under what conditions is such an interpretation possible, why is a judicial decision present in this case, why is the individual norm created thereby a legal norm belonging to a valid legal order and therefore ought to be applied? The answer is: Because this individual norm was created in applying a criminal law that contains a general norm according to which (under conditions present in the case concerned) the death penalty ought to be inflicted. If we ask for the reason for the validity of this criminal law, then the answer is: the criminal law is valid because it was created by the legislature, and the legislature, in turn, is authorized by the constitution to create general norms. If we ask for the reason of the validity of the constitution, that is, for the reason of the validity of the norms regulating the creation of the general norms, we may, perhaps, discover an older constitution; that means the validity of the existing constitution is justified by the fact that it was created according to the rules of an earlier constitution by way of a constitutional amendment. In this way we eventually arrive at a historically first constitution that cannot have been created in this way and whose validity, therefore, cannot be traced back to a positive norm created by a legal authority; we arrive, instead, at a constitution that became valid in a revolutionary way, that is, either by breach of a former constitution or for a territory that formerly was not the sphere of validity of a constitution and of a national legal order based on it. If we consider merely the national legal order, not international law, and if we ask for the reason of the validity of the historically first constitution, then the answer can only be (if we leave aside God or "nature") that the validity of this constitution—the assumption that it is a binding norm—must be *presupposed* if we want to interpret (1) the acts performed according to it as the creation or application of valid general legal norms; and (2) the acts performed in application of these general norms as the creation or application of valid individual legal norms. Since the reason for the validity of a norm can only be another norm, the presupposition must be a norm: not one posited (i.e., created) by a legal authority, but a presupposed norm, that is, a norm presupposed if the subjective meaning of the constitution-creating facts and the subjective meaning of the norm-creating facts established according to the constitution are interpreted as their objective meaning. Since it is the basic norm of a legal order (that is, an order prescribing coercive acts), therefore this norm, namely the basic norm of the legal order concerned, must be formulated as follows:

Coercive acts sought to be performed under the conditions and in the manner which the historically first constitution, and the norms created according to it, prescribe. (In short: One ought to behave as the constitution prescribes.) The norms of a legal order, whose common reason for their validity is this basic norm are not a complex of valid norms standing coordinatedly side by side, but form a hierarchical structure of super- and subordinate norms. This structure of the legal order will be discussed later.

d) *The Basic Norm as Transcendental-logical Presupposition*

To understand the nature of the basic norm it must be kept in mind that it refers directly to a specific constitution, actually established by custom or statutory creation, by and large effective, and indirectly to the coercive order created according to this constitution and by and large effective; the basic norm thereby furnishes the reason for the validity of this constitution and of the coercive order created in accordance with it.[70] The basic norm, therefore, is not the product of free invention. It is not presupposed arbitrarily in the sense that there is a choice between different basic norms when the subjective meaning of a constitution-creating act and the acts created according to this constitution are interpreted as their objective meaning. Only if this basic norm, referring to a specific constitution, is presupposed, that is, only if it is presupposed that one ought to behave according to this specific constitution—only then can the subjective meaning of a constitution-creating act and of the acts created according to this constitution be interpreted as their objective meaning, that is, as objectively valid legal norms, and the relationships established by these norms as legal relations.

In presupposing the basic norm referring to a specific constitution, the contents of this constitution and of the national legal order created according to it is irrelevant—it may be a just or unjust order; it may or may not guaranteee a relative condition of peace within the community established by it. The presupposition of the basic norm does not approve any value transcending positive law.

---

[70] A special case of the basic norm is discussed later; cf. pp. 225 f. It is not considered here.

Insofar as only the presupposition of the basic norm makes it possible to interpret the subjective meaning of the constitution-creating act (and of the acts established according to the constitution) as their objective meaning, that is, as objectively valid legal norms, the basic norm as represented by the science of law may be characterized as the transcendental-logical condition of this interpretation, if it is permissible to use by analogy a concept of Kant's epistemology. Kant asks: "How is it possible to interpret without a metaphysical hypothesis, the facts perceived by our senses, in the laws of nature formulated by natural science?" In the same way, the Pure Theory of Law asks: "How is it possible to interpret without recourse to meta-legal authorities, like God or nature, the subjective meaning of certain facts as a system of objectively valid legal norms describable in rules of law?" The epistemological answer of the Pure Theory of Law is: "By presupposing the basic norm that one ought to behave as the constitution prescribes, that is, one ought to behave in accordance with the subjective meaning of the constitution-creating act of will—according to the prescriptions of the authority creating the constitution." The function of this basic norm is to found the objective validity of a positive legal order, that is, to interpret the *subjective* meaning of the acts of human beings by which the norms of an effective coercive order are created, as their *objective* meaning. The foundation of the validity of a positive norm, that is, one established by an act of will and prescribing a certain behavior, is the result of a syllogistic procedure. In this syllogism, the major premise is the assertion about a norm regarded as objectively valid, according to which one ought to obey the commands of a certain person, that is, one ought to behave according to the subjective meaning of these commands; the minor premise is the assertion of the fact that this person has commanded to behave in a certain way; and the conclusion is the assertion of the validity of the norm: that one ought to behave in this particular way. Thus the norm whose validity is stated in the major premise legitimizes the subjective meaning of the command, whose existence is asserted in the minor premise, as the command's objective meaning. For example: One ought to obey God's commands. God has commanded to obey the commands of the parents. Hence, one ought to obey the commands of the parents. Thus the subjective meaning of the act by which a father commands a certain behavior of his son is legitimized as its objective meaning, that is, as a binding norm.

The norm whose validity is asserted in the major premise is a basic norm if its objective validity is not questioned. It is not questioned if its validity cannot be based on a syllogistic procedure. And it cannot be so based, if the statement of the fact that this norm was established by an individual's act of will is not possible as the minor premise of a syllogism. This is the case when the person whose commands one ought to obey according to the norm now in question, is regarded as a highest authority, for example, God. Then the norm prescribing to obey the commands of this person has to be placed at the top of the syllogism as its major premise without it being possible that the norm itself is stated in the form of a conclusion of a further syllogism. This means: the norm is *presupposed* as a basic norm.

For this reason, the norm: "One ought to obey the commands of God" is a basic norm on which the validity of the norm: "One ought to obey the commands of one's parents," is based. A theological ethics that regards God as the highest norm-creating authority cannot state that somebody else has ordered to obey the commands of God—because this would have to be an authority higher than God. And if the norm: "One ought to obey the commands of God" were presumed to be posited by God, it could not be the reason for the validity of God-created norms, because it would itself be a God-created norm. Nor can theological ethics in itself create such a norm (that is, command to obey the commands of God) because as cognition it cannot be a norm-creating authority. Therefore, the norm: "One ought to obey the commands of God," as the basic norm, cannot be the subjective meaning of an act of will; it can only be the meaning of an act of thinking. That means: Theological ethics can only state: "The command of the parents has the character of an objectively binding norm if we presuppose in our thinking the norm: 'One ought to obey the commands of God' (who has commanded to obey the commands of the parents)." [71]

Since a positivistic science of law regards the creator of the his-

---

[71] A norm which is the meaning of an act of thinking is not a norm whose content is directly evident. The Basic Norm of a positive legal order, as developed in that which follows, is by no means directly evident. Cf. p. 221.

torically first constitution as the highest legal authority and therefore cannot maintain that the norm to obey the commands of the
creator of the constitution is the subjective meaning of the act of
will of an authority higher than the creator of the constitution—
such as God's or nature's—so therefore, the science of law cannot
base the validity of this norm on a syllogistic procedure. A positivistic science of law can only state that this norm is presupposed as a
basic norm in the foundation of the objective validity of the legal
norms, and therefore presupposed in the interpretation of an
effective coercive order as a system of objectively valid legal norms.
Since this basic norm cannot be the meaning of an act of will; and
since this norm (rather: the statement about it) is logically indispensable for the foundation of the objective validity of positive
legal norms, it can only be the meaning of an act of thinking;
the science of law can state no more than: the subjective meaning
of the acts by which legal norms are created can be interpreted as
their objective meaning only if we presuppose in our juristic
thinking the norm: "One ought to obey the presciptions of the
historically first constitution."

The science of law does not prescribe that one ought to obey the
commands of the creator of the constitution. The science of law
remains a merely cognitive discipline even in its epistemological
statement that the basic norm is the condition under which the
subjective meaning of the constitution-creating act, and the subjective meaning of the acts performed in accordance with the constitution, are interpreted as their objective meaning, as valid
norms, even if the meaning of these acts is so interpreted by the
legal science itself.[72]

By offering this theory of the basic norm, the Pure Theory of
Law does not inaugurate a new method of legal cognition. It
merely makes conscious what most legal scientists do, at least un-

---

[72] The question: "Who presupposes the basic norm?" is answered by the Pure
Theory as follows: The basic norm is presupposed by whoever interprets the
subjective meaning of the constitution-creating act, and of the acts created according to the constitution, as the objective meaning of these acts, that is, as objectively
valid norm. This interpretation is a cognitive function, not a function of the will.
Since the science of law, as cognition, can only describe norms, and not prescribe
anything, hence cannot create norms, I have occasionally expressed doubt against
the view that the basic norm is also presupposed by the science of law ("Was ist
ein Rechtsakt?" *Oesterreichische Zeitschrift für Oeffentliches Recht,* 1952). These
doubts are eliminated by the distinction, presented in the text, between positing
and presupposing a norm.

consciously, when they understand the mentioned facts not as causally determined, but instead interpret their subjective meaning as objectively valid norms, that is, as a normative legal order, without basing the validity of this order upon a higher, meta-legal norm, that is, upon a norm enacted by an authority superior to the legal authority; in other words, when they consider as law exclusively positive law. The theory of the basic norm is merely the result of an analysis of the procedure which a positivistic science of law has always applied.

e) The Logical Unity of the Legal Order; Conflict of Norms

Since the basic norm is the reason for the validity of all norms belonging to the same legal order, the basic norm constitutes the unity of the multiplicity of these norms. This unity is expressed also by the fact that a legal order may be described in rules of law that do not contradict each other. To be sure, it is undeniable that legal organs may create conflicting norms—that they perform acts whose subjective meaning is an "ought" and which may be in conflict with each other if their subjective meaning is interpreted as their objective meaning. Such a conflict of norms is present, if one norm prescribes a certain behavior, and another norm prescribes another behavior incompatible with the first. For example, if one norm prescribes that adultery ought to be punished, and another norm that it ought not to be punished; or if one norm prescribes that theft ought to be punished by death, and another by imprisonment. This conflict, however, as has been demonstrated earlier,[73] is not a logical contradiction in the strict sense of the word, even though it is usually said that the two norms "contradict" each other. For logical principles, especially the principle of the exclusion of contradictions, are applicable to assertions that can be true or false; if a logical contradiction exists between two assertions, only the one or the other assertion can be true; if one is true, the other must be false. But a norm is neither true nor false, but either valid or invalid. However, the assertion describing a normative order by saying that a certain norm is valid according to that order can be true or false; and particularly so the rule of law describing a legal order by saying that, according to that order,

---

[73] Cf. pp. 74 f.

a certain coercive act ought to or ought not to be performed under certain conditions. Therefore, logical principles in general, and the Principle of the Exclusion of Contradictions in particular, are applicable to rules of law describing legal norms and therefore indirectly also to legal norms. Hence it is by no means absurd to say that two legal norms "contradict" each other. And therefore only one of the two can be regarded as objectively valid. To say that *a* ought to be and at the same time ought not to be is just as meaningless as to say that *a* is and at the same time that it is not. A conflict of norms is just as meaningless as a logical contradiction.

But since the cognition of law, like any cognition, seeks to understand its subject as a meaningful whole and to describe it in noncontradictory statements, it starts from the assumption that conflicts of norms within the normative order which is the object of this cognition can and must be solved by interpretation. Since the structure of the legal order is a hierarchy of higher and lower norms, whereby the higher norm determines the creation of the lower one, the problem of norm conflicts within the same legal order presents itself in two forms, depending on whether the conflict is between two norms of the same level or between a higher and a lower norm.

To begin with, we shall consider conflicts between norms of the same level. If we have a conflict between general norms, created by the same organ at different times, then the validity of the later norm supersedes the validity of the earlier, contradictory, one according to the principle *lex posterior derogat priori*. Since the norm-creating organ—the king or the parliament—is normally authorized to prescribe changeable and therefore abolishable norms, the principle *lex posterior derogat priori* may be presumed to be included in the authorization. The principle also applies if the conflicting norms are prescribed by two different organs; for example, if the constitution authorizes the king and the parliament to regulate the same subject by general norms, or if legislature and custom are both established as law-creating facts. However, the conflicting norms may have been prescribed simultaneously, by the same act and by the same organ, so that the mentioned principle is not applicable, for example if contradictory clauses are contained in the same statute, such as: adultery is punishable and adultery is not punishable; or: everybody who committed a certain delict is punishable and persons of less than fourteen years of age are not punishable. Then the following possibilities for the solution of the conflict exist: Either the two norms can be understood to be subject to a choice by the law-applying organ, e.g., the judge; or if, as in the second example, the two norms are only partly contradictory, then the one norm can be understood to be limiting the validity of the other. The law-describing rule does not say: "Adultery ought to be punished *and* ought not to be punished"; it says: "He who commits adultery ought to be punished *or* he ought not to be punished." Nor does the law-describing rule say: "Everybody who commits a certain delict ought to be punished *and* persons below the age of fourteen ought not to be punished"; it says: "Everybody who has committed a certain delict, with the exception of persons below the age of fourteen, ought to be punished." If neither the one nor the other interpretation is possible, then the legislator creates something meaningless; we then have a meaningless act of norm creation and therefore no act at all whose subjective meaning can be interpreted as its objective meaning; no objectively valid legal norm is present, although the act has been posited according to the basic norm. The basic norm does not bestow the objective meaning of a valid norm upon every act, but only upon an act that has a meaning— the subjective meaning that individuals ought to behave in a certain way. The act must be meaningful in this normative sense. If the act has a different meaning (such as the meaning of an assertion, for example of a theory propounded in a statute) or no meaning at all (for example, if a statute contains nonsensical words or prescriptions incompatible with each other), then no subjective meaning is present that can be interpreted as objective meaning; no act is present whose subjective meaning is capable of being legitimized by the basic norm.

A conflict may also exist between two individual norms, such as two court decisions, particularly if the two norms have been created by different organs. A law might authorize two courts to decide the same case without giving the decision of the one court the authority to abolish the decision of the other. To be sure, this is a most inadequate legal technique, but it is not impossible and has happened. In that case it may well be that an accused person is condemned by one court and acquitted by another, that is, he ought to be punished according to the one norm and not punished according to the other; or it may be that one court may find for the plaintiff as claimed and another court may dismiss the action, which means that according to the one norm civil execution ought to be directed into the property of the defendant, but according to the other norm that civil execution ought not to be directed. The conflict is solved by giving the executive organ the choice between the two decisions. If civil execution is carried out as prescribed by the one norm, then the other norm remains permanently ineffective and therefore loses its validity; if execution is not carried out, it is the other way around. This interpretation is advanced according to the basic norm. For the basic norm prescribes: "Force ought to be exerted under the conditions and in the manner prescribed by the by and large effective constitution and by the by and large effective general and effective individual norms created according to the constitution." Effectiveness is stipulated as a condition for the validity by the basic norm. If a conflict is present within the same court decision (for example if the judge is insane), then the act is simply meaningless and therefore no objectively valid legal norm exists. In this way the basic norm makes it possible to interpret the material submitted to legal cognition as a meaningful whole, which means, to describe it in logically noncontradictory sentences.

No conflict is possible between a higher norm and a lower norm, that is, between one norm which determines the creation of another norm and this other norm, because the lower norm has the reason for its validity in the higher norm. If a lower norm is regarded as valid, it must be regarded as being valid according to a higher norm. How this is done will be discussed in the description of the hierarchy of the legal order.[74]

f) Legitimacy and Effectiveness

The function of the basic norm becomes particularly apparent if the constitution is not changed by constitutional means but by revolution; when the existence—that is, the validity—of the entire legal order directly based on the constitution, is in question.

It was said earlier that a norm's sphere of validity, particularly

---

[74] Cf. § 35a.

its temporal sphere of validity may be limited; the beginning and
end of its validity may be determined by the norm itself or by a
higher norm regulating the creation of the lower one. The norms
of a legal order are valid until their validity is terminated according to the rules of this legal order. By regulating its own creation
and application, the legal order determines the beginning and end
of the validity of the legal norms. Written constitutions usually
contain special rules concerning the method by which they can be
changed. The principle that a norm of a legal order is valid until
its validity is terminated in a way determined by this legal order or
replaced by the validity of another norm of this order, is called the
principle of legitimacy.

This principle is applicable to a national legal order with one
important limitation only: It does not apply in case of a revolution. A revolution in the broader sense of the word (that includes
a coup d'état) is every not legitimate change of this constitu-
ion or its replacement by an other constitution. From the point of
view of legal science it is irrelevant whether this change of the
legal situation has been brought about by the application of force
against the legitimate government or by the members of that government themselves, whether by a mass movement of the population or by a small group of individuals. Decisive is only that the
valid constitution has been changed or replaced in a manner not
prescribed by the constitution valid until then. Usually a revolution abolishes only the old constitution and certain politically important statutes. A large part of the statutes created under the old
constitution remains valid, as the saying goes; but this expression does not fit. If these statutes are to be regarded as being valid
under the new constitution, then this is possible only because they
have been validated expressly or tacitly by the new constitution.
We are confronted here not with a creation of new law but with
the reception of norms of one legal order by another; such as the
reception of the Roman Law by the German Law. But such reception too is law creation, because the direct reason for the validity
of the legal norms taken over by the new revolutionary established
constitution can only be the new constitution. The content of
these norms remains unchanged, but the reason for their validity,
in fact the reason for the validity of the entire legal order, has
been changed. As the new constitution becomes valid, so simul-

taneously changes the basic norm, that is, the presupposition according to which are interpreted as norm-creating and norm-applying facts the constitution-creating fact and the facts established according to the constitution. Suppose the old constitution had the character of an absolute monarchy and the new one of a parliamentary democracy. Then the basic norm no longer reads: "Coercive acts ought to be carried out under the conditions and in the manner as determined by the old, no longer valid, constitution," and hence by the general and individual norms created and applied by the constitutionally functioning monarch and the organs delegated by him; instead, the basic norm reads: "Coercive acts ought to be carried out under the conditions and in the manner determined by the new constitution," and hence by the general and individual norms created and applied by the parliament elected according to that constitution and by the organs delegated in these norms. The new basic norm does not make it possible—like the old one—to regard a certain individual as the absolute monarch, but makes it possible to regard a popularly elected parliament as a legal authority. According to the basic norm of a national legal order, the government, which creates effective general and in-individual norms based on an effective constitution is the legitimate government of the state.

The change of the basic norm follows the change of the facts that are interpreted as creating and applying valid legal norms. The basic norm refers only to a constitution which is actually established by legislative act or custom, and is effective. A constitution is "effective" if the norms created in conformity with it are by and large applied and obeyed. As soon as the old constitution loses its effectiveness and the new one has become effective, the acts that appear with the subjective meaning of creating or applying legal norms are no longer interpreted by presupposing the old basic norm, but by presupposing the new one. The statutes issued under the old constitution and not taken over are no longer regarded as valid, and the organs authorized by the old constitution no longer as competent. If the revolution is not successful there would be no reason to replace the old basic norm by a new one. Then, the revolution would not be regarded as procedure creating new law, but—according to the old constitution and the criminal law based on it and regarded as valid—would be interpreted as high treason. The principle applied here is the principle of effectiveness. The principle of legitimacy is limited by the principle of effectiveness.

g) *Validity and Effectiveness*

This limitation reveals the repeatedly emphasized connection (so important for a theory of positive law) between the validity and the effectiveness of law. The correct determination of this relationship is one of the most important and at the same time most difficult problems of a positivistic legal theory. It is only a special case of the relationship between the "ought" of the legal norm and the "is" of natural reality. Because the act by which a positive legal norm is created, too, is an "is-fact" (German: *Seinstatsache*) just as the effectiveness of the legal norm. A positivistic legal theory is faced by the task to find the correct middle road between two extremes which both are untenable. The one extreme is the thesis that there is no connection between validity as something that ought to be and effectiveness as something that is; that the validity of the law is entirely independent of its effectiveness. The other extreme is the thesis that validity and effectiveness are identical. An idealistic theory of law tends to the first solution of this problem, a realistic theory to the second. The first is wrong for it is undeniable that a legal order in its entirety, and an individual legal norm as well, lose their validity when they cease to be effective; and that a relation exists between the *ought* of the legal norm and the *is* of physical reality also insofar as the positive legal norm, to be valid, must be created by an act which exists in the reality of being. The second solution is wrong because it is equally undeniable that there are many cases—as has been shown before [75]— in which legal norms are regarded as valid although they are not, or not yet, effective. The solution proposed by the Pure Theory of Law is this: Just as the norm (according to which something *ought* to be) as the meaning of an act is not identical with the act (which actually *is*), in the same way is the validity of a legal norm not identical with its effectiveness; the effectiveness of a legal order as a whole and the effectiveness of a single legal norm are—just as the norm-creating act—the condition for the validity; effectiveness

---

[75] Cf. pp. 11 and 87 f.

is the condition in the sense that a legal order as a whole, and a single legal norm, can no longer be regarded as valid when they cease to be effective. Nor is the effectiveness of a legal order, any more than the fact of its creation, the reason for its validity. The reason for the validity—that is, the answer to the question why the norms of this legal order ought to be obeyed and applied—is the presupposed basic norm, according to which one ought to comply with an actually established, by and large effective, constitution, and therefore with the by and large effective norms, actually created in conformity with that constitution. In the basic norm the fact of creation and the effectiveness are made the condition of the validity—"effectiveness" in the sense that it has to be added to the fact of creation, so that neither the legal order as a whole nor the individual legal norm shall lose their validity. A condition cannot be identical with that which it conditions. Thus, a man, in order to live, must have been born; but in order that he remain alive other conditions must also be fulfilled, for example, he must receive nutrition. If this condition is not fulfilled, he will lose his life. But life is neither identical with birth nor with being nourished.

In the normative syllogism leading to the foundation of the validity of a legal order, the major premise is the ought-sentence which states the basic norm: "One ought to behave according to the actually established and effective constitution"; the minor premise is the is-sentence which states the facts: "The constitution is actually established and effective"; and the conclusion is the ought-sentence: "One ought to behave according to the legal order, that is, the legal order is valid." The norms of a positive legal order are valid *because* the fundamental rule regulating their creation, that is, the basic norm, is presupposed to be valid, not because they are effective; but they are valid only *as long as* this legal order is effective. As soon as the constitution loses its effectiveness, that is, as soon as the legal order as a whole based on the constitution loses its effectiveness, the legal order and every single norm lose their validity.

However, a legal order does not lose its validity when a single legal norm loses its effectiveness. A legal order is regarded as valid, if its norms are *by and large* effective (that is, actually applied and obeyed). Nor does a single legal norm lose its validity if it is only exceptionally not effective in single cases. As mentioned in another connection, the possibility of an antagonism between that which is prescribed by a norm as something that ought to be and that which actually happens must exist; a norm, prescribing that something *ought* to be, which, as one knows beforehand *must* happen anyway according to a law of nature, is meaningless—such a norm would not be regarded as valid. On the other hand, a norm is not regarded as valid which is never obeyed or applied. In fact, a legal norm may lose its validity by never being applied or obeyed—by so-called *desuetude*. *Desuetudo* may be described as negative custom, and its essential function is to abolish the validity of an existing norm. If custom is a law-creating fact at all, then even the validity of statutory law can be abolished by customary law. If effectiveness in the developed sense is the condition for the validity not only of the legal order as a whole but also of a single legal norm, then the law-creating function of custom cannot be excluded by statutory law, at least not as far as the negative function of *desuetudo* is concerned.

The described relation between validity and effectiveness refers to general legal norms. But also individual legal norms (judicial decisions, administrative decrees) that prescribe an individual coercive act lose their validity if they are permanently unexecuted and therefore ineffective, as has been shown in the discussion of a conflict between two legal decisions.[76]

Effectiveness is a condition for the validity—but it is not validity. This must be stressed because time and again the effort has been made to identify validity with effectiveness; and such identification is tempting because it seems to simplify the theoretical situation. Still, the effort is doomed to failure, not only because even a partly ineffective legal order or legal norm may be regarded as valid, and an absolutely effective norm which cannot be violated as invalid because not being regarded as a norm at all; but particularly for this reason: If the validity, that is, the specific existence of the law, is considered to be part of natural reality, one is unable to grasp the specific meaning in which the law addresses itself to reality and thereby juxtaposes itself to reality, which can be in conformity or in conflict with the law only if reality is not identical with the validity of the law. Just as it is impossible in

[76] Cf. p. 207.

determining validity to ignore its relation to reality, so it is likewise impossible to identify validity and reality. If we replace the concept of reality (as effectiveness of the legal order) by the concept of power, then the problem of the relation between validity and effectiveness of the legal order coincides with the more familiar problem of the relationship between law and power or right and might. And then, the solution attempted here is merely the scientifically exact formulation of the old truism that right cannot exist without might and yet is not identical with might. Right (the law), according to the theory here developed, is a certain order (or organization) of might.

h) The Basic Norm of International Law

We shall now also consider the international legal order in relation to national legal orders; and we shall assume—as it is frequently assumed—that international law is valid for a state only if its government on the basis of an effective constitution has recognized international law; then our answer given so far to the question as to why law is valid, is still the same: the reason for the validity of law is a presupposed basic norm referring to an effective constitution. For in this case, international law is only a part of the national legal order, regarded as sovereign—and the reason for the validity of the national legal order is the basic norm referring to the effective constitution. The basic norm, as the reason for the validity of the constitution, is at the same time the reason for the validity of international law, recognized on the basis of the constitution.

The situation is different, however, if international law is not regarded as part of the national legal order, but as a sovereign legal order, superordinated to all national legal orders, limiting them in their spheres of validity; if, in other words, one does not assume the primacy of the national legal orders, but the primacy of the international legal order.[77] The latter does, in fact, contain a norm that represents the reason for the validity of the individual national legal orders. Therefore the reason for the validity of the individual national legal order can be found in positive international law. In that case, a positive norm is the reason for the valid-

---

[77] Cf. § 43d, subsection "Primacy of the international legal order."

ity of this legal order, not a merely presupposed norm. The norm of international law that represents this reason for the validity usually is described by the statement that, according to general international law, a government which, independent of other governments, exerts effective control over the population of a certain territory, is the legitimate government; and that the population that lives under such a government in this territory constitutes a "state" in the meaning of international law, regardless of whether this government exerts this effective control on the basis of a previously existing constitution or of one established by revolution. Translated into legal language: A norm of general international law authorizes an individual or a group of individuals, on the basis of an effective constitution, to create and apply as a legitimate government a normative coercive order. That norm, thus, legitimizes this coercive order for the territory of its actual effectiveness as a valid legal order, and the community constituted by this coercive order as a "state" in the sense of international law—regardless of whether the government came to power in a "legitimate" way (in the sense of the previous constitution) or by revolution. According to international law, this power is to be regarded as *legal* power. This means that international law legitimizes a successful revolution as a law-creating procedure. If a positive norm of international law is recognized as the reason for the validity of a national legal order the problem of the basic norm is shifted, because the reason for the validity of the national legal orders, then, is no longer a norm only presupposed in juristic thinking but a positive norm of international law; and then the question arises as to the reason for the validity of the international legal order to which the norm belongs on which the validity of the individual national legal order is founded—the norm in which this legal order finds its direct, although not its ultimate, reason for the validity. This reason of validity, then, can only be the basic norm of international law, which, therefore, is the indirect reason for the validity of the national legal order. As a genuine basic norm, it is a presupposed —not a positive norm. It represents the presupposition under which general international law is regarded as the set of objectively valid norms that regulate the mutual behavior of states. These norms are created by custom, constituted by the actual behavior of the "states," that is, of those individuals who act as governments according to national legal orders. These norms are interpreted as legal norms binding the states, because a basic norm is presupposed which establishes custom among states as a law-creating fact. The basic norm runs as follows: "States—that is, the governments of the states—in their mutual relations ought to be-have in such a way"; or: "Coercion of state against state ought to be exercised under the conditions and in the manner, that con-forms with the custom constituted by the actual behavior of the states." [78] This is the "constitution" of international law in a transcendental-logical sense.[79]

One of the norms of international law created by custom au-thorizes the states to regulate their mutual relations by treaty. The reason for the validity of the legal norms of international law cre-ated by treaty is this custom-created norm. It is usually formulated in the sentence: *pacta sunt servanda.*

The presupposed basic norm of international law, which insti-tutes custom constituted by the states as a law-creating fact, ex-presses a principle that is the basic presupposition of all customary law: the individual ought to behave in such a manner as the others usually behave (believing that they ought to behave that way), applied to the mutual behavior of states, that is, the behavior of the individuals qualified by the national legal orders as govern-ment organs.[80]

No affirmation of a value transcending positive law is inherent in the basic norm of international law, not even of the value of peace guaranteed by the general international law created by cus-tom and the particular international law created by treaty. Inter-national law and—if its primacy is assumed—the subordinated na-tional legal orders are not valid "because" and "insofar as" they realize the value that consists in peace; they may realize this value if and so far as they are valid; and they are valid if a basic norm is presupposed that institutes custom among states as a law-creating fact regardless of the content of the norms thus created. If the rea-son for the validity of national legal orders is found in a norm of

---

[78] Cf. § 42b–d.

[79] Cf. § 34d.

[80] The theory held by many authors (and at one time also by myself) that the norm of *pacta sunt servanda* is the basis of international law is to be rejected because it can be maintained only with the aid of the fiction that the custom established by the conduct of states is a tacit treaty.

international law, then the latter is understood as a legal order superior to the former and therefore as the highest sovereign legal order. If the states—that is, the national legal orders—are nevertheless referred to as "sovereign," then this "sovereignty" can only mean that the national legal orders are subordinated *only* to the international legal order.

i) The Theory of the Basic Norm and the Theory of Natural Law

If the question as to the reason for the validity of positive law, that is, the question why the norms of an effective coercive order ought to be applied and obeyed, aims at an ethical-political justification of this coercive order, which means at a firm standard according to which a positive legal order may be judged as "just" and therefore as valid or "unjust" and therefore as invalid, then the basic norm of the Pure Theory of Law does neither yield such a justification nor such a standard. For positive law—as pointed out [81]—is justified only by a norm or normative order with which positive law according to its contents, may or may not conform, hence be just or unjust. The basic norm, presented by the Pure Theory of Law as the condition for the objective validity of law, establishes the validity of *every* positive legal order, that is, of every coercive order created by acts of human beings and by and large effective. According to the Pure Theory of Law, as a positivistic legal theory, no positive legal order can be regarded as not conforming with its basic norm and hence as not valid. The content of a positive legal order is entirely independent from its basic norm. For—the point must be stressed—only the validity, not the content of a legal order can be derived from the basic norm. Every by and large effective coercive order can be interpreted as an objectively valid normative order. The validity of a positive legal order cannot be denied because of the content of its norms. This is an essential element of legal positivism; and it is precisely in its theory of the basic norm that the Pure Theory of Law shows itself as a positivistic legal theory. The Pure Theory describes the positive law as an objectively valid normative order and states that this interpretation is possible only under the condition that a basic norm is pre-

---

[81] Cf. § 13.

supposed according to which the subjective meaning of the law-creating acts is also their objective meaning. The Pure Theory, thereby characterizes this interpretation as possible, not necessary, and presents the objective validity of positive law only as conditional—namely conditioned by the presupposed basic norm. The fact that the basic norm of a positive legal order *may* but *need not* be presupposed means: the relevant interhuman relationships may be, but need not be, interpreted as "normative," that is, as obligations, authorizations, rights, etc. constituted by objectively valid norms. It means further: they can be interpreted without such presupposition (i.e., without the basic norm) as power relations (i.e., relations between commanding and obeying or disobeying human beings)—in other words, they can be interpreted sociologically, not juristically.[82] Since the basic norm, as shown, as a norm presupposed in the foundation of the validity of positive law, is only the transcendental-logical condition of this normative interpretation, it does not perform an ethical-political but only an epistemological function.[83]

A consistent theory of natural law differs from a positivistic theory of law in that the natural-law theory seeks the reason for the validity of positive law in a natural law, different from positive law, and hence in a normative order with which the positive law, according to its contents, may or may not conform; so that the positive law, if not in conformity with natural law, must be re-

---

[82] In earlier publications I used as an example for the fact that the presupposition of the basic norm is possible but not necessary: An anarchist does not presuppose the basic norm. This example is misleading. The anarchist emotionally rejects the law as a coercive order; he objects to the law; he wants a community free of coercion, a community constituted without a coercive order. Anarchism is a political attitude, based on a certain wish. The sociological interpretation, which does not presuppose a basic norm, is a theoretical attitude. Even an anarchist, if he were a professor of law, could describe positive law as a system of valid norms, without having to approve of this law. Many textbooks in which the capitalist legal order is described as a system of norms constituting obligations, authorizations, rights, jurisdictions, are written by jurists who politically disapprove of this legal order.

[83] Therefore, the doctrine of the basic norm is not a doctrine of recognition as is sometimes erroneously understood. According to the doctrine of recognition positive law is valid only if it is recognized by the individuals subject to it, which means: if these individuals agree that one ought to behave according to the norms of the positive law. This recognition, it is said, actually takes place, and if this cannot be proved, it is assumed, fictitiously, as a tacit recognition. The theory of recognition, consciously or unconsciously, presupposes the ideal of individual liberty as self-determination, that is, the norm that the individual ought to do only what he wants to do. This is the basic norm of this theory. The difference between it and the theory of the basic norm of a positive legal order, as taught by the Pure Theory of Law, is evident.

garded as invalid. Therefore, according to a true theory of natural law, not *any* by and large effective coercive order may be interpreted as objectively valid normative order. The possibility of a conflict between natural law and positive law includes the possibility of regarding such a coercive order as invalid. Only to the extent that the content of positive law may or may not conform with natural law and may therefore not only be just but also unjust and therefore invalid—only to that extent can natural law serve as ethical-political standard and therefore as a possible ethical-political justification of positive law. This is precisely the essential function of natural law. If a legal theory that presents itself as natural-law doctrine formulates the norm or normative order which functions as the reason for the validity of positive law in such a way that a conflict between the so-called natural law and positive law is excluded (for example, by asserting that nature commands to obey every positive legal order, regardless of the kind of behavior this order demands), then such a legal theory divests itself of its character as a theory of natural law, that is, a theory of justice. It thereby abandons the function, essential to natural law, as an ethical-political value standard and therefore as a possible justification of positive law.

According to a positivistic theory of law the validity of positive law rests on a basic norm, which is not a positive but a presupposed norm, hence not a norm of the positive law whose validity is founded on the basic norm; and according to the natural-law doctrine, the validity of positive law likewise rests on a norm that is not a norm of positive law and functions as a value standard of this law. In this fact one might see a certain limitation imposed upon the principle of legal positivism and one might describe the difference between a positivistic theory of law and a theory of natural law as relative rather than absolute. But the difference between the two is large enough to exclude the view (which ignores this difference) that the positivistic theory of a basic norm, as advanced by the Pure Theory of Law, is a theory of natural law.

j) The Basic Norm of Natural Law

Since the Pure Theory of Law, as a positivistic legal theory, by its doctrine of the basic norm of positive law does not provide a standard for justice or injustice of positive law and therefore does not provide its ethical-political justification, it has frequently been criticized as unsatisfactory. What is much sought is a criterion by which positive law may be judged as just or unjust— most of all: justified as just. The natural-law theory can provide such a criterion only if the norms of the natural law presented by that theory—the norms that prescribe a certain behavior as just—have the absolute validity they claim to have; this means: if they exclude the validity of norms which prescribe the opposite behavior as just. However, the history of the natural-law theory shows that this is not the case. As soon as the natural-law theory undertakes to determine the content of the norms that are immanent in nature (may be deduced from nature) it gets caught in the sharpest contrasts. The representatives of that theory have not proclaimed *one* natural law but *several* very different natural laws conflicting with each other. This is particularly true for the fundamental questions of property and form of government. According to one natural-law theory only individual property, according to another only collective property; according to one only democracy, according to another only autocracy are "natural," that is, "just." Any positive law that conforms with the natural law of one theory and therefore is judged "just" is in conflict with the natural law of the other theory and therefore is judged "unjust." Natural-law theory as it actually was developed—and it cannot be developed differently—is far from providing the criterion expected of it.

Similarly, the assumption that a natural-law theory gives an absolute answer to the question as to the reason for the validity of positive law, is an illusion. Such a theory sees the reason for the validity of positive law in the natural law, that is, in an order established by nature as a highest authority standing above the human legislator. In this sense natural law, too, is "posited," that is, positive law—posited, however, not by a human but by a superhuman will. True, a natural-law theory can assert—although it cannot prove as a fact—that nature commands that men ought to behave in a certain way. But since a fact cannot be the reason for the validity of a norm, so therefore a logically correct natural-law theory cannot deny that a positive law, conforming with natural law, can be interpreted as valid only if the norm is presupposed that says: "One ought to obey the commands of nature." This is the basic norm of natural law. The natural-law theory, too, can give only a conditional answer to the question as to the reason for the validity of positive law. If the natural-law theory asserts: "The norm that one ought to obey the commands of nature is self-evident," the theory errs. This assertion is untenable. Not only in general because there can be no self-evident norms of human behavior; but also in particular, because this norm, much less than any other, can be said to be self-evident. From the point of view of science, nature is a system of causally determined elements. Nature has no will and therefore cannot enact norms. Norms can be assumed as immanent in nature only if the will of God is assumed to be manifested in nature. To say that God in nature as a manifestation of his will commands men to behave in a certain way, is a metaphysical assumption, which cannot be accepted by science in general and by legal science in particular, because scientific cognition cannot have as its object a fact which is assumed to exist beyond all possible experience.

35. The Hierarchical Structure of the Legal Order

a) The Constitution

The peculiarity of the law that it regulates its own creation, has been pointed out before in these pages. This can be done by a norm determining merely the procedure by which another norm is to be created. But it can be done also by a norm determining, to a certain extent, the content of the norm to be created. Since, because of the dynamic character of law, a norm is valid because, and to the extent that, it had been created in a certain way, that is, in a way determined by another norm, therefore that other norm is the immediate reason for the validity of the new norm. The relationship between the norm that regulates the creation of another norm and the norm created in conformity with the former can be metaphorically presented as a relationship of super- and subordination. The norm which regulates the creation of another norm is the higher, the norm created in conformity with the former is the lower one. The legal order is not a system of coordinated norms of equal level, but a hierarchy of different levels of legal norms. Its unity is brought about by the connection that results from the fact that the validity of a norm, created according to another norm, rests on that other norm, whose creation in turn, is determined by a third one. This is a regression that ultimately ends up in the presupposed basic norm. This basic norm, therefore, is the highest reason for the validity of the norms, one created in conformity with another, thus forming a legal order in its hierarchical structure.

Considering, to begin with, only a national legal order, the constitution represents the highest level of positive law. "Constitution" is understood here in its material sense, that is, we understand by constitution the positive norm or norms which regulate the creation of general legal norms. The constitution may be created by custom or by a specific act performed by one or several individuals, that is, by a legislative act. In the latter case it is always formulated in a document and hence called a "written" constitution, in contradistinction to the "unwritten" constitution brought about by custom. The material constitution may consist partly of norms of written and partly of unwritten law. The unwritten norms of the constitution may be codified; and if this codification is the work of a law-creating organ and therefore acquires binding force, it becomes a written constitution.

The constitution in the material sense must be distinguished from the constitution in the formal sense, namely a document called "constitution," which, as written constitution, may contain not only norms regulating the creation of general norms (that is, legislation), but also norms concerning other politically important subjects; and, besides, regulations according to which the norms contained in this document may be abolished or amended —not like ordinary statutes, but by a special procedure and under more rigorous conditions. These regulations represent the constitutional form, and the document to whose content these regulations refer, represents the constitution in a formal sense, which may include any desired content. The purpose of the regulations which render more difficult the abolition or amendment of the content of the constitution in a formal sense is primarily to stabilize the norms designated here as "material constitution" and which are the positive-legal basis of the entire national legal order.

In a modern legal order, the creation (regulated by the material constitution) of general legal norms has the character of legislation. The constitutional regulation of legislation determines the organs authorized to create general legal norms—statutes and ordinances. If the courts should be regarded as authorized to apply customary law also, they must be authorized by the constitution to do so in the same way as they must be authorized to apply statutes. In other words: the constitution must institute as a law-creating fact the custom constituted by the habitual behavior of the individuals subject to the national legal order—the "subjects." If the application of customary law by courts is considered to be legitimate although the written constitution contains no such authorization, then the authorization cannot be considered to proceed from an unwritten custom-created constitution [84] but must be *presupposed,* in the same way that it must be presupposed that the written constitution has the character of an objectively binding norm if the statutes and ordinances issued in accordance with it are regarded as binding legal norms. Then the basic norm (the constitution in the transcendental-logical sense) institutes not only the act of the legislator, but also custom as law-creating facts.

The constitution of the state, as a written constitution, can appear in the specific form of a constitution, that is, in norms that may not be abolished or amended as ordinary statutes but only under more rigorous conditions. But this need not be so. It is not so if there is no written constitution, if the constitution is created by custom and is not codified; then, even norms which have the character of a material constitution may be abolished or amended by simple statutes or by customary law.

It is possible that the organ specifically and formally authorized to create, abolish, or amend statutes having the character of a constitution is different from the organ authorized to create, abolish, or amend ordinary statutes. For example, the former function may be rendered by an organ different from the latter organ in composition and electoral procedure, such as a constituent national assembly. But usually both functions are performed by the same organ.

The constitution regulating the creation of general norms (statutes) may also determine the content of future statutes: positive constitutions do this frequently by prescribing or excluding certain contents. The former case represents usually only a promise of statutes to be created, not an obligation to create such

[84] Cf. p. 226.

statutes, because for legal-technical reasons the noncreation of statutes with a certain content cannot easily be connected with a sanction. The exclusion of statutes with certain contents, however, can be effected easier by a constitution. The catalog of fundamental rights and freedoms, which typically constitutes a part of modern constitutions, is essentially an attempt to prevent such statutes. The attempt is effective if the creation of such a statute (for example, a law that violates freedom of conscience or equality) is placed under the personal responsibility of certain officers participating in its creation, such as the chief of state or a minister, or if the possibility of contesting and abolishing such statutes is provided; all this under the presupposition that the ordinary statute does not have the power to abolish or amend a statute having the character of a constitution because it determines the ordinary statute's creation and content; that this statute can be abolished or amended only under more rigorous conditions, such as qualified majority, increased quorum, and the like. This means that the constitution prescribes for its abolition or amendment a procedure different from and more difficult than the procedure provided for ordinary legislation; that there exists besides the form of ordinary statutes a specific form of statutes having the character of a constitution.

b) Legislation and Custom

Next step down in the hierarchy, after the constitution, are the general norms created by legislation or custom. The constitutions of modern states institute special legislative organs authorized to create the general norms to be applied by the courts and administrative organs. The level of creating the constitution is followed by the level of creating ordinary statutes which, in turn, is followed by the level of judicial and administrative procedures. However, there need not always be three levels. It is possible that the constitution does not create a special legislative organ, but directly authorizes courts and administrative organs to create themselves the norms they consider expedient or just to be applied in concrete cases. We shall discuss such instances later. For the present we shall only consider the normal situation: a legal order which institutes a special legislative organ.

The nature of the legislative organ is one of the most important factors determining the so-called form of government. If the organ is a single individual, a hereditary monarch or a dictator who acquired his power by a revolution, we speak of autocracy; if it is an assembly of the entire population or a parliament elected by the people, of democracy. Only in a domocratic legislation are regulations required that determine the legislative procedure, which here means: participation in the popular assembly or in the election of the parliament, the number of its members, the proceedings to pass resolutions. All these regulations are part of the material constitution, even if they do not in all cases appear in the form of a constitution but as ordinary statutes. If, in addition to the ordinary legislative organ, a constituent national assembly exists, and if in a constitutional statute created by this latter organ (for example, in a statute that amends the legislative procedure), the ordinary legislative organ is authorized to enact an electoral statute, then the level of the material constitution is again split in two levels.

General legal norms created by legislation are consciously posited norms. The acts that constitute legislation are norm-creating acts, that is, their subjective meaning is an "ought." The constitution elevates this subjective meaning to an objective one, establishing the fact of legislation as a law-creating fact. But the constitution may also establish custom as law-creating fact. This fact is, as discussed earlier,[85] characterized by the circumstance that men belonging to the legal community behave under the same circumstances in the same way; that this behavior takes place for a sufficiently long time; and that in the individuals whose acts constitute the custom the collective will arises that one *ought* to behave in that way. Then the subjective meaning of the facts that constitute the custom is an "ought"—the meaning that one ought to behave according to custom. However, the subjective meaning of the fact of custom may be interpreted as objectively valid legal norm only if the thus qualified fact is instituted by the constitution as norm-creating.

Traditional science of law assumes that *opinio necessitatis* is an essential component of the facts of custom. That is to say that the acts which constitute the custom must take place in the belief that

---

[85] Cf. pp. 9 and 53 f.

they ought to take place. But this opinion presupposes an individual or collective act of will whose subjective meaning is that one ought to behave according to custom. If customary law, like statutory law, is positive law, then there must be an individual or collective act of will whose subjective meaning is the "ought"—that is interpreted as objectively valid norm, as customary law.

As stated earlier, customary law may be applied by the law-applying organs only if they can be regarded as authorized thereto. If this authorization is not conferred by the constitution in the positive-legal sense (that is: if custom is not instituted by the constitution in the positive-legal sense as a law-creating fact), then it must be presupposed that custom as a law-creating fact is already instituted in the basic norm as the "constitution" in the transcendental-logical sense. This means: a basic norm must be presupposed which institutes not only the fact of the creation of a constitution, but also the fact of a qualified custom as law-creating fact.

This is so also if the constitution of the legal community is not created by a legislative act but by custom, and if the law-applying organs are considered authorized to apply customary law. This situation cannot be interpreted to mean that custom is instituted as a law-creating act by the custom-created, that is, positive-legal, constitution. This would be a *petitio principii.* For if the positive-legal constitution, that is, a norm that regulates the creation of general norms, can be created by custom, then it must already be presupposed that custom is a law-creating fact. This presupposition can only be the basic norm, that is, the constitution in the transcendental-logical sense. Then the earlier-mentioned fact [86] is present, that the basic norm does not refer directly to a constitution in the positive-legal sense and only indirectly to the legal order established in accordance with that constitution, but *directly* to the legal order created by custom. This is particularly true with respect to the basic norm of general international law, whose norms are created by international custom and applied by the organs of the individual states.

Statutory law and customary law cancel each other according to the principle of the *lex posterior.* However, a constitutional law in the formal sense may not be abolished by an ordinary statute—only

---

[86] Cf. p. 201.

again by a constitutional law; but customary law does have a canceling effect in relation to a formal constitutional law, and even in relation to a formal constitutional law that expressly excludes the application of customary law.

The view that custom is a law-creating fact is opposed by another view according to which this fact has no constitutive but only declaratory character; that, as Savigny has said, "Custom is the badge, and not the origin, of positive law." [87] This merely expresses the theory advanced by the German Historical School that law is neither created by legislation nor by custom but only by the Popular Spirit (*Volksgeist*); that either method merely ascertains the existence of a law that had been valid before. The same thought is advanced by a French sociological theory with the difference that here the law is not created by *Volksgeist* but by *solidarité sociale* (Leon Duguit, *L'Etat, le droit objectif et la loi positive*, 1901, pp. 80 ff., 616).

According to both theories, the law, only declaratively ascertained (not created) by legislation or custom, can claim validity because, and so far as, it is the reproduction of a pre-existing law. Both theories are merely variants of the natural-law doctrine, whose dualism (of one law created by nature and one created by man) is reflected in the dualism of one law produced by *Volksgeist* or *solidarité sociale* and one law reproduced by legislation or custom. What has been said against the natural-law doctrine is applicable to these two theories. From the point of view of a positivistic theory of law which can neither assume the existence of an imaginary *Volksgeist* nor of an equally imaginary *solidarité sociale*, the constitutive, that is, the law-creating, function of custom is as indubitable as that of legislation.

The question of whether a law-creating custom is present may be decided only by the law-applying organ. This fact was occasionally the basis of the doctrine that a rule expressing the customary behavior of men becomes a legal norm only by recognition on the part of a law court which applies this rule; and that therefore the norms of customary law are created by the law courts. Yet, the relation of the law-applying organ (especially the law court)

<hr>

[87] "Gewohnheit [ist] das Kennzeichen des positiven Rechts, nicht dessen Entstehungsgrund." Friedrich Karl von Savigny, *System des heutigen Römischen Rechts*, 1840, p. 35.

toward customary law is no different from that toward statutory law. For an organ who has to apply a norm created by custom ascertains the fact of custom (that is, decides the question whether a norm he is about to apply was actually created by way of custom) precisely in the same manner as an organ who has to apply a norm created by legislation ascertains the fact of legislation (that is, decides the question whether a norm he is about to apply was created by way of legislation). This latter question may be easier to answer, and these organs may therefore be less conscious of it than of the question whether a norm had been created by custom, especially if the statutes have been published in an official gazette. Yet, the law-applying organ's function, namely to ascertain the existence of a norm to be applied (that is, its constitutional creation), is the same in both instances. And in both instances does a general legal norm exist, created before the law-applying act. To be true, the ascertainment of the fact by the law-applying organ has constitutive character, as we shall have occasion to discuss in detail; but this constitutive ascertainment has retroactive force. The fact is considered to be existent from the time ascertained by the law-applying organ, not from the time of the ascertainment.[88]

The validity of customary law within the legal community is limited insofar as the application of the general custom-created norms to concrete cases may take place only through statutory law—that is to say through decisions representing individual norms enacted by acts of will of law-applying organs, especially courts. The difference between the law-creating function of a legislative organ and the law-creating function of a court consists in that norms created by the former have—normally—a general, the norms created by the latter, normally, an individual character.[89]

A politically important difference between statutory law and customary law is the fact that the former is created by a relatively centralized, the latter by a relatively decentralized procedure. Statutes are created by special organs who are appointed for this purpose and who function according to the principle of division of labor. The norms of customary law, on the other hand, are created by the behavior of the individuals who are subject to the legal order. In the former, the norm-creating authority and the norm-

---

[88] Cf. p. 239.
[89] Cf. § 35g.

THE DYNAMIC ASPECT OF LAW

subjected individuals are not identical; in the latter they are, at least to some degree. To consider the fact of a law-creating custom as being existent, it is not necessary for all individuals obligated or entitled by the custom-created norm, to participate in the creation of the custom; it is sufficient that the overwhelming majority do; thus it is possible that individuals are bound by a custom-created norm in whose creation they did not take part. This is particularly true in a norm of customary law that had become valid some time ago. For this reason it is incorrect to interpret customary law as "a tacit contract," as is sometimes done, especially with respect to international customary law.

c) *Statute and Ordinance*

The level of the creation of general legal norms—regulated by the constitution—in the formation of the national legal order is usually divided into two or more levels. At this point we mention only the distinction between statutes and ordinances; it is important especially when the constitution confers the creation of general norms (statutes) in principle upon a popularly elected parliament, but permits the detailed elaboration of the statutes through general norms which are issued by administrative organs; or authorizes the government, instead of the parliament, to issue all necessary or certain general norms in the event of exceptional circumstances. The general norms issued by an administrative authority are called "ordinances" and may either elaborate or replace statutes. The latter are called ordinances with statutory effect. There exists, therefore, a specific statutory form, just as there exists a specific constitutional form. We speak of law in the formal sense in contradistinction to law in the material sense. The latter designates any general legal norm; the former either a general legal norm in the form of a statute, that is, a general legal norm adopted by parliament and published in a certain way as determined by most constitutions; or otherwise any content appearing in this form. Therefore, the term "law in the formal sense" is ambiguous. Unambiguous is merely the concept of statutory form in which may appear not only the general norms, but also other contents, including those whose subjective meaning is not even a norm. In this case we are dealing with a legally irrelevant content of a statute. We have discussed this in a different context.[90]

d) *Material and Formal Law*

The general legal norms created by acts aiming at the creation of law (statutes and ordinances), and the general legal norms created by custom, are to be applied by the organs competent to exercise this function—courts and administrative authorities. These law-applying organs have to be designated by the legal order, that is: it must be determined under which conditions a certain individual functions as a judge or administrative organ. Besides, the procedure has to be determined in which his function—the application of general legal norms—is to be exercised. The general norm, which attaches to an abstractly determined fact an abstractly determined consequence, needs individualization in order to be applied in a concrete case. It must be ascertained whether *in concreto* a fact is present which the general norm has determined *in abstracto;* and for this concrete case a concrete coercive act must be ordered and then executed—also determined *in abstracto* by the general norm. Therefore the application of a general norm to a concrete case consists in the creation of an individual norm—in the "individualization" or "concretization" of a general norm. Consequently the function of the general norm to be applied may also consist in determining the content of the individual norm to be created by an act of the judicial or administrative authority. Hence the general norms to be applied by judicial or administrative organs have a double function: (1) determination of these organs and of the procedure to be observed by them; (2) determination of the content of the individual norms to be created in the judicial or administrative procedure.

These two functions correspond with the two categories of legal norms usually distinguished: the norms of formal law and the norms of material law. Formal law is the general norms regulating the organization and procedure of the courts and administrative authorities, namely the civil, criminal, and administrative proceedings. Material law is the general norms that determine the contents of judicial and administrative acts, and which are re-

---

[90] Cf. § 6d.

ferred to as civil law, criminal law, and administrative law, although the norms that regulate the procedures of the law courts and administrative agencies are civil law, criminal law and administrative law no less. Also, when speaking about the norms to be applied by these organs one usually thinks of the material civil law, criminal law, and administrative law only, although material civil, criminal, and administrative laws cannot be applied without simultaneously applying formal (procedural) law. Material and formal law are inseparably connected with each other. Only in their organic combination do they constitute law that regulates its own creation and application. Each rule of law that completely describes this law must contain the formal as well as the material elements. A rule of law describing a norm of criminal law must be formulated—much simplified even at that—approximately as follows: "If an individual has committed a crime determined in a general legal norm, then an organ designated in a general legal norm (a law court) ought to order a sanction, determined in the former legal norm in a procedure determined in a general legal norm." We shall see later that a still more complicated formulation is necessary, namely: "If an organ, whose nomination is determined by a general legal norm, has ascertained, in a procedure determined by a general legal norm, that facts are present to which a general legal norm attaches a certain sanction, then this organ ought to order a sanction determined in the earlier-mentioned legal norm, in a procedure determined by a general legal norm." This formulation of the rule of law, then, shows—and therein lies the essential function of the rule of law describing the law—the systematic connection between the so-called formal and the so-called material law (that is, between the determination of the delict and the sanction on the one hand and the determination of the law-applying organ and his procedure on the other).

The relation between the general legal norms and their application by judicial or administrative organs is essentially the same as that existing between the constitution and the creation of general legal norms determined by it. The creation of general legal norms is an application of the constitution in the same way that the application of the general legal norms by judicial or administrative organs is the creation of individual legal norms. Just as the general legal norms created by legislation or custom are formally, and perhaps also materially, determined by the norms of the constitution (that is, by norms of a higher level) in the same way are the individual norms created by judicial or administrative acts—materially as well as formally—determined by general norms of statutory or customary law (that is, norms of a higher level). But the relation between the formal and the material element is different in the two instances. The constitution (in the material sense of the word) usually only determines the organs and the procedure of legislation and leaves the determination of the content of the statutes to the legislative organs. The constitution determines only exceptionally (and effectively only in a negative sense) the contents of the statutes to be created, by excluding certain contents.

As for law creation by custom, the constitution can delegate only the procedure characterized as "custom." The constitution cannot exclude a certain content of the legal norms created by custom, because the constitution itself—even a formal, written constitution—can be changed by legal norms created by custom. The general legal norms created in accordance with the constitution, however, not only determine the organs by which, and the procedures in which, they are to be applied, but also—albeit in various degrees—the content of the individual norms that represent the judicial decisions and administrative decrees. In criminal law the predetermination of the content of judicial decisions usually goes very far, so that the discretion of the criminal court in creating the individual legal norm represented by its decision is relatively limited. In administrative law the discretion is usually extensive. In other words: The constitution has predominantly the character of formal law, whereas the immediately inferior level of law creation has the character both of formal and material law.

e) The So-called Sources of Law

Legislation and custom are often referred to as the two "sources" of "law"—meaning by law only the general norms of national law. But the individual norms are also "law," just as much parts of the legal order as the general norms on which their creation is based. And if international law is considered, then only custom and treaty, not legislation, can be considered to be the "source" of this law.

Source of law is a figure of speech, which has more than one meaning. It can mean only the methods just mentioned, but all methods of law creation, or every higher norm in relation to a lower norm whose creation it regulates. Therefore, by "source of law" may also be meant the reason for the validity of a law, particularly the ultimate reason, the basic norm of a legal order. Actually, however, only the positive reason for the validity of a legal norm, that is, the higher positive legal norm that regulates its creation, is called "source." In this sense, the constitution is the source of the general legal norms created by legislation or custom; a general legal norm is the source of the judicial decision (i.e., of the individual norm) by which the general norm is applied; but the judicial decision itself may be regarded as the source of the obligation or right of the contending parties established by the decision, or as the source of the authorization of the organ who has to execute this decision. According to a positivistic theory of law, the source of law can only be law.

The expression, however, is used also in a nonjuristic sense, if thereby all conceptions are designated which actually influence the law-creating or law-applying function, such as moral and political principles, legal theories, expert views. These sources must be distinguished from sources in the sense of a positivistic law theory. The difference between them is this: the latter are legally binding, whereas the former are not, unless a positive legal norm delegates them as legal sources, that is, makes them mandatory. In that case, however, they assume the character of a higher legal norm, which determines the creation of a lower legal norm. The ambiguity of the term "source of law" makes it rather unsuitable for scientific discussion. It seems preferable to replace this figure of speech by a term which unambiguously describes the legal phenomenon one has in mind.

f) Creation, Application, and Observance of Law

As has been said, the legal order is a system of general and individual norms connected in such a way that the creation of each norm of this system is determined by another and ultimately by the basic norm. A norm is part of a legal order only because it had been created according to the provision of another norm of this order.

This regression leads eventually to the presupposed basic norm, which is not created according to the provision of another norm. Speaking not only of the legal order, but also of a legal community (constituted by that order), we can say that a legal norm is part of a certain legal order if it was created by an organ of that community and, therefore, by the community. But the individual who created a norm is an organ of the legal community because and insofar as his function is determined by a norm of the legal order that constitutes the community and can therefore be attributed to the community.[91] The attribution of the law-creating function to the legal community is based exclusively on the legal norm that determines this function. Just as the legal community consists only in the legal order, in the same way the sentence saying that a norm is part of a legal order because it is created by an organ of the legal community, only means that a norm is part of the legal order because it is created according to the provision of a norm of this legal order and, ultimately, according to the basic norm of this legal order. The realization of this is important especially if a national legal order is in question and therefore the legal community is the state—it is important for the understanding of the usual assertion that it is the state that creates the law.

A norm that determines the creation of another norm is applied by the creation of that other norm. Application of law is at the same time creation of law. These two concepts are not in absolute opposition to each other as assumed by traditional theory. It is not quite correct to distinguish between law-creating and law-applying acts. Because apart from the borderline cases—the presupposition of the basic norm and the execution of the coercive act—between which the legal process takes place, every legal act is at the same time the application of a higher norm and the creation of a lower norm. If the national legal order is considered without regard to a higher international legal order, then the basic norm in fact determines the creation of the constitution without being itself the application of a higher norm. But the constitution is created in application of the basic norm. In application of the constitution the general legal norms are created by legislation or custom; and in application of these general legal norms the individual norms of judicial decisions and administrative decrees are created. Only

---

[91] Cf. § 30c.

the execution of the coercive act prescribed by these individual norms—this final act in the law-creating procedure—takes place in application of the individual norms without being itself the creation of a norm. Law application, then, is the creation of a lower norm on the basis of a higher norm, or the execution of the coercive act authorized by a norm.

It has been pointed out that the creation of a lower norm by a higher one can be determined in two directions: the higher norm can determine the organ by whom and the procedure by which the lower norm is to be created; but it can also determine the content of that norm. Even if the higher norm only determines the organ, that is, the individual, who is to create the lower norm, while leaving both the procedure and the content of the norm to be created to the discretion of this organ, still the higher norm is applied in the creation of the lower one. Determining the organ is the minimum that must be accomplished in the relation between higher and lower norm. For a norm whose creation is not determined by a higher norm cannot be considered as a norm created within the legal order and therefore cannot be a part of it; and an individual cannot be considered as an organ of the legal community (his function cannot be attributed to the community), unless he has been determined by a norm of the legal order, that is: unless he has been authorized by such a higher norm to perform his function. Each law-creating act must be a law-applying act—it must be the application of a legal norm that preceded the act in order to be considered as an act of the legal community. Therefore law creation must be understood as law application, even if the higher norm determines only the personal element, the individual, who has to render the law-creating function. This higher norm, the norm that determined the organ, is applied in every act of the organ. In Plato's ideal state, in which judges may decide all cases entirely at their discretion, unhampered by any general norms issued by a legislator, every decision is, nevertheless, an application of the general norm that determines under what conditions an individual is authorized to act as a judge. Only on the basis of this norm he can be considered as a judge of the ideal state; only then can his decision, as having been reached within the ideal state, be attributed to this state.

The creation of a lower norm may be determined by a higher in different degrees. But this determination must never be so weak that the act in question cannot be considered as an act of law application, and it can never go so far that the act can no longer be considered as an act of law creation. Even if—as in the case of a judicial decision reached on the basis of a statute—not only the organ and the procedure are determined, but also the content of the decision that is to be rendered, this still does not represent merely law application but also law creation. The question whether an act has the character of law creation or law application depends on the degree to which the function of the act-rendering organ is predetermined by the legal order. But there are acts which are only law application, not law creation. These are the acts, mentioned before, by which the coercive acts, authorized by the legal norms, are executed. And there is an act of positive law creation, which is not the application of a positive legal norm: the enactment of the historically first constitution, which takes place in application of the presupposed, not positively created, basic norm.

The creation and application of law must be distinguished from the observance of law. Law is observed by that behavior to whose opposite is attached the coercive act of the sanction. It is that behavior, primarily, that avoids the sanction; it is the fulfillment of the legal obligation constituted by the sanction. Creation, application, and the observance of law are "legal functions" in the widest sense of the term. Making use of a positive permission may also be designated as the observance of law. In the narrower, specific sense of the term, only law creation and law application are called legal functions.

g) Jurisdiction

The constitutive character of the judicial decision

Traditional jurisprudence sees law application primarily, if not exclusively, in the decisions of civil and criminal law courts. These courts, in fact, when deciding a litigation or imposing a punishment upon a criminal usually apply general legal norms created by legislation or custom. But law is also applied, as has been said, when general legal norms are created, when decrees are issued by administrative officials, and (as will be discussed later) when legal transactions are performed; and the courts apply the general legal norms by creating individual norms whose content is determined by the general norms which authorize a concrete sanction: civil execution or punishment.

Contemplated from the point of view of the dynamics of the law, the creation of individual norms by the courts represents a transitional stage of the process that begins with the establishment of the constitution, continues via legislation or custom to the judicial decision, and leads to the execution of the sanction. This process, in which the law keeps renewing itself, as it were, proceeds from the general (abstract) to the individual (concrete); it is a process of increasing individualization and concretization.

In order to individualize the general norm, the court must first ascertain whether in a given case the conditions for a sanction determined *in abstracto* in the general norm are present *in concreto*. This ascertainment includes the ascertainment of the existence of the general norm to be applied, that is, the ascertainment that a general norm is valid which attaches a sanction to the facts present. The court has to answer the *quaestio juris* as well as the *quaestio facti*. After these two ascertainments have been made, the court has to order *in concreto* the sanctions prescribed by the general norm *in abstracto*. These ascertainments and this order are the essential functions of the judicial decisions. In this respect a certain difference exists between a civil and a criminal decision: in the former the concrete sanction is usually ordered conditionally. The civil court sentences the defendant to render a certain performance to the plaintiff, and orders the sanction only on condition that this performance is not rendered within a certain time. Punishment, on the other hand, is usually ordered unconditionally, although it may also be conditioned inasmuch as its execution may be made dependent on the sentenced person's committing another delict within a stipulated time.

A judicial decision does not have merely declaratory character as is sometimes assumed. The court does not merely "find" (in German: *das Recht finden*) the law whose creation had been previously entirely completed; the court's function is not only juris-"dictio," the pronouncement of law in this declaratory sense. The finding of law is present only when the general norm to be applied in the concrete case is to be ascertained; and even this ascertainment has a constitutive, not merely a declaratory, character. The court that has to apply the general valid norms of a legal order to a concrete case, must decide the question whether the norm to be applied is constitutional, that is, created in a legislative procedure determined by the constitution or by custom delegated by the constitution.[92] This fact, to be ascertained by the court, is as much a condition for the sanction stipulated by the court in a concrete case as the fact, to be ascertained by the court, that a delict had been committed. The legal rule describing this situation —for example when a criminal law of a democratic legal order is applied—is this: if the constitutionally elected parliament, by way of a procedure prescribed by the constitution, has passed a statute, according to which a certain behavior ought to be punished, as a crime, in a certain way; and if the court has ascertained the fact that a certain individual has behaved in that way; then the court ought to impose the punishment prescribed by the statute. This formulation of the rule of law reveals the position of the so-called constitutional law (that is, the norms regulating the creation of general legal norms)—within the framework of a legal order. They are not independent, complete norms because they determine only one of the conditions of the coercive act stipulated by other norms. They are legal norms only in connection with these norms. Therefore, the fact that the norms of constitutional law do not stipulate coercive acts is not sufficient reason to reject, as is sometimes done, the definition of law as a coercive order. Only by the ascertainment implied in the judicial decision that a general norm, to be applied by the court, is valid—and it is valid if it was created according to the constitution—does the norm become applicable in the concrete case, and thereby a legal situation is created for this case which did not exist before the decision.

That the ordering of a concrete sanction has constitutive character hardly needs much proof. The individual norm stipulating that a certain sanction ought to be directed against a certain individual has been brought into existence by the judicial decision; it did not exist before. Only the lack of insight into the normative function of the judicial decision, only the prejudice that the law consists merely of general norms, only the ignoring of the exist-

---

[92] For limitations by positive law of this right of the courts and other law-applying organs, cf. § 35j, subsection "The 'unconstitutional' statute."

ence of individual legal norms obscured the fact that the judicial decision is a continuation of the law-creating process, and has led to the error to see it in a merely declaratory function.

It is important to realize that even the ascertainment of the fact that a delict had been committed represents an entirely constitutive function of the court. If a legal order attaches a certain consequence to a certain fact as condition, then this order must also determine the organ who and the procedure by which the existence of the conditioning fact is to be ascertained in a concrete case. The legal order may authorize the organ to determine the procedure at his own discretion; but the organ and the procedure must be determined—directly or indirectly—by the legal order, so that the general norm can be applied to the concrete case. With regard to a fact stipulated by the legal order as the condition of a certain consequence, the first question of the jurist must be which legal organ is competent, according to the legal order, to ascertain this fact in the concrete case, and which is the procedure prescribed by the legal order. It is only by this ascertainment that the fact reaches the realm of law; only then does a natural fact become a legal fact —is it created as a legal fact. The objection: "The moment at which the legal fact is to be regarded existent is identical with the moment at which the natural fact occurred," may be answered by the statement: "The ascertainment of the fact by the law-applying organ has retroactive force." The fact is not considered to be established at the moment of the ascertainment, but at the moment determined by the law-applying organ, that is, at the moment at which—according to the ascertainment of the law-applying organ —the natural fact occurred. The ascertainment of the conditioning fact by the court, therefore, is constitutive in every sense. If a general legal norm attaches a punishment to murder, then this situation is not correctly described by the statement—the fact that an individual has committed murder is the condition of the sanction. Not the fact in itself that an individual has committed a murder is the condition stipulated by the legal order, but the fact that an organ, authorized by the legal order, in a procedure prescribed by the legal order, has ascertained that an individual has committed murder. If it is said: "A court ascertained that a certain individual committed a certain murder, although 'in reality' this individual did not commit it"; or if it is said: "The court ascertained that a certain individual did not commit a certain murder, although 'in reality' he did''—then, this means that the court ascertained the existence or nonexistence of a fact which, according to the opinion of individuals legally not competent to ascertain this, did not exist or existed.

From the point of view of a legal order that is to be applied by individuals, relevant are only the opinions of individuals whether an individual has committed a murder. These opinions are more or less reliable, they may be contradictory, the suspected individual himself may admit or deny the fact. But if the general legal norm is to be applied, only *one* opinion can be decisive. Which one, must be determined by the legal order. This opinion is expressed in the court decision. It alone is legally relevant, the opinions of all others are irrelevant. Still, a judicial decision may be contested by way of appeal if the ascertainment of the conditioning fact, contained in the decision, is considered erroneous by the parties authorized by the legal order to make such an appeal. This means that the *subjective* meaning of the act of such a decision need not yet be accepted definitely as its *objective* meaning. The subjective meaning of the act will become definitely its objective meaning only when the judicial decision has acquired the force of a final judgment: when it cannot be canceled by a further procedure. In that case the opinion that an innocent individual was sentenced is legally excluded. This is so because the legal rule does not say: "If a certain individual has committed murder, then a punishment ought to be imposed upon him." The legal rule says: "If the authorized court in a procedure determined by the legal order has ascertained, with the force of law, that a certain individual has committed a murder, then the court ought to impose a punishment upon that individual." In juristic thinking the ascertainment of the fact by the competent authority replaces the fact in itself that in nonjuristic thinking is the condition for the coercive act. Only this ascertainment is the conditioning "fact," and concerning the question whether this fact exists in the concrete case, whether the ascertainment was made at all or by the authorized organ or in the prescribed procedure—concerning all these questions just as many different opinions are possible as concerning the question whether the ascertainment was "correct." Just as it is possible to appeal against a judicial decision on the grounds of incorrectness of the ascertainment of the fact (that a certain delict was committed by a certain individual), so it is possible to appeal against the execution of a sanction on the grounds of nonexistence of a judicial decision, or on the grounds of incompetence of the organs or faultiness of the procedure. The situation that, according to the view of the parties, the execution of a sanction was ordered without a preceding judicial procedure, is analogous to the situation that the court ascertained the commission of a delict although, according to the opinion of the parties, no such delict was committed. In this case, the commisssion of the delict can be ascertained again in an appeal procedure or, if the noncommission of the delict is ascertained by the court of appeal, the order of the execution of the sanction can be rescinded. In the former case, the fact contested by the parties, that the order of the execution of the sanction was preceded by a court procedure, can be ascertained in an appeal procedure or, if this fact cannot be ascertained, a new court procedure can be instituted. The situation that, according to the view of the parties, the judicial decision was rendered by a court incompetent to sit, or in a faulty procedure, is analogous to the situation that the delict was committed by an individual other than the sentenced one or that the delict which he actually did commit was different from the one for which he was sentenced. In all these cases a court procedure is the subject of another court procedure. If this appeal from one procedure to another is limited by a positive legal order, then there is finally a court procedure that can no longer be the subject of another court procedure. Then the borderline case of an ultimate court procedure must be accepted as a fact in itself. This happens when the decison of the court of last instance acquires the force of law. This means that now the subjective meaning of the act of decision of the court of last instance has to be accepted as its objective meaning. If in this decision the party-contested fact is ascertained that a court procedure preceded the ordering of the execution of the sanction or that the competence of the earlier court, denied by the parties, cannot be denied or that the faultiness of the previous court procedure asserted by the parties does not exist—then any other opinion is legally excluded.

Although the court procedure that ascertains the fact that is the condition for the sanction, is not a procedure of scientific cognition, but of creation of law, still, a certain parallel exists between this procedure and the procedure by which scientific cognition of natural facts is attained, provided that we assume that the procedure of scientific cognition has a constitutive character. In this parallel the organ of the constitutive court procedure corresponds to the subject of the constitutive procedure of scientific cognition. Just as the object of this cognition is "created" in the procedure of cognition, so the fact that is the condition for the sanction is created in the court procedure. And just as the court procedure as a fact can itself become the object of a court procedure, so the procedure of cognition itself may become the object of a procedure of scientific cognition in the theory of cognition (epistemology). But the cognition whose object is scientific cognition as a fact cannot be again, as a fact, the object of cognition. The regression from the procedure of scientific cognition to another procedure of scientific cognition whose object the former is, is limited. There exists the borderline case of a procedure of scientific cognition, which must be accepted as a fact in itself, which means, as a fact that cannot be created in another procedure of scientific cognition.

The relation between a court decision and the general legal norms to be applied

The act by which the individual norm of judicial decision is created is usually predetermined, as has been said, by general norms of formal and material law. In that case, two possibilities present themselves in a concrete case to be decided by a court. Either the court ascertains that the defendant or accused has committed the delict as claimed by the plaintiff or public prosecutor and has thereby violated an obligation imposed on him by the legal order; then the court must find for the plaintiff or condemn the accused by ordering a sanction prescribed in the general norm. Or the court ascertains that the defendant or accused has not committed the delict and therefore has not violated an obligation imposed on him by the legal order; then the court must dimiss the action or acquit the accused—that is, the court must order that no sanction ought to be directed against the defendant or accused. Whether the court (a) finds for the plaintiff or condemns the accused or (b) dismisses the action or acquits the accused, the judicial decision applies the valid legal order; this is particularly so when the court dismisses the action or acquits the accused on the grounds that, according to the court's view, no valid general norm exists which attaches a sanction to the defendant's or accused's behavior alleged by the plaintiff or public prosecutor. It has been explained earlier [93] that the legal order regulates human behavior not only positively by ordering a certain behavior, but also negatively by permitting a certain behavior by not prohibiting it. That which is legally not prohibited is legally permitted. The court, by dismissing an action or acquitting the accused, applies the legal order which permits the defendant or accused the behavior against which was directed the action or accusation not founded on the legal order.

As discussed earlier, the legally not prohibited, and in this sense permitted, behavior of an individual can be guaranteed by the legal order by obligating other individuals to tolerate this behavior, that is, not to prevent or impair it. This is always the case insofar as a general prohibition of the application of physical force exists, and this application of force is reserved to organs of the legal community. But it is possible that the permitted behavior of one individual is opposed by a behavior, not consisting in the application of physical force, of another individual—a behavior that likewise is permitted. Then—as mentioned before—a conflict of interests is present which the legal order does not prevent; no legal order can prevent all possible conflicts of interests. In this situation the court must dismiss the action even if it is directed against a permitted behavior of the defendant by which a permitted behavior of the plaintiff is prevented or impaired without application of physical force and the court has to acquit the accused even if his behavior against which the accusation is directed has this character. In this case too the judicial decision applies the legal order—it is law application. The application of valid law may be considered unsatisfactory in such a case because it refrains from protecting an interest which, from some points of view, is regarded as worthy of protection. But since a legal order cannot protect all possible interests but only specific interests by prohibiting their violation it has to leave unprotected the ever-present counter-interests. So therefore the conflict between a permitted behavior of

---

[93] Cf. § 4d.

one individual and the permitted behavior of another individual is inevitable. Such conflict is always present when the action is dismissed only, or the accused acquitted only, because his behavior is not prohibited and therefore the interest violated by his behavior is not protected by a general norm attaching a sanction to this behavior.

It is also possible, however, that the legal order authorizes the court not to dismiss the action or not to acquit the accused, but, if the court considers the lack of such a general norm as unjust or unequitable, that is, unsatisfactory, to find for the plaintiff or to sentence the accused. This means that the court is authorized to create in this case an individual legal norm whose content is in no way predetermined by a general legal norm created by legislation or custom. In this case the court does not apply such a legal norm but the norm that authorizes the court to create new law. It is usually said that the court is authorized to function as a legislator. This is not quite correct if by "legislating" is meant the creation of general legal norms. For the court is only authorized to create an individual norm, valid for the single, present case. But the court creates this individual norm by applying a general norm which the court considers "just" or desirable—a norm which the positive legislator failed to create. The court-created individual norm is justifiable only as application of such a not positive, general norm.

There is only a difference in degree between the case in which the court is authorized to function as a "legislator" and the case in which the court must—in the absence of a positive general norm that predetermines the content of the judicial decision—dismiss the action or acquit the accused. The difference is one of degree not only because, even in the former case, the court applies a general, even though not a positive, norm of material law, but also, especially, because even in the latter case the function of the court is law creation, namely the creation of an individual norm. Only, in this case, the discretion of the court is much more limited than in the former case in which the discretion is, in fact, so little limited as the discretion which the constitution ordinarily allows the legislator in creating general legal norms. But even in the case in which the content of the individual legal norm to be created by the court is predetermined by a positive general legal norm, a certain amount of discretion must be reserved for the law-creating function of the court. The positive general norm cannot predetermine all the factors which make up the peculiarities of the concrete case—such as, for example, the amount of damage to be determined by the court which has to be compensated for by the court-ordered civil execution in the property of the defendant; or the moment at which the jail sentence to be imposed by the court should begin or end; or the day when a death sentence is to be executed. In the procedure in which a general norm is individualized, the organ applying the general norm must always determine the facts which are not yet, and cannot be, determined by the general norm. The general norm is always only a frame within which the individual norm is to be created. But this frame can be narrower or wider. It is widest when the positive general norm contains only the authorization for the creation of the individual legal norm, without predetermining its content.

If the content of such a court-created individual legal norm is in no way predetermined by a general norm, then the individual norm has retroactive force. A legal norm is said to have retroactive force, if the fact to which the sanction is attached occurred before the norm became valid; the fact, then, was at the time of the creation of the norm not yet a delict, but was made into one by this norm afterward.

This is so when the court applies to the case which it has to decide an individual legal norm whose content is not predetermined by a positive general legal norm; that means: if this individual legal norm attaches a sanction to a behavior of the defendant or accused, a sanction which at the time the behavior occurred was not yet a delict but was made into one only by the individual legal norm of the judicial decision.

The so-called gaps in the law

It follows from what has been said that a positive legal order can always be applied by a court to a concrete case, even when the legal order does not contain, according to the court's view, a general norm positively regulating the behavior of the defendant or accused; that is to say, when the legal order does not contain a general norm imposing upon the defendant or accused the obligation of a behavior which he, according to the action of the private plaintiff or the accusation of the public prosecutor, did not perform. For in this case his behavior is regulated negatively, that is, legally not prohibited, and in this sense permitted. But traditional jurisprudence interprets this case, under certain circumstances, as a "gap" in the legal order.

In order to judge the theory of "gaps" in the law it is necessary to determine the circumstances under which, according to that theory, a "gap" in the law occurs. According to this theory, the valid law is not applicable in a concrete case if no general legal norm refers to this case; therefore the court is obliged to fill the gap by creating a corresponding norm. The essential argument is that the application of the valid law, as a conclusion from the general to the particular, is logically impossible in this case because the necessary condition—the validity of a general norm referring to the case—is missing. This theory is erroneous because it ignores the fact that the legal order permits the behavior of an individual when the legal order does not obligate the individual to behave otherwise. The application of the valid legal order is not impossible in this case in which traditional theory assumes a gap. The application of a single legal norm, to be true, is not possible, but the application of the legal order—and that, too, is law application—*is* possible. Law application is not excluded. In fact, the existence of a gap is in no way assumed in all cases in which the obligation of the defendant or accused as asserted by the plaintiff or public prosecutor is not established by a norm of the valid law. Upon closer inspection it turns out that the existence of a gap is assumed only when the absence of such a legal norm is regarded as politically undesirable by the law-applying organ; when, therefore, the logically possible application of the valid law is rejected for this political reason, as being inequitable or unjust according to the opinion of the law-applying organ. But the application of the valid legal order may be regarded as inequitable or unjust not only when this order lacks a general norm imposing upon the defendant or accused a definite obligation, but also when it contains such a norm. The fact that a legal order lacks a legal norm that stipulates punishment for the theft of electricity may be regarded as inequitable or unjust as much as the fact that a legal order contains a legal norm applicable to murder with robbery in the same way as to the case in which a son kills his incurably ill father upon the latter's request. A gap in the sense of the inapplicability of the valid law is no less present in the one case as in the other; and it is at least inconsistent to assume a gap only in one case and not in the other. Besides, the judgment, according to which the lack of a legal norm of a certain content is inequitable or unjust, represents a very subjective value judgment which in no way excludes an opposite value judgment. If, for example, a legal order does not contain a general legal norm which imposes upon the employer the obligation to compensate for damage caused by an employee in the employer's business, and if, therefore, the court must dismiss the action against the employer and can find only for the plaintiff if the action is directed against the employee, then the application of the valid legal order will be judged as unsatisfactory by a Socialist, but entirely satisfactory by a Liberal. The lack of a general legal norm which results in the dismissal of the plaintiff's action or the acquittal of the accused will usually be regarded as satisfactory, and therefore as equitable and just by the defendant or the accused, but as unsatisfactory and therefore as inequitable or unjust by the plaintiff or public prosecutor.

In spite of all these objections the gap theory plays an important role in the technique of modern legislation. The following rule of the Swiss Civil Code is typical: "The law is applicable to all legal problems for which it contains a rule explicitly or by interpretation. If no prescription is contained in the law, the judge shall decide according to custom and, where this too is lacking, according to the rule which he would establish were he a legislator." This rule presupposes the possibility that Swiss law is inapplicable to a concrete case to be decided by a Swiss civil court. But since this is actually not possible, since a legal order is always applicable and is actually applied even when the court must dismiss the action on the grounds that the legal order does not contain a general rule imposing upon the defendant the obligation asserted by the plaintiff, so therefore the supposition, on which the cited rule is based, is a fiction. The fiction consists in this: a lack, based on a subjective, moral-political value judgment, of a certain legal norm within a legal order is presented as the impossibility of its application.

The legislator may be induced to use this fiction through the consideration that the application of a statute created by him may lead to an unsatisfactory result under certain unforeseen and unforeseeable circumstances; and that it is desirable therefore to authorize the court, not to apply in such cases the statute that predetermines the content of its judgment, but to create an individual norm, whose content is not determined by a statute but adapted to the circumstances not foreseen by the legislator. If he were to formulate this authorization in a theoretically correct fashion, that is, without fiction, he would have to say: "If the application of the valid legal order is unsatisfactory according to the moral-political opinion of the court in the present case then the court may decide the case according to its own discretion." But such a formulation would allow far too great authority to the court. The judge would be authorized to decide according to his own discretion whenever he considers the application of the valid legal order as unsatisfactory even when he considered as unsatisfactory the application of a general legal norm which imposes upon the defendant or accused the obligation which he has violated according to the plaintiff or public prosecutor. If the moral-political opinion of the judge replaces that of the legislator, then the legislator abdicates in favor of the judge. The attempt to limit the authorization to cases which the legislator has been foreseen is bound to fail because the legislator is unable to predetermine these cases; if he could predetermine them he would positively regulate them himself. The assumption of the court that a case had not been foreseen by the legislator and that the legislator would have formulated the law differently if he had foreseen the case usually rests on an unprovable guess. The legislator's intention is recognizable with sufficient certainty only insofar as it is expressed in the law he has created. It is for *this* reason that the legislator, to limit the authorization of the courts which he regards as indispensable, uses the fiction that the valid legal order is inapplicable in certain cases for objective —and not for subjective, moral-political reasons; that the judge may function as a legislator only when the law has a gap.

But since the valid law is always applicable, since it has no gaps in this sense, the formula, when its fictitious character has been exposed, does not provide the intended limitation of the authorization granted to the court but its self-abolition. But if the court accepts the assumption that the law has gaps, then this theoretically

untenable fiction may—practically—have the intended effect. For
the judge—especially one controlled by a higher court—who is not
inclined to assume the responsibility for creating new law will assume the existence of a gap only very rarely and therefore only
rarely make use of his authorization to take the place of the legislator.

Beside the so-called true gaps, sometimes "technical" gaps are
distinguished which are considered possible even by those who
deny, from their positivistic point of view, the existence of true
gaps. Such a technical gap is present when the legislator fails to
prescribe something which he would have had to prescribe if it
should be technically possible at all to apply the law. However,
that which is described as a technical gap is either a gap in the
original sense of the word, that is, a difference between a positive
law and a desired law, or that kind of uncertainty that results from
the frame character of the general norm. The former is present if,
for example, the law according to which in case of a sale, the seller
is obligated to deliver the merchandise or, if he does not deliver, to
compensate for the caused damage, does not determine who is running the risk when the sold merchandise perishes before it is
handed over, through no fault of either party. It is not true, however, that the legislator prescribes "nothing" for this case, but only
that he does not prescribe that the seller is discharged from the obligation to deliver the merchandise or render compensation; a prescription, which is presumably regarded as desirable by those who
assert that a gap exists here; a prescription which, however, in no
way needs to be supplied to make the law applicable. Since the law
does not even in the described case exempt the seller from the obligation to deliver the merchandise or render compensation, the
law in fact prescribes that the seller is running the risk.

The second case is present if the law prescribes, for example,
that an organ should be established by election but does not regulate the election procedure. This means, that any type of election
is in accordance with the law. The organ authorized to carry out
the election may determine the electoral procedure according to
his own discretion. The determination of this procedure is left to a
lower norm. Another example: a law prescribes, among other
things, that a committee, in order to function, must be convoked
by its chairman; but it also prescribes that it must elect its own

chairman. If it is not possible to interpret these norms to mean that any type of convocation is lawful in case no chairman is as yet elected, but only that, even in this situation, the committee ought to be convoked by its chairman, then this committee cannot function lawfully. But no gap is present here, either. For the law wants that the committee be convoked by its chairman even if it doesn't have one. If the law had not prescribed anything for the convocation of the committee in such a situation, any kind of convocation would be lawful. The law simply prescribes something nonsensical. Since laws are man-made, this is not impossible.

Creation of general legal norms by the courts; flexibility of the law and legal security

A court, especially one of highest instance, may be authorized to create by its judgment not only an individual norm binding for the present case, but a general norm. This happens when the judicial decision becomes a so-called precedent, that is, when the decision of a case is giving direction to the decision of similar cases. A judicial decision may have the character of a precedent when the individual norm created by the decision is not, in its content, predetermined by a general norm of statutory or customary law or is ambiguously worded and therefore permits different interpretations. In the former case the court's precedential decision creates new law; in the second case the interpretation implicit in the decision assumes the character of a general norm. In both cases, the court that creates the precedent functions in the manner of a legislator precisely like the organ authorized by the constitution to legislate. The judicial decision of a concrete case gives direction to the decision of similar cases in that the individual norm which the judicial decision represents is generalized. This generalization, that is, the formulation of the general norm, may be done by the court that created the precedent; but it can also be left to other courts bound by the precedential decision. In that case it is not excluded that different courts may generalize the precedential decisions in different ways; which does not help the purpose of the institution, namely, to achieve a uniform judicature. Since the precedential decision can give direction only to the decision of similar cases, the question whether a case is similar to the precedential case is of decisive importance. Since no case is similar to another in every respect, the "similarity" of the two cases in question here can consist only in that they correspond to each other in certain essential points, just as two sets of facts which constitute the same delict are not similar in all points, but only in certain essential points. But the question in which points they have to correspond in order to be considered "similar" can be answered only on the basis of a general norm that defines the fact by determining its essential elements. Whether two cases are similar can therefore be decided only on the basis of the general norm created by the precedential decision. The formulation of this general norm is the supposition under which the precedential decision can give direction to the decision of "similar" cases.

The law-creating function of the courts becomes particularly visible when a court is authorized to create a general norm by establishing a precedent. To give such an authorization to a court, especially to a court of last instance, is particularly commendable when the court is authorized to decide a case under certain circumstances not by applying a general norm of an already existing law, but according to its own discretion; in other words, if the court is authorized to create an individual legal norm whose content is not predetermined by a general norm of positive law. To bestow the character of a precedent upon such a decision is only a consistent enlargement of the court's law-creating function.

If courts are authorized to create individual *and* general norms, they compete with the legislative organ established by the constitution; this means a decentralization of the legislative function. With respect to the relationship between the legislative organ and the courts, two technically different types of legal system are distinguishable. Within the first system the creation of general legal norms is entirely centralized, that is, reserved for a central legislative organ, and the courts are restricted to apply the general norms created by the legislative organ in concrete cases by the individual norms to be created by them. Since the legislative procedure, in order to function, has to surmount many obstacles, especially in a parliamentary democracy, it is difficult to accommodate the law in such a system to changing circumstances. This system has the disadvantage of lacking flexibility. It has the advantage, however, of legal security; this means that the judicial decisions are foreseeable to a certain extent, and therefore calculable enough that the individuals subject to the law can adapt their behavior to the foreseeable judicial decisions.

The principle, to bind decisions of concrete cases by general norms that are to be created beforehand by a central legislative organ, can be extended analogously to the functions of administrative authorities. The principle, in this general form, represents the principle of the *Rechtstaat,* that is, a state governed by law. It is essentially the principle of legal security, *Rechtssicherheit.*

In direct opposition to this system is the one within which no central legislative organ exists at all, but judges and administrative authorities decide individual cases according to their own free discretion. The justification of this system is the assumption that no case is exactly like any other case; and that therefore the application of general norms, which predetermine the judicial decision or the administrative decree and thus prevent the respective organs to do justice to the peculiarities of the individual cases, may lead to undesirable results. This is the system of the so-called *freie Rechtsfindung* (free jurisdiction); it is a system that Plato proposed for his ideal state. Because of its radical decentralization of law creation, this system is distinguished by great flexibility, but lacks all legal security. For under such a legal order the subjected individuals can in no way anticipate the decisions of concrete cases in which they may participate as accused or prosecutor, as defendant or plaintiff. Therefore they cannot know in advance what is legally permitted and prohibited, what they are legally authorized to do or not authorized to do. They can learn this only through the decision in which they are punished or acquitted, in which their action is dismissed or decided in their favor.

Free jurisdiction that guarantees flexibility of the law is often demanded in the name of justice—a justice presupposed to be absolute. "Just" in this sense is said to be the decision of a concrete case only if it takes into consideration all peculiarities of the case. But since no case is exactly like any other, the application of a general norm to a concrete case can never—so it is said—lead to a just decision. For a general norm necessarily presupposes similar cases, which in reality do not exist. Therefore all law must have individual character only, and the decision of concrete cases must not be bound by general norms.

Against this justification of free jurisdiction the following may be objected: what actually happens, when the decisions of concrete cases are not determined with respect to content by general norms, is by no means the complete elimination of general norms from the process of law creation. If the organ, who is about to decide a concrete case, is to make a "just" decision, he can do this only by applying a general norm he considers as just. If such a general norm is not already created by legislation or custom, the organ must proceed in the same way as a legislator who is guided in formulating the general norms by a certain ideal of justice. Since different legislators may be guided by very different ideals of justice, the value of justice which they realize can only be relative; and equally relative is the justice of the general norm by which the organ is guided who is called upon to decide the concrete case. From the point of view of an ideal of justice—possible only as a relative value—the difference between the system of free jurisdiction and of the jurisdiction determined by statutory or customary law is this: in place of the general norm of positive law and the general norm constituting the legislator's ideal of justice functions the general norm of the ideal of justice of the organ who is to render the decision of the concrete case.

The presupposition of this general norm is indispensable, as has been said, if the decision of the concrete case is to be regarded as "just." For the question why a certain decision is just is provoked by the need to justify the decision, to give a reason for the validity of the individual norm established by it. And such justification or foundation of the validity is only possible by showing that the individual norm conforms with a higher general norm presupposed to be just. The norm constituting the value of justice must, according to its nature, have a general character.

A special variant in the demand for a free jurisdiction not predetermined by general norms is a doctrine that has appeared recently under the influence of existentialist philosophy.[94] According to it, reality, which is essentially concrete, cannot be comprehended by abstract concepts, or regulated by general norms, but must be "lived." Since the concrete cases to be decided by the

---

[94] Cf. Georg Cohn, *Existenzialismus und Rechtswissenschaft* (Basel: 1955) and Hans Kelsen, "Existenzialismus in der Rechtswissenchaft?" Archiv für Rechts- und Sozialphilosophie, 43:2 (1957), 161 ff.

courts are thoroughly different, the correct decision—that is, the one which considers all peculiarities of the case—cannot be found in a general norm that has been brought on from the outside, but only in the reality of the concrete case itself. The just law is immanent in social reality and can only be found by a careful analysis of this reality, not in general norms created by legislation. In this respect existentialist theory of law is merely a variant of the doctrine of natural law and, like it, the hopeless attempt of a logically impossible deduction from an *is* to an *ought*.

Between these two extreme types of a jurisdiction bound by state legislation and a jurisdiction free of state legislation are (a) those types in which a central legislative organ is established, yet the courts are authorized to create not only individual norms within the framework of the general norms created by the legislative organ but also—under special circumstances, described above —individual norms outside this framework; and (b) that system in which the courts are authorized to create general legal norms in the form of precedential decisions. These different systems represent different degrees of centralization or decentralization of the law-creating function and thereby different degrees of the realization of the principle of flexibility of law, which is in inverse relation to the principle of legal security.

A system of a special kind is that in which general norms are, in the main, not created by a central legislative organ, but by custom, and applied by the courts. Since in case of custom-created general norms the adaptation of the law to changing circumstances is more difficult than in case of creation by a central legislative organ, than the system of customary law has a favorable climate for the development of precedential jurisdiction. It is understandable, therefore, that such jurisdiction flourished especially in the sphere of Anglo-American common law, which essentially is customary law.

We have already pointed out that the application of a general legal norm created by custom is distinguished from the application of a general norm created by legislation in that the ascertainment of the validity of a norm of customary law to be applied —that is, the ascertainment that a law-creating custom is present— plays a much more prominent and clear role in the judge's conscience than the ascertainment of the validity of a norm created by

legislation and published in the official gazette. This explains why
the view is sometimes held that customary law is court-made law.
If the courts have to apply usually customary law, as in the sphere
of the Anglo-American common law, and if they, besides, have the
authority to create precedents, a theory can easily develop in such
an area that all law is court-made law; that no law exists before the
judge's decision; that a norm becomes a legal norm only because it
is applied by the court.[95] Such a theory can be maintained only by
regarding the norms applied by the courts as "sources of law," not
as law, whereby this figure of speech is used as a description for all
factors that actually influence the judicial decision, such as moral-
political value judgments, expert opinions, and the like. Influenced by the paramount importance which the courts have within
the systems of customary law and precedential jurisdiction, this
theory ignores the essential difference between "sources" of law
that are legally binding and those that are not. The theory errs in
not recognizing that the "source" of law in the specific sense of the
term (that is, the origin of law, that from which law arises, that
which creates law) can be "law" only because it is a peculiarity of
the law to regulate its own creation.

The theory that only the courts create law, a theory grown upon
the soil of Anglo-American common law, is just as one-sided as the
theory, grown on the soil of European-Continental statutory law,
that the courts do not create law at all, but only apply already created law. The latter theory amounts to the view that only general
legal norms exist, the former that only individual legal norms
exist. The truth is in between. The courts do create law—usually
individual law; but within a legal order that establishes a legislative organ, or that recognizes custom as law-creating fact, the
courts do this by applying general law previously created by legislation or custom. The judicial decision is the continuation, not the
beginning, of the law-creating process.

If from a legal-political viewpoint the difference between jurisdiction bound by general norms created by legislation or custom
and a jurisdiction not bound by such norms is considered to constitute a principal antagonism between two legal systems, it must

---

[95] This theory is developed in John Chipman Gray, *The Nature and Sources of
the Law*, 2d ed. (1927). Cf. Kelsen, *General Theory of Law and State*, pp. 150 ff.

be taken into consideration that this antagonism is considerably lessened by the fact that a judicial decision may have the force of a final judgment (*Rechtskraft*). This will be discussed later.

h) The Legal Transaction

The legal transaction as law-creating fact

The individual legal norm represented by the judicial decision prescribes a sanction which has the character of a punishment (in a criminal procedure) or of a civil execution (in a civil procedure). The purpose of the civil sanction is compensation, especially compensation for damage.[96] The behavior which causes the damage is unlawful, a civil delict, if it is the condition of a civil execution. Two types óf such causes of damage are distinguishable depending on whether they are connected or not connected with a preceding legal transaction. Cause of damage of the second type is present if, for example, somebody damages or destroys intentionally or negligently an object that is somebody else's property; or if somebody causes damage to somebody else by a criminal delict such as bodily harm or theft. In the latter case the civil sanction is added to the criminal sanction. Cause of damage of the first type is present if, for example, two parties conclude a contract, and the one party to the contract damages the other party by not fulfilling his contractual obligation. In this case the facts that are the condition for the civil sanction consist of two parts: the conclusion of the contract and a behavior that is contrary to the terms of the contract; or, expressed in more general terms: the performance of a legal transaction and a behavior that is opposed to the terms of the transaction.

A behavior may be considered as being opposed to the terms of a legal transaction because the subjective meaning of the act (or acts) that constitutes the legal transaction is a norm. The legal transaction is a norm-creating fact. In traditional legal terminology the term "legal transaction" is used to designate both the norm-creating act and the norm created by the act. The typical legal transaction is the contract. In a contract the parties agree that they ought to behave mutually in a certain way. This "ought"

---

[96] Cf. § 27a and § 28 f.

is the subjective meaning of the legal transaction. But it is also its
objective meaning. This means: the act is a norm-creating fact, if
and so far as the legal order bestows this quality upon the fact; and
the legal order does this by making the establishment of the fact of
the legal transaction, together with the behavior that is opposed to
the terms of the legal transaction, the condition for a civil sanction. The legal order, by instituting the legal transaction as a law-
creating fact, authorizes the individuals subject to the law to regulate their mutual relations within the framework of general legal
norms created by legislation or custom, by norms created by way
of legal transactions. These norms created by legal transactions,
which do not prescribe sanctions but a behavior whose opposite is
the condition for the sanction established by the general norms,
are not independent legal norms. They are legal norms only in
connection with the general sanction-establishing legal norms.
The civil court which decides a controversy resulting from a legal
transaction must determine not only the validity of the general
norm on which the legal transaction was based, but also the fact
that the legal transaction was performed, that a behavior is present
that is opposite to the terms of the legal transaction, and that the
damage thus caused has not been repaired; and must issue the
following individual norm on the basis of these determinations:
if the court-determined damage has not been repaired within
a prescribed period, a sanction ought to be executed, which is
prescribed by the general legal norm to be applied by the court.
The sanction prescribed in the general legal norm constitutes—as
the main obligation—the obligation to refrain from behaving in
opposition to the terms of the legal transaction and thus to refrain
from causing damage; and, in case this obligation is violated, constitutes—as a substitute obligation—the obligation to repair the
damage caused. The sanction may be avoided either by fulfillment of the obligation directly created by the legal transaction
or, in case of nonfulfillment of this obligation, by fulfillment
of the obligation to repair the damage. This obligation takes
the place of the main obligation. The same is true when the damage is not caused by a behavior opposite to the terms of a legal
transaction, but neither by a punishable behavior. But if the damage is caused by a behavior that is the condition of a punishment
—such as severe bodily harm—then this sanction cannot be avoided

by fulfillment of the obligation to compensate for the damage caused by the punishable delict; for then the civil sanction constituting this obligation is added to the criminal sanction constituting the obligation to refrain from committing the criminal delict. In relation to this obligation, the obligation to repair the damage is not a substitute obligation.

The legal transaction, like the delict of behaving in opposition to the terms of the legal transaction and the delict not to repair the thus-caused damage are the conditions for the civil sanction. The difference between the legal transaction and the delict is that the transaction creates, according to the legal order, the norm which is its meaning, whereas the delict is not a norm-creating fact instituted as such by the legal order. The coercive act of the civil sanction is not directed against the individual who has performed a legal transaction, but against the individual who, after he has performed a legal transaction, behaves in opposition to the terms of it or fails to compensate for the damage caused by this behavior.

The contract

Depending on the way in which a legal transaction is performed, that is to say, whether it is constituted by the act of one individual or the acts of two or more individuals, unilateral and bilateral (or multilateral) legal transactions are distinguished. By far the most important legal transaction of modern law is the bilateral (or multilateral) legal transaction of the contract.

In a contract two or more individuals declare their agreement, that is to say, they make concordant declarations of will directed toward their mutual behavior. The legal order may, but need not, prescribe a form which these declarations of will have to have to constitute a legally binding contract, that is, to create norms which impose obligations or confer rights upon the contracting individuals—for example, the law may prescribe that the declarations of will have to be made in writing, not merely orally or by gestures. At any rate, the individuals must express their will in some way, that is, make their will apparent. Otherwise it would be impossible to ascertain in a law-applying procedure, especially a judicial procedure, the fact that a contract was concluded.

Between the actual will of a party and his declaration may be a discrepancy, because the other contracting party or the law-applying organ may attribute to the declaration a meaning different from that which the party himself intended to express. The consequence of such a discrepancy cannot be determined by the science of law, but only by the legal order. The legal order may stipulate that a law-creating contract has not been concluded if one party is able to prove that the intended meaning of his declaration is different from that attributed to it by the other party. But the legal order may also stipulate that such a discrepancy is of no importance for the validity of the contractually created norm; that the discrepancy is legally irrelevant; that what matters is only the meaning which, according to the opinion of the law-applying organ, may normally be attributed to the declaration by the other party. The legal order may either place more weight upon the declaration than on the actual will or more weight upon the actual will than on the declaration. Which of these two solutions is preferable depends on the principles of legal policy which guide the legislator. The ideal of security in the course of business may lead to one solution, the ideal of individual freedom to another.

For a contract to be concluded, the declaration of one party is to be directed to the other, and must be accepted by that other party. The contract, therefore, consists, as it is said, of offer and acceptance. By the acceptance of the offer, a norm becomes legally valid that regulates the mutual behavior of the contracting parties. If this norm stipulates an obligation of the offering party, then the offer has the character of a promise. The differentiation between offer and acceptance presupposes that the two declarations do not occur simultaneously. The offer must precede the acceptance. The questions therefore arise: Does the offering party have to maintain the will expressed in the offer until the moment of acceptance, so that at the moment of acceptance both wills must agree and that, if this is not the case (because the offering party has meanwhile changed his mind and has expressed this change of will by retracting his offer) no contract has been concluded? or: Is, after the offer has been made, the change of will irrelevant, so that the offer cannot be retracted? and: If it cannot be retracted, how long is the offering party bound by his offer? These are questions that can be answered only according to the positive norms of the legal order.

If the order permits retraction of the offer before acceptance at any time, then the conclusion of a contract between individuals not present in the same place at the same time is made difficult. To remove this difficulty the legal order sometimes prescribes that the offering party is bound by his offer under certain circumstances and for a certain time. This means, that the contract is validly concluded if the offer is accepted within that time, even if the offering party changes his declared will. By accepting the offer a norm can be created which, in this case, obligates the offering party even against his will.

For a contract to be concluded concordant declarations of the will of the contracting parties must be present—declarations according to which the parties want the same thing. Thereby a norm is created whose content is determined by concordant declarations. The contract as a norm-creating fact, and the norm created by this fact, need to be clearly distinguished. In traditional terminology, however, the word "contract" is used to designate both. One speaks of the conclusion of a contract and means by this the acts which constitute the norm-creating set of facts. And one speaks of the validity of a contract and means by this the norm created by these facts; for only a norm—not an act—can be "valid." The temporal sphere of validity of a contractually created norm may be determined in its content; a contract may be concluded to be valid for a certain period of time. The norm may stipulate that the validity of the contract may be terminated at any time by a unilateral declaration of one of the parties. According to positive law this may be so also if the contract had been concluded with validity for an undetermined time. If the period of validity is determined in the contractually created norm itself, the period cannot be terminated by a unilateral declaration of one of the parties. Termination before the end of the stipulated time may then be brought about only by a norm created by both parties. In other words, the contract may be terminated only by another contract concluded by the same parties.

Ordinarily only obligations and rights of the contracting parties can be stipulated by a contractually created norm. This is the so-called principle of private autonomy. But a legal order may also permit contracts by which individuals who are not contracting parties are obligated or receive rights—so-called contracts to the debit or in favor of third persons. The contractually created norm may impose the same obligations and bestow the same rights upon the contracting parties. But it may also impose different obligations upon the different parties or it may impose an obligation on only one party and bestow only a right on the other. But this content must always be intended by all contracting parties. The contractually created norm has individual character, such as for example in a contract of sale by which one party is obligated to deliver only once to the other a certain object, and the other party is obligated only once to pay a certain sum of money.

The contract, however, may also have general character, that it, it may not obligate the parties to a single performance or performance-and-counterperformance, but to render an undetermined number of performances or performances-and-counterperformances; such as the contract in which an insurance company binds itself to compensate an individual in each case of sickness for the costs of medical treatment, and the insured individual binds himself to pay to the insurance company a certain amount of money every month.

Some international treaties contain a provision concerning accession to the treaty. Such a provision authorizes any state or some states to accede to the treaty. The accession may take place by a unilateral declaration or by a proposition which must be accepted by the parties to the treaty, by a majority of them, or by an organ instituted by the treaty. In the latter case the accession takes place by a new treaty; in the former case by a unilateral submission under the treaty. By accession to the treaty, the treaty becomes valid for the acceding party.

A special kind of contracts or treaties by which general norms are created are those which establish the statutes of an association (in national law) or the constitution of an international organization, like the League of Nations or the United Nations (in international law). Accession to an association or to an international organization means accession to the contract or treaty by which the association or international organization is constituted. If such accession is possible only with the consent of an organ of the association or international organization, then the accession is based on a contract between the association or international organization on the one hand and the acceding subject on the other hand. If the accession can be accomplished by a unilateral declaration of the acceding subject, then submission to a valid partial legal order takes place. By the act of accession the norms of the association's statute or the organization's constitution are put into force for the acceding subject; this means: they are created with validity for this subject.

Such accession of a private individual to an association, or of a state to an international organization, is a unilateral legal transaction, in contradistinction to a contract or treaty. Such a unilateral legal transaction is—in private law—also the publicly announced promise of a reward for a performance. In both cases a norm or norms are created by the act of a subject, through which the act-performing subject is obligated. Thus these unilateral legal transactions are distinguished from legislative acts, judicial decisions, and administrative decrees, all of which create norms that obligate other subjects than those who perform these acts.

i) Administration

Besides legislation and jurisdiction, traditional theory regards administration as one of the three essential functions of the state. Legislation and jurisdiction are legal functions in the narrower sense of the term, that is, functions by which the norms of the national legal order are created and applied—whereby the application of a legal norm consists in the creation of another norm or in the execution of the coercive act prescribed by the norm.[97] The individuals performing the functions are organs of the law. As such they are organs of the state, that is, their function is attributed to the "state" (the legal community constituted by the national legal order). That means that these functions are referred to the personification of the coercive order constituting this community.

This coercive order is a national legal, that is, a coercive order constituting a state because (1) it institutes for these legal functions organs working according to the principle of division of labor—organs directly or indirectly called to their functions, that is to say, relatively central organs; (2) this coercive order is limited in its territorial sphere of validity to a strictly defined area, the so-called territory of the state; and (3) it is pre-

---

[97] Cf. § 30c.

supposed to be the highest order, or an order inferior only to the international legal order. It is to be noted, however, that legal functions—the creation and application of norms of the national legal order—are performed not only by central organs, but also in decentralized procedures; thus the creation of general legal norms through custom and of individual and general legal norms through legal transactions. The individuals who perform these legal functions are organs of the law just like the legislative organs or the judges, and their function may be attributed to the state just as much as legislation and jurisdiction. Traditional terminology, however, is not in accord with this. Legal norms created by custom or legal transactions are not characterized as law created by the state, although these norms belong to the national (or state) legal order just as much as the norms created by legislation or jurisdiction. Traditional terminology has the tendency to designate as "state organs" only more or less central legal organs—the tendency to attribute only functions performed by such organs to the legal community, the state. It is characteristic in this respect that, as mentioned, the parliament is considered a state organ, but the electorate or the individual voter is not.[98]

The function called state administration is largely of the same type as legislation and jurisdiction, namely a legal function in the narrower sense of creation and application of legal norms. The function of the highest administrative organ, the government, consists in its participation—delegated to it by the constitution— in the legislation, in the exercise of its constitution-delegated authorization to conclude international treaties, in the issuance of ordinances and administrative commands directed at its subordinated administrative organs and subjects—that is, in the creation and application of general and individual norms. From the point of view of legal technique, there is no difference between an administrative statute that obligates the legal subjects to behave in a certain way by prescribing sanctions in matters of health, trade, or traffic, and a criminal or civil law. The administrative authorities subordinated to the government (especially the police organs), have to apply general legal norms prescribing sanctions and these functions differ from the jurisdiction of courts not in their content, but only in the nature of the functioning organ. The judge

---

[98] Cf. § 30c.

in his function is independent of a higher organ, that is, he is bound only by the general norms he is to apply; whereas the administrative organ in exercising his function has to observe the instructions of his superior organ. But this is not an absolute difference, since the highest administrative organs—for lack of higher ones—are just as independent as the judges. Apart from the independence of the judicial organs there is no difference between the function of a court which in case of theft imposes jail and in case of insult a fine, and the function of an administrative organ who in case of a violation of tax, sanitary, or traffic law orders the execution of analogous sanctions. Besides, the execution of a sanction even if ordered by a court, is an administrative act; and the executive organ is not a judicial, but an administrative organ.

A functional difference between judicial and administrative functions exists when the coercive act does not have the character of a sanction—when legal norms are applied which prescribe the forcible internment of patients, the forcible expropriation or destruction of property, and similar coercive acts, which do not represent themselves as reactions against an illegal behavior.[99]

Essentially different from the two mentioned types of state administrative activity, which constitute legal functions in the narrower sense, is that which does not consist in the creation or application, but in the observation of legal norms by specifically qualified individuals, called "state officials." This activity, called state administration, is of the same type as the economic or cultural activity of private individuals. Precisely like the latter, the state can build and operate railroads, construct schools and hospitals, sponsor education, and give medical care to the sick. These activities, as state administration, do not differ in their content from like activities performed by private individuals, but in that the individuals performing these activities are legally qualified as state officials. This means: these functions, when performed under certain conditions, namely by certain qualified individuals, are not attributed to the individuals, but to the state. The nature of this qualification will be discussed later.[100] At this point it needs to be stressed that this activity, interpreted as state administration, is the content

---

[99] Cf. § 6b, subsection "Coercive acts other than sanctions."
[100] Cf. pp. 296 f.

of specific official obligations. These official obligations are constituted by legal norms which attach so-called disciplinary penalties to the nonexercise or faulty exercise of official functions. According to the usual terminology, only the function performed in fulfillment of an official obligation is attributed to the state, not this official obligation; precisely as the disciplinary penalty to be imposed for nonfulfillment of this official obligation is not regarded as directed against the state. If the parliament, in the form of a statute, decides that a state ought to build and operate a railroad, and if this decision is interpreted to constitute an "obligation" of the state, then it is not the official obligation of the organs here concerned which is attributed to the state. These official obligations also exist if the state, according to the wording of the statute, is merely authorized to build and operate a railroad. If the terminology of "obligation of the state" is used here, this is not an obligation strictly in the legal sense of the word.[101] If the activity interpreted as state administration does not consist in the creation and application but in the observation of legal norms, that is, in the fulfillment of official obligations by state officials; if, in other words, not a law-creating or law-applying, but a law-obeying function is attributed to the "state," then, according to traditional language use, the behavior to be attributed to the state must not only be determined in the legal order that constitutes the community, but must also be the function of an individual qualified as a "state official." But it is to be noted that law-applying and law-creating functions may also be the specific official obligations of the individuals qualified as state officials. Not only administrative organs who perform jurisdictional functions but also independent judges may have the character of state officials; and the administrative activity of the state includes also the conducting of legal transactions that create legal norms, and the fulfillment of the obligations created by such legal transactions and the exercise of the rights created by them. This means: these functions, too, as the content of the legal obligations of officials (and hence as law-obeying functions) can be attributed to the state—they can be interpreted as acts of the state administration. Primarily they have the character of law-obeying functions because they are performed

---

[101] Cf. pp. 302 f.

in fulfillment of official obligations of official organs; and only secondarily do they have—if acts of legal transactions are concerned—the character of norm-creating functions.

The norms regulating the behavior of these individuals by imposing specific official obligations upon them and bestowing specific competences on them constitute, within the total legal order that regulates the behavior of all individuals within its territorial sphere of validity, a partial legal order that constitutes only the partial community of officials: the state as a bureaucratic machinery, headed by the government. This narrower concept of state must be distinguished from the wider concept that includes all individuals living on the state territory. The latter includes the former. The one is the personification of the total legal order regulating the behavior of all individuals living on the state territory; the other is the personification of a partial legal order regulating the functions of the officials. The attribution of these functions to the state means the relation to the unity of this partial legal order. But by relating these functions to the unity of the partial legal order, they are at the same time related to the unity of the total legal order that includes this partial order. The attribution to the state in the narrower sense implies the attribution to the state in the wider sense.

If it is regarded as a purpose of the national legal order—or of "the state," which is the same thing—to bring about lawful, obligation-fulfilling, sanction-avoiding behavior and to make legally possible a certain behavior by establishing rights and positive permissions—insofar as this behavior is not attributed to the state, is not interpreted as function of the state—then the purpose of the state is realized only indirectly through the state (or legal) function, which consists in prescription and execution of coercive acts. If, however—as in the case of the state administration which does not, or not primarily, have the character of creation or application but of observation of the law—the behavior of the official is attributed to the state, interpreted as a function of the state in the narrower sense, then the purpose of the state in the wider sense is directly realized by this function of the state in the narrower sense. Then we can distinguish an indirect state administration whose function is not different from jurisdiction but, like it, is law-creating and law-applying; and a direct state administration which is essentially

different from jurisdiction because it is a law-*obeying* function—
and if it is also a law-creating function, it has the character of a
legal transaction, not of jurisdiction.

It follows that, from the point of view of a structural analysis of
the law, two different functions are designated by the term "state
administration" and that the borderline between these functions
runs right through the area which in traditional theory is differentiated as state administration from the function designated as jur-
diction. This differentiation expresses not a difference of functions,
but the difference of two bodies of officials (administration and ju-
diciary). The coming into existence of these two bodies in the
modern state can be explained only historically, not justified from
the point of view of a juristic systematization.

j) Conflict between Norms of Different Levels

The "unlawful" judicial decision

Since the legal order represents a hierarchy of superordinated and
subordinated norms, and since a norm belongs to a certain legal
order only because and so far as it is in accord with the higher
norm that determines its creation, the problem arises of a possible
conflict between a higher and a lower norm. The question then
arises: What is the law, if a norm is not in conformity with the
norm that prescribes its creation and, especially, if it is not in conformity with the norm predetermining its content. Such a conflict
seems to be present if certain expressions usual in traditional science of law are taken literally; such expressions are "unlawful"
judicial decisions and "unconstitutional" statutes, which give the
impression that such a thing as "a norm contrary to a norm" in general and a "legal norm contrary to a legal norm" in particular
were possible. Indeed, the law itself seems to be taking into
account the possibility of a law contrary to law and takes various
precautions for the purpose of abolishing such "unlawful" law.
A "norm contrary to a norm," however, is a self-contradiction; a
legal norm which might be said to be in conflict with the norm that
determines its creation could not be regarded as a valid legal norm
—it would be null, which means it would not be a legal norm at
all. That which is null cannot be annulled. To annul a norm can-

not mean to annihilate the act whose meaning is the norm. Something that actually happened cannot be made to unhappen. To annul a norm means to deprive an act, whose subjective meaning is a norm, of the objective meaning of a norm; and this means: to terminate the validity of one norm by another norm. If a legal order authorizes the annulment of a norm it must first recognize this norm as an objectively valid, that is, lawful, legal norm, as the following analysis will demonstrate.

The question whether in a concrete case the facts are present to which a legal norm attaches a sanction must be connected with the question who is authorized to answer that first question. In the same way, the question whether a norm created by a legal organ conforms to the higher norm that determines its creation or content, cannot be separated from the question of who is authorized by the legal order to decide the first question. Both questions can only be decided by the organ authorized for the purpose by the legal order and in the procedure established by the legal order. To say that a judicial decision or an administrative decree is unlawful can only mean that the procedure in which the individual norm was created does not conform to the general norm determining this procedure or that its content does not conform to the general norm determining this content. To simplify matters, let us explore only the case in which it is questioned whether the individual norm of the judicial decision conforms to the general norm which determines the individual norm's content.

If the legal order were to permit everybody to decide this question, a judicial decision binding the parties would hardly come to pass. Hence, according to positive national law, this question can only be decided by the court itself or by a higher court. If the court decides a concrete case and asserts to have applied a general legal norm, then the question is positively decided and remains so decided unless and until the decision is rescinded by the decision of a higher court. For the decision of the first court—and this means the individual norm created by this decision—is not null according to positive law, even if it is regarded as "unlawful" by the court authorized to decide the question. The norm is merely annullable, that is, it can be invalidated by a procedure determined by the legal order. Only if the legal order provides such a procedure can the decision be contested by the parties, if they question the "lawfulness" of the decision. But if the procedure in

which a judicial decision may be contested is terminated; if there
is a court of last instance whose decision cannot be appealed; if a
decision has the force of a final judgment (*Rechtskraft*), then the
"lawfulness" of the decision can no longer be questioned. But
what does it mean: the legal order confers the force of final judgment to the decision of last instance? It means that: even if a
general norm, to be applied by the court, is valid, which predetermines the content of the individual norm to be created by the
court, an individual norm, created by the court of last instance, can
become valid whose content does not conform to this general norm.
That the legal order confers the force of a final judgment to a decision of a court of last instance means that not only is a general norm
valid that predetermines the content of the judicial decision, but
also a general norm according to which the court may itself determine the content of the individual norm to be created by the court.
The two norms form a unit: the court of last instance is authorized
to create either an individual legal norm whose content is predetermined by the general norm, *or* an individual norm whose content
is not so predetermined, but is to be determined by the court of
last instance itself. But also the fact that the decision of the court
of first instance and of any court except the one of last instance are
only annullable (that is, valid until annulled by a higher court)
means: these organs are authorized by the legal order to create either an individual norm whose content is predetermined by the
general norm *or* an individual norm whose content is not predetermined, but to be determined by the organs themselves; with the
difference that the validity of these norms is only provisional (that
is, may be rescinded), in contrast to individual norms created by
courts of last instance and having attained the force of final
judgment. *Their* validity is definitive. But both the provisional
validity of the one norm and the definitive validity of the other
rest on the legal order, which means: on a general norm that
exists before the individual norms come into existence. If the content of these individual legal norms is determined by the pre-
existing general legal norm, it is so in the sense of the alternative
mentioned here. As long as a judicial decision is valid it cannot be
"unlawful." Therefore there can be no conflict between the court-
created individual norm and the general norm to be applied by
the court—even in case of a decision of a court of first instance, a
decision that can be contested, that is "voidable." The objective

reason that it can be voided is not its "unlawfulness" (the fact that it does not conform to the general norm to be applied; if it did not conform it would be null, not merely annullable), but the possibility, provided by the legal order, to bring about, in a procedure established for this purpose, the definitive validity of the other alternative, the one not realized by the contested decision. If the court-created individual norm can be contested at all, it may be rescinded by the decision of a court of last instance not only if the court of first instance makes use of the alternative to determine provisionally itself the content of the norm it created, but also if the content of the individual norm created by the court of first instance conforms to the general norm that predetermines it. If a judicial decision may be contested at all, then it can be contested objectively in both cases by the parties and can be repealed by the higher court, even if the parties subjectively justify the appeal by the fact that the decision does not conform to the predetermining general norm. The parties can count on the fact that, if a decision of last instance attains the force of a final judgment, it is impossible to prevent that an individual norm becomes valid whose content is not predetermined by any general legal norm. They avail themselves of the possibility to contest a judicial decision only when the decision is prejudicial to their interests. It is irrelevant whether they consider the decision subjectively as being in conformity with or contrary to law—even if the law prescribes that a judicial decision may be contested only for the reason that it is "unlawful" in some respect, which means that it is considered by the parties as being contrary to law. For the question whether a decision is "contrary to law" is not to be decided by the parties, but by the court of appeals, and the decision of last instance attains the force of a final judgment in any case. If there were any sense in speaking of a judicial decision being "per se" lawful or unlawful, then one would have to grant that even a lawful decision may be rescinded by a decision having the force of a final judgment.

This shows that the possibility of predetermining by general norms the individual norms to be created by the courts is very limited. But this fact does not justify the mentioned view that no law exists at all before the judicial decision, that all law is judge-made law, that no general legal norms exist, but only individual legal norms.

The "unconstitutional" statute

The statement that a valid statute is "unconstitutional" is a self-contradiction; for a statute can be valid only on the basis of the constitution. If one has reason to assume that a statute is valid, the reason for its validity must be the constitution. Of an invalid statute one cannot say that it is unconstitutional, for an invalid statute is no statute at all; it is legally nonexistent, and no legal statement can therefore be made about it. If the assertion, usually made by traditional theory, that a statute is unconstitutional, were to have a possible juristic meaning, it cannot be taken literally. The meaning of the assertion can only be that the statute in question can be repealed not only in the ordinary procedure according to the constitution, namely according to the rule *lex posterior derogat priori,* but also according to a special procedure provided for by the constitution. But until it is rescinded it must be considered as being valid; and as long as it is valid it cannot be unconstitutional.

Since the constitution regulates the organs and the procedure of legislation and sometimes also determines to some degree the content of future statutes, the legislator must take into consideration the possibility that the norms of the constitution (as it is expressed in the usual way) are not always and not entirely observed—that an act subjectively claims to have created a statute although the procedure in which this act was brought about or the content of the statute created by the act do not conform to the constitution. This raises the question whom the constitution should authorize to decide whether in a concrete case the norms of the constitution were observed; whether a text, whose subjective meaning is to be a statute according to the constitution, should be considered to be one also in its objective meaning.

If the constitution were to authorize everybody to decide this question, a statute binding the subjects and organs of the law would hardly ever see the light of day. In order to avoid such a situation, the constitution has to authorize one specific legal organ to decide this question. If only one central legislative organ exists, the decision of this legal question by a higher legislative organ is excluded. Only the existing legislative organ itself, or a different organ—such as the court which has to apply the statute, or a special court—can be authorized to decide the question of the constitutionality of a statute. If the constitution contains no provision concerning the question who is authorized to examine the constitutionality of statutes, then the organs competent to apply statutes, that is, especially, the courts, have the power to perform this examination. Since they are authorized to apply the statutes, they have to determine whether something whose subjective meaning is to be a statute has objectively this meaning; and it does have the objective meaning only if it conforms to the constitution.

But the constitution may authorize organs to apply statutes and expressly exclude from this authorization the examination of the constitutionality of the statutes to be applied. Constitutions sometimes contain the stipulation that courts and administrative authorities are not to examine the constitutionality of the statutes they are to apply. This restriction, however, is possible only to a certain degree. The law-applying organs cannot reasonably be authorized to apply as a statute everything that presents itself subjectively as such. A minimum of power to examine the constitutionality of the statutes to be applied must be granted to them. Where statutes, to be binding, must according to the constitution be published in an official gazette by the government, the limitation of the power to examine means only that the law-applying organ, especially the courts, merely have to check whether that which has the subjective meaning of a statute is published in the gazette. The law-applying organs are not authorized to examine whether that which is published as "statute" was created by the constitutional organ, in the constitutionally prescribed procedure, and with the constitutionally determined content. To verify these points, the government organ, not identical with the legislative organ, entrusted by the constitution with the publication of statutes, may be authorized. This authorization, too, can be limited only to a certain extent. The government organ authorized to publish the statute or—if official publication is not required—the organ authorized to apply statutes, must be entitled to examine at least whether that which presents itself subjectively as a statute was even decided upon by the organs authorized by the constitution to legislate, even though the organ entitled to such limited verification is not authorized to examine whether the procedure in which

THE DYNAMIC ASPECT OF LAW

that which presents itself as statute was decided upon or the content of this decision was constitutional. The organ cannot be obliged to publish as statute or to apply as statute everything that presents itself subjectively as statute. Then only the legislative organ itself is authorized to decide whether the statute passed by it is constitutional; then the positive decision of this question is implied in the legislative act. This means that everything which the legislative organ issues as a statute has to be considered as statute within the meaning of the constitution; and that the norms which are the subjective meaning of a legislative act have the objective meaning of legal norms even if the statute—according to somebody else's view—is not in conformity with the norms of the constitution regulating the legislative procedure and the contents of statutes. The legislative organ is then in a situation analogous to that of a court of last instance whose decision has attained the force of a final judgment. The meaning of the constitution regulating legislation is not that valid statutes may come into being only in the way directly stipulated by the constitution, but also in a way determined by the legislative organ itself.

The provisions of the constitution which regulate legislation have an alternative character. The constitution includes a direct and an indirect regulation of legislation; and the legislative organ has to choose between them. The author of the constitution and the legislator may not be aware, or not fully aware, of this situation. But an objective description of the legal situation created consciously or unconsciously by a constitution that does not confer the examination of the constitutionality of statutes upon an organ different from the legislator must come to this conclusion.

The legal situation is entirely changed if the constitution confers upon an organ different from the legislative organ the power to examine the constitutionality of statutes and authorizes this organ to repeal a statute considered as "unconstitutional." This function may be conferred upon a special court or upon the supreme court or upon all courts. If every court is authorized to examine the constitutionality of a statute to be applied by this court in a concrete case, then the court, if it considers the law "unconstitutional," is usually only authorized to refuse the application of this statute in the concrete case, that is, to suspend its validity for the concrete case; but the statute remains valid for all other cases to which it refers, and has to be applied by all courts in these cases unless they, in turn, refuse application. If the examination of the constitutionality of statutes is reserved for one special court, this court may be authorized not only to suspend the statute's validity for a concrete case, but to rescind the statute altogether. Until then, however, the statute is valid and has to be applied by all law-applying organs. Such a law may be valid and applied for many years before it is rescinded by the competent court as "unconstitutional." But this means that the provisions of the constitution concerning the repeal of statutes that do not conform to the norms of the constitution directly regulating legislation have this meaning: even statutes that do not conform to these norms ought to be considered as valid until and to the extent that they are not rescinded in the manner prescribed by the constitution. The so-called unconstitutional statutes are constitutional statutes which, however, may be rescinded in a special procedure. In these cases too, provisions of the constitution regulating legislation have the mentioned alternative character. The legislative organ has the choice between two paths: the one prescribed explicitly by the constitution and the one to be decided by the legislative organ itself. The difference, however, consists in that the statutes created by the latter method may be repealed in special procedure, even though they are, until then, valid.

This shows that the constitution, while being unable to exclude the second path, prefers the first. This preference may also be expressed by the provision that certain persons who according to the constitution participate (beside the parliament) in the legislative procedure, such as the head of state who promulgates the statutes or the minister who countersigns the acts of the former, may be punished by a special court for their part in bringing about a so-called unconstitutional statute. This procedure may, but need not, be connected with a procedure aimed at the repeal of the statute.

The personal responsibility of an organ for the legality of a norm he created comes less in question in the relation between constitution and statute than in the relation between constitution and ordinance, and between statute and ordinance. The constitution may authorize administrative organs, especially the government, to issue under certain circumstances general legal norms in the form of ordinances, which do not execute already existing statutes but regulate certain matters *in lieu* of statutes. If the government issues such an ordinance under circumstances other than those prescribed by the constitution, the members of the government who issued the ordinance may be called to account and punished. This procedure may, but need not, be connected with a procedure aiming at the repeal of the ordinance. Similarly, administrative organs authorized to issue ordinances on the basis of statutes may be accountable for the issuance of unlawful ordinances, without this "unlawful" ordinance necessarily being repealed. If the ordinance is valid until it is rescinded, or if it cannot be rescinded at all, this means that the administrative organ is authorized to issue it; that the author of the constitution or the legislator prefers, however, to have ordinances issued which conform to the explicit provisions of the constitution or keep within the statutes.

In all these cases, an act by which valid legal norms are created, since it is the condition of a sanction, has the character of a delict. These cases show that the principle *ex injuria jus non oritur,* regarded by traditional theory as universally valid, has exceptions.

According to the foregoing remarks, then, the examination of the constitutionality of statutes by the organs authorized to publish or apply them, can be restricted only in some degree but not entirely excluded; these organs have to decide at least the question whether that which presents itself subjectively as a statute has been enacted by the organ authorized by the constitution. If this question is decided negatively by the organ—for example for the reason that that which claims to be a valid statute was issued not by the constitutionally authorized parliament but by a usurper— the organ authorized to examine the constitutionality of that which presents itself as statute will refuse the publication or application. If this is not done, and if, therefore, the general norms issued by the usurper become effective, then we are faced by a revolutionary change of the constitution and therefore by a constitutional statute because it conforms to the new constitution.

In the same way that the publication or application of that which presents itself subjectively as a statute can be denied by the competent organ, so also that which subjectively presents itself as a decision of the court of last instance may be rejected by the organ authorized to execute court decisions, for the reason that, according to the opinion of that organ, the decision was not rendered by individuals who, according to the constitution, form the Supreme Court, but by individuals who have usurped this position. If nevertheless their decisions are executed and thereby become effective, then no revolutionary total change of the constitution has taken place, as in the previous situation, but only a revolutionary partial change; hence a constitutional judicial decision is valid.

The question of the legality of a judicial decision or the constitutionality of a statute, generally formulated, is the question whether an act that claims to be creating a legal norm conforms to the higher norm which regulates its creation or content. If the question is to be decided by an organ authorized for this purpose then the question may arise whether the individual who rendered the decision is in fact the competent organ, that is, the organ authorized for this purpose by a valid legal norm. This question may again be decided by another organ who for this reason is to be regarded as a higher organ. This regression to higher organs, however, must stop somewhere. There must be highest organs whose authority may no longer be examined by still higher organs; whose character as highest legislative, administrative, or judicial organs may no longer be questioned. They prove to be highest organs by the fact that the norms issued by them are by and large effective. For then the norm that authorizes them to issue these norms is presupposed as valid constitution. The principle that a norm may be created only by the competent organ is the principle of legitimacy. It is limited by the principle of effectiveness.

It follows from this analysis that no conflict is possible between statute and judicial decision, constitution and statute, constitution and ordinance, statute and ordinance, or, formulated generally: no conflict is possible between a higher and lower norm of a legal order, which would destroy the unity of this system of norms by making it impossible to describe it in noncontradictory rules of law.

k) Nullity and Annullability

It follows from what has been said that "nullity" cannot exist in a legal order—that a legal norm belonging to a legal order cannot be null, but only "annullable." But the annullability provided for by the legal order may have different degrees. As a rule, a legal norm is annulled (i.e., repealed) only with effect to the future, so that the legal effects brought about by it are left undisturbed. But, exceptionally, it can also be annulled retroactively, so that all legal effects brought about by it are annulled; such as, for example, the annulment (repeal) of a penal statute with simultaneous annulling of all judicial decisions based on it, or of a civil statute with simultaneous annulling of all legal transactions and civil-court decisions based on *it*. But until its annulment the statute was valid; it was not null from the beginning. It is therefore incorrect if the decision annulling the statute is designated "declaration of nullity" (German: *Nichtigkeitserklärung*) and if the organ who annuls the statute declares in his decision that the statute was null "from the beginning." His decision has a constitutive, not a merely declarative, character. The meaning of an act by which a norm is annulled, like the meaning of an act by which a norm is created, is a norm. The legal order may authorize one specific organ to annul a norm created by another organ, or it may authorize everybody to decide whether something that claims to be a legal norm objectively has this meaning and is therefore binding. If the decision is decentralized in such a manner—for example, if the legal order, as in general international law, does not institute organs working according to the principle of division of labor for the creation and application of the legal norms—this decision may differ if rendered by different individuals: one individual may declare a norm to be valid, another to be null. The decision, however, so far as the validity of a legal norm is in question at all, has a constitutive character. The norm in question is not null from the beginning. The decision that it is "null" annuls it retroactively for the deciding subject. Even within a relatively centralized, national legal order it cannot be excluded that an individual considers as "null" something that presents itself subjectively as legal norm. But this individual may do this only at his own risk, namely the risk that that which he considers null is declared to be a valid legal norm by the competent organ, and that, consequently, the execution of the sanction prescribed in this legal norm will be ordered.

It is undeniable that there are cases in which something, especially a command that claims to be a legal norm, need not be so regarded by anybody without the legal order authorizing everybody to maintain such a position, that is, without, in fact, an act of nullification rendered by a special organ being necessary—for example, if a patient in an insane asylum issues a "statute." If we assume that in these cases nullity exists *a priori*, then such nullity falls outside the sphere of law. Nor is it possible to determine such cases legally. The legal order cannot ascertain the conditions under which something that claims to be a legal norm is to be considered *a priori* as null and not as being a norm which needs to be annulled by a procedure prescribed by the legal order. When, for example, the legal order stipulates that a norm is to be considered as *a priori* null (and therefore does not require a nullifying act) if the norm was not created by the competent organ, or if it is created by an individual who does not even have the quality of an organ, or if the norm has a content excluded by the constitution, then the legal order would have to prescribe who has to establish the existence of these conditions of nullity; and since this establishment has constitutive character (since the nullity of the norm in question is the result of this establishment and cannot legally be asserted before the establishment), this establishment means the retroactive nullification of a norm to be regarded as valid until then, even if the establishment is formulated as a "declaration of nullity." In this respect the law is like King Midas: just as everything he touched turned to gold, so everything to which the law refers assumes legal character. Within the legal order, nullity is only the highest degree of annullability.

VI

LAW AND STATE

36. CREATION OF LAW
AND FORM OF GOVERNMENT

The doctrine of the hierarchy of the legal order comprehends the law in motion, in its perpetually renewed process of self-regeneration. It is a dynamic theory of law as opposed to a static theory which attempts to comprehend the law without consideration of its creation, only as created order—its validity, sphere of validity, and so on. In the center of the problems of a dynamics of law is the question of the different methods of law creation. If those legal norms are considered that constitute the main part of a legal order, namely those that attach a sanction to a certain human behavior, and if it is recognized that an individual is obligated to a certain behavior by the fact that the opposite behavior is made the condition of a sanction, then it is possible to distinguish two types of legal norms establishing legal obligations: those in whose creation the individual to be obligated participates, and those in which he does not participate. The principle underlying this distinction is the principle of freedom in the sense of self-determination. From the point of view of the individual subjected to norms, the decisive question is whether the obligation is established with his consent, or without, or even against his consent. This is the difference usually described as the difference between autonomy and heteronomy, two principles which the legal theory considers as essential within the sphere of constitutional law. Here the difference appears as the distinction between democracy and autocracy or between republic and monarchy; and here it leads to the usual classification of the forms of government. But that which is comprehended as form of government is only a special method of the creation of law. The form of government is merely the method of creating law at the highest level of the legal order, namely at the level of the constitution. The concept of the "form of government" characterizes the method of creating of general legal norms as regulated by the constitution. If we understand as the form of government (German: *Staatsform*) only the constitution as the determination of the method of legislation, that is, the creation of general legal norms, and if we, thus, identify the state with the constitution as the determination of the method of creating general legal norms, then we merely follow the usual way to comprehend law. It is usual to see in law simply a system of general norms without realizing that the individualization of the general norms, the progression from the general to the individual norm, also must fall within the framework of the legal order. The identification of the form of government with the constitution corresponds exactly to the prejudice of identifying law with general norms. The problem of the form of government as the question of the method of law creation arises, however, not only at the level of the constitution, hence not only for legislation as the creation of *general* legal norms, but at all levels of law creation and especially for the various cases of creating *individual* norms: acts of administration, judicial decisions, and legal transactions.

37. PUBLIC AND PRIVATE LAW

As an especially characteristic example let us discuss the distinction between public and private law, which is so basic for the systematization of law by modern legal science. Until this day it has not been possible to achieve an entirely satisfactory definition of the difference. According to the majority view we are confronted here with a classification of legal relationships: private law represents a relationship between coordinated, legally equal-ranking subjects; public law, a relationship between a super- and a subordinated subject, that is, between two subjects of whom one has a higher legal value as compared with that of the other. The typical public-law relationship is that between state (or government) and subject (in German, characteristically, *Untertan*). Private-law relationships are called simply "legal relationships" in the narrower sense of the term, to juxtapose to them the public-law relationships as "power relationships" or relationships of "dominion." In general, the differentiation between private and public law tends to assume the meaning of a difference between law and a nonlegal, or at least a half legal, power, and, particularly, between law and state. A closer analysis of the higher value attributed to certain subjects, of their superordination over others, discloses that we are confronted here with a differentiation between law-creating facts. And the decisive difference is the same as that which is the basis for the classification of forms of government. The legal plus-value assigned to the state— that is, to its organs in relation to the subjects—consists in that the legal order concedes to individuals qualified as officials (or at least to some of them) the power to obligate the subjects by a unilateral expression of their will (commands). A typical example of a public-law relationship is the one established by an administrative order, that is, an individual norm issued by an administrative organ obligating legally the addressee to behave in conformity with the order. A typical example of a private-law relationship is the one established by a legal transaction, especially the contract (that is, the individual norm created by the contract), by which the contracting parties are legally obligated to a mutual behavior. Whereas here the subjects participate in the creation of the norm that obligates them—this is, indeed the essence of contractual law creation—the subject obligated by the administrative order under public law has no part in the creation of the norm that obligates him. It is the typical case of an autocratic norm creation, whereas the private-law contract represents a typically democratic method of law-making. Therefore the sphere of legal transactions is characterized as the sphere of private autonomy.

38. The Ideological Character of the Dualism of Public and Private Law

If the decisive difference between private and public law is comprehended as the difference between two methods of creating law; if the so-called public acts of the state are recognized as legal acts just as the private legal transaction; if, most of all, it is understood that the acts constituting the law-creating facts are in

both cases only the continuations of the process of the creation of
the so-called will of the state, and that in the administrative order
just as much as in the private legal transaction only the individualization of general norms are effected—then it will not seem so
paradoxical that the Pure Theory of Law, from its universalistic
viewpoint, always directed toward the whole of the legal order
(the so-called will of the state), sees in the private legal transaction just as much as in an administrative order an act of the state,
that is, a fact of law-making attributable to the unity of the legal
order. By doing so, the Pure Theory of Law "relativizes" the contrast between private and public law "absolutized" by the traditional science of law, changes it from an extra-systematic difference, that is, a difference between law and nonlaw or between law
and state, to an intra-systematic one. The Pure Theory proves to
be a true science by dissolving the ideology connected with the absolutizing of the difference in question. For if the contrast between public and private law is presented as the absolute contrast
of power and law or at least of state power and law, then the idea is
conveyed that in public law, especially in the politically important constitutional and administrative law, the principle of law is
not valid in the same sense and with the same intensity as in private law, which is regarded as the "true" sphere of law as it were.
According to this ideology law in the strict sense of the word does
not prevail in so-called public law—as it prevails in private law—
but rather the interest of the state, the public welfare which under
all circumstances must be realized; consequently the relationship
between general norm and executive organ in public law is different from that in private law: not (as in private law) strict application of statutes to concrete cases, but the unfettered realization of
the state's purposes merely within the framework of the law and,
in an emergency (in case of what is called in German political theory *Staatnotrecht*) even against the law. But a critical analysis reveals that this whole differentiation has no basis in positive law,
inasmuch as it means more than referring to the fact that the activities of the legislative, governmental, and administrative organs
are, as a rule, less restricted by general legal norms than the activities of the courts; that the courts usually are allowed less discretion
in positive law than those organs. Furthermore, the theory insist-
ing on an essential difference between public and private law is

trapped in the contradiction by characterizing as "legal principle" the freedom *from* law, which this theory claims for the sphere of public "law" as the life sphere of the state, by presenting this principle as the specific quality of public law. At best, therefore, the theory could speak of two technically different spheres of law, but not of an absolute difference between the essence of state and law. The logically entirely untenable dualism has no theoretical, but only an ideological character. Developed by constitutional doctrine, it is designed to secure for the government and its administrative machinery a freedom deduced, as it were, from the nature of public affairs; a freedom not from law, which—from the point of view of a legal theory—is impossible; but from statutes, from the general legal norms created by the parliament as the representation of the people, and not only in the sense that a far-reaching legal restriction of the power of governmental and administrative organs is asserted to be incompatible with the essence of their functions, but also in the sense that, where such restriction exists it may be ignored when necessary. And this tendency, as an effect of the habitual antagonism between government and parliament, can be observed not only in constitutional monarchies but also in democratic republics.

On the other hand, the "absolutizing" of the contrast between public and private law also creates the idea that the political dominion is restricted to public law, that is, primarily to constitutional and administrative law, but entirely excluded from private law. It has been shown earlier that this difference between the "political" and the "private" within the sphere of rights (law in a subjective sense) does not exist, that the private rights are political rights in the same sense as those rights which alone are so described; for both allow, even though in different ways, participation in the formation of the so-called will of the state, that is, in political dominion. The differentiation in principle between a public (or political) and a private (or unpolitical) legal sphere is designed to prevent the recognition that the "private" right created by the legal transaction of a contract is just as much the theater of the political dominion as the public law created by legislation and administration. But the so-called private law, the complex of norms whose core is the legal institution of individual property, is (from the point of view of the function that this part

of the legal order occupies within the total legal order) a method
of creating individual norms, characteristic of the capitalistic system. This method of norm creation conforms with the principle of
self-determination and, in this sense, has a democratic character.
But the creation of general legal norms within a capitalistic system
may have just as much autocratic as democratic character. The
most important capitalistic states of our time have democratic constitutions, but the institution of private property and the creation
of individual legal norms according to the principle of self-determination are also possible in absolute monarchies and have, in fact,
existed in them. Within the legal order of a socialistic economic
system, so far as it admits only of collective property, the creation
of individual legal norms may have an autocratic character insofar
as the private-law contract is replaced by the public-law administrative act. But this system too is just as much compatible with a
democratic as with an autocratic creation of general legal norms—
compatible, that is, with either a democratic or an autocratic constitution.[102]

The lacking insight in the hierarchy of law prevented the cognition that different law-making methods may be applied upon the
different levels of the same legal order; and that a democratic creation of general legal norms may be combined with an autocratic
creation of individual legal norms and vice versa.[103]

39. The Traditional Dualism
of State and Law

The contrast assumed by traditional legal theory between public and private law clearly displays the fundamental dualism
that dominates modern legal science and thereby our entire social
thinking: the dualism between state and law. If traditional theory
of law and state opposes the state to the law as an entity different
from the law, and at the same time asserts that the state is a legal
being, they accomplish this by comprehending the state as a subject of obligations and rights, that is, as a legal person, and at the

---

[102] Cf. Hans Kelsen, "Foundations of Democracy," *Ethics*, LXVI: 1 (1955), Part II,
pp. 1–101.
[103] Cf. Hans Kelsen, *Allgemeine Staatslehre* (1925), pp. 361 ff. and *General Theory
of Law and State* (1945), pp. 283 ff.

same time attributing to it an existence independent of the legal order.

Private-law theory originally assumed that the legal personality of the individual logically and temporally precedes the legal order; in the same way the public-law theory assumes that the state, as a collective unit and subject of willing and acting, exists independent of, and even preceding, the law. According to this theory the state fulfills its historic mission by creating the law, "its" law, the legal order, and submits itself to it afterward, which means the state imposes obligations and confers rights upon itself by means of its own law. Thus, the state, as a meta-legal being, as a kind of powerful macro-anthropos or social organism, *is presupposed by the law*—and at the same time, as a subject of the law, i.e., as subjected to it, obligated and authorized by it, *presupposes the law*. This is the doctrine of the two sides and self-obligation of the state which manages to maintain itself with unequaled tenacity despite the manifest contradictions which it implies.

40. THE IDEOLOGICAL FUNCTION OF THE DUALISM OF STATE AND LAW

Traditional theory of state and law cannot abandon this doctrine and the dualism of state and law manifested by it. For it renders an ideological service of extraordinary importance that cannot be overestimated. The state must be represented as a personal being different from the law, in order that the law can justify that state, which creates and submits itself to that law. And the law can justify the state only, if it is presupposed as an order essentially different from the state, opposed to the state's original nature, namely power, and thereby as order in some sense "right" or "just." In this way the state is transformed from a bare fact of power to a legal institution justifying itself as a community governed by law (*Rechsstaat*). To the same degree that a religious-metaphysical justification of the state becomes ineffectual, this doctrine of the state as a community governed by law must become the only possible justification of the state. This "theory" is not discredited by the contradiction that it makes the state as a juristic person the object of legal cognition, and at the same time

stresses with greatest emphasis that the state—as power and therefore different in essence from law—cannot be comprehended juridically. Indeed, contradictions, inherent in ideological theories,
are never a serious embarrassment to them. For ideologies are not
aimed at deepening cognition, but at determining the will. The
aim of the dualistic "theory" is not so much to understand the essence of the state, but to strengthen the state's authority.

41. The Identity of State and Law

a) The State as a Legal Order

A cognition of the state free of ideology, and hence of metaphysics and mysticism, can grasp its essence only by comprehending this social structure as an order of human behavior. It is usual
to characterize the state as a political organization. But this merely
expresses the idea that the state is a coercive order. For the specifically "political" element of this organization consists in the coercion exercised by man against man, regulated by this order—in the
coercive acts prescribed by this order. These are precisely the coercive acts which the legal order attaches to certain conditions stipulated by it. As a political organization, the state is a legal order.
But not every legal order is a state. Neither the pre-state legal
order of primitive society, nor the super- (or inter-) state international legal order represent a state. To be a state, the legal order
must have the character of an organization in the narrower and
specific sense of this word, that is, it must establish organs who, in
the manner of division of labor, create and apply the norms that
constitute the legal order; it must display a certain degree of centralization. The state is a relatively centralized legal order.

This centralization distinguishes the state as a legal order from
the primitive pre-state order and the super-state order of general
international law. In neither order are the general legal norms
created by a central legislative organ but by way of custom, which
means that the creation of general legal norms is decentralized.
Neither the pre-state nor the super-state legal order establishes
courts authorized to apply the general norms to concrete cases, but
authorizes the individuals subjected to the legal order themselves
to render this function and, particularly, to execute, by way of self-
help, the sanctions prescribed by the legal order. According to

primitive law, it is the members of the murdered man's family who take blood revenge against the murderer and his family, which means, they are authorized to carry out the primitive punishment; it is the creditor himself who can satisfy his claim against the debtor by taking some property of the debtor and holding it in pawn. It is the government of the individual state which, according to general international law, is authorized to resort to war or take reprisals against a law-violating state, which means: against the subjects of the state whose government has violated the law. True, the individuals who in the pre-state and in the super-state community create (by custom) or apply the law and execute the sanctions, are legal organs and thus organs of the legal community; but they are not functioning in the manner of division of labor and therefore not centralized organs like a government, a legislature, and courts under a national legal order. The legal order of primitive society and the general inter-national law order are entirely decentralized coercive orders and therefore not states.

If the state is comprehended as a social community, it can be constituted only by a normative order.[104] Since a community can be constituted by only *one* such order (and is, indeed, identical with this order), the normative order constituting the state can only be the relatively centralized coercive order which is the national legal order.

In traditional theory the state is composed of three elements, the people of the state, the territory of the state, and the so-called power of the state, exercised by an independent government. All three elements can be determined only juridically, that is, they can be comprehended only as the validity and the spheres of validity of a legal order.

The state's population is the human beings who belong to the state. If it is asked why an individual together with other individuals does belong to a certain state, no other criterion can be found than that he and the others are subject to a certain, relatively centralized, coercive order. All attempts to find another bond that holds together and unites in one unit individuals differing in language, race, religion, world concept, and separated by conflicts of interests, is doomed to failure. It is particularly impossible to demonstrate the existence of some sort of psychic interaction which,

---

[104] Cf. pp. 85 f. and 150.

independent of any legal bond, unites all individuals belonging to a state in such a way that they can be distinguished from other individuals, belonging to another state, and united by an analogous interaction as two separate groups. It is undeniable that no such interaction exists uniting all individuals belonging to one state, and only them; and it is undeniable that individuals belonging to different states may be connected spiritually much closer than those belonging to the same state. For they belong to this state only legally. They certainly may have a psychic relation to their state, as the saying goes; they may love it, even deify it, and be prepared to die for it. But they belong to it even if they do not feel that way, if they hate it, even betray it, or are indifferent to it. The question whether an individual belongs to a state is not a psychological but a legal question. The unity of individuals constituting a state's population can only be seen in the fact that the same legal order is valid for these individuals, that their behavior is regulated by the same legal order. The state population is the personal sphere of validity of the national legal order.

The state territory is a certain delimited space. It is not a delimited piece of the earth's surface, but a three-dimensional space which includes the space below the ground and the space above the territory enclosed by the so-called frontiers of the state. It is obvious that the unity of this space is not a natural, geographic one. The same state territory may include areas separated by the ocean, which is not the territory of *one* state, or by the territory of another state. No natural science, but only legal cognition can answer the question what criteria determine the frontiers of the space which is that of one state territory, what constitutes its unity. The so-called state territory can only be defined as the spatial sphere of validity of a national legal order.[105]

A special case within the question of the spatial sphere of validity of the norms constituting the national legal order is the nature of those legal entities that result from a territorial division of the state. This is the problem of centralization and decentralization.[106] From this point of view we may comprehend administrative decentralization, self-governing bodies, provinces, state

---

[105] Cf. Hans Kelsen, *Der soziologische und der juristische Staatsbegriff*, 2d ed. (Tübingen, 1928).
[106] Cf. § 41d.

fragments, and so on, but particularly also the union of states, con-
federacies of states, and federal states. Besides, the traditional theory of state overlooks the fact that the state has not only spatial but
also temporal existence, that time must be considered as an element of the state just as much as space, that the existence of the
state is limited in time as much as in space since states can come
into existence and pass away. And just as the existence of the state
in space is the spatial sphere of validity, so the state's existence in
time is the temporal sphere of validity of the national legal order.
And just as the question of the territorial borders of the state, so
the question of its temporal borders, that is, the question when a
state begins and when it ceases to exist, is a legal question and not
a question that can be answered by a cognition directed toward
natural reality. As we shall see, it is general international law
which determines the spatial and temporal sphere of validity of
the national legal orders, delimits them against each other, and
thus makes it legally possible that states exist beside each other in
space and follow each other in time.

It is almost self-evident that the so-called state power which is
exercised by a government over a state's population within a state
territory is not simply the power which some individual actually
has over another individual consisting in the former's ability to induce the latter to behave as the first one desires. Many such actual
power relationships exist without the one who has such power
over another being regarded as an organ of the state. The relationship designated as state power is distinguished from other power
relationships by the fact that it is legally regulated, which means
that the individuals who exercise this power in their capacity as
members of a state government are authorized by a legal order to
exercise this power by creating and applying legal norms—that the
state power has normative character. The so-called state power is
the validity of an effective national legal order. That the government exerting the state power must be independent means that it
must not be bound by any other national legal order; that the national legal order is inferior, if to any other legal order at all, only
to the international legal order.

In the exercise of the state's power one usually sees the manifestation of a power which one considers as such an essential attribute
of the state that one speaks of states as of "powers," even if they are

not so-called "great powers." The "power" of a state can show itself only in the specific means of power which are at the disposal of
a government; in the fortresses and prisons, the guns and gallows,
the individuals uniformed as policemen and soldiers. But these
fortresses and prisons, these guns and gallows, are dead objects;
they become tools of state power only so far as they are used by a
state government or by individuals according to orders directed to
them by the government, only so far as the policemen and soldiers
obey the norms that regulate their behavior. The power of the
state is no mystical force concealed behind the state or its law; it is
only the effectiveness of the national legal order.

Thereby the state whose essential elements are population, territory, and power is defined as a relatively centralized legal order,
limited in its spatial and temporal sphere of validity, sovereign or
subordinated only to international law, and by and large effective.

b) The State as a Juristic Person

The problem of the state as a juristic person, that is, as an acting
subject and as the subject of obligations and rights, is essentially
the same problem as that of the corporation as a juristic person.
The state too is a corporation, that is, a community constituted by
a normative order which institutes organs directly or indirectly
called upon to perform their functions, according to the principle
of division of labor. The order constituting this community is the
legal order, designated as national legal order in contradistinction
to the international legal order. Just as the corporation constituted
by a statute is subject to the national legal order which imposes
obligations and confers rights upon it as a juristic person, so the
state may be considered as being subject to the international legal
order which imposes obligations and confers right upon the state
as a juristic person. And thus external and internal obligations
and rights may be distinguished with respect to the state as a corporation subject to international law just as with respect to a corporation subject to the national legal order: external obligations
and rights of the state are stipulated by the international, internal
ones by the national legal order. In the following section we will
discuss, first, only the problem of the state as a juristic person re-

gardless of international law which imposes obligations and confers rights upon the state.

The state as an acting subject; the organ of the state

If the state is presented as an acting subject, if it is said that the state has done this or that, the question arises which is the criterion according to which certain acts performed by certain individuals are attributed to the state, are qualified as acts or functions of the state, or, what amounts to the same, why certain individuals in performing certain acts are considered to be organs of the state. The answer to this question is the same as the one given earlier to the analagous question concerning the juristic person of the corporation subject to the national legal order. The attribution of the behavior of an individual to the state only expresses that this behavior is determined by the national legal order as a condition or consequence. Since the problem of the state as an acting person—particularly as a person fulfilling legal obligations and exercising legal rights—is a problem of attribution, it is necessary to know the nature of this mental operation in order to comprehend the meaning of the problem.

The question whether a certain behavior, particularly whether a certain act, a certain function is an act or function of the state, that is, whether it is the state as a person that performs an act or exercises a function, is not a question directed toward the existence of a fact like the question whether a certain human being has performed a certain action. If the question did have this meaning, it could never be answered affirmatively. For in fact it is never the state but always a certain individual who is acting. Only if the state as an acting person is represented as a real being, as a reality different from a human being, as a kind of superman, that is, if the auxiliary construction of a person is hypostatized, can the question whether a state function is present have the meaning of a question directed toward the existence of a fact—only then can the answer to the question be that a certain act or a certain function *is* or *is not* a state act or state function. In this sense, for example, the question has been discussed in the literature of constitutional law whether legislation is a function of the state and has sometimes been answered affirmatively and sometimes negatively. But since the state as an acting person is not a reality but an auxiliary construction of legal thinking, the question whether a function is a state function cannot be directed toward the existence of a fact. If the question is posed in this sense and answered, then it is erroneously posed and erroneously answered. Correctly posed, its meaning can only be: whether and under what circumstances a function rendered by a certain human being may be attributed to the state.

From the point of view of cognition directed toward the law, only a function determined by the legal order—that is a legal function in the narrower or wider sense of the term—can be comprehended as a function to the state. Since the attribution of a function determined by the legal order and performed by a certain human being to the state as a person is only a way of expressing the idea that a function is referred to the unity of the legal order which determines this function, any function determined by the legal order may be attributed to the state as the personification of this legal order. Using a metaphor, it may be said of any function determined by the legal order that it is performed by the state as a person. For by this it is only expressed that the function is determined by the legal order. One *may* use this metaphor, but need not because the facts may be described without it; one uses it if this is regarded as advantageous for some reason. Since the problem of the state as an acting person is a problem of attribution, and since this attribution is expressed in linguistic usage, in answering the question whether a certain function is a state function we first have to ascertain whether this function is attributed to the state in linguistic usage. This usage, however, is not uniform and not consistent. To return to the question whether legislation is a function of the state: this function is, as a rule, presented as of the state, that is, it is attributed to the state. But some authors do not do so. They refuse to interpret legislation as a function of the state.[107] They are free to do so; but they err if they mean by that, that legislation, in contradistinction to other functions, can actually not be performed by the state; that the state can conclude treaties, punish criminals, run railroads, but can not make statutes. The true meaning of their refusal is that, for some reason, they do

---

[107] Thus, in my *Hauptprobleme der Staatsrechtslehre*, pp. 465 ff., I interpreted myself legislation not as a function of the state but of society.

not make use of the existing possibility of attributing legislation to the state, just as, usually, one does not attribute a delict, determined by the legal order, to the state, although this would be possible in the same sense in which any function is attributed to the state. For such attribution of a function to the state merely means that the function is determined in the legal order constituting the state community.

If the linguistic usage is analyzed, that is, if one attempts to discover under which conditions in legal terminology certain functions determined by the national legal order are attributed to the state by saying that the state, through a certain individual as its organ, performs a certain function, then it appears that in general a function is attributed to the state, is interpreted as a state function only if it is performed by an individual called upon for this purpose by the legal order and functioning according to the principle of division of labor; or, what amounts to the same, that an individual is regarded as an organ of the state only when he is called upon by a procedure determined by the legal order, to perform this function. By relating the function to the unity of the legal order that determines it, and thus attributing it to the state, and representing it as a function of the state, this legal order is personified. The state as a social order is the above-defined national legal order. The state as a person is the personification of that order. But it is to be noted, as stated earlier, that beside this concept of the state a second concept, different from it but closely related to it and included in it, is being applied. This state, if represented as an acting person, is also only the personification of a legal order—not of the total legal order that regulates the behavior of all individuals living within its territorial sphere of validity and thus constituting the state as a legal community to which all individuals belong who live within a certain territory, but a partial legal order which regulates the behavior of individuals who have the character of organs functioning as "officials" according to the principle of division of labor. This partial legal order constitutes a partial community to which only these individuals belong. To this partial community are attributed only the functions of these individuals. It is the state as the bureaucratic machinery of officials, headed by the government.

Since this problem of attribution to a juristic person was dis-

cussed in the preceding analysis of the juristic person of the corporation, repetitions in the presentation of the problem of the state
as person are unavoidable. They may be justified by the fact that
the insight, here presented, into the nature of this operation,
which plays an important role in juristic thinking, entails a con-
siderable revision of traditional views. Since this insight destroys
the erroneous concept of the state person as a substance different
from law, it cannot be emphasized enough.

The functions attributed to the state by the traditional theory
of state fall into three categories: legislation, administration (including government), and jurisdiction. As shown, all three are
legal functions—either legal functions in the narrower sense,
namely functions of law creation and law application, or functions
in the wider sense which also includes the law-obeying function. If
legislation is interpreted as a function of the state, it is because this
function is performed by a parliament, that is, according to the
principle of division of labor—by a parliament elected in a procedure prescribed by the legal order. It is to be noted that the individuals who perform the legislative function (the members of parliament) are not state officials; they do not have this quality which
is decisive for the attribution to the state of other functions. But
the individuals who elect the parliament, exercising their rights of
voting, ordinarily are not called state organs and their function is
not called a state function. Although it is said that the state makes
laws, it is not said that the state elects the parliament. Still, this
could be said just as much, because the function involved here, the
creation of the law-making organ, is an essential part of the procedure by which the laws are created. In the main, this procedure
falls into two steps: the creation of the organ by elections and the
creation of the general norm by the organ in a legislative procedure. It is significant for the nature of the attribution manifesting
itself in current linguistic usage—the attribution on which the idea
of the state as an acting person is based—that the creation of general norms by custom is not attributed to the state, is not interpreted as a function of the state. Indeed, those who assert that state
and law are two different phenomena cite customary law as an argument for their contention that law need not necessarily be created by the state—that there is a kind of law which comes into
being entirely independent of the state. But since by custom, pre-

cisely as by legislation, general legal norms are created, custom could be attributed to the state just as much as legislation. If the creation of customary law is not attributed to the state, this is so only because it is not, like legislation, the function of an organ that operates according to the principle of division of labor and is called upon, in a special procedure, to perform this function. But the attribution of the legislative function to the state takes place, as has been said, without the organ, functioning in the manner of division of labor, being qualified as an official of the state. We might recall here the circumstance, mentioned in a different connection, that the individual legal norm representing a judicial decision is looked upon as a function of the state, but not the bringing of a suit (which constitutes an essential part of the procedure in which this individual norm is created); this can only be explained by the fact that the court, but not the plaintiff, is an organ functioning according to the principle of division of labor and called upon to perform this function. But if, as in a criminal procedure, the judicial decision is conditioned by the indictment of a public prosecutor appointed by the government, then this function too is interpreted as a function of the state, because it is performed by division of labor—by an organ called upon for this purpose. It is said that the state accuses the criminal as it is said that the state condemns the criminal. For the same reason the contractual creation of general and individual norms is not called a state function, unless it is performed by state officials functioning by division of labor, although the execution of legal transactions by "private persons," like legislation and jurisdiction is a legal function, in the narrower sense, as determined by the legal order.

We have seen earlier [108] that the activity designated as state administration consists of two parts, different in their legal structures. The function of the government (the chief of state, the members of the cabinet, the ministers or state secretaries, and largely the administrative officials subordinated to the government) is specifically a legal function in the narrower sense of the term, namely the creation and application of general and individual legal norms by which the individuals subjected to the law, the "subjects," are obligated to a certain behavior because a coercive act is attached to the opposite behavior, and the execution of this

---

[108] Cf. § 35i.

coercive act is attributed to the state. If it is assumed that the behavior which is the content of the legal obligation, constituted by the sanctions, is intended by the legal order, because it is to be brought about by the threat of a sanction, and if the intention of the legal order is represented as the purpose of the state—just as the territorial sphere of validity of the national legal order is represented as the territory of the state—then one can say that this purpose of the state is realized *indirectly,* because it is realized in the obligated behavior of the individuals, which is not attributed to the state. But a great part of the activity interpreted as state administration represents a *direct* realization of the state's purpose. It is a behavior attributed to the state which constitutes the contents of the legal obligations. The function attributed to the state is not a law-creating and law-applying, but a law-obeying function. The obligations whose observance is attributed to the state (is interpreted as a state function), are obligations of "officials" functioning according to the principle of the division of labor. State functions in which the state's purpose is directly realized are present (or: direct state adminstration is present), if, as the saying goes, the state does not limit itself to bringing about a certain state of affairs by issuing laws by which the individuals subjected to the state are obligated to a behavior which brings about this state of affairs; and by applying these laws to concrete cases and executing the sanctions prescribed in the laws; but if the state itself brings about the intended state of affairs, that is, by its organs, in a manner which—according to the prevailing linguistic usage—is attributable to it: if, for example the state operates railroads, builds schools and hospitals, provides education, offers medical care—in brief, if the state engages in economic, cultural, or humanitarian activities in the same manner as private individuals. The "nationalization" of these activities means, so to speak, their "officialization," that is to say—their performance by organs qualified as "officials" and functioning according to the principle of division of labor. In what does this qualification as "officials" consist?

First, in that these individuals are called to their functions by an administrative act of the government or of an authorized administrative authority, and are legally subordinated to the government. Second, in that the execution of their function is made the content of a specific obligation, the official duty, whose fulfillment is guaranteed by disciplinary penalties. It is to be noted that the activity that presents itself as direct state administration may be made the official duty of an organ in such a way that the organ in fulfillment of his duty is allowed more or less latitude. This latitude may be so wide, the discretionary power of the official may be so little limited, that the element of "obligation" seems to be absent. But it still must be assumed to be present—even if reduced to a minimum—so far as official duty is considered to be an essential element of the character of an official. Third, in that these organs have to carry out their functions not occasionally and temporarily, but permanently (perhaps until they have reached an age limit) and professionally, which means at the exclusion of other gainful activity and therefore against consideration. They get a salary from the state; this means the compensation for their services is taken from the state's treasury, a central fund whose administration, income, expenses, and use are legally regulated. The treasury is formed mainly by taxes paid by the individuals subjected to the law, who are obligated by statutes to pay them, and is administered by state officials. Not only the salary of the state officials but also other expenses of the state administration are covered by the state property (in the wider sense of the term, comprising all the financial rights of the state, *Staatsvermögen*). If the activity interpreted as direct state administration has the character of a commercial enterprise (such as the operation of a railroad or a tobacco monopoly), then the assets and the liabilities of this enterprise belong to the state property. This constitutes a significant difference between the activity of direct administration attributed to the state and the analogous activity of private individuals, not attributed to the state. The legal nature of the treasury will be discussed later.

If the state whose internal function is limited to legislation, jurisdiction, and execution of the sanctions is called a "jurisdictional" state (*Gerichtsstaat*), then it can be said that with the establishment of direct state administration the state becomes a "jurisdictional and administrative" state (*Gerichts-und Verwaltungsstaat*). It is the result of a long development closely connected with the growing centralization of the legal order, especially with the growth of a central governing organ and the extension of its competence. The organ of the administrative state is the completely developed type of the state official. But there are numerous in-between levels, not exhibiting all mentioned characteristics: there are state officials who are not permanently employed, have no fixed salary or none at all; and state officials who are appointed not by an administrative act, but by way of a civil-law contract.

The "officialization," that is, the confering of state functions to officials, goes hand in hand with the transition from a jurisdictional to an administrative state. At first only certain legal functions in the narrower sense of the term are transfered to officials, especially the execution of the coercive act, the police function and the conduct of war, by the establishment of a standing army and the appointment of career officers. But once such a machinery of officials is created it can be charged with legal functions other than those in the narrower sense. The state administration increasingly becomes the direct realization of the state's purposes; but even this realization has the character of a legal function in the wider sense, that is, a law-obeying function. It is also in the direct state administration that the state manifests its legal character. Since the partial legal order, which constitutes the state in the narrower sense (the state as a machinery of officials, headed by the government), is an integral part of the total legal order, which constitutes the state in the wider sense (the state whose subjects are the personal sphere and whose territory is the territorial sphere of validity of the legal order, and whose power is the effectiveness of this legal order), so therefore the attribution of a function to the state in the narrower sense (as a reference to the unity of the partial legal order) implies the attribution to the state in the wider sense (as a reference to the unity of the total legal order).

The transition to the administrative state and the increasing importance of the machinery of officials is connected with a certain tendency to identify the concept of state organ with that of the state official; that means: to limit the attribution to the state to functions determined by the legal order, performed by individuals functioning according to the principle of division of labor and qualified as officials. It may be on account of this tendency that some writers refuse to designate parliamentary legislation as a state function, since it is not a function performed by state officials. Yet, the parliament sometimes has certain features which are characteristic of state officials: for example, its members receive compensation from the treasury. The chief of state in the absolute and constitutional monarchy is considered a state organ, even if he is not subjected to official duties. The chief of state in a democratic republic and the cabinet members in a monarchy and in a republic perform their functions, which essentially are legal functions, as official duties; but these are not constituted by the general disciplinary law, but by special regulations which establish a specific responsibility. They, too, are state organs, not as state officials but so far as they perform a function determined by the legal order, according to the principle of division of labor.

Representation

The attribution of the described function to the fictitious person of the state is not the only possible one. In fact, linguistic usage employs another, which is closely connected with—if not included in—the attribution to the person of the state. It is the attribution implied in the concept of representation. Sometimes attribution to the person of the state is identified with representation, when it is said that the state organ "represents" the state. But in the specific sense the concept of representation is used only to express attribution of a function to the people. Of certain organs, such as parliament, it is said that, in performing their functions, they represent the people, but this does not mean that attribution to the person of the state, that is, the characterization of these organs as state organs, is excluded. To be sure, one speaks of representation of the people usually only when the function is rendered by an organ elected by the people. But linguistic usage is not consistent. Representation also designates the attribution of a function of an organ not elected, and not only attribution to the people, but also to another organ. Thus it is also said of an absolute monarch and a dictator who usurped power that they represent the people; and of a judge, appointed by a monarch in a monarchy transformed from an absolute to a constitutional monarchy, that he represents the monarch. "Representation" means substitution. We say: an individual who has no capacity to act does not act himself, but he acts through his legal substitute as his representative; that is to say, one attributes to the individual who lacks the capacity to act himself the acts of his statutory representative, because the latter has to realize the interests of the represented.[109] If we say that an organ in the exercise of his functions represents the people—the individuals who constitute the state community—if we thus attribute his functions to these individuals, we mean by this that the individual whose function may also be attributed to the state and who, therefore, may be considered as an organ of the state, is legally or morally obligated to exercise his function in the interest of the people. Since in juristic language "interest" and "will" are more or less identified (because it is assumed that an individual "wills" that which is in his interest) the essence of representation is believed to be that the will of the representative is the will of the represented—that the representative by his actions does not realize his own will but the will of the represented. This is a fiction, even if the will of the representative is more or less bound by the will of the represented, as in the case of a contractual representation or of a state divided into estates whose constitution obligates the representatives of the estates to follow the instructions of their voters who have the power of recalling the representatives. For even in these cases the will of the representative is different from the will of the represented. Still more patent is the fiction of identity of will, where the will of the representative is not bound by the will of the represented, as in the case of statutory representation of the individual lacking the capacity to act or the representation of the people by a modern parliament whose members, in the exercise of their functions, are legally independent; which is usually characterized by saying they have a "free mandate." The same fiction is present when it is said that the judge, in a constitutional monarchy, represents the monarch, that the judicial decision is the will of the monarch; and when it is even said that the monarch is invisibly present at the moment the judge pronounces his sentence. Attribution essentially always involves a fiction, whether the function or the will realized by the function of a definite individual is attributed to another individual or to a juristic person. The fact that the parliament is elected by the people, that the judge is appointed by the monarch, does not change the fictitious character of the attribution embedded in the concept of representation. Therefore the method by which an organ is created is irrelevant for the possibility of attributing his function to another

[109] Cf. pp. 159 f.

organ or to the people. Decisive is merely the assumption that the function is to be performed in the interest of that individual or those individuals to whom the function is attributed. Therefore the view found in certain political doctrines that an absolute monarch or a dictator [110] is the "true" representative of the people, expresses an attribution which is just as fictitious as that assumed in traditional theory according to which the parliament elected by the people represents the people, the statutes are created by the people (where a parliament exists), "the people are the source of law," or "the law emanates from the people," as it is said in the constitutions of some democratic republics.

The only question is under what conditions a scientific presentation of law may use the fiction that consists in the attribution of the function performed by one individual to a juristic person or to another individual; or, in other words: under what conditions the use of the concepts of "organ" (German: *Organschaft*), "substitute," or "representative" are scientifically legitimate. The answer is: the use is legitimate provided that one is aware of the nature of the attribution, and that one wishes to express by attributing a function performed by a definite individual to a juristic person, or by characterizing this individual as an "organ" of the community presented as a juristic person, nothing else but the relationship of this function to the unity of the legal order constituting the community; and that one wishes to express by attributing a function performed by one individual to another individual or to other individuals, especially to the individuals forming the people of a state, nothing else but that the individual exercising the function is legally or morally-politically bound to exercise this function in the interest of the individual or individuals to whom, for this reason, the function is attributed. The use of fiction is scientifically illegitimate, however, in the following cases: (1) if by attribution of a function to a juristic person (by asserting that the juristic person of a corporation or the state as a juristic person performs this function, fulfills an obligation, exercises a right through an organ) is meant that the juristic person (as the performer of this function; as the subject of obligation that is fulfilled by the function; as the subject of the right that is exercised by the function) *is a*

---

[110] Cf. Hans Kelsen, *The Political Theory of Bolshevism* (1955), p. 51 and "Foundations of Democracy," Ethics, LXVI: 1 (1955), Part II, pp. 6 ff.

real being, different from the members of the corporation or the state; (2) if in case of a statutory representation of an individual incapable of acting his legal capacity is feigned; (3) if, by characterizing the parliament as the representative of the people the fact is to be concealed that the democratic principle of the people's self-determination is essentially modified where this principle is restricted to the election of the parliament by a more or less extensive group of citizens; and (4) if, by asserting that an absolute monarch or a dictator represent the people, the validity of this principle of democracy is simulated, though in fact it is entirely abolished. Therefore the fiction that the independent judge repre-sents the monarch is utterly unjustifiable. Because by this is not meant, and cannot be meant, that the judge has to perform his function in the interest of the monarch, but only that this function is actually the monarch's prerogative who delegates it for some reason to the judge appointed by him. But this fiction is in conflict with positive law even if the legislator himself uses it—even if the law orders the judge to pronounce his sentence "in the name of" the monarch. This fiction has no other purpose than the political one to raise the monarch's authority by attributing to him a function of which he was explicitly deprived when the absolute monarchy was changed to a constitutional monarchy.

The state as a subject of obligations and rights

The obligations and rights of a state as a juristic person, whose structure is analyzed below, are not those imposed upon or granted the state by a higher legal order, international law. They are obligations and rights stipulated by the national legal order. The obligations and rights stipulated by international law, which are analogous to those of corporations stipulated by national law, will be discussed in the presentation of the relationship between international and national law.

Obligations of the state: state obligation and state delict; liability of the state.—In a juristically inexact sense, "obligations" of a state are often talked about, without a precisely defined concept of legal obligation being applied. If such a concept is presupposed, especially the one accepted here, according to which a legal obligation to behave in a certain way exists if the legal order attaches to the opposite behavior a coercive act as a sanction, then usually no legal obligation attributed to the state is present, but only a moral-political obligation. This is so, for example, when it is said that the state is obligated to punish the evildoer, although inflicting a punishment upon the evildoer is not the content of a legal obligation, because the noninfliction of the punishment is not made the condition of a sanction—the law-applying organ is not obligated, but merely authorized, to inflict the punishment. If such an obligation exists as an official obligation of the law-applying organ, this obligation can be attributed to the state only—if one is consistent—if its violation is also attributed to the state, because subject of a legal obligation is he by whose behavior the obligation may be violated—the potential delinquent. If the official obligation to punish the evildoer is constituted by a criminal sanction, and if, as is usual, no punishable delict is attributed to the state, then—if one is consistent—the obligation in question cannot be attributed to the state either. But in everyday terminology it is not this official obligation of the organ at all that is attributed to the state. As an official obligation it is regarded as a duty of the individual whose behavior constitutes the content of this duty. With this the need for the existence of a subject of the obligation is met; and an attribution to the juristic person of the state is therefore unnecessary. For this reason, when speaking of the state's obligation to punish one does not mean the official duty of the organ, but expresses by this only a moral-political postulate directed at the legal order.

It is customary to juxtapose to the constitutionally guaranteed so-called fundamental rights and civil liberties of the subjects of the state corresponding obligations of the state not to violate by statutes the equality or liberty that is the content of these rights, or, in other words, not to intervene in the thus protected sphere of individuals by statutes restricting or abolishing this sphere. In the earlier analysis of these fundamental rights and civil liberties [111] it was demonstrated that these are not rights in the specific sense of the term; that the "prohibition" to issue certain statutes violating the constitutionally guaranteed equality or liberty does not create a legal obligation of the legislative organ, but only the possibility

---

[111] Cf. pp. 140 f.

to annul a so-called unconstitutional statute by special procedure. Since a legal obligation of the legislative organ to refrain from creating violative statutes does not exist, and since the possibly existing legal obligation of the chief of state or the cabinet members not to participate in the creation of such statutes is regarded as an obligation of these organs and therefore does not require attribution to the juristic person of the state, so therefore the so-called obligation of the state to respect the equality and liberty of the subjects merely means the moral-political postulate, directed at the legal order, mentioned above.

   If it is assumed that a legal obligation to a certain behavior exists only if the legal order attaches a sanction to the opposite behavior; if, then, legally obligated to a certain behavior is that individual who by his behavior can not only *fulfill* the obligation but also *violate* it, then the subject of the obligation attributed to the state is the individual who—as a state organ—has to fulfill this obligation by his behavior and therefore also is able to violate this obligation by his behavior; and then it would be consistent to attribute to the juristic person in general and to the juristic person of the state in particular a legal obligation if not only the observance but also the violation of the obligation by the organ is attributed to it—especially if one assumes that the state can commit a delict. But since attribution is only a possible mental operation, not a necessary one, and always involves a fiction since it is actually never the state as a juristic person but a certain human being that fulfills or violates the obligation stipulated by the legal order, it is possible to attribute to the state an obligation and the behavior that represents its fulfillment, without also attributing to the state the violation of the obligation; it is possible, moreover, to maintain—in the interest of the authority of the state, and that means, of its government—the idea that the state can do right, but not wrong.

   To be sure, if the delict is a fact determined by the international legal order and consists in the violation of an obligation imposed by that order upon the state as a juristic person, then the attribution of the delict to the state meets with no difficulty in common terminology. For, as we shall see later, the national legal order may authorize a state organ to behave in a way prohibited by international law. This behavior represents a delict only according

to international law, not according to national law. The norm of
the national legal order that authorizes the behavior violating international law is not annullable according to international law.
General international law merely attaches to this behavior one of
its sanctions: war or reprisal resorted to by the state whose interests protected by international law are violated. In prevailing
usage of language no resistance is offered to the assertion that a
state has violated its international legal obligations or that the
sanctions provided for by international law are directed against the
delinquent state itself; this means that the state is liable for the delict it has committed.[112]

The situation is different, however, if the question is to be answered whether the facts constituting a delict according to the national legal order may be attributed to the state as the personification of *this* legal order and whether a sanction stipulated by the
national legal order may be interpreted as being directed against
the state. Here the tendency becomes apparent not to attribute
to the state a behavior that has the character of a delict according
to the national legal order; the tendency to consider as an organ of
the state an individual called to perform a definite function only
insofar as his behavior does not constitute a delict according to the
national legal order. This tendency is expressed in the formula:
The State Can Do No Wrong. This formula is justified by the idea
that the state whose "will" is the law cannot will the wrong and
therefore cannot do wrong. If a delict is committed, it can only be
the delict of an individual, brought about by the individual's behavior, but not the delict of the state as whose organ this individual behaves only if his behavior is authorized by the legal order in
the sense that his behavior is creation, application, or observance,
but not violation of the law. Law violation falls outside the authority given the organ and therefore is not attributable to the
state. A wrong-doing state would be a contradiction in itself.

Such restriction of the attribution to the state is entirely possible. But it is not necessary in the sense that attribution of a delict
to the state would constitute a logical contradition. That the law is
the "will" of the state is a metaphor that expresses no more than
that the community constituted by the legal order is the state, and
that the personification of this legal order is the person of the

---

[112] Cf. pp. 322 and 326.

state; and the "wrong" (the delict) is not a negation of the law
—as is assumed in rejecting the concept of a delict committed
by the state—but, as demonstrated, a condition to which the law
attaches a specific consequence. The statement that a behavior is
"unlawful" (illegal) does not express a logical, but only a teleological contrast between it and the "lawful" (legal) behavior so
far as one assumes that the legal order attempts to prevent the
former but not the latter by attaching to the illegal behavior a sanction against the individual behaving in that way. Since the delict
is a fact determined by the legal order, it may be related to the
unity of the legal order personified, that is to say, it may be
attributed to the state. This is in fact done in certain cases. The
principle that the state cannot commit a delict is maintained in
common usage of language only with significant exceptions.

To be true, the delict constituted by a punitive sanction is
usually not attributed to the state. As the subject of the obligation
to whose violation a punishment is attached, the individual is regarded by whose behavior the obligation was violated. Since, according to common usage of language, only those obligations are
attributed to the state which are to be fulfilled by individuals
functioning according to the principle of division of labor and
called to this fulfillment by the legal order, it is assumed that such
an individual in violating the obligation constituted by a punitive sanction does not act as an organ of the state. So far as only a
behavior consisting in the fulfillment of the obligation (not in its
violation) is attributed to the state, an obligation is attributed to
the state which the state can fulfill but not violate. It has been explained earlier why the objection that such an attribution is incompatible with the concept of legal obligation here developed is
immaterial.[113]

In fact, the violation of an obligation stipulated by the national
legal order—and hence also this obligation—is attributed to the
state only when its contents is a financial performance, when it is
to be fulfilled from the state property, and when the execution (if
such applies) is to be directed into the property of the state. The
legal order may prescribe: if it has been ascertained in a judicial
procedure that an innocent individual was punished, not only the
sentence should be annulled and therefore the forcible depriva-

---

[113] Cf. § 33e, subsection "Obligations of the juristic person."

tion of life or liberty not be considered as punishment, but also the material damage caused to the individual concerned or his family should be repaired by a payment from the state's property. To execute this payment, a certain state organ is obligated. If the payment is not made, then—so it is said—the state may be sued and condemned by a court to make the payment; and if this sentence is not carried out—which will hardly ever happen, but which is possible—execution directed into the property of the state could take place. In this case it is said that the state has violated his legal obligation to repair the damage caused an innocent individual. That is to say the obligation as well as its fulfillment *and* violation are attributed to the state; and, assuming that the property in question is interpreted to be the property of the state, even the suffering of the sanction is attributed to the state.

The same attribution takes place when an individual in his capacity as a state organ performs a legal transaction by which are created obligations of the state which are to be fulfilled from the property interpreted to be that of the state. The attribution to the person of the state, of the delict that consists in the nonfulfillment of the obligation is possible, because the facts constituting the delict are determined in the national legal order as conditions of the sanction—that is, as conditions of the execution to be directed into the state's property. If, however, the property in question can be interpreted as the collective property of the individuals belonging to the legal community called "state"—this will be discussed later —then this obligation may be attributed to these individuals, and then we may speak of collective obligations of the members of the state. The official duty violated by the organ in not fulfilling the obligation of the state or—what amounts to the same—the collective obligation of the members must be distinguished from this obligation. For this obligation is constituted by the possible execution into the state's property, the official duty of the organ by a disciplinary sanction directed against the organ. Only the first-mentioned obligation, not the official duty of the organ, is attributed to the state.

Execution into the state's property seems to be an absurd interpretation if the coercive act itself is attributed to the state, and thus the state seems to be carrying out an execution against itself. But this interpretation is avoidable. The actual situation is this:

the execution has to take place against the will of the organ in whose competence falls the administration of the property in question. His refusal to carry out the order of the state's executive organ is a violation of his official duty. The coercive act, if in fact it should become necessary, would actually be directed against this individual. Since attribution is only a possible, not a necessary, mental operation, the attribution to the state of the suffering of the evil that constitutes the coercive act is by no means necessary, and must not take place if one wishes to avoid the idea of an execution by the state against itself. The execution, then, takes place into the property of the state, but is not directed against the person of the state. The individual against whom the execution into a property is directed need not necessarily be the subject of the right which constitutes the property.

The state's financial obligations are, then, if described without the aid of attribution, obligations of the state's organ whose behavior constitutes the content of these obligations. They are obligations to be fulfilled from the property interpreted as property of the state. They are constituted by the establishment of sanctions, namely of an execution, interpreted to be directed into this property, but not against the person of the state. The execution is directed against the person of the state's organ who administers this property. If this property is attributed to the state as the subject of the right constituting the property, then the state is liable with its property for the delict which an individual has committed by nonfulfillment of the obligation which he has to fulfill in his capacity as an organ of the state. Whereas in case of the obligations imposed on the state by *international* law the obligation *and* the suffering of the coercive act that constitutes the obligation are attributed to the person of the state, in case of the obligations imposed on the state by the *national* legal order only the obligation, not the suffering of the coercive act, is attributed to the person of the state. According to common terminology, the state as a juristic person can commit a delict by not fulfilling, and thus violating, a financial obligation imposed on him by the national legal order; but the execution directed into the property of the state, which the national legal order attaches as a sanction to this delict of the state, is not interpreted as being directed against the person of the state. This means: the state is not liable with his person, but only with his property for the delict attributed to "him," but the organ acting contrary to his duty is liable with his person for this delict of the state. If the state's property can be interpreted as the collective property of the members of the state, then, as will be shown later, the liability of the state is the collective liability of its members.

Rights of the State.—If a right in the technical sense of the word is understood as a reflex right equipped with the legal power to be exercised as a reaction against nonfulfillment of the obligation identical with the reflex right and if the subject of the right is the individual on whom the legal order bestows this legal power, then the rights interpreted to be those of the state are the rights of the individual who, in his capacity as organ of the state, has to exercise this legal power. If we attribute the exercise of this legal power to the state we refer it to the national legal order which stipulates that the legal power has to be exercised by a certain individual. The obligation against whose nonfulfillment the legal power is exercised is also interpreted as an obligation toward the state, and the reflex right identical with this obligation is interpreted as a reflex right of the state. In fact the obligated behavior of one individual can only take place toward another individual or other individuals. But the exercise of the reflex right may be the function of an individual who has the quality of a state organ; that is, this behavior may be attributed to the state. This is true of certain obligations, for example, the obligation to render military service or pay taxes. The performance of military service is accepted by the state's military organs, the payment of taxes by the state's financial organs, and this acceptance constitutes the content of their official duty. But, it is said, they do not accept the performances for themselves, like an employer accepting the performance of the employee or a creditor accepting the payment of the debtor. They accept the performances "for the state." This means that the acceptance is interpreted as a state function—it is attributed to the state. In case of the obligation to pay taxes one has to add that the payment does not flow into the property of the individual functioning as a state organ, but into property interpreted as state property. The obligations to render military service and to pay taxes are characterized as public-law obligations. But the same situation exists in case of private-law obligations (to render a performance) created by legal transactions executed by the state, that is, by a certain individual as a state organ, authorized to do so by the legal order. The exercise of the legal power to start proceedings leading to the execution of the sanction prescribed as reaction against the nonfulfillment of the duties here concerned, this exercise, too, is carried out by a state organ, and is attributed to the state as a state function. Considering that these duties are not established in the interest of the individuals who accept the services and are charged with reacting against nonfulfillment, and assuming that it is a state interest which is guaranteed by establishing these duties, then this can only mean—since only living human beings can have "interests"—that these duties are established in the interest of all individuals belonging to the legal community. It is possible then to attribute the acceptance of the performance and the exercise of the legal power not to the fictitious person of the state, but to the individuals of the legal community. This means: we may designate the individuals accepting the performances not only as organs of the state, but also as organs of the people who belong to the legal community. To this extent it is possible to interpret the rights in question as the collective rights of these individuals.

Sometimes the obligations to refrain from a certain behavior, which make up the bulk of criminal law, are interpreted in that way that they exist not only in relation to the individuals directly affected by their violation, but also indirectly in relation to the state; we say that the state has the right that its subjects refrain from committing these delicts—this especially in view of the fact that it is the public prosecutor who reacts against the violation of these obligations. That it is in relation to the state that the delict must not be committed, presupposes that the delict is not merely a behavior which is injurious to the individual directly affected but a behavior violating the interest of all individuals of the legal community; and this is expressed by the fact that it is prosecuted not by the directly affected individual but by an organ of the community in the interest of the community. On the basis of these considerations we can speak, in this case too, of collective rights of the members of the state.

Sometimes one speaks of the state's "right" to punish the evildoer. Such a right—as a reflex right—is present only if a legal obligation exists to tolerate the punishment, that is, if the behavior by which the evildoer escapes the punishment to which he is sentenced is connected with an additional punishment.

Of particular importance are real rights (*Sachenrechte*) and especially property rights in the narrower sense (*Eigentumsrechte*) of the state. For these constitute the core of the property in the wider sense, interpreted as state property (*Staatsvermögen*), which plays such an important role in the attribution of functions to the state as a bureaucratic machinery of officials and therefore plays an important role in the attribution of that function which is designated as direct state administration.

An individual's property right with respect to an object consists in that all other individuals are obligated to tolerate the actual disposal of the object on the part of this individual—its use, non-use, even its destruction—and that the individual toward whom the others' obligation to tolerate exists has the legal power both to dispose of the object by a legal transaction and to react against the nonfulfillment of the others' obligation by bringing an action against them. Ordinarily it is the same individual who is entitled to the (actual or contractual) disposal and to the exercise of the legal power. This individual is the owner of the object. If we describe, without the aid of attribution, the set of facts interpreted as the property right of the state with respect to a certain object, we must say that the (actual and contractual) disposal of the object is reserved for certain individuals, who dispose of the object in fulfillment of an official duty, in such a way that all other individuals are obligated to tolerate these acts of disposal and are thereby excluded from the disposal of the object; and that, also, legal power to react by an action against the nonfulfillment of the obligations to tolerate is bestowed upon certain individuals who have the same qualifications as those for whom the (actual or contractual) disposal is reserved. Obviously it is not the same individual who is entitled to this disposal of the object and who has to exercise the legal power; the functions are distributed among different individuals. It is to be noted that the actual disposal of the object which is considered to be owned by the state—particularly its use —is not due to all members of the state. A house or a vehicle belonging to the state may be used only by certain individuals in a legally regulated manner. But even if all functions in question were combined in the hand of a single individual, which never happens, this individual would still not be regarded as the owner, for it would be assumed that in this case too, as in the others, the functions are conferred upon the exercising individual not in his own interest, but in the interest of all individuals of the community; in other words: it would be assumed that the right in question does not serve the protection of the interest of the mentioned individuals but of the interest of the community. The assumption of such a community interest supplies the criterion for an attribution of the functions, performed by officials, and thereby of the respective right, to the community members. In fact, this attribution to the members of the state community is included in the attribution of property rights to the fictitious person of the state. The nationalization of property is always understood as socialization, communization of property. In this sense, state property is collective property of the members of the state; that means that precisely as property can be attributed to the person of the state, it can be attributed also to the real human beings who form the community called "state." In both cases the attribution implies a fiction. In common terminology the one is included in the other. If one is stressed, we say that the individuals rendering the property function are organs of the state, and then the property is state property; if the other is stressed, we say the individuals represent the people, and the property is the people's property.

c) The So-called Self-obligation of the State; the State Governed by Law (Rechtsstaat)

Only on the basis of the analysis of the concept of state, exhibited above, is it possible to understand what traditional theory calls "self-obligation of the state" and describes as a fact that the state, existing as a social reality independent of law, creates the law and then subjects itself to it, voluntarily as it were. Only then is it a state governed by law, a *Rechtsstaat*. A state not governed by law is unthinkable; for the state only exists in acts of state, and these are acts performed by individuals and attributed to the state as a juristic person. Such attribution is possible only on the basis of legal norms which specifically determine these acts. That the state creates the law merely means that individuals, whose acts, on the basis of law, are attributed to the state, create the law. But this means that the law regulates its own creation. It does not happen, and never can happen, that a state, which in its existence precedes the law, creates the law and then submits itself to it. It is not the state which submits itself to the law, but it is the law which regulates the behavior of man and, particularly, their behavior directed at the creation of law, and which thereby subjects these men to law.

We can speak of a self-obligation of the state only in the sense that the obligations and rights attributed to the person of the state are stipulated by the same legal order whose personification is the state. This attribution of obligations and rights to the state—that is, referring them to the unity of the legal order and thus to the personification performed thereby—is a mere mental operation, as must be repeated for emphasis. What actually exists as the object of cognition, is only the law.

If the state is comprehended as a legal order, then every state is a state governed by law (*Rechtsstaat*), and this term becomes a pleonasm. In fact, however, the term is used to designate a special type of state or government, namely, that which conforms with the postulates of democracy and legal security. A *Rechtsstaat* in this specific sense is a relatively centralized legal order according to which jurisdiction and administration are bound by general legal norms—norms created by a parliament elected by the people; a chief of state may or may not participate in this creation; the members of the government are responsible for their acts; the courts are independent; and certain civil liberties of the citizens, especially freedom of religion and freedom of speech, are guaranteed.

d) Centralization and Decentralization [114]

If the state is comprehended as an order of human behavior and hence as a system of norms valid in time and space, then the problem of territorial subdivisions of the state into provinces or so-called member states becomes a special problem of the territorial sphere of validity of the norms forming the order called "state." The normal concept of the state starts from the supposition that all norms of the national legal order are valid equally for the entire state territory or—if they are related to the norm-creating organ—

[114] Cf. Kelsen, *Allgemeine Staatslehre*, pp. 163 ff.

emanate from a single authority; and that a single authority rules over the entire territory from a center. In this last concept—the concept of the so-called unitary state—the idea of the territorial sphere of validity of the norms forming the state order is mixed up with the idea of the singularity or multiplicity of the norm-creating organs. Yet, both ideas must be kept clearly separate. And to the extent that the contrast between centralization and decentralization is expressed by the concept of a "unitary state"—to the extent, as the unitary state as a centralized legal community is opposed to the type of decentralized legal community—this contrast can be presented solely from the point of view of the territorial sphere of validity of the norms which form the national legal order—that is, it can be described by a static theory of law without regard to the dynamic element of the unity or multiplicity of the norm-creating organs.

The idea that the norms of the national legal order are equally valid for the entire territory of the state is supported by the assumption that this legal order, the order of the state, consists only of general norms—that the order of the state is identical with the norms enacted as statutes. For the situation that the laws of the state are valid for the entire territory of the state—that there are no laws of the state valid for only a part of the state territory—is quite frequent. If we identify the power of the state with the legislative power, then there is little conflict between the idea of the state as a centralized legal community and the historical legal reality, that is, the positive legal orders. But if we also think of the individual norms created by judicial decisions and administrative acts concretizing the general norms created by the legislative organ, because these norms, too, belong to the national legal order as the order called "state," then it appears that a positive state hardly ever conformed with the idea of a unitary state as a centralized legal community. For even if the general legal norms created by legislation are valid for the entire territory of the state, the concretization of these general legal norms takes place, as a rule, in individual norms valid only for parts of the territory; for these individual norms are created by organs whose norm-creating competence is territorially limited to a part of the total area. The historical states, that is, the positive national legal orders, are neither entirely centralized nor entirely decentralized; they are always only partly centralized, and, accordingly, partly decentralized, appoaching sometimes the one, sometimes the other ideal type.

Conceptually a centralized legal community is one whose order consists exclusively of legal norms valid for the entire territory, whereas a decentralized community is one whose norms are valid only for parts of the territory. That a legal community is divided in partial legal communities means that the norms of the legal order constituting the legal community, or some of these norms, are valid only for parts of the territory. Then the legal order constituting the community is composed of norms which have different territorial spheres of validity. In case of total (not partial) decentralization, there cannot exist norms valid for the entire territory beside norms valid only for parts of the territory. Since the unity of the territory is constituted by the unity of the legal order valid for this territory, it seems questionable whether in the ideal case of total decentralization we can still speak of a total territory and of *one* legal order. Decentralization can exist only in case of the subdivision of the one and the same legal community, of one and the same territory. If decentralization were to go so far that several legal communities, several legal orders with independent (separate) territorial spheres of validity, were to exist side by side, without the possibility that these subdivisions could be looked upon as parts of a total territory, then the limit of possible decentralization seems to be overstepped. A multitude of legal communities or legal order standing side by side without a total order including and mutually delimiting these legal orders, and constituting a total legal community is unthinkable as will be shown.[115] And just as all states—so far as they are considered to be coordinated legal communities—must be regarded as members of a comprehensive international legal community, so also all state territories must be regarded as partial territorial spheres of validity of the universal legal order.

If complete decentralization—according to its idea—exists only where there are no norms valid for the entire territory, then this can be understood—with regard to the necessary unity of the order—only in the sense that there must be no *positive* norms valid for the entire territory, but that at least the presupposed basic

---

[115] Cf. § 43c.

norm is valid for the entire territory. The unity of the entire territory and the unity of the total legal order, comprising the partial
legal orders, must be constituted at least by this basic norm. The
borderline case of decentralization is therefore at the same time
the borderline case of the side-by-side existence of a multitude of
legal communities. The minimum condition under which it is still
possible to speak of decentralization is at the same time the minimum condition for the assumption of the coexistence of a multitude of legal communities. But we can speak also of decentralization in a narrower sense only if the unity of the entire territory is
constituted by positive norms and not merely by the presuppoesd
basic norm. But this is hardly important, because the legal reality
does not overstep this narrower limit, either. The extreme case of
decentralization that comes into consideration within positive law,
the subdivision of the international community into national
states too, conforms with this concept of decentralization in the
narrower sense.

If the norms of a legal order have different spheres of territorial
validity, then the possibility, although not the necessity, is present
that norms of different content are valid for the various subdivisions. In the theoretical borderline case, where the unity of the
territory is constituted merely by the presupposed basic norm and
where all positive, that is, posited, norms are valid for subdivisions
only, one legal order exists without any positive legal norm having a definite material content being valid for the entire territory.

The requirement of norms with different contents for different
subdivisions may have various reasons: geographical, national, religious differences within the material that is to be legally regulated may require a territorial subdivision of the legal community;
and this all the more the larger is the total territory and the larger
the possibility of differentiation within the social relations that
need to be regulated. This territorial differentiation of the legal
order must be distinguished from a merely personal differentiation of the legal order. It is possible to issue legal norms of different content, valid for the entire territory, for individuals who
differ with respect to their language, religion, race, sex, or profes-
sion. If, in this case, we speak of a "division" of the state, it is a

"division" according to the personality principle, not according to the territoriality principle.

It follows from what has been said that the problem of centralization and decentralization is primarily a problem of the territorial sphere of validity of the norms of the legal order. Secondarily, however, to this static element of the spatial sphere of the norms' validity, a dynamic element is added which, although entirely different from and independent of the former, is still used in a muddled mixture with it when centralization and decentralization are being talked about. Whereas from the first point of view the valid norms are being looked upon merely with consideration of their different territorial spheres of validity, from the latter point of view, the consideration is directed at the method of creating these norms, that is to say, at the act of norm creating and therefore at the norm-creating organs. A distinction is made whether the norms, valid for the entire territory or parts thereof, are created by a single organ or a plurality of organs. And although a centralized and a decentralized legal community (in the static sense) is possible whether the norms are created by one organ or a number of organs, yet one normally associates with "centralization" the concept of norms (valid for the entire area) created by a single organ, constituting as it were the center of the community and somehow physically sitting in the center of it; whereas one associates with "decentralization" the concept of a plurality of organs, not stationed in the center, but dispersed over the entire territory, each authorized to create norms valid for one partial territory only.

It is to be noted that not only the creation of legal norms, but also their application, indeed all functions stipulated by a legal order, may be centralized or decentralized in this dynamic sense, that is, to be performed by one organ or several. Centralization in the dynamic sense reaches its highest degree when all functions are performed by a single organ and, especially, when all norms of a legal order, the general and the individual, are created and applied by the same individual. Decentralization in the dynamic sense reaches its highest degree if all functions may be performed by all individuals subject to the legal order. Both cases are only ideal borderline cases which do not occur in social reality.

e) Abolition of the Dualism of Law and State

Once it is recognized that the state, as an order of human behavior, is a relatively centralized coercive order and that the state as a juristic person is the personification of this coercive order, the dualism of state and law is abolished as one of those duplications that originate when cognition hypostatizes the unity of its object (the concept of "person" being the expression of such unity). Then the dualism of the person of the state and the legal order parallels, when seen from an epistemological viewpoint, the likewise contradictory theological dualism of God and the world.[116] Precisely as theology asserts will and might as the essence of God, so the theory of law and state regards will and power as the essence of the state. Precisely as theology asserts God's transcendence in relation to the world and at the same time his immanence in the world, so the dualistic theory of law and state asserts the transcendence of the state in relation to the law (the state's meta-legal existence) and at the same time its immanence in the law. Precisely as the world-creating God in the myth of his incarnation must come into this world, must submit to the laws of the world (and this means: to the order of nature), must be born, suffer, and die, so too must the state, in the doctrine of its self-obligation, submit to the law created by the state itself. And precisely as the path to true science of nature is opened by pantheism, which identifies God with the world (and this means: with the order of nature), so is the identification of law and state (the recognition that the state is a legal order) the presupposition of a true science of law. If the identity of state and law is discovered, if it is recognized that the law—the positive law, not the law identified with justice—is this very coercive order as which the state appears to a cognition which is not mired in anthropomorphic metaphors but which penetrates through the veil of personification to the man-created norms, then it is simply impossible to justify the state through the law; just as it is impossible to justify the law through the law, unless this word is used on one occasion as meaning positive law and on another as meaning the "right" law, that is, justice. And then the attempt to

---

[116] Cf. Kelsen, *Der soziologische und der juristische Staatsbegriff*, 2d ed. (Tübingen, 1928), pp. 205 ff.

legitimize the state as governed by law, as a *Rechtsstaat,* is revealed as entirely useless because, as we have said, every state is "governed by law" in the sense that every state is a legal order. This, however, represents no political value judgment. The mentioned restriction of the *Rechtsstaat* concept to a state which conforms with the postulates of democracy and legal security involves the assumption that only such a coercive order may be regarded as a "true" legal order. This assumption, however, is a prejudice based on natural law. A relatively centralized, autocratic coercive order which, if its flexibility is unlimited, offers no legal security is a legal order too; and—so far as order and community are differentiated—the community, constituted by such a coercive order, is a legal community and as such, a state. From the point of view of a consistent legal positivism, law, like the state, cannot be comprehended otherwise than as a coercive order of human behavior. The definition says nothing about the moral value or justice of positive law. Then the state can be juristically comprehended no more and no less than law itself.

This critical abolition of the dualism of state and law also represents the most radical annihilation of one of the most effective ideologies of legitimacy; hence the passionate resistance with which traditional theory of law and state opposes the doctrine of the identity of state and law, as founded by the Pure Theory of Law.

VII

STATE AND INTERNATIONAL LAW

42. The Essence of International Law

a) *The Legal Nature of International Law*

According to the traditional definition, international law is a complex of norms regulating the mutual behavior of states, the specific subjects of international law. We shall discuss below what it means to say that the subjects of international law are states and whether it is true that only states are subjects of international law. At this point we shall answer the question whether international law is "law" in the same sense as national law, and therefore a possible object of a science of law.

In accordance with the concept of law here accepted, so-called international law is "law," if it is a coercive order, that is to say, a set of norms regulating human behavior by attaching certain coercive acts (sanctions) as consequences to certain facts, as delicts, determined by this order as conditions, and if, therefore, it can be described in sentences which—in contradistinction to legal *norms* —may be called "rules of law."

It will be demonstrated below that international law regulates the behavior of human beings, even where it regulates the behavior of states. At the moment we want to answer the question whether international law regulates the behavior of states in such a way that it reacts against a certain behavior as a delict by providing for a sanction as the consequence of the delict. The decisive question, then, is: does international law establish coercive acts as sanctions?

The specific sanctions of international law are reprisals and war.

It is easy to demonstrate that this assumption is correct with respect to reprisals. For it is a principle of general international law that a state which considers some of its interests violated by another state, is authorized to resort to reprisals against the state responsible for the violation. A "reprisal" is an interference—under normal circumstances forbidden by international law—in the sphere of interest of a state; it is an interference that takes place without and against the will of the state concerned and is in this sense a coercive act, even if it is executed without physical force (*i.e.*, without force of arms) when the affected state does not resist. However, the application of physical force is not excluded. Reprisals may be executed by force of arms if necessary. But this coercive act has the character of a reprisal only as long as the action of the armed force has not assumed—because of its intensity and magnitude—the character of war.

The difference between armed reprisal and war is only one of degree. A reprisal is limited to the violation of certain interests, war is unlimited interference in the sphere of interest of another state. By "war" is understood an armed action of one state against another even if there is no similar reaction, that is to say, no counterwar.[117] Since reprisals are admissible only as reactions against the violation of certain interests of one state by another, they have the character of sanctions; and the violation of interests conditioning the reprisals have the character of a violation of international law, that is, the character of an international delict. In this way international law protects some—not all possible—interests of the states subject to it. The interests of a state protected by general international law are precisely those against whose violation the state is authorized by international law to use reprisals. The limited interference in the sphere of interest of another state is itself an international delict if it is not a reaction against a violation of the law (*i.e.*, a reprisal). The interference, then, is either a sanction or a delict.

Does this also apply to the unlimited interference in the sphere of interests of another state, called "war"? In this respect two opposing views are maintained. The first holds that according to general international law, war is neither a delict nor a sanction, every state may go to war for whatever reason, without violating inter-

---

[117] Cf. Hans Kelsen, *Principles of International Law* (New York: 1952), pp. 25 ff.

national law. The second holds that war, even according to general international law, is permissible only as a reaction against a violation of international law. War, like reprisal, is itself a delict, unless it is a sanction. This is the so-called principle of *bellum iustum*.

The view that this principle is part of positive international law was at the basis of the peace treaties concluding the First World War, the Covenant of the League of Nations, being a part of these treaties. Since then, however, this principle has become unequivocally the content of two important treaties—the Briand-Kellogg Pact and the Charter of the United Nations. The former has been joined by practically all nations, and the latter claims in this respect validity for all states of the world.

In view of these facts it is hardly possible to say any longer today that according to valid international law any state, unless it has obligated itself otherwise, may wage war against any other state for any reason without violating international law; it is hardly possible, in other words, to deny the general validity of the *bellum iustum* principle.[118] The assumption, then, that war, like reprisals, is a sanction of international law, is well founded.

These sanctions, like the sanctions of national law, consist in the forcible deprivation of life, liberty, and other goods, notably economic values. In a war, human beings are killed, maimed, imprisoned, and national or private property is destroyed; by way of reprisals national or private property is confiscated and other legal rights are infringed. These sanctions of international law are not different in content from those of national law. But they are "directed against the state" as the saying goes. If war and reprisals have the character of sanctions, and if these sanctions are described as being directed against the state although they are directly directed against human beings, that is, if the suffering of the sanctions is attributed to the state, then this attribution expresses the idea that the human beings who suffer the sanctions "belong" to the state, that is, are subject to the legal order whose personification is the state as the subject of international law, and, as such, the subject of the international delict which is the condition for the sanctions.

---

[118] *Ibid.* pp. 33 ff.

b) *International Law as a Primitive Legal Order*

International law, as a coercive order, shows the same character as national law, *i.e.*, the law of a state, but differs from it and shows a certain similarity with the law of primitive, *i.e.*, stateless society in that international law (as a general law that binds all states) does not establish special organs for the creation and application of its norms. It is still in a state of far-reaching decentralization. It is only at the beginning of a development which national law has already completed. General norms are created by custom or treaty, which means: by the members of the legal community themselves, not by a special legislative organ. And the same is true for the application of the general norms in a concrete case. It is the state itself, believing its rights have been violated, which has to decide whether the fact of a delict exists for which another state is responsible. And if this other state denies the asserted delict, and if no agreement can be reached between the two parties concerned, no objective authority exists competent to decide the conflict in a legally regulated procedure. And it is the state whose rights have been violated which is authorized to react against the violator by reprisals or war as the coercive acts provided for by international law. The technique of self-help, characteristic of primitive law, prevails.

c) *The Hierarchy of International Law*

International law consists of norms which originally were created by custom, that is, by acts of the national states or, more correctly formulated, by the state organs authorized by national legal orders to regulate interstate relations. These are the norms of "general" international law, because they create obligations or rights for all states. Among those norms one is of special importance, known as the principle *pacta sunt servanda*. It authorizes the states as the subjects of the international community to regulate by treaty their mutual behavior, that is, the behavior of their own organs and subjects in relation to the organs and subjects of other states. By the consensus of the authorized organs of two or more states norms are created by which obligations are imposed upon the contracting states, and rights are conferred on them. International law created by treaties, as valid today, apart from certain exceptions, does not have general but only particular character; its norms arc not valid for all states, but only for two or a larger or smaller group of states; they constitute only partial communities. It is to be noted that particular international law created by treaties and general international customary law are not to be regarded as norms on the same level. Since the basis of the one group of norms is a norm that is part of the other group, the two have a relation of a higher and a lower level in a hierarchy. And if we consider also the legal norms created by international courts and by other international organs, established by treaties, a third level appears in the structure of international law. For the function of such an organ is itself based on an international treaty, that is to say, on a norm of the second level of international law. Since this second level, that is, the international law created by international treaties, rests upon a norm of general customary international law (the highest level), the presupposed basic norm of international law must be a norm which establishes custom constituted by the mutual behavior of states as law-creating fact.

d) Indirect Obligating and Authorizing by International Law

International law obligates and authorizes states. It obligates states to a certain behavior by attaching "sanctions" (reprisals or war) to the opposite behavior; in this way international law forbids this behavior as a delict and prescribes its opposite. Delicts are not connected with the sanctions by tying certain delicts to the one kind of sanctions and other delicts to the other kind of sanctions; the state whose rights have been infringed has a choice between the two. Besides, the wronged state is not obligated, but only authorized, according to general international law, to react with a sanction against an infringement. The right of the one state which is the reflex of the obligation of the other state is equipped with the authorization to execute the sanctions, established by international law, against the state which violates its obligation. This constitutes the subjective right (in the specific technical sense) of the wronged state.

This right is different from a right of private law in that the

sanctions need not be ordered by a court decision and need not
be executed by a special organ; therefore the wronged state has no
legal power to institute a legal procedure directed toward a sanction, but has the legal power to decide itself that in the present
case a sanction is to be directed against a state, and also itself to
execute the sanction.

This does not mean—as is sometimes assumed—that international law does not obligate or authorize individuals. Since all law
essentially regulates human behavior, both a legal obligation and a
legal right can have nothing else as their content but human behavior; and this cannot be anything but the behavior of individual
human beings. That international law obligates and authorizes
states merely means this: it does not obligate and authorize individuals directly, like the national legal order, but only indirectly,
through the medium of the national legal order (whose personification is "the state"). The obligation and authorization of the state
by international law has the same character as the obligation and
authorization of a corporation as a juristic person by the national
legal order. The state is a juristic person, and the norms of international law, by which the states as such are obligated or authorized, are incomplete norms. They determine merely the material,
not the personal element of human behavior, which by necessity is
their content. They determine only *what* ought to be done or
what ought not to be done, but not *who* (which human being)
has to perform the prescribed action or observe forbearance. His
identification is left by international law to the national legal
order. The behavior of this individual commanded or prohibited
by international law constituting the fulfillment or violation of
the obligation established by international law, and consequently
this obligation, is attributed to the state, that is to say: is referred
to the unity of the national legal order, insofar as this behavior
is determined by the national legal order as the function of an
individual acting as a special organ of the state. The same is true
of the behavior that consists in the exercise of the right and
the authorization to react with reprisals or war against the violation of the obligation whose reflex is the right. There is no difficulty in attributing to the state a behavior prohibited by international law, that is, in assuming that a state can commit an international delict. The national legal order can very well authorize

and even obligate an organ of the state to a behavior to which international law attaches a sanction, and which, therefore, has the character of an international delict.

As has been said, the statement that reprisals and war as sanctions of international law are directed against the state, means that the suffering of the evil constituted by these sanctions which in fact is suffered by human beings belonging to the state, is attributed to "the person of the state." The situation can be described, however, in a more realistic fashion without the aid of this fictitious attribution. In so far as international delicts, which are the conditions for sanctions, are committed by human beings who function as the government of their states, whereas the sanctions are directed not against them, but against other human beings, the meaning of the statement that the sanctions are directed "against the state" can be interpreted to mean: the sanctions stipulated by international law (war and reprisals) constitute collective liability of the members of the state for the international delicts committed by the government.[119]

This collective liability is an absolute liability or liability without fault, because the behavior which constitutes the international delict is not the behavior of the individuals against whom the sanction is directed, and therefore the violation of interests created by the delict is neither intentionally nor negligently brought about by these individuals.

This collective liability also constitutes a similarity between general international law and the law of a primitive community.

According to general international law, acts of war ought to be directed only against members of the armed forces who are organs of the state. Attributing their suffering to the state can therefore also express the idea that the acts of war are directed against organs of the state. But it is not excluded that in fact the acts of war affect people who are not members of the armed forces; at the present stage of technical warfare this is no longer avoidable.

---

[119] The use of this attribution is very characteristic in a civil war. The insurgents will not say that their warlike actions are directed against the state but only against the actual government; that means, they attribute the suffering of the evil inflicted upon human beings not to the state. But the government against which, according to the statement of the insurgents, the revolutionary action is directed and which—as long as it is in effective control of the subjected individuals —is the legitimate government representing the state, will characterize these acts, in conformity with the usage of language of some penal statutes as "hostile to the state," that is, as directed against the state.

The legal meaning of the peculiarity of international law, according to which "only states are obligated and authorized" and according to which "only states are subjects of international law," is completely expressed in the statement: international law delegates to the national legal orders the task of identifying the individuals by whose behavior the obligations established by international law are fulfilled or violated, and the rights established by international law are exercised. By this statement nothing else is expressed but the indirect obligation and authorization of the individual by international law.

This indirect obligation and authorization of individuals by international law, however, is a rule which has some important exceptions both in general and in particular international law. There are cases in which a norm of international law directly obligates an individual—cases in which international law not only determines *what* ought to be done or omitted, but also which human being ought to behave in that way. In these cases individuals appear directly as subjects of international law.

If individuals are directly obligated by international law, such obligation is not brought about by attaching the specific sanctions of international law (reprisals or war) to the behavior of the individual. The obligations directly imposed upon individuals are constituted by sanctions which are characteristic for national law, namely punishment and civil execution. International law may leave the determination and execution of these sanctions to a national legal order, as in the case of the international delict of piracy. Or the sanctions may be determined by an international treaty, and their application in concrete cases may be charged to an international court created by an international treaty; this happened, for example, in the case of the prosecution of war criminals according to the London Treaty of August 8, 1945.

To the extent that international law penetrates areas that heretofore have been the exclusive domain of national legal orders, its tendency toward obligating or authorizing individuals directly increases. To the same extent collective and absolute liability is replaced by individual liability and liability based on fault. This development is paralleled by the establishment of central organs for the creation and execution of legal norms—a development that up to now is observable only in particular international communities. This centralization applies, in the first place, to jurisdiction; it aims at the formation of international courts. In this respect the evolution of international law is similar to that of national law. Here, too, centralization begins with the establishment of tribunals.

43. INTERNATIONAL LAW
AND NATIONAL LAW

a) The Unity of International and National Law

The entire legally technical movement, as outlined here, has—in the last analysis—the tendency to blur the border line between international and national law, so that as the ultimate goal of the legal development directed toward increasing centralization, appears the organizational unity of a universal legal community, that is, the emergence of a world state. At this time, however, there is no such thing. Only in our cognition of law may we assert the unity of all law by showing that we can comprehend international law together with the national legal orders as one system of norms, just as we are used to consider the national legal order as a unit.

Traditional theory, on the contrary, sees in international and national law two different, mutually independent, isolated, norm systems, based on two different basic norms. This dualistic construction—or rather, "pluralistic" construction, in view of the multitude of national legal orders—is untenable, if both the norms of international law and those of the national legal orders are to be considered as simultaneously valid legal norms. This view implies already the epistemological postulate: to understand all law in one system—that is, from one and the same standpoint—as one closed whole. Jurisprudence subsumes the norms regulating the relations between states, called international law, as well as the norms of the national legal orders under one and the same category of law. In so doing it tries to present its object as a unity. The negative criterion of this unity is its lack of contradiction. This logical principle is also valid for the cognition in the realm of norms. It is not possible to describe a normative order by asserting the validity of the norm: "a ought to be" and at the same time "a ought not to be." In defining the relation between international and national law, it is important, above all, to answer the question whether there can be an insoluble conflict between the two systems of norms. Only if this question has to be answered in the affirmative, the unity of international and national law is excluded. In that case, indeed, only a dualistic or pluralistic construction of the relations between international and national law would be possible. If so, however, we cannot speak of both being valid at the same time. This is demonstrated by the relation between law and morals. Here, indeed, such conflicts are possible—for example, if a certain moral order forbids taking of human life under all circumstances, while at the same time a positive legal order prescribes the death penalty and authorizes the government to go to war under the conditions determined by international law. In this dilemma, an individual who regards the law as a system of valid norms has to disregard morals as such a system, and one who regards morals as a system of valid norms has to disregard law as such a system. This is expressed by saying: From the viewpoint of morals, the death penalty and war are forbidden, but from the viewpoint of law both are commanded or at least permitted. By this is only expressed, however, that no viewpoint exists from which both morals and law may simultaneously be regarded as valid normative orders. No one can serve two masters.

If an insoluble conflict existed between international and national law, and if therefore a dualistic construction were indispensable, one could not regard international law as "law" or even as a binding normative order, valid simultaneously with national law (assuming that the latter is regarded as a system of valid norms). The relations concerned could be interpreted only either from the viewpoint of the national legal order or from that of the international legal order. Insofar as this is assumed by a theory which believes that insoluble conflicts exist between international and national law, and which does not look upon international law as a "law" but only as a kind of international morality, nothing could logically be objected. But most representatives of the dualistic theory feel obliged to regard both international and national law as valid legal orders, independent of each other in their validity and subject to possible conflicts with each other. Such a theory, however, is untenable.

b) No Conflict between International and National Law

The view that national and international law are two different legal orders, independent from each other in their validity, is usually justified by the existence of insoluble conflicts between them. Upon closer examination, however, it becomes manifest that what is regarded as conflict between the norms of international law and the norms of national law is not a conflict of norms at all; that the situation can be described in rules of law which in no way contradict each other.

Such a conflict is seen primarily in the fact that a national law can be in conflict with an international treaty. For example: A state can be obligated by treaty to grant the members of a minority the same political rights as the members of the majority, but a national statute deprives the members of the minority of political rights—this contrast, however, does not affect the validity of either the treaty or the statute. The situation is exactly analogous to a situation within the state's legal order, without, on that account, causing any doubt as to its unity. The so-called unconstitutional statute, too, is and remains a valid law, without the constitution having to be suspended or changed because of it. The so-called illegal decision, too, is a valid norm and stays valid until its validity is abolished by another decision. It has been shown before that a norm contrary to a norm does not mean a conflict between a norm of a lower level and a norm of a higher level, but only means that the validity of the lower may be abolished or the responsible organ may be punished. It is to be noted particularly that the act by which a "norm contrary to a norm" is established may constitute a delict to which the legal order may attach its specific sanctions. It follows from what has been said that a delict does not constitute a negation of law (as the German term *Un-recht* indicates)— something that is not "law"—but is only a condition to which the law attaches specific consequences; in other words, that there is no contradiction between law and delict. The fact that valid legal norms may be created by an act which has the character of a delict does not meet with any logical difficulty. The creating of a norm may be connected with sanctions, yet the created norm may be valid; valid, that is, not only in the sense that it remains valid until abolished by a legal act, especially provided by the legal order for this purpose, but also in the sense that such a norm may not be abolished at all in such a procedure, because the legal order does not provide a special procedure of this kind. This is the situation in the relationship between international and national law. The meaning of the fact that international law imposes on the state the obligation to perform acts, especially to create norms of a special content, is merely this: The opposite acts or the creation of norms with opposite content, is the condition to which international law attaches its sanctions: reprisals or war. But the norm of the national legal order, created in "violation" of international law, remains valid—even from the point of view of international law, because international law provides no procedure in which the norm can be abolished. The relationship of international law to a norm of national law which—as one says—is contrary to international law, is the same as the relationship of the constitution of a national legal order, which, for example in its provisions concerning fundamental rights, determines the content of future statutes to a statute which violates fundamental rights and therefore is considered to be unconstitutional—if the constitution does not provide for a procedure in which statutes, because of their unconstitutionality, may be abolished, but contains only the provision that certain organs may be tried in court personally for their part in the establishment of the "unconstitutional" statute. International law determines the content of the national legal order in the same way as the constitution, which does not establish a judicial control of the constitutionality of statutes, determines the contents of future statutes. The possibility of another content than the one prescribed is not excluded, and the creation of a norm with such a content is thereby—if only secondarily—delegated. Such a norm is disqualified only insofar as the creation of such a norm is qualified as delict according to international law without prejudice to the validity of this norm. Neither this delict, nor the norm created thereby and labeled as "contrary to international law" logically contradict international law. This situation, therefore, does not prevent the assumption of a unity of international and national law.

c) *The Mutual Relationship between Two Norm Systems*

The unity of international and national law may be understood in two different ways; and if both systems are considered to be simultaneously valid orders of binding norms, it is inevitable to comprehend both as *one* system which can be described in noncontradictory rules of law.

Two norm complexes of the dynamic type, like international law and a national law, can form a single system in the way that the one order turns out to be subordinated to the other, because one contains a norm which determines the creation of the norms of the other, and hence the latter has the reason of its validity in the former. The basic norm of the higher order, then, is also the reason for the validity of the lower order. But two norm complexes may form a single system of norms also in that fashion that both orders are coordinated, that is, that their spheres of validity are delimited against each other. This coordination, however, presupposes a third, higher, order which determines the creation of the other two, delimits their spheres of validity against each other, and thus coordinates them. Determination of the sphere of validity means determination of an element of content of a lower order by a higher order. The determination of the creating procedure may be direct or indirect: a norm of the higher may determine the procedure itself by which the norms of the lower order are created, or the higher order may confine itself to authorize an organ to create, according to its own discretion, norms for a certain sphere. In this case we speak of "delegation"; and the unity of the normative system in which the higher and the lower order are connected has the character of "connection by delegation." Hence the relation of a higher order to lower orders delegated by the former, must be, at the same time, the relation of a total order to the partial orders it comprises. For, since the norm that constitutes the reason for the validity of the lower order, is a part of the higher order, so therefore the former may be conceived as partial order, contained in the latter as the total order. The basic norm of the higher order—as the highest level of the hierarchy—represents the highest reason for the validity of all norms, including those of the lower orders.

If national and international law form a single system, then their mutual relationship must be one of the two types here described. International law must be conceived either as a legal order delegated by, and therefore included in, the national legal order; or as a total legal order comprising all national legal orders as partial orders, and superior to all of them. Both interpretations represent a monistic construction. The one implies the primacy of the national legal order, the other the primacy of the international legal order.

d) A Monistic Construction Is Inevitable

Recognition of international law by the state:
primacy of the national legal order

As has been stressed, the representatives of a dualistic construction regard international law as a system of binding norms, valid beside the norms of national law. They are therefore obliged to answer the question why the norms of international law obligate the individual state—the question of the reason for their validity. In answering this question they start from the validity of their own national order, which they consider as self-evident. However, if one starts from the validity of a national legal order, the question arises how from this starting point the validity of international law can be established; and then the reason for the validity of international law must be found in the national legal order. This is done by assuming that general international law is valid for a state only if it is recognized by this state as binding—recognized, that is, as it is shaped by custom at the moment of recognition. Such recognition may take place either expressly by an act of the legislature or of the government or tacitly by actual application of the norms of international law, by the conclusion of international treaties, or by respecting the immunities established by international law, etc. Since all states recognize international law in this way, international law actually is valid for all states. However, international law becomes valid for the individual state only by this expressed or tacit recognition. This view prevails in Anglo-American jurisprudence, and is confirmed in modern constitutions by the statement that general international law is to be regarded as a part of national law; thereby general international law is recognized and made a part of the national legal order whose constitution contains such a provision. The recognition of international law by the individual state is not a condition of its validity for this state stipulated by international law itself. A valid norm of international law cannot establish such a condition, because the validity of this norm itself cannot depend on such a condition. But nothing prevents law courts and other law-applying organs to regard international law as valid for their own state only if that state has recognized it as binding. The result of such a view is that international law is not binding for a state which has not recognized it. The view that international law is not valid for a state, that the state's relations to other states are not subject to international law, is quite possible.

International law, according to its own intention, is applicable to the relation of a state to another community as a state only under the condition that this community has been recognized by the state as a "state" in the sense of international law. This recognition of a community as a "state," required by international law, is not to be confounded with the recognition of international law by a state. If, in answering the question for the reason of the validity of international law, one starts from the validity of one's own national legal order—if one asks why international law is valid for the state already conceived of as a legal order, the only possible answer is: International law has to be recognized by this state in order to be valid for it. The formulation of the question contains already the assumption that the reason for the validity of international law must be found in the national legal order, that is, the assumption of the primacy of the national legal order, its "sovereignty," or—what amounts to the same—the sovereignty of the state for which the validity of international law is in question.

The sovereignty of the state is the decisive factor for assuming the primacy of the national legal order. Sovereignty is not a sensually perceptible or otherwise objectively cognizable quality of a real object, but a presupposition. It is the presupposition of a normative order as the highest order whose validity is not derivable from any other higher order. The question of whether the state is sovereign cannot be answered by an analysis of natural reality. Sovereignty is not a maximum of real power. States which, in comparison with the so-called great powers, have very little real power are considered as "sovereign" powers just as the great powers. The question whether a state is sovereign is the question whether the national legal order is presupposed as supreme. This is done, if international law is regarded as a legal order delegated by the national legal order, and not as a legal order standing above the national legal order—in other words, if international law is regarded as valid for the state only if the state has recognized it. This is just as possible, as it is possible to regard the national legal order as valid for the individual human being only if he has recognized it. If the reason for the validity of the national legal order is seen in the recognition of that order by the individual, then one has started from the sovereignty of the individual, his freedom—in the same way as one starts from the sovereignty of the state, if one sees the reason for the validity of international law in its recognition by the individual state. For a state to be "sovereign" merely means that the establishment of the historically first constitution is presupposed as a law-creating fact without a positive norm of international law taken into account which institutes this fact as a law-creating fact.

International law, then, appears not as a supranational legal order, nor as one independent of the national legal order, and isolated from it, but—if as law at all—as a part of the national legal order. It has been called "external law of the state," assuming that it regulates the relations of a state toward "the outside," toward other states. But international law cannot be defined according to the object matter regulated by its norms. As already pointed out, international law regulates not only the behavior of states, and therefore indirectly the behavior of individuals, but regulates also directly this behavior. International law can be defined solely by the way in which its norms are created. It is a system of legal norms created by the custom of states, international treaty, and international organs established by treaty. If the norms, thus created, are regarded as valid only if they have become parts of a national legal order by recognition, if, therefore, their ultimate reason of validity is the presupposed basic norm of this legal order, then the unity of international law and national law is established —not on the basis of the primacy of the international legal order, but on the basis of the primacy of the national legal order.

The dualistic construction becomes impossible as a consequence of its indispensable assumption that the validity of the norms of international law for a state depends on the recognition of this law by the state. For if international law is regarded as merely a part of national law, then it cannot be a legal order different from, and its validity cannot be independent of, national law; hence there can be no conflict between the two, because both are based on the "will" of the same state, according to the terminology of traditional jurisprudence.

Primacy of the international legal order

The second method to establish the unity of international law and national law starts from international law as a valid legal order. If we start, as in the preceding pages, from the validity of a national order, the question arises how then the validity of international law can be established; it can only be done by the recognition of international law on the part of the state for which international law is valid. This means primacy of the national legal order. If one starts, however, from the validity of international law, the question arises how from this starting point the validity of the national legal order can be established; in that case the reason for the validity of this order must be found in international law. This is possible, because, as we mentioned in a different context,[120] the principle of effectiveness (which is a norm of positive international law), determines both the reason for the validity and the territorial, personal, and temporal sphere of validity of the national legal orders; and these, therefore, may be conceived as being delegated by international law and therefore subordinated to it—conceived, in other words, as partial legal orders included in a universal world legal order; the coexistence of the national legal orders in space and their succession in time is then made legally possible by international law. This primacy of international law is compatible with the fact that the constitution of a state contains a provision to the effect that general international law is valid as a part of national law. If we start from the validity of international law which does not require recognition by the state, then the mentioned constitutional provision does not mean that it puts into force international law for the state concerned, but merely that international law—by a general clause—is transformed into national

---

[120] Cf. § 34h.

law. Such transformation is needed, if the organs of the state, especially its tribunals, are only authorized (by the constitution) to apply national law; they can, therefore, apply international law only if its content has assumed the form of national law (statute, ordinance) that is, if it has been transformed into national law. If, in default of transformation, a norm of international law cannot be applied in a concrete case, then (if we start from the validity of international law) this does not mean that this norm of international law is not valid for the state; it only means that, if it is not applied and therefore international law is violated by the state's behavior, the state exposes itself to the sanctions prescribed by international law.

Since international law regulates the behavior of states, it must determine what is a "state" in the sense of international law—it must determine under what conditions individuals are to be regarded as the government of a state; therefore, under what conditions the coercive order under which they function is to be regarded a valid legal order; under what conditions their acts are to be regarded as acts of state, that is, legal acts in the meaning of international law. Positive international law stipulates that individuals are to be regarded as the government of a state if they are independent of other organs of the same type and able to bring about permanent obedience for the coercive order on which their functions are based—obedience on the part of the individuals whose behavior is regulated by this coercive order; in other words: if this relatively centralized coercive order, subordinated only to international law, is by and large effective, regardless of the way in which the individuals functioning as government have obtained their positions. This means that the community constituted by such a coercive order is a "state," and the coercive order that constitutes this community is a valid legal order in the sense of international law. International law also stipulates that the state's territory, the territorial sphere of validity of the national legal order, extends as far as this order is permanently effective; and that all individuals living on this territory (with certain exceptions determined by international law) are subject to this and not to another national legal order. According to international law, a state may, on principle, function in its capacity as a coercive machinery only inside its own territory—the territory guaranteed to this state by international law. To formulate this differently: the national legal order must stipulate that its specific coercive acts are to be performed only within the sphere of validity granted it by international law. In this way the spatial coexistence of a multitude of states—a multitude of coercive orders—becomes legally possible. But not only coexistence in space, also the succession in time (that is, the temporal sphere of validity of national legal orders) is determined by international law. Beginning and end of the validity of a national legal order are determined by the legal principle of effectiveness. The coming into existence and the downfall of the state, then, present themselves, from this point of view, as legal phenomena comparable to the creation and dissolution of a corporation as a juristic person within the framework of national law. But international law is important also for the material sphere of validity of the national legal order. Since the norms of international law, especially those created by international treaty, may refer to all kinds of subject matters, including those which up till then had been regulated only by national law, international law limits the material sphere of validity of national law. Although the individual states remain competent, in principle (even under international law) to regulate everything, they retain their competence only so far as international law does not regulate a subject matter and thereby withdraws it from free regulation by national law. Under the assumption of international law as a supranational legal order, the national legal order, then, has no longer an illimitable competence (*Kompetenzhoheit*). However, its competence is limitable only by international law but it is not restricted by international law from the first to definite subject matters. The national state, then, in its legal existence appears determined in all directions by international law, that is, as a legal order delegated by international law in its validity and sphere of validity. Only the international legal order, not the national legal order, is sovereign. If national legal orders or the legal communities constituted by them, i.e. the states, are denoted as "sovereign," this merely means that they are subject only to the international legal order.

It may be objected that the individual state cannot be conceived as an order delegated by international law, because historically the states—the national legal orders—preceded the creation of general international law, which was established by custom prevalent among states. This objection, however, is based on the lack of differentiation between the historical relation of facts and the logical relation of norms. The family too, as a legal community, is older than the state which embraces many families; and yet the validity of family law is based upon the national legal order. In the same way, the validity of the order of a single member state is based upon the constitution of the federal state, although the latter's creation is later in time than the formerly independent states which only subsequently are gathered together in a federal state. Historical and normative-logical relations should not be confounded.

If we start from international law as a valid legal order, then the concept of "state" cannot be defined without reference to international law. From this point of view, the state is a relatively centralized partial legal order, subject only to international law—the territorial, temporal, and material sphere of validity of this partial legal order being limited only by international law.

The difference between the two monistic constructions

The international law which from the viewpoint of the primacy of national law is regarded as merely a part of national law, is in content the same international law which from the viewpoint of the primacy of the international legal order is regarded as a legal order superior to all national legal orders delegating these legal orders. The difference between the two monistic constructions of the relationship between national and international law concerns only the reason for the validity of international law, not its content. For the first, starting from the validity of a national legal order, the reason for the validity of international law is the presupposed basic norm, according to which the establishment of the historically first constitution of the state is a law-creating fact. For the second, starting from international law, the reason for its validity is the presupposed basic norm, according to which the custom of the states is a law-creating fact. Custom of the states is a law-creating fact also within the framework of an international law which is regarded only as part of a national legal order. But here custom of the state is a law-creating fact not because of a merely presupposed norm according to which custom of states creates law, but because of a positive legal norm established by the act of recognition—the reason for the validity of this positive norm being ultimately the presupposed basic norm of the national legal order which constitutes the starting point of the construction.

Since in both cases international law has the same content, it has also in both cases the same functions: it determines, through the principle of effectiveness, the reason and sphere of validity of the national legal orders. One of these national legal orders is the one from which the construction presupposing the primacy of that order starts out; it is the one which according to this construction contains international law as a part. This can be only *one,* though any, national legal order; if international law is looked upon as a part of the national legal order, then it is necessary to distinguish between a national legal order in the narrower sense and a national legal order in the wider sense. The national legal order in the narrower sense comprises the norms of the constitution and the norms created—in accordance with the constitution—by the acts of legislation, jurisdiction, and administration. The national legal order in the wider sense is the starting point of the construction insofar as it also includes the recognized international law, that is, the norms created by international custom and international treaty. The international law that forms a part of this national law determines, through its principle of effectiveness, the reason for the validity of all national legal order—of those which are not the starting point of the construction and of the one which is and which therefore includes international law as a part. It fulfills this function in the latter case, as a part of the national legal order in a wider sense, only with respect to the national legal order in a narrower sense. Therefore the relationship of the two parts of this national legal order in the wider sense is not to be regarded a relationship of coordination, but as one of sub- and superordination. That part of the national legal order which is the international law is at a higher level than the part that is the national legal order in the narrower sense. Figuratively speaking we may say: the state which recognizes international law thereby submits to international law. However, the effectiveness principle of international law, constituting a part of the national legal order, is not the ultimate reason for the validity of the national legal order in the narrower sense; the ultimate reason is the presupposed basic norm of this legal order—the basic norm which, at the same time, is the ultimate reason for the validity of the international law that is part of this national legal order. Only between this national legal order in the wider sense and the international legal order contained in it exists that relationship between national and international law characterized here as primacy of the national legal order.

The other function, too, which international law performs by its principle of effectiveness—the limitation of the sphere of validity of the national legal orders—is performed as a part of a national legal order only with respect to the other part of this legal order, the national legal order in the narrower sense of the word. Only the latter's sphere of validity is limited by the international law which is part of the national legal order in the wider sense. And, again, the principle of effectiveness of this international law is not the last reason for the validity of this limitation—the last reason is the presupposed basic norm of this national legal order of which international law is a part.

As far as the other legal orders come into question, from the point of view of the legal order that constitutes the starting point of the construction and includes international law, their relationship to international law differs from that which exists according to the primacy of international law only so far as the principle of effectiveness of international law is not the ultimate reason for their validity and for the limitation of their spheres of validity; the ultimate reason, from the viewpoint of the national legal order which is the starting point of the construction, is the presupposed basic norm of this national legal order. This national legal order therefore—taken in its wider sense including the recognized international law—is alone sovereign in the sense of a highest legal order over which no higher one is presupposed. Since, however, within this national legal order in the wider sense one part (the national legal order in the narrower sense) is subordinated to the other part (the international legal order), this national legal order in the narrower sense is not sovereign, but—like the other national legal orders that are not the starting points of the construction—subject only to international law. The national legal order which is the starting point of the construction becomes, in virtue of the international law which is part of it, a universal legal order delegating all other national legal orders. The result is the same as that to which the primacy of the international legal order leads: the cognitive unity of all valid law. But while the starting point of the construction in the case of the primacy of international law can only be this international law, the starting point of the construction in the case of the national legal order can be—as has been said—every legal order, although only one each time. And only if the construction of the relationship between international law and national law starts from a national legal order, must the primacy of this national order be assumed—indeed, is this primacy already presupposed.

As has been emphasized, the choice of one or the other construction has no influence on the content of international law. The international law which is considered part of the national legal order has the same content as the international law considered superior to the national legal orders. In addition, the content of national law also remains unaffected by the construction of its relationship to international law. Therefore it is an abuse of the one construction or the other if (as happens repeatedly) decisions are deduced from them which can only be drawn from positive international law or from positive national law. Thus, those who presuppose the primacy of international law assert that it follows from the fact that international law is superior to national law—that in case of a conflict between the two, international law has precedence of national law; that means that the norm which is contrary to international law is null. As we can see from what has been said, such a conflict of norms between international law and national law can never occur. A norm of national law cannot be null, it can only be "annullable" and can be annulled for reasons of being "contrary to international law" only if international law or national law themselves are providing for a procedure in which this norm may be annulled. General international law does not provide for such procedure. The fact that international law is conceived as being superior to national law does not make superfluous such a provision. It is widely assumed to be possible to deduce from the subjection of the states to international law the fact that the sovereignty of the states is essentially restricted, and that therefore an effective legal organization of the world is possible. The primacy of international law plays a decisive role in the political ideology of pacifism. The sovereignty of the state—which is entirely excluded by the primacy of international law—is something quite different from the so-called sovereignty of the state restricted by international law. The former means: highest legal authority; the latter: freedom of action for the state. This freedom of action is restricted by international law whether international law is conceived as superordinated or subordinated to the national legal order and hence conceived as part of the national legal order. An effective legal organization of the world is possible whether the one or the other construction is accepted.

The primacy of the national legal order, based on the assumption of the sovereignty of the state is even more exposed to such abuse than the primacy of international law. From the fact that international law is valid only because of its being recognized by the state and therefore being a part of the national legal order, one concludes that the state is not necessarily bound by the treaties which it had concluded; or that it is incompatible with the sovereignty of a state to subject itself to an international court—even by a treaty concluded by that state—or to be bound by a majority decision of a collegiate organ, even if this collegiate organ and its procedure had been created by a treaty concluded by the state. Just as the primacy of international law plays a decisive role in the pacifist ideology, so the primacy of the national legal order, the sovereignty of the state, plays a decisive role in imperialistic ideology. In both the ambiguity of the concept of sovereignty is an aiding and abetting factor. But if a state has recognized international law, and if, therefore, international law is valid for that state, then it is valid in the same way as if it were valid as a supranational legal order. In that case the international law principle of *pacta sunt servanda* is valid, regardless of what content the states have given the contractually created norms. According to international law, no content can be excluded from a norm created by international treaty for being "incompatible" with the nature of the contracting state, specifically with its sovereignty. The fact that the sovereignty of a state is unhampered by a superordinate international law is entirely compatible with the fact that the state having recognized, on the basis of its sovereignty, international law and therefore having made it part of its national law, *itself* restricts its "sovereignty," which now means its freedom of action, by accepting the obligations established by general international law and by the treaties concluded by that state. The question of how far the sovereignty of a sovereign state may be limited by the international law recognized by the state, can only be answered on the basis of the content of international law, and cannot be deduced from the concept of sovereignty. The restriction of national sovereignty as the state's freedom of action is not limited by positive international law. An international treaty could create an international organization which is so centralized that it has itself the character of a state, so that the states which have concluded this treaty and are members of the organization lose their character as states. To decide, however, how far a government ought to or is permitted to restrict the freedom of action of its own state, is a question of politics. The answer can neither be deduced from the primacy of international law nor from the primacy of national law.

44. THEORY OF LAW AND VIEW OF THE WORLD

The contrast of the two monistic constructions of the relationship between international law and national law—that is, of the two approaches by which the cognitive unity of all valid law is achieved—has a striking parallel in the contrast that exists between a subjectivistic and an objectivistic world view. The subjectivistic view starts from the sovereign Self in order to conceive the external world which, therefore, is not conceived as an external but as an internal world, as idea and will of the Self; in the same way the construction based on the primacy of national law starts from its own sovereign state in order to conceive the external world of law, i.e., international law and the other national legal orders, and can, therefore, conceive of this external law only as internal law, as a part of its own national legal order. The subjectivistic, egocentric interpretation of the world leads to solipsism, that is, the view that only one's Self exists as a sovereign being, and everything else exists only in it or as a result of its thinking, feeling, and willing, and therefore cannot honor the claim of other beings that they, too, are sovereign Selves; in the same way the primacy of the national legal order means that only one's own state can be conceived as being sovereign, because the sovereignty of the one state (one's own) excludes the sovereignty of all other states. With this in mind, we can describe the primacy of one's own national legal order as state subjectivism, indeed as state solipsism. The objectivistic world view starts from the reality of the external world in order to conceive the Self—not only the Self of the observer but all Selves—but does not allow this Self to exist as a sovereign being and as the center of the world, but only as an essential part of the world; in the same way the construction described as primacy of the international legal order starts from the external world of law, international law, as valid legal order, to conceive of the legal existence of the individual states, but cannot afford to consider them as sovereign authorities—only as partial legal orders integrated into international law. The scientific cognition of reality is not affected by the antithesis between a subjectivistic and an objectivistic world view; the world as object of cognition, the laws of nature describing this world, remain the same whether this world is conceived as the internal world of the Ego or the Ego is thought of as being inside the world; in the same way the contrast between the two legal constructions does not affect the content of the law; be it international law or national law, the rules of law describing their content remain the same whether international law is conceived as included in national law, or national law in international law.

The antithesis between the two legal constructions may also be compared with the antithesis between the geocentric Ptolemaic and the heliocentric Copernican view of the universe. Just as according to one construction the own state is in the center of the world of law, in the Ptolemaic view of the world our earth is the center around which the sun turns. Just as according to the other construction international law is the center of the world of law, so in the Copernican view the sun is the center around which our earth turns. However, this contrast between two astronomic views of the universe is only a contrast between two different reference systems. Max Planck [121] says: "If we start from a reference system that is firmly connected with our earth, we must say that the sun moves in the sky; but if we transfer the reference system to a fixed star, then the sun does not move. The contrast between the two

---

[121] Max Planck, *Vorträge und Erinnerungen* (Stuttgart: 1949), p. 311.

formulations implies neither a contradiction, nor an obscurity—only two modes of viewing things are presented. According to the physical theory of relativity, which may be looked upon today as firmly established in science, both reference systems and the corresponding modes of viewing things are equally correct and justified, and it is impossible, in principle, to decide between them—without arbitrariness—by measurement or computation." The same is true of the two legal constructions of the relationship between national and international law. Their contrast rests on the difference between two systems of reference. One is anchored in the legal order of one's own state, and the other in the international legal order. Both systems are equally correct and equally justified. It is impossible to decide between them on the basis of the science of law. This science can do no more than describe them both, and state that the one or the other reference system must be accepted if the relationship between national and international law is to be determined. The decision itself lies outside the science of law. It can be made only on the basis of nonscientific, political considerations. He who treasures the idea of the sovereignty of his state, because he identifies himself in his increased self-consciousness with the state, will prefer the primacy of the national legal order. He who values the idea of a legal organization of the world, will prefer the primacy of international law.

This does not mean, as has been stressed, that the theory of the primacy of national law is less favorable to the idea of a legal organization of the world than the theory of the primacy of international law. But the theory of the primacy of national law seems to supply the justification for a policy that rejects far-reaching restrictions of the state's freedom of action. This justification is based on a fallacy, caused by the ambiguity of the concept of sovereignty as either highest legal authority or unlimited freedom of action. But the existence of this fallacy has to be accepted as an essential element of the political ideology of imperialism, which operates with the dogma of state sovereignty. The same is true, *mutatis mutandis*, for preferring the primacy of international law. This idea is in no way less favorable to the ideal of an unlimited sovereignty in the sense of a state's freedom of action than the primacy of a national legal order; but it seems to justify much more a far-reaching limitation of a state's freedom of action than the primacy of the national legal order. This too is a fallacy; but this fallacy plays a decisive part in the political ideology of pacifism.

By unmasking both fallacies, by depriving them of the appearance of logical proofs that—as such—would be irrefutable, and by reducing them to political arguments that can be met with corresponding counterarguments, the Pure Theory of Law opens the road to either the one or the other political development, without postulating or justifying either, because as a theory, the Pure Theory of Law is indifferent to both.

VIII

INTERPRETATION

45. The Nature of Interpretation

If law is to be applied by a legal organ, he must determine the meaning of the norms to be applied: he must "interpret" these norms. Interpretation, therefore, is an intellectual activity, which accompanies the process of law application in its advance from a higher to a lower level. In the case we usually think of when we talk about interpretation, the interpretation of a statute, the question needs to be answered as to what content is to be given to the individual norm of a judicial decision or an administrative decree in deducing this individual norm from the general norm of the statute to be applied in a concrete case. But there also exists an interpretation of the constitution, if it is necessary to apply the constitution on a lower level, such as in the procedure of legislation, in issuing emergency regulations, or in the performance of other acts authorized directly by the constitution; and there also exists an interpretation of the norms created by international treaties or of the norms of general international law created by custom, if these norms are to be applied in a concrete case by a government or an international or national court or an administrative organ. And there also exists an interpretation of individual norms, judicial decisions, administrative commands, legal transactions, and so on—in short, of all legal norms that are to be applied.

But also the individuals who have to *obey* the law by behaving in a way that avoids sanctions, must understand the legal norms and therefore must ascertain their meaning. And finally the science of law, too, when describing positive law, must interpret its norms.

348

Hence we have two kinds of interpretations which must be clearly distinguished: the interpretation of law by the applying organ, and the interpretation of the law by a private individual and especially by the science of law. First we shall consider the interpretation by the law-applying organ.

a) Relative Indefiniteness of the Law-applying Act

The relationship between a higher and a lower level of the legal order, such as constitution and statute, or statute and judicial decision, is a relationship of determining or of binding: the higher-level norm regulates the act by which the lower-level norm is created, or the act of execution; the higher-level norm determines not only the procedure in which the lower norm is created or the act of execution is performed, but—possibly—also the content of that norm or that act.

This determination can never be complete. The higher norm cannot bind in every direction the act by which it is applied. There must always be more or less room for discretion, so that the higher norm in relation to the lower one can only have the character of a frame to be filled by this act. Even the most detailed command must leave to the individual executing the command some discretion. If the organ A orders organ B to arrest subject C, the organ B must, according to his own discretion, decide when and where and how to carry out the order of arrest—decisions that depend on extraneous circumstances which the ordering organ has not foreseen and to a certain extent cannot foresee.

b) Intentional Indefiniteness of the Law-applying Act

Hence every law-applying act is only partly determined by law and partly undetermined. The indefiniteness may concern either the conditioning facts or the conditioned consequences. The indefiniteness can be intentional, that is, intended by the organ who creates the norm to be applied. Hence a merely general norm is always created with the assumption that the creation of the individual norm by which the general norm is applied will continue the process of determination which constitutes the meaning of the hierarchy of the legal order. Here are two examples: A law prescribes that at the outbreak of an epidemic the inhabitants of a town have to take, by pain of punishment, certain measures to prevent the spreading of the disease; the administrative authority is authorized to determine the various measures according to the various diseases. A criminal law provides in case of a certain delict a fine or imprisonment leaving it to the judge to decide in the concrete case for the one or the other, and also to determine the extent of either; whereby the law may provide an upper and a lower limit.

c) Unintended Indefiniteness of the Law-applying Act

The indefiniteness of the legal act may also be the unintended result of the way in which the legal norm is formulated that is to be applied by the act in question. This happens usually when a word or clause used in formulating the norm has more than one meaning: the linguistic expression of the norm is ambiguous; different interpretations of the wording are possible. The same happens when the individual who has to apply the norm believes that there is a discrepancy between the wording of the norm and the will of the norm-creating authority—regardless in which way this will can be found out. It must be regarded as possible to find out that will from sources other than the words of the norm itself. The possibility that the so-called will of the legislator or the intention of parties in a legal transaction does not conform with the expressed words is generally recognized by traditional jurisprudence. The discrepancy between will and expression may be total or partial— the latter, when the will of the legislator or the intention of the parties conforms at least with one of the interpretations which the words of the norms allow. Finally, the indefiniteness of the legal act that is to be performed may also be the result of the fact that two norms which both claim validity—perhaps because they are both included in the same statute—partly or wholly contradict each other.

d) The Law to Be Applied Is a Frame

In all these cases of intended or unintended indefiniteness at the lower level, several possibilities are open to the application of law.

The legal act applying a legal norm may be performed in such a way that it conforms (a) with the one or the other of the different meanings of the legal norm, (b) with the will of the norm-creating authority that is to be determined somehow, (c) with the expression which the norm-creating authority has chosen, (d) with the one or the other of the contradictory norms; or (e) the concrete case to which the two contradictory norms refer may be decided under the assumption that the two contradictory norms annul each other. In all these cases, the law to be applied constitutes only a frame within which several applications are possible, whereby every act is legal that stays within the frame.

If "interpretation" is understood as cognitive ascertainment of the meaning of the object that is to be interpreted, then the result of a legal interpretation can only be the ascertainment of the frame which the law that is to be interpreted represents, and thereby the cognition of several possibilities within the frame. The interpretation of a statute, therefore, need not necessarily lead to a single decision as the only correct one, but possibly to several, which are all of equal value, though only one of them in the action of the law-applying organ (especially the court) becomes positive law. The fact that a judicial decision is based on a statute actually means only that it keeps inside the frame represented by the statute; it does not mean that it is *the* individual norm, but only that it is *one* of those individual norms which may be created within the frame of the general norm.

Traditional jurisprudence, however, expects from interpretation not only the ascertainment of the frame, but the fulfillment of another task, and sees in the latter actually its main function: interpretation is to develop a method that makes it possible correctly to fill the ascertained frame. Traditional theory will have us believe that the statute, applied to the concrete case, can always supply only *one* correct decision and that the positive-legal "correctness" of this decision is based on the statute itself. This theory describes the interpretive procedure as if it consisted merely in an intellectual act of clarifying or understanding; as if the law-applying organ had to use only his reason but not his will, and as if by a purely intellectual activity, among the various existing possibilities only one correct choice could be made in accordance with positive law.

e) *The So-called Methods of Interpretation*

From a point of view directed at positive law, there is no criterion by which one possibility within the frame is preferable to another. There simply is no method (that can be characterized as a method of positive law), by which only one of several meanings of a norm may gain the distinction of being the only "correct" one—provided, of course, that several possible interpretations are available. Despite all efforts of traditional jurisprudence it has not been possible so far to solve in an objectively valid fashion the conflict between will and expression in favor of the one or the other. All methods of interpretation developed so far lead only to a possible, not a necessary, result, never to one which is alone correct. From the point of view of positive law, one method is exactly as good as the other—to neglect the wording and adhere to the presumed will of the legislator or to observe strictly the wording and pay no attention to the (usually problematical) will of the legislator. If it occurs that two norms of the same statute contradict each other, then, according to positive law, the mentioned possibilities of applying the law are of equal weight. It is a futile endeavor to try to justify "legally" one at the exclusion of the other. That the *argumentum a contrario* and analogy as means of interpretation are entirely worthless can be seen from the fact that both lead to opposite results and that no criterion exists to decide when the one and when the other should be applied. Similarly, the principle called "weighing of interests" (*Interessenabwägung*) is merely a formulation of the problem, not a solution. It does not supply the objective measure or standard for comparing conflicting interests with each other and does not make it possible to solve, on this basis, the conflict. It is impossible to derive this measure or standard from the norm that is to be interpreted, or from the statute that contains the norm, or from the entire legal order, as has been asserted by the theory of the so-called "weighing of interests." For the need for an "interpretation" results precisely from the fact that the norm to be applied or the system of norms leaves open several possibilities—and this means that it contains no decision as to which of the interests in question has a higher value than the others, but leaves this decision to an act of norm creation to be performed, for example in rendering a judicial decision.

46. Interpretation As an Act
of Cognition or Will

The idea on which traditional theory of interpretation is based, namely that the determination (of the legal act to be performed) not rendered by the norm that is to be applied could be gained by some cognition of the existing law, is a contradictory fallacy because it is incompatible with the presupposed possibility of an interpretation. The question which of the possibilities within the frame of the law to be applied is the "right" one is not a question of cognition directed toward positive law—we are not faced here by a problem of legal theory but of legal politics. The task to get from the statute the only correct judicial decision or the only correct administrative act is basically the same as the task to create the only correct statutes within the framework of the constitution. Just as one cannot obtain by interpretation the only correct statutes from the constitution, so one cannot obtain by interpretation the only correct judicial decisions from the statute. To be sure, there is a difference between these two cases, but it is only one of quantity, not of quality; the difference is merely that the constraint exercised by the constitution upon the legislator, as far as the content of the statutes is concerned which he is authorized to issue, is not as strong as the constraint exercised by a statute upon the judge who has to apply this statute—that the legislator is much freer in creating law than the judge. But the judge too creates law, and he too is relatively free in this function. For the creation of an individual norm, within the frame of a general norm in the process of applying the law, is a function of the will. So far as in applying the law a cognitive activity of the law-applying organ can take place, beyond the necessary ascertainment of the frame, within which the act to be performed is to be kept, it is not cognition of positive law, but of other norms that may flow here into the process of law-creation—such as norms of morals, of justice, constituting social values which are usually designated by catch words such as "the good of the people," "interest of the state," "progress," and the like. From the point of view of positive law nothing can be said about their validity. Seen from the point of view of positive law, all these norms can be characterized only negatively; they are norms that are not of positive law. With respect to this law, the establishment of a legal act, so far as it takes place within the framework of the legal norm to be applied, is free, that is, within the discretion of the organ called upon to establish the act—unless positive law itself delegates some meta-legal norms like morals or justice; but then these norms are transformed into norms of positive law.

If not only the interpretation of the statutes by courts or administrative authorities, but the interpretation of law in general by law-applying organs is to be characterized, the following may be said: In the application of law by a legal organ, the cognitive interpretation of the law to be applied is combined with an act of will by which the law-applying organ chooses between the possibilities shown by cognitive interpretation. This act of will creates either a lower-level norm or is the execution of a coercive act stipulated in the legal norm to be applied.

This act of will differentiates the legal interpretation by the law-applying organ from any other interpretation, especially from the interpretation of law by jurisprudence.

The interpretation by the law-applying organ is always authentic. It creates law. To be sure, we speak of "authentic interpretation" only if this interpretation assumes the form of a statute or an international treaty and has general character, that is, if it creates law not only for a concrete case but for all similar cases—in other words, if the act described as authentic has the character of the creation of a general norm. However, the interpretation by a law-applying organ is authentic (law-creating) also if it creates law only for a concrete case, that is, if the organ creates only an individual norm or executes a sanction. Here it is to be noted: By way of authentic interpretation (that is, interpretation of a norm by the law-applying organ) not only one of the possibilities may be realized that have been shown by the cognitive interpretation of the norm to be applied; but also a norm may be created which lies entirely outside the frame of the norm to be applied.

By such authentic interpretation law can be created not only in a case in which the interpretation has general character (where we are, then, confronted with "authentic interpretation" in the traditional sense) but also in a case in which an individual legal norm is created by a law-applying organ, as soon as the validity of this norm cannot be rescinded, as soon as this norm has gained the force of a final judgment. It is well known that much new law is created by way of such authentic interpretation, especially by courts of last resort.

The interpretation by a law-applying organ is different from any other interpretation—all other interpretations are not authentic, that is, they do not create law.

If an individual wishes to obey a legal norm that regulates his behavior, that is, if he wishes to fulfill a legal obligation by behaving in a way to whose opposite the legal order attaches a sanction, then this individual, too, must make a choice between different possibilities if his behavior is not unambiguously determined by the norm. But this is not an authentic choice. It does not bind the organ who applies this norm and therefore always runs the risk of being regarded as erroneous by that organ, so that the individual's behavior may be judged to be a delict.

47. INTERPRETATION BY THE SCIENCE
OF LAW

The interpretation of law by the science of law (jurisprudence) must be sharply distinguished as nonauthentic from the interpretation by legal organs. Jurisprudential interpretation is purely cognitive ascertainment of the meaning of legal norms. In contradistinction to the interpretation by legal organs, jurisprudential interpretation does not create law. The view that it is possible to create new law by merely cognitive interpretation of valid law is the basis of the so-called Conceptual Jurisprudence (German: *Begriffsjurisprudenz*) which the Pure Theory of Law rejects. The purely cognitive interpretation by jurisprudence is therefore unable to fill alleged gaps in the law. The filling of a so-called gap in the law is a law-creating function that can only be performed by a law-applying organ; [122] and the function of creating law is not performed by jurisprudence interpreting law. Jurisprudential interpretation can do no more than exhibit all possible meanings of a legal norm. Jurisprudence as cognition of law cannot decide between the possibilities exhibited by it, but must leave the decision to the legal organ who, according to the legal order, is authorized to apply the law. An attorney who, in the interest of his client,

---

[122] Cf. § 35g, subsection "The so-called gaps in the law."

propounds to the judge only one of several possible interpretations of the legal norm to be applied in this case, or a writer who in his commentary extolls a specific interpretation among many possible ones as the only "correct" one, does not render a function of legal science, but of legal politics. He seeks to influence legislation. This, of course, he cannot be denied. But he cannot do this in the name of legal science (jurisprudence) as so frequently is done. Jurisprudential interpretation must carefully avoid the fiction that a legal norm admits only of one as the "correct" interpretation. Traditional jurisprudence uses this fiction to maintain the ideal of legal security. In view of the ambiguity of most legal norms this ideal is only approximately attainable. It should not be denied that the fiction of legal norms having but one meaning may have great advantages from some political point of view. But no political advantage can justify the use of this fiction in a scientific description of positive law. It is, from a scientific and hence objective point of view, inadmissible to proclaim as solely correct an interpretation that from a subjectively political viewpoint is more desirable than another, logically equally possible, interpretation. For in that case a purely political value judgment is falsely presented as scientific truth. Besides, the strictly scientific interpretation of a statute or international treaty, exhibiting on the basis of a critical analysis all possible interpretations (including the politically undesired ones and those not intended by the legislator or the contracting parties, yet included in the wording chosen by them) may have a practical effect by far outweighing the political advantage of the fiction of unambiguousness, of "one meaning only": such scientific interpretation can show the law-creating authority how far his work is behind the technical postulate of formulating legal norms as unambiguously as possible, or, at least, in such a way that the unavoidable ambiguity is reduced to a minimum and that thereby the highest possible degree of legal security is achieved.